A Guidebook for Teaching
About the
ENGLISH LANGUAGE

A Guidebook for Teaching About the ENGLISH LANGUAGE

JOHN CORMICAN
Utica College of Syracuse University

GENE STANFORD
Utica College of Syracuse University

Allyn and Bacon, Inc.   Boston · London · Sydney

This book is part of A GUIDEBOOK FOR TEACHING Series

Library of Congress Cataloging in Publication Data

Cormican, John, 1940–
  A guidebook for teaching about the English language.

  (A Guidebook for teaching series)
  Includes bibliographies.
  1. English language—Study and teaching (Secondary)
I. Stanford, Gene, joint author. II. Title. II. Series.
LB1631.C68   1978   420'.7'12   78-8514
ISBN 0-205-06119-2

For Elin

About the authors

John Cormican, who has taught English language courses for more than fifteen years, and has served as Associate Professor of English at Utica College of Syracuse University, received his Ph.D. from the University of Michigan. A regular contributor to *The Old English Newsletter*, he has also published in a number of other journals including: *Ball State University Forum, Papers in Linguistics, Social Casework, Geriatrics, Child: Care, Health and Development* and *University of South Florida Language Quarterly*. His articles cover the study of the English language from Old English linguistics and Germanic philology to today's sociolinguistics.

Gene Stanford, a former high school English teacher, received his Ph.D. from the University of Colorado. He has served as Associate Professor of Education and Director of Teacher Education Programs at Utica College of Syracuse University. Dr. Stanford is the author of numerous books, including *A Guidebook for Teaching Composition, A Guidebook for Teaching Creative Writing,* and *Human Interaction in Education*, and is Consulting Editor for the *Guidebook for Teaching* Series, all published by Allyn and Bacon, Inc.

Contents

Preface

From its inception, this book has been designed to serve a unique purpose: providing the English teacher with so many specific ideas and resources for teaching about the English language that he or she could never use them all. There are already too many books that outline in a general way what high school students need to know about their own language, that convey the content of language study without providing specific suggestions for how to help students learn that content.

By contrast, we have tried to produce a comprehensive handbook with an emphasis on practicality. For each aspect of language that a teacher might wish to introduce students to, *A Guidebook for Teaching About the English Language* provides instructional objectives, a summary of the basic concepts related to that area of the content, classroom activities, discussion questions, small-group activities, projects, individual assignments, annotated lists of materials, and even sample tests. Perhaps the most valuable feature of the book is the section of Reproduction Pages, which can be used to make masters for spirit duplication or transparencies for the overhead projector—saving the teacher hours of preparation time.

Although the book often suggests a sequence of activities that might be useful in teaching a particular concept, the teacher can choose those materials and strategies that he or she wants to use without being locked into prescribed lesson plans. In general, for each topic the book provides:

1. A brief introduction to the concepts that the chapter deals with, along with a brief discussion of why these concepts might be important for students to study and an outline of what choices the teacher may need to make in organizing instruction of these concepts

2. A list of objectives that the methods and materials in the chapter help the student achieve, saving teachers the tedium of writing behavioral objectives of lesson plans

3. An overview of the content of the chapter, which serves a dual purpose: first, to remind the teacher of the basic content of that particular area of language study; and second, to provide the raw material for brief lectures by the teachers if he or she wishes to utilize this teaching method

4. A wealth of learning experiences to involve the student actively in the study of the concepts of the chapter

5. Sample tests to determine how well the student has achieved the objectives of the unit

6. Annotated lists of materials, including books, films, filmstrips, cassettes, and slide-tape programs

Rather than promote a single approach to teaching about language, our goal has been to suggest activities and materials that teachers with a wide variety of teaching styles and philosophies will find useful. Thus, for example, although we describe numerous activities that put students to work in small groups (since we believe this is an extremely effective approach that many teachers have neglected), we also include activities that allow the students to work individually. The reader is encouraged to understand the rationale for each of the approaches and to choose those which are most consistent with his or her own goals and students' needs.

However, we do have our own set of biases—our own viewpoint, if you will—based on our own ideas of what language study should be and our own philosophy of education developed from a number of years of teaching English in many different settings. This viewpoint is likely to be evident throughout the book. We believe, for example, that students need to be exposed to new ideas clearly; that students learn more when they are given the opportunity to relate new ideas to their own experience; that students learn from discussions with their fellow students as well as from listening to the teacher; that in order to be valuable education must also be dangerous or controversial at times; and finally that language is intrinsically interesting because language is human behavior.

Most of the activities and approaches included in this book were developed for, and used successfully with, our own classes. We feel confident, therefore, that many other teachers will find them practical and useful. But we have no way of knowing whether *A Guidebook for Teaching About the English Language* has been helpful without feedback from those who use it. We invite you to write us your comments about the book, using the Feedback Form that appears at the end of the book (p. 458). It can be torn out and mailed with a minimum of inconvenience. We promise you a personal reply and will sincerely appreciate your suggestions. They will help us decide what kinds of changes to make when we revise this book.

Our gratitude is extended to the producers of educational materials who supplied us with review copies and to the following copyright holders who gave us permission to use material published previously: Harcourt Brace Jovanovich, St. Martin's Press, John Wiley and Sons, Houghton Mifflin Company, University of Michigan Press, Prentice-Hall, and the Ohio Historical Society.

John Cormican
Gene Stanford

A Guidebook for Teaching About the ENGLISH LANGUAGE

1

Language as a System of Human Behavior

This chapter introduces language, differentiates it from things with which it is commonly confused, and explains the systematic way that a child acquires language. A practical result of this unit is that students should lose their fear of speaking, since, by definition, all normal children learn the "correct" system of their language at an early age. An ancillary result is that students should develop a heightened awareness of nonverbal types of human communication and of nonhuman communication.

First, the student should be made aware that language is only one method of human communication, but also the most precise one. This idea may be illustrated by using gestures, body language, and writing to express simple ideas like "Come here" and "I am afraid of you." One should also point out initially that preschoolers communicate clearly before they learn to write.

Next, the student should notice how limited his or her communication would be if he or she were limited to the types of nonlinguistic modes of communication that other species have and that he or she was limited to as an infant. Obvious examples that students are likely to be familiar with are dogs and cats. This awareness should increase the student's appreciation for language as a unique human attribute, since only humans have the potential to develop language.

Finally, the student may be introduced to the idea that language is developed by each child in a systematic way with various stages. This topic can serve as an introduction to the concept that language has structure.

The first two topics in this chapter are essential to the study of language as language. The teacher will have to decide whether he or she wishes to introduce the third topic as well.

OBJECTIVES

If all the topics in this chapter are chosen by the teacher, the student should, at the end, be able to:

1. Define language
2. Explain the relationship and difference between language and writing
3. Give examples of nonverbal communication used by humans
4. Explain why the communication systems of species other than humans are not language
5. Demonstrate that language is arbitrary in selecting sequences of sound to represent a particular concept
6. Give at least one example of the systematic nature of the English language
7. Give evidence that a language is learned rather than inborn
8. Identify the stages of language development in a small child

---

CONTENT OVERVIEW

What Language Is

Language is a learned *oral* system of arbitrary symbols used for communication among human beings. Language is arbitrary because each language reflects the peculiar experiences of its speakers, that is, their culture. Nevertheless, each language has its own systematized or patterned way in which these oral symbols may be combined.

It will be obvious to students that a baby is not born speaking English or Spanish or Japanese. It may be less obvious, however, that a child has no particular predisposition toward learning one language as opposed to another. Instead, a child is born with an innate ability to learn language, and the particular one or ones he or she learns are determined by the language or languages he or she hears in the immediate environment.

Since students mastered their language before they came to school and have spent a great deal of time in school reading and writing, it is necessary to emphasize that language is oral and that writing is only an attempt to approximate a particular language graphically. These points may be made by noting that writing is a relatively recent development in the history of man—the earliest writing systems more advanced than picture drawing are only about five thousand years old—while language has been used as long as man has been *Homo sapiens,* since the thinking and cultural developments that define *Homo sapiens* could not exist without language. It should also be noted that many cultures in the world, as well as illiterate members of the literate cultures, have developed language but make no use of writing systems; the converse is never true: no culture ever developed a writing system without first developing a language to be recorded by that writing system.

That language is a system should be readily apparent to students who speak or have studied more than one language. To reinforce this concept or to introduce it to those unfamiliar with more than one language, it will be useful to contrast the parts of different language systems illustrated by the "same" sentence in different languages: *The book is large*; Latin *magnus liber* (literally, "large [is] book"); German *Das Buch ist gross;* Hebrew *hasefer gadol* (literally, "the book [is] large"). It might also be useful to point out the system, that is, word order, inflections, derivational affixes, function words, and intonation patterns, in simple English sentences like *The beautiful girl reads very well, The beautiful girl reads very well?* and *Does the beautiful girl read very well?*

That language is arbitrary can be shown by pointing out that while the biological function of fatherhood is a universal human phenomenon, words for that function do not sound very similar: Spanish *padre*; German *Vater*; Yoruba *baba*; Irish *athir*; and English *father, daddy,* and *pop.* Even onomatopoetic words are arbitrary despite the claim that such words sound like the things they represent in nature. For instance, the following words for the sounds of a dog barking—Japanese *wung-wung*, Urdu *vow-vow*, French *gnaf-gnaf*, Irish *amh-amh*, and Serbo-Croatian *av-av*—do not sound much like the English onomatopoetic words *bow-wow*, *arf-arf*, and *ruff-ruff* (which do not sound all that similar to each other). Similarly, dropping a book on a desk and asking English-speaking students to write the word for the sound of the book dropping will elicit conventional and dissimilar-sounding words like *thud, bang, boom, plop, bam,* and some creative contributions from the students.

The combinations of sounds used in a language are also symbolic, that is, they stand for something in that particular language. In English, the word *kitten* stands symbolically for a particular thing commonly found in the environment of English-speaking people. The word *nettik* does not. Similarly, the syntactic arrangement of the words in the sentence *The teacher can read a book very rapidly* represents a possible relationship between things common to the English-speaking culture; *a book rapidly very can teacher the read,* on the other hand, is not English and does not stand for anything (despite the fact that it is made up of individual English words, i.e., meaningful combinations of sound).

Since language is symbolic and human, it follows that humans use it to communicate ideas among themselves. While some communication could be carried on if people carried around objects they wanted to communicate about so they could point to them, or if they could draw clear pictures, no one could carry everything around with him or her that he or she might want to talk about, and not all persons can draw intelligible pictures. The most important function of language, however, is in communicating abstract ideas like love, morality, and history; without language, one could not communicate the humane ideas which separate *Homo sapiens* from other species.

Only humans have language. Of course, other species are able to communicate by bodily movements (often instinctive) just as humans can. Many species also communicate orally; the important differences between the oral communications of other species and human languages are that the oral communications of other species are instinctive rather than learned, limited in number as opposed to infinite, restricted to the immediate environment as opposed to capable of representing things not present, and nonspecific rather than specific. For example, a mother chicken may cluck in such a way as to indicate danger to her chicks without having to teach them the meaning of these clucks, but she cannot communicate danger ahead of time so that the chicks will know what to fear, nor can she indicate that the danger is represented by two foxes seventy yards away in some tall grass as opposed to a hawk flying toward the chicks from the northeast. She also cannot communicate a very large repertoire of things to her chicks other than warnings or calls to approach her.

Other Methods of Communication

Humans also have other ways of communicating than through language and the graphic attempts to represent language, that is, writing. Attempts to represent writing and thus language secondarily like Morse code, semaphore, and Braille are interesting but peripheral. More important, however, are gestures, which are conscious body movements (usually of hands and arms), and kinesics, which are largely unconscious body movements and may involve the whole body. Gestures of greeting and farewell are the easiest to illustrate and, of course, vary from culture to culture. Students will also be familiar with standardized insulting gestures and hand movements to indicate that someone else is crazy. They will be less familiar with how the whole body is used to communicate, but even here they should be able to grasp how certain emotions like fear are communicated by the body. They may be made aware of how certain body movements are made to emphasize important words if they are shown silent movies or sound movies or television with the sound turned off.

How Children Learn a Language

Just as a child makes random body movements before he or she learns to use his or her body to communicate, a child makes random oral noises before learning to use the sounds as part of language. The child makes crying sounds initially, cooing sounds during the third month after birth, and babbling sounds in the fifth or sixth months. It is not until sometime between the ages of eight and eighteen months that the child begins to use the sounds he or she makes to approximate the sounds that an adult would make in order to express an idea, that is, to use language.

At the first or holophrastic stage of language development, the child speaks one-word sentences. *Eat* may mean *I want to eat,* for example. At the second or analytic stage, the child recognizes the different elements in his or her holophrastic sentences and may say sentences like *Me eat.* At the third or syntactic stage, the child has established classes of words and makes substitutions from among these classes in his telegraphic sentences (those sentences devoid of grammatical morphemes like articles, prepositions, and noun and verb inflections); the child may say *Mommy eat* and *Daddy eat* as well as *Me eat,* and *Me drink* and *Me sleep* as well as *Me eat.* The structural stage ends when the child starts using subordinate clauses like *Will you read to me if I drink my milk?* At the last or stylistic stage of language development, the child develops a repertoire of ways to say "the same thing" and knows that they have the same meaning, such as *Give the ball to me* and *Give me the ball.* Even in the stylistic stage, initially the child's language will differ significantly from that of an adult in some ways, such as avoiding passive sentences and using *because* and *therefore* to express time relationships rather than causal ones; at the end of the stylistic stage, the child will not only speak like an adult, but he will also be an adult linguistically.

LEARNING EXPERIENCES

Topic I: What Language Is

- Have students break up into groups of four or five and assign each group to come up with a definition of language. Have a member from each group write that group's definition of language on the board. Let the class arrive at the definition of language by discussing the groups' definitions, but be prepared to ask relevant questions to elicit aspects of language that the groups may all have overlooked.

- Ask a student who speaks Pig Latin or any other concealment language to explain how to speak it. The important thing to emphasize here is that the concealment language is systematic (in this case, a systematic changing of an already systematic language).

- Ask students who speak a non-English language to contrast a short sentence in that language with its English equivalent in terms of word order of subject-verb-(object) and modifiers, that is, adjectives before or after nouns, and grammatical categories like grammatical gender or inflections for case. The point to be made here is that English has a system, too, but one that most speakers of English have not thought about consciously.

- Drop an object or break a stick and ask the students to write down the word for the sound they have just heard. You will probably elicit several conventional words from the students. You should then point out that the words may be quite dissimilar and yet are used to describe the same sound. The point here is that even so-called onomatopoetic words are arbitrary; they, like all other words, have no natural connection to the sounds they are alleged to represent but are only conventional, arbitrary symbols for those sounds.

- Ask the students to write down the sound that a dog makes while barking and then ask them what they wrote. If responses include things like *bow-wow, woof, arf-arf,* and *ruff-ruff,* point out how dissimilar and arbitrary these words are and that none of them really reflects the sound a barking dog makes. If there are students in the class who speak a non-English language, ask them what the words for the barking of a dog are in those languages. They should be different enough from the English words to make the point clearly about language sounds being arbitrary.

- To demonstrate that language is oral and that writing is secondary and sometimes a poor representation of language, have the students say the following phrases, which may be written the same way but that are said differently and have different meanings (students may provide other examples):

  1. Frank's Body Works (car repair shop)
     Frank's Body Works (newspaper headline about a superior athlete)

  2. old maid (spinster)
     old maid (elderly servant)

  3. hot line (direct phone communication)
     hot line (wire with electrical current)

  4. little woman (wife)
     little woman (small female)

  5. old man (father)
     old man (elderly male)

  6. look over the fence (examine it)
     look over the fence (peer on the other side)

- To prove that the English language has a system, ask the students to indicate whether the following sentences are English or not. Although the students may not be able to explain why some sentence is not English, the point to emphasize is that they *know* the system or they could not classify the sentences as English or non-English:

  1. Bill often eats here.
  2. Bill never eats here.
  3. Never, Bill eats here.
  4. Often, Bill eats here.
  5. John writes a lot.
  6. Writes John a lot?
  7. Does John write a lot?
  8. Mary saw door.
  9. Mary saw the door.
  10. He arrived today.
  11. He arrived tomorrow.
  12. He arrived yesterday.
  13. He saw a dog.

14. He saw two dog.

15. He saw a deer.

16. He saw two deer.

- Have each student write a short essay relating an experience where he or she has misinterpreted the communications of a pet or a small baby.

Topic II: Other Methods of Communication

- Divide the class into groups of three or four and instruct them to write a story that will be acted out without words or in mime. Let the rest of the class attempt to determine what the story was about. If your students are good actors, you may discover that they communicate well with gestures and kinesics. If so, emphasize the idea of nonlinguistic communication. If no one can figure out the stories, emphasize the importance of language in human communication.

- As a variation on the activity above, let each member of the group acting out the story say *one* key word as he or she acts. This may help the rest of the class interpret the body movements more accurately and see the importance of body movements accompanying speech in communication.

- Show silent movies or sound movies or television with the sound turned off and let the class carry on a running commentary about what is happening on the screen. They may be able to interpret the screen action quite well.

- If there are any Boy Scouts or other students in the class who can signal messages with flags, have them demonstrate this method of communication.

- Use your state's driver's license manual to illustrate the traditional hand signals for turns and stops while driving a car. It will be necessary to point out to students that for many years cars did not come equipped with turn signals.

- Ask your students what is communicated by traffic signals when the red, yellow, and green lights are on and what flashing red lights and flashing yellow lights mean when one is driving.

- Ask your students to demonstrate how they would warn each other that you were coming back to the classroom if you had left it momentarily after telling them to remain quietly in their seats while you were gone.

- Ask your students to demonstrate gestures with which they are familiar. Be prepared for the worst gestures, but try to elicit handshakes, kisses, salutes, bowing, and kneeling.

- If any of your students plays catcher on a baseball or softball team, ask him or her to demonstrate signals he or she uses with the pitcher.

- Ask students with pets to tell how their pets communicate with them and specifically *what* they can communicate.

- Tape a dog barking, a cat meowing, a cow mooing, a baby crying, etc., and ask the students to interpret what each sound means. There will probably be wide discrepancies in their interpretations.

- Identify students wearing rings or jewelry and ask them to show them to the rest of the class. Have the rest of the class interpret the message conveyed by the jewelry. Class rings, birthstone rings, crosses, and Stars of David will be obvious communicators, but there may also be more subtle messages. You might also want to mention what wedding rings communicate.

- Have each student write a short essay on the many ways he or she communicates with a close friend or relative.

- Have each student observe a sports activity or a ceremony such as a wedding, a funeral, or any religious ritual and report back to the class on the paralinguistic and kinesic aspects of the event.

Topic III: How Children Learn a Language

- Assign different groups to approximate how a child at the ages of one month, one year, two years, and three years would convey the following different messages to its parents: *I am tired; I am hungry; my stomach hurts; I wet my diaper (or pants)*. Be prepared for the groups dealing with the child at the first two ages to become frustrated, but use that frustration to point out that babies must often be frustrated too and that language is probably more important to the students now than they may have realized.

- Arrange for some students who have younger brothers, sisters, nephews, or nieces to have them brought to school so the students can talk to their younger relatives and elicit linguistic responses from them. This activity should obviously be coordinated with parents' day or be conducted sometime when adults would be visiting the school anyway in order to inconvenience the parents of the small children as little as possible. The young child will be most likely to talk (coo or babble) with a familiar person, that is, the student who is related to the child.

- Show a film or play a record or a tape of young children talking. If the child is still an infant, no doubt an adult will be talking with the child. You may then point out how the adult stimulates the child to talk and reinforces the child's attempts. If the child is old enough to be corrected by the adult, point out that this correction is necessary for the child to learn the language of the surrounding adult world.

- From a film or their own observations, ask the students to pick out examples of how an adult talking to a small child changes his or her speech pattern to help the child learn; for example, saying, *Give Mommy a kiss* rather than *Give me a kiss*, using short sentences with no subordinate clauses, and using simple words.

- From a film or tape of a baby or observation of a baby, ask the students to pick out which sounds the child can make or if the child is a little older which sounds or sequences of sound he cannot make.

- From a film or tape or direct observation of a baby, have the students listen for intonation patterns which sound like English sentences (even if the words are unintelligible).

- From a film or tape or observation, have the students pick out the kinds of words small children use first (verbs, nouns, pronouns) and the kinds omitted (articles, conjunctions, prepositions, adverbs).

- Ask the students to visit their former kindergarten or first-grade teacher to listen to his or her speech patterns. The students will often discover that the teacher continues to modify his or her speech patterns to make them appropriate for small children even when the teacher is not talking to small children. Specifically, ask the students if they felt their former teacher was treating them as if they were still small children.

- Ask each student to write down a short conversation he or she has outside of class with a small child. Have each student read the conversation to the class, which can then pick out changes from the student's normal speech pattern.

- Have each student write an essay on what he or she imagines he or she thought or felt about life as a one-year-old.

ASSESSING ACHIEVEMENT OF OBJECTIVES

Ongoing Evaluation

The extent to which students have mastered the concepts covered under the three topics can be measured by any of the activities assigned to class members as individuals, particularly the writing activities.

Final Evaluation

For an overall evaluation of the students' grasp of the concepts in the chapter, if all topics in the chapter have been taught, a test constructed directly from the list of student objectives for the chapter as listed on page 2 can be used. As an alternative, one might compose a test from the following items:

1. Defend the statement that only human beings use language.

2. Explain why children learn to speak before they learn to read or write.

3. Identify three ways that human beings communicate other than by the use of language.

4. To what extent should onomatopoeia be taken seriously?

5. Give three different words for the same thing in English.

6. Explain why *The girl big sat outside the chair* is not an English sentence.

7. List five words that you know that you would not expect a three-year-old child to know and tell why you do but he or she doesn't know them.

8. Tell why, if you were a bird with hungry children, you would have difficulty explaining to them that you couldn't find any food for them.

9. Suppose you had laryngitis. How would you convey messages to other people?

10. Give examples of the types of sentences a child might speak at the holophrastic, analytic, syntactic, structural, and stylistic stages of language development.

RESOURCES FOR TEACHING ABOUT LANGUAGE AS A SYSTEM OF HUMAN BEHAVIOR

Below is a selected and annotated list of resources useful for teaching the topics in this chapter and arranged in order of ascending difficulty. Special strengths and weaknesses are mentioned in the annotations. Addresses of publishers or distributors can be found in the alphabetical list on pages 263–265 in Appendix A. Films are black and white unless otherwise indicated.

I. WHAT LANGUAGE IS

Audiovisual Materials

Speaking of Language. Sound filmstrip (sound on LP record or cassette tape), 25 minutes, 1971, Guidance Associates. Discusses the nature of language and the external history of the English language.

Nature of Language. Film, part of *Principles and Methods of Teaching a Second Language* Series, 28 minutes, 1961, Indiana University Audio-Visual Center. Defines language, contrasts language with writing, and shows how different languages have different sound and grammatical systems.

Definition of Language, A. Film, part of *Language and Linguistic* Series, 30 minutes, 1958, Indiana University Audio-Visual Center. Defines language and shows the relationship between language and culture.

Print

"Characteristics of Language," pp. L16–L24 in *Purpose and Change* by Albert R. Kitzhaber et al. Presents a simple discussion of language emphasizing its systematic and symbolic nature. Hardbound, Holt, Rinehart, and Winston, 1974.

"Human Speech" and "Language as Social Behavior," pp. 3–13 in *The Structure of American English* by W. Nelson Francis. Gives one of the clearest definitions of what language is. Hardbound, The Ronald Press Co., 1958.

"A Definition of Language," pp. 3–8 in *Introduction to Linguistics* by Ronald Wardhaugh. Presents a clear, detailed discussion of what language is. Paperbound, McGraw-Hill, 1972.

"Some Traits of Language," pp. 11–18 in *Aspects of Language* by Dwight Bolinger. Presents a clear, detailed analysis of what language is but lacks a coherent definition. Paperbound. Harcourt, Brace and World, 1968.

"Some Traits of Language," pp. 13–19 in *Working with Aspects of Language* by Mansoor Alyeshmerni and Paul Taubr. Consists of exercises showing the systematic and arbitrary nature of language. Paperbound, Harcourt, Brace and World, 1970.

"For Different Languages, Different Systems," pp. 12–13 in *Problems in the Origins and Development of the English Language,* 2nd ed., by John Algeo. Provides an exercise showing differences among the language systems of English, Pidgin English, Latin, and Esperanto. Paperbound, Harcourt Brace Jovanovich, 1971.

II. OTHER METHODS OF COMMUNICATION

Audiovisual Materials

Introduction. Film, part of *Language and Linguistics* Series, 29 minutes, 1958, Indiana University Audio-Visual Center. Focuses primarily on how the words people use influence the way they see the world and the way they think, but also discusses and illustrates kinesics and paralanguage.

Language, Signs and Symbols: How Man Communicates. Sound-slide set (sound on LP record or cassette tape), 15- and 18-minute programs, 1972, The Center for Humanities, Inc. Provides an excellent correlation of visual artworks on slides with discussions of language as medium of communication and reflector of culture (part 1) and writing, body language, and other symbols used in communication (part 2).

Language and Meaning. Film, part of *Language and Linguistics* Series, 29 minutes, 1958, Indiana University Audio-Visual Center. Discusses the relationship of paralanguage and kinesics to language and meaning and shows how congruence or incongruence of the various types of human communication may be used to analyze psychiatric interviews.

Print

"Animal Communication" and "Who Can Learn Human Language?" pp. L5-L15 and L24-L32, in *Purpose and Change* by Albert R. Kitzhaber et al. Presents a cursory survey of the communication systems of several species but a very good description of bees' communications and a summary of attempts to teach human language to other species. Provides discussion questions. Hardbound, Holt, Rinehart and Winston, 1974.

"Nonverbal Communication," pp. 1-21 in *Patterns of Communicating* (Grade 8) by Allan A. Glatthorn and Jane Christensen. Presents a simple but fairly complete analysis of human nonverbal communication with suggested exercises. Hardbound, D.C. Heath and Co., 1975.

"Cats and Babies," by Stuart Chase, pp. 24-29 in *Language and Literature for Composition*, edited by Sanford R. Radner and Susan G. Radner. Discusses in easily understood terms the limitations of communication systems of nonhuman species and contrasts these systems with human

language. Paperbound, Thomas Y. Crowell Co., 1973.

"Nonlinguistic Human Communication" and "Animal Communication," pp. 17-24 in *Introduction to Linguistics* by Ronald Wardhaugh. Discusses the various aspects of paralanguage, introduces kinesics, and provides some information about the communication systems of jackdaws, bees, gibbons, and dolphins. Paperbound, McGraw-Hill, 1972.

"Masculinity and Femininity as Display," pp. 39-46 in *Kinesics and Context* by Ray L. Birdwhistle. Points out how members of seven cultures identify certain body movements used in communication as masculine or feminine, with emphasis on speakers of American English. Paperbound, University of Pennsylvania Press, 1972.

"Toward Analyzing American Movement," pp. 99-110 in *Kinesics and Context* by Ray L. Birdwhistle. Discusses characteristic body movements which systematically co-occur with American speech. Paperbound, University of Pennsylvania Press, 1972.

"Winking, Blinking, and Nods," by Julius Fast, pp. 501-510 in *Language,* edited by Virginia P. Clark et al. Discusses the use of eyes in communication and focuses on cultural and sexual differences. Paperbound, St. Martin's Press, 1972.

"The Sounds of Silence," by Edward T. Hall and Mildred Reed Hall, pp. 459-470 in *Language,* edited by Virginia P. Clark et al. Provides a nontechnical discussion of kinesics (particularly eye movements) and proxemics, or the way space is used in human communication. Paperbound, St. Martin's Press, 1972.

"In Other Words," pp. 231-247 in *Word Play* by Peter Farb. Discusses cultural determination of body language, its use in television game shows and psychological experiments, and various sign languages. Paperbound, Bantam Books, 1974.

"When Space Is Invaded," by Julius Fast, pp. 531-543 in *Language,* edited by Virginia P. Clark et al. Analyzes the manipulation of space and kinesic defenses against invasion of space in the business world. Paperbound, St. Martin's Press, 1972.

"Nonverbal Communication and the Education of Children" by Paul Byers and Happie Byers, pp. 3-31 in *Functions of Language in the Classroom,* edited by Courtney B. Cazden et al. Focuses on problems of nonverbal communication by teachers to minority students. Paperbound, Teachers College Press, 1972.

"Movement with Speech," pp. 110–127 in *Kinesics and Context* by Ray L. Birdwhistle. Provides a discussion of kinesic markers co-occuring with American speech. Paperbound, University of Pennsylvania Press, 1972.

"Kinesic Stress in American English," pp. 128–143 in *Kinesics and Context* by Ray L. Birdwhistle. Presents a difficult and complex analysis of body-movement correlations with the four stress phonemes of American English. Paperbound, University of Pennsylvania Press, 1972.

III. HOW CHILDREN LEARN A LANGUAGE

Audiovisual Materials

Development of the Child: Language Development. Film, 20 minutes, 1972, Harper and Row. Shows acquisition of sounds, syntax, and semantics during the first four years of life.

Organization of Language. Film, part of *Principles and Methods of Teaching a Second Language* Series, 33 minutes, 1961, Indiana University Audio-Visual Center. Shows how children learn grammatical patterns and how grammatical patterns differ from language to language with primary foci on English and German.

Print

"They Learn the Same Way All Around the World" by Dan I. Slobin, pp. 19–28 in *Current Topics in Language,* edited by Nancy Ainsworth Johnson. Explains that children learning different languages go through the same stages of language acquisition. Paperbound, Winthrop Publishers, 1976.

"How Babies Learn Their Language," pp. 187–193 in *The Way of Language* by Fred West. Provides a good general introduction to how a child develops the sound and syntactic systems of a language. Paperbound, Harcourt Brace Jovanovich, 1975.

"Native Language Acquisition: What Children Learn," pp. 231–242 in *Linguistics and Language* by Julia S. Falk. Provides the most complete short summary of the stages of development by English-speaking children of the phonological and syntactic systems of English. Paperbound, Xerox, 1973.

"The Pattern of Early Speech" by David McNeill in *Current Topics in Language,* edited by Nancy Ainsworth Johnson. Discusses holophrastic and telegraphic speech in small children. Paperbound, Winthrop Publishers, 1976.

"Born to Speak," pp. 1–8 in *Aspects of Language* by Dwight Bolinger. Discusses the stages of syntactic development in a child's language in a concise and organized manner. Paperbound, Harcourt, Brace and World, 1968.

"Stages of Language Acquisition," p. 11 in *Working with Aspects of Language* by Mansoor Alyeshmerni and Paul Taubr. Provides an exercise on the five stages of syntactic development by children. Paperbound, Harcourt, Brace and World, 1970.

"Acquiring Negation and Questions" by Edward S. Klima and Ursula Bellugi, pp. 70–81 in *Current Topics in Language,* edited by Nancy Ainsworth Johnson. Uses transformational rules in a fairly difficult essay to show how negatives and questions are produced at three periods of a child's syntactic development. Paperbound, Winthrop Publishers, 1976.

2

The Influence of Language on Perception and Thought

This chapter focuses on how language forces us to think and to perceive reality within the constraints of the particular language we speak. A practical application of this phenomenon is the development of an awareness of how the English language causes us unconsciously to form stereotypes based on sex and ethnic backgrounds due to attitudes inherent within the language. Another practical application is the development of an awareness of how others may consciously manipulate us through their use of language.

Initially, the student should be made aware that the language he or she speaks does influence the way he or she sees the world and that speakers of other languages may very well interpret the things they see differently from the way he or she does because of differences in the languages. This can be illustrated with the use of words from other languages for concepts that do not occur in English, with the use of multiple vocabulary items centering around an important aspect of another culture which is represented by only a few words in English (i.e., Eskimo words for *snow,* Aymará Indian words for *potato,* or Australian aborigine kinship terms), or even a little child's use of *dog* to stand for all animals or *car* to stand for all vehicles.

Then the student will be ready to examine how the denotations and connotations of words in the English language help the speaker of English develop certain prejudices toward people. The student will also be prepared to examine how other people use the emotional content of words to attempt to manipulate him or her. Finally, the student will be able to analyze the underlying significance of our resorting to euphemisms as an attempt to deny unpleasant parts of the reality we perceive.

Only the first topic must be introduced sequentially. The others may be rearranged, and the teacher may choose to omit any of them.

OBJECTIVES

If all of the topics in this chapter are chosen by the teacher, the student should be able to:

1. Illustrate how he or she and the speaker of another language might see and describe the same thing or event differently
2. Explain how a positive or negative stereotype of a particular ethnic group is reinforced by the English language
3. Give an example of the sexist use of the English language
4. Explain the connotative differences between pairs of alleged synonyms in English
5. Identify misleading language in advertisements and explain why it was used
6. Identify the use of confusing or misleading language in newspapers, political pamphlets, and persuasive speeches
7. Express the same ideas euphemistically and directly
8. Express the same ideas with positive, negative, and neutral words
9. Differentiate related words using semantic feature matrices

CONTENT OVERVIEW

How Language Creates Different Realities

The Whorf-Sapir hypothesis is that a person's perception of the world is determined, in large part, by the language he speaks because of the inherent categories, both grammatical and substantive, within that particular language. Benjamin Lee Whorf, who had been Edward Sapir's student, demonstrated the contrasting verb categories of tense inherent in European languages—present, past, and future—with those for aspect in several American Indian languages which do not have tense markers. From these grammatical differences, he extrapolated a difference in world views between the speakers of European languages and the speakers of American Indian languages, essentially time orientation as opposed to process orientation. If one recalls Bacon's "Idols of the Mind," he may remember the idol dealing with the names of things that do not exist; however, the Whorf-Sapir hypothesis states that those things do exist in the world of the speaker of a language which has names for them. The pantheism of both the ancient Greeks and American Indians, for example, manifested itself in words in their languages for the different gods which were part of their worlds, even though these names refer to nothing in the world of a nonpantheist.

At a perhaps more familiar level, speakers of English who study foreign languages probably have encountered concepts in these foreign languages that do not have exact counterparts in English, and vice versa. The second person singular pronouns like German *du* or Spanish and French *tu* allow for a contrast in number that modern English *you* does not (except in those dialects which have created a new plural form like *you-all, youse,* or *you'uns*) and also for a contrast of familiarity versus politeness when addressing one person as in German *du* versus *Sie,* Spanish *tu* versus *usted,* and French *tu* versus *vous.* Similarly, words like Spanish *compadre* and Italian *compare* are poorly translated by the English word *friend,* since these languages have other words that mean *friend,* while *compadre* and *compare* mean something more than that. Even more familiar to students of foreign languages, the use of grammatical gender by some foreign languages rather than the English natural or sex-linked gender of nouns and the use of the subjunctive mood (nearly gone in modern English) of verbs in some languages present problems for many English speakers learning these languages. Speakers of European languages also find it strange that singular and plural are not required categories for nouns in Chinese, Japanese, or Korean and that Algonquin classifies nouns on the basis of animateness versus inanimateness while Navaho has twelve classes of nouns based on shape. While these language differences may seem superficial, there are others that reflect even more clearly a difference in perception by the speakers of various languages.

We who speak English usually think that colors as natural phenomena are universals and that everyone divides the color spectrum the way we do, but such is not the case. Bassa, a language spoken in Liberia, divides the spectrum into only two parts, while Shona, a language spoken in Rhodesia, divides it into three. The principle involved here may be shown most familiarly by pointing out that in general in Western cultures women have more color words in their vocabulary and make finer color distinctions than do men, unless, of course, the men happen to be artists, interior decorators, or color chemists.

How Language Reflects and Perpetuates Prejudicial Stereotypes

Color terms applied to racial stocks are equally arbitrary. For example, both Guyana and the Union of South Africa set up three racial categories—black, white, and colored (for racially mixed people)—whereas the United States uses only two terms to cover the same range. Incidentally, in South Africa, Japanese are white but Chinese are not. However, the color terms used for racial stocks in the United States also are highly connotative words; *white* generally has positive connotations in English (e.g., white wedding gowns symbolize purity), while *black* and *yellow* generally have negative connotations. The slogan "Black is beautiful" is a direct reaction to these negative connotations.

Just as the highly connotative words for races influence judgments about people who are labeled with those terms, the ethnic designations for hyphenated Americans also carry the stereotyped connotations felt to be true by many people (almost always erroneously). One feature of an ethnic designation is to signal that a person is somehow different from other people, and that difference is often assumed to be a negative one. The negative nature of such a designation is shown by the fact that there is always a more overtly derogatory term that can be substituted for the hyphenated American designation. My name is Irish in origin, but if someone wanted to offend me, he might call me a *mick* rather than an *Irish-American*. My wife's background is Finnish, but someone might choose to use the term *squarehead* rather than *Finnish-American* to refer to her. Since these ethnic labels often override other possible labels that could be used to designate a person such as teacher, social worker, blond, redhead, New Yorker, or Hoosier, they tend to falsify reality by focusing on one feature of a person and ignoring all other features while replacing those other features with stereotyped features associated with the ethnic label.

Other Misleading Language

Language is often misleading in other ways. Some professions, such as medicine and the law, use language that is confusing to many persons out of a certain necessity for precision. Others, however, do so out of choice rather than a desire for preciseness. Indeed, it is not totally unfair to accuse some advertising people and politicians of consciously using language in order to be imprecise. The "false comparative" in advertisements is a good example, for "better," "more," and other comparative forms that are not followed by "than X" phrases give the appearance of saying something they do not. Most teachers are aware of how common this practice has become after having read student papers and trying to explain the logical necessity of a comparison when a comparative form is used. Another conscious use of misleading or slanted language is the use of highly connotative words to influence people on an emotional rather than on a rational level to accept or reject certain ideas.

One way to encourage the students to use language carefully and to react to others' use of language carefully is to insist on clear definitions of highly connotative words. This precise definition may consist of identifying the precise semantic features underlying the words, or it may be something as simple as teaching that all members of a class are not identical, that is, dog_1 is not dog_2 or $socialist_1$ is not $socialist_2$. Another way to encourage students to use language carefully is to get them to examine the reality that euphemisms are invented to disguise, found, for example, in death being referred to as "eternal rest."

LEARNING EXPERIENCES

Topic I: How Language Creates Different Realities

- Hold up sheets of construction paper of various nonprimary colors and ask the students to write down the names of the color. Discuss the differences in the color words used to describe each sheet of paper and whether these differences might lead to problems in communication. If there are differences between the number of color words used by male and female students (females usually have more color words), discuss how this difference came about through acculturation and how it might interfere with communication between the sexes.

- Ask the students to list as many types of saws and of cakes as they can think of. If there is a difference in lengths of the two lists between the sexes, discuss how this difference is also culturally determined and how it might contribute to misunderstandings.

- Ask the students what *it* refers to in *It is rainy* or *It is warm today*. Point out that the pronoun *it* usually has a specific antecedent in English, but the structure of the language sometimes forces us to create fake subjects to sentences since sentences in English normally have a subject and a predicate.

- If you and your students speak or have studied a modern European language, show with comparative examples how certain concepts are shown in that language that are not shown in English. Possible concepts include the subjunctive versus the indicative mood of verbs, the imperfect versus the perfect tense of verbs, or gender as in Spanish or Italian *primo* versus *prima*, French *cousin* versus *cousine*, or German *Amerikaner* versus *Amerikanerin*.

- Ask each student to prepare a list of vocabulary items that he or she uses in pursuing some special interest or hobby such as skiing, tropical fish, football, and so on, or which his parent uses at his job such as farming, automotive mechanics, social work, law, and so on. Then ask the students to compare lists to see how many of the words in their own reality are not known by their classmates.

- Make lists of pairs of antonyms in English like *innocent* and *guilty, cheap* and *expensive.* Then see if the class can come up with words that stand between these polar opposites. Frequently, there will be none, since English tends to operate with absolutes. In some legal systems, however, the question is not whether one is innocent or guilty but rather how much guilt he has.

**Topic II: How Language Reflects and
Perpetuates Prejudicial Stereotypes**

- Ask the students to come up with English clichés involving *right* and *left*, like *right-hand man* and *out in left field*. After lists are made, examine them to see how many of those involving *right* are positive and how many involving *left* are negative and whether these clichés show a negative attitude toward left-handed people. You might add that the negative terms *sinister* and *gauche* originated from terms meaning "left-handed" in Latin and French, respectively, while the positive terms *dextrous* and *adroit* come from terms meaning "right-handed" in those languages.

- Go through the language of the Declaration of Independence and parts of the Constitution in class to determine the attitude of the founding fathers toward women. The absence of specific references and of feminine pronouns should give a clue.

- Ask the class if there is any significance to a married woman adopting the last name of her husband or even to becoming Mrs. *John* Smith. You might also arouse a lively discussion as to whether the women's liberationists are correct in finding the use of *Miss* and *Mrs.* an indication of a double standard by signaling availability whereas *Mr.* for men indicates nothing about availability.

- Show large pictures of various persons and get the class's guesses as to the personalities of these people from their appearance. Then attach ethnic-sounding names to the same pictures and record any changes in personality attribution that the class makes. Then discuss the changes made in supposed personalities because of the ethnic designation as evidence of stereotypes carried by ethnic names.

- Elicit from the class their stereotypes of members of various ethnic groups as shown in the activity above. Then talk about persons with ethnic-sounding names that do not fit each stereotype. The class will usually be able to provide these counterexamples, but you should have some well-known counterexamples in mind in case the class does not come up with them.

- When teaching primarily black students, we have asked them to describe what they think the white stereotype of blacks is and then to describe their own stereotype of whites. The stereotypes have turned out to be similar enough to point out the meaninglessness of stereotypes associated with labels for people. Again, counterexamples help to invalidate both stereotyped lists of features. We would, of course, urge caution in using this activity or modification of it, but it can be useful if a class is predominantly from one ethnic background if the teacher focuses initially on the stereotype associated with that ethnic background.

- Ask the class for clichés in English that reflect prejudices toward one group or another. Be sure that all such clichés are exposed as false, however.

- In order to show how all ethnic terms imply a negative difference, list all of the hyphenated-American terms for Americans of different ethnic backgrounds and elicit their corresponding derogatory terms from the class. Begin with your own ethnic-background terms, both hyphenated and derogatory, in order to show that no one should take offense from the derogatory terms.

- After the stereotypes associated with ethnic names have been shown to be false, ask the students to explain why such stereotypes and labels remain. Possible areas of discussion are: desire to have a quick key to the personality of people one meets; simply repeating what a person has heard; and compensating for one's own feelings of inferiority by putting others down.

- Have each student write a paper on a stereotype he or she is familiar with and whether it is an accurate description of *all* members of the group to which it is applied.

- Have each student write a paper on how a label attached to him or her has influenced his or her life, either positively or negatively.

- Have each student write an essay describing how he or she feels after having been called a derogatory term.

Topic III: Connotations and Euphemisms

- Give the students a list of words like the following with the directions to think of as many words as they can which persons use to avoid these unpleasant or taboo words:

1.	bathroom	6.	drunk	11.	janitor	16.	poor
2.	corpse	7.	false teeth	12.	Jesus (profanity)	17.	pregnant
3.	crippled	8.	fat	13.	murder	18.	retarded
4.	damn	9.	God (profanity)	14.	old person	19.	stupid
5.	death	10.	insane	15.	pimples	20.	war

- After the students have made their lists, ask them why some persons avoid the words in the original list.

- Although Americans are often uncomfortable about certain bodily functions, it is generally acceptable when one must discuss them to use Latinate terms, which, in essence, function as euphemisms for the Anglo-Saxon terms. *Defecate* and *urinate* are such Latinate terms used euphemistically to avoid the Anglo-Saxon terms, which are considered obscene. (It is not necessary to mention them; your students already know them.) Ask your students to think of other euphemistic terms for *defecate* and *urinate*. As a hint, you might ask them to think of terms that little children use.

- Hand out an exercise like the following list of alleged synonyms to the class and ask each student to pick the word in each set that sounds the best and the one that sounds the worst.

    1. antiquated, antique, old
    2. conservative, old-fashioned, unchanged
    3. aromatic, stinking, odorous
    4. firm, indomitable, stubborn
    5. complimentary, flattering, laudatory
    6. enthusiastic, fanatical, zealous
    7. preowned, secondhand, used
    8. slim, skinny, thin
    9. parsimonious, stingy, tight
    10. plan, scheme, strategy
    11. funeral director, mortician, undertaker
    12. custodian, janitor, maintenance man
    13. change, progress, reaction

14. attorney, lawyer, shyster
15. bachelor girl, old maid, unmarried women
16. cop, policeman, police officer
17. apparel, clothes, getup
18. alcohol, booze, liquor
19. broad, lady, woman
20. gentleman, guy, man
21. abdomen, belly, stomach
22. bribe, payment, reward
23. cemetery, graveyard, memorial park
24. flick, motion picture, movie
25. minister, pastor, preacher
26. home, house, residence
27. daydream, meditate, think
28. acquire, obtain, take
29. intercede, interfere, intervene
30. liquidate, kill, murder
31. brainwash, indoctrinate, teach
32. build, construct, make
33. puke, regurgitate, vomit
34. conserve, hoard, save
35. good morning, hello, hi

There should be general agreement on most words that can then lead into a general discussion of connotations versus denotations.

- Set up a connotation scale from 1 to 5 or 1 to 10, with 1 being the most negative connotation and the highest number being the most positive connotation. Then have the class rate common nouns like *mother, father, sister, brother, cat, dog, rat, teacher,* and so on, for their degree of positive or negative connotation on a piece of paper. This exercise should show how certain things are generally perceived the same way within the culture. The same process may be repeated with adjectives easily and less easily with verbs and adverbs.

Topic IV: The Use of Misleading Language

- Bring newspaper or magazine articles to class and have the students pick out things in an article that imply that something is true but avoids making clearly untrue statements.

- Have students bring advertisements to class that use misleading words and have the rest of the class pick out the misleading words.

- Have students bring advertisements to class that use words with positive connotations in order to attach positive connotations to the products advertised.

- Examine the connotations behind well-known brand or product names to determine what market they were designed to appeal to and how. Brand names of soaps, clothes, and cars would be good places to begin.

- Have students examine statements by politicians that either beg the questions asked or that imply something without committing the politician to a particular course of action. The statements of politicians may also be examined for their use of highly connotative words.

- Have students examine newspaper or magazine editorials or articles for evidence of slanted or highly connotative writing whose purpose is to influence the reader's opinion at an emotional level.

- Have each student write an essay showing how he or she or someone else avoided trouble by using misleading language but avoiding lying.

SEMANTIC DISTINCTIONS

Directions: *Fill in the feature matrices below to describe these common English kinship terms with + if the word has the feature and − if the feature is absent. Notice that English does not specify one feature for cousin that it does for the other terms. The first term is marked for you.*

Term / Feature	Mother	Father	Sister	Brother	Aunt	Uncle	Cousin	Grand-mother	Grand-father
Same generation as speaker	−	−	+	+	−	−	+	−	−
One generation older than speaker									
Two generations older than speaker									
Female									

Directions: *Fill in the feature matrices below to describe these common domesticated animals with + if the word is associated with the feature and − if the feature is absent. Notice that the features might be different for the same word in different cultures. What other features might have been used?*

Term / Feature	Cow	Horse	Cat	Dog	Sheep	Goat	Pig
Pet							
Source of milk							
Source of meat							
Source of transportation							
Skin used by man							
Hair used by man							
Guard animal							

MORE SEMANTIC DISTINCTIONS

Directions: *Take common breeds of dogs and define them in terms of feature matrices. Some common breeds and some possible features are given, but you may add other breeds and other features to differentiate the breeds further.*

Term / Feature	Irish setter	German shepherd	Chihuahua	Collie				
Large								
Hunting								
Watchdog								
Stock dog								
Long hair								
Solid color								

- Have each student write a speech that a politician in your area might give in order to appeal to the voters' prejudices. The best ones should prove entertaining when read in class.

- Have each student write two short essays or stories in which the same ideas or events are seen from two different points of view and reported in such a way as to convey those different points of view.

Topic V: Semantics

- Discuss how arguments often result from two people using the same word like *best* to mean different things.

- Ask the students for words that mean one thing when they use the words with people their own age and something entirely different when they are used by older people, that is, *bad* meaning "good," *foxy* meaning "attractive" versus "sly."

- Discuss how students' slang often gives new meanings to old words in order to confuse adults. Some examples of your own student slang would be helpful.

- Using Reproduction Pages 1 and 2, duplicate the exercises that appear on p. 20 on semantic distinctions using feature matrices and distribute them in class. The first one might well be done individually by the students and then compared in class.

ASSESSING ACHIEVEMENT OF OBJECTIVES

Ongoing Evaluation

The extent to which students have mastered the concepts covered under each topic can be measured by any of the activities assigned to the class as individuals, particularly the writing activities.

Final Evaluation

For an overall evaluation of the students' mastery of the concepts in the chapter, if all topics in the chapter have been taught, a test constructed directly from the list of student objectives for the chapter as listed on page 14 can be used. As an alternative, one might consider a test composed of the following items:

1. Show with examples how negative attitudes toward left-handedness are reflected by the connotation of *right* and *left* in American English idioms and clichés.

2. Explain the difference and meaning and connotations between the sets of words (a) *white person, WASP,* and *honkie,* or (b) *black person, Negro,* and *nigger.*

3. What sex do you associate with each of these professions: *doctor, nurse, lawyer, secretary,* and *interior decorator*? Discuss whether these sexual stereotypes are valid. If you think they are valid, discuss whether they should be or not.

4. Give examples of how words or phrases in the English language reflect negative attitudes toward three different ethnic groups.

5. Explain the Whorf-Sapir hypothesis.

6. Give examples of sexist attitudes toward women reflected in the English language.

7. Illustrate with examples the use of misleading language found in advertisements.

8. Illustrate with examples the slanted or loaded language used by some politicians or editorial writers.

9. Although nearly all human hair is a shade of brown, what stereotypes are associated within American culture with the labels *blonde, brunette,* and *redhead*? Are there counterexamples to these stereotypes?

10. Illustrate how pairs of antonyms in English get positive or negative connotations because of the pattern of positive and negative associated with English antonyms such as *right* and *wrong, innocent* and *guilty, true* and *false.* For instance, what happens to pairs like *practical* and *theoretical, production* and *research,* and *work* and *leisure?*

RESOURCES FOR TEACHING ABOUT THE INFLUENCES OF LANGUAGE ON PERCEPTION AND THOUGHT

Below is a selected and annotated list of resources useful for teaching the topics in this chapter, divided into audiovisual materials and print materials and arranged in order of ascending difficulty. Special strengths and weaknesses are mentioned in the annotations. Addresses of publishers or distributors can be found in the alphabetical list of pages 263–265 in Appendix A. Films are black and white unless otherwise indicated.

I. HOW LANGUAGE CREATES DIFFERENT REALITIES

Audiovisual Materials

Language of Man, The: How Words Change Our Lives. Sound-slide set (sound on LP records or cassette tape), 16- and 22-minute programs, 1974, The Center for Humanities, Inc. Provides an excellent correlation of visual artworks and literary excerpts on slides with discussions of how words create different realities or distort reality, and how words have several meanings and are never the same as the thing they symbolize.

Words and Their Meanings. Film, part of *Principles and Methods of Teaching a Second Language* Series, 31 minutes, 1961, Indiana University Audio-Visual Center. Shows that there is no one-to-one correlation between words in different languages and that events are viewed differently by speakers of different languages.

What Is Language? Film, part of *Language in Action* Series, 30 minutes, 1958, Indiana University Audio-Visual Center. Shows how words have different meanings in different cultures.

Talking Ourselves into Trouble. Film, part of *Language in Action* Series, 30 minutes, 1958, Indiana University Audio-Visual Center. Explicates ideas of the Whorf-Sapir hypothesis and shows problems in communication caused by words.

On the Difference Between Words and Things. Film, 30 minutes, 1961, Indiana University Audio-Visual Center or Syracuse University Film Rental

Library. Shows how words distort reality and influence behavior and how time is reflected in the English language.

Print

"Control By Language," pp. 252–257 in *Aspects of Language* by Dwight Bolinger. Discusses the Whorf-Sapir hypothesis with regard to time in Hopi and color words in various American Indian languages. Paperbound, Harcourt, Brace and World, 1968.

"Man at the Mercy of Language," pp. 191–213 in *Word Play* by Peter Farb. Discusses how language reflects culture using examples from many languages. Paperbound, Bantam Books, 1974.

"English and Nootka," by Benjamin Lee Whorf, pp. 63–67 in *Reading About Language*, edited by Charles Laird and Robert M. Gorrell. Discusses the necessity of creating fictional entities in nature because of the grammatical structure of English and contrasts the world view of speakers of English and the speakers of Nootka. Paperbound, Harcourt Brace Jovanovich, 1971.

"Language and Logic," by Benjamin Lee Whorf, pp.

259–270 in *A Linguistic Reader*, edited by Graham Wilson. Advances the Whorf-Sapir hypothesis and contrasts the world view of speakers of English and those of speakers of Shawnee and Nootka. Paperbound, Harper and Row, 1967.

"How Language Shapes Our Thoughts," by Stuart Chase, pp. 97–107 in *Language: An Introductory Reader*, edited by J. Burl Hogins and Robert E. Yarber. Explicates the Whorf-Sapir hypothesis using examples from Chinese and American Indian language. Paperbound, Harper and Row, 1969.

"Language, Thought, and Culture," by Peter Woolfson, pp. 5–10 in *Language*, edited by Virginia P. Clark et al. Examines the Whorf-Sapir hypothesis and recent cross-cultural attempts to verify it. Paperbound, St. Martin's Press, 1972.

"Language and the Mind," by Noam Chomsky, pp. 77–86 in *Reading About Language*, edited by Charlton Laird and Robert M. Gorrell. Presents a different argument that there is a universal innate basis for all languages, so that differences in the world view of speakers of various languages are more apparent than real. Paperbound, Harcourt Brace Jovanovich, 1971.

II. HOW LANGUAGE REFLECTS AND PERPETUATES PREJUDICIAL STEREOTYPES

Audiovisual Materials

Labels: If You Label It This, It Can't Be That. Film, 14 minutes, 1972, Filmfair or Syracuse University. Shows how labels perpetuate misconceptions about people and erroneous stereotypes.

Roots of Prejudice. Film, 30 minutes, Indiana University Audio-Visual Center. Discusses stereotypes and how they are perpetuated.

Print

"WCBS Radio Report," by Charles Osgood, pp. 14–15 in *Language Awareness*, edited by Paul A. Eschholz et al. Shows how words are used to dehumanize various ethnic and social groups. Paperbound, St. Martin's Press, 1974.

"Linguistic Factors in Prejudice," by Gordon All-

port, pp. 107–117 in *Language Awareness*, edited by Paul A. Eschholz et al. Shows how certain labels placed on persons have "primary potency" and overshadow other words that might also be used to label the same person and how people's attitudes toward different ethnic groups can be triggered by an ethnic last name. Paperbound, St. Martin's Press, 1974.

"Prejudice: Linguistic Factors," by Gordon Allport, pp. 313–320 in *Language: An Introductory Reader*, edited by J. Burl Hogins and Robert E. Yarber. Shorter version of preceding resource. Paperbound, Harper and Row, 1969.

"The English Language Is My Enemy," by Ossie Davis, pp. 120–121 in *Language Awareness*, edited by Paul A. Eschholz et al. Examines the connotations of synonyms for *black* and *white* in a thesaurus to show the racial prejudice inherent in the English language. Paperbound, St. Martin's Press, 1974.

"How 'White' Is Your Dictionary?" by William Walter Duncan, pp. 243-245 in *Language* edited by Virginia P. Clark et al. Examines the connotations of *black* and *white* in modern dictionaries and finds that positive connotations of *black* are not given. Paperbound, St. Martin's Press, 1972.

"Does Language Libel the Left-Handed?" by Scott, Foresman and Co., pp. 131-132 in *Language Awareness* edited by Paul A. Eschholz et al. Shows the negative connotations of *left* and the positive connotations of *right* in English clichés. Paperbound, St. Martin's Press, 1974.

"From Nobody Ever Died of Old Age," by Sharon R. Curtin, pp. 148-149 in *Language Awareness,* edited by Paul A. Eschholz et al. Shows how older persons are dehumanized by labels placed on them. Paperbound, St. Martin's Press, 1974.

"As I Listened to Archie Say 'Hebe.' . . ." by Laura Z. Hobson, pp. 442-450 in *Language,* edited by Virginia P. Clark et al. Examines the derogatory terms for ethnic groups used in "All in the Family" and points out that the most derogatory terms are not used, only the "polite" derogatory terms. Paperbound, St. Martin's Press.

"The Language of Sexism," by Haig A. Bosmajian, pp. 122-129 in *Language Awareness,* edited by Paul A. Eschholz et al. Shows how the English language reflects traditional male supremacy and traditional second-class status of women. Paperbound, St. Martin's Press, 1974.

"Classification," by S. I. Hayakawa, pp. 296-305 in *Language: An Introductory Reader,* edited by J. Burl Hogins and Robert E. Yarber. Explains arbitrary nature of labels, their use in stereotyping, and possible ways to lessen the effect of labels. Paperbound, Harper and Row, 1969.

The Language of Oppression by Haig A. Bosmajian. Provides erudite discussions of the languages of anti-Semitism, white racism, Indian derision, sexism, and war. Recommended for teachers. Paperbound, National Council of Teachers of English, 1974.

III. CONNOTATIONS AND EUPHEMISMS

Print

"Words at Work: Labeling Our Mental Maps," pp. 53-65 in *Making Sense* by Robert P. Potter. Discusses the consequences of labeling, denotation and connotation, and euphemisms. "With-it" style may be offensive to some. Paperbound, Globe Book Co., 1974.

"Control Through Language," pp. 260-264, in *Aspects of Language* by Dwight Bolinger. Discusses euphemisms and connotations of alleged synonyms. Paperbound, Harcourt, Brace and World, 1968.

"Taboo and Euphemism," by Louis B. Salmon, pp. 144-148 in *Reading About Language,* edited by Charlton Laird and Robert M. Gorrell. Presents a good, short, relatively inoffensive discussion of the subjects. Paperbound, Harcourt Brace Jovanovich, 1971.

"American Euphemisms for Dying, Death, and Burial," by Louise Pound, pp. 312-319 in *Language,* edited by Virginia P. Clark et al. Lists a collection of euphemisms connected with death as used by various social groups. Paperbound, St. Martin's Press, 1972.

"Occupational Euphemisms," by H. L. Mencken, pp. 49-55 in *Language Awareness,* edited by Paul A. Eschholz et al. Shows how persons in various businesses and professions use euphemisms to conceal what they really do. Paperbound, St. Martin's Press, 1974.

"The Speakable and the Unspeakable," pp. 83-106 in *Word Play* by Peter Farb. Gives a very explicit discussion of taboo words and euphemisms in English with interesting examples from Zuni and Nupe. Not recommended for younger students. Paperbound, Bantam Books, 1974.

IV. THE USE OF MISLEADING LANGUAGE

Audiovisual Materials

Communication Is Power: Mass Media and Mass Persuasion. Sound-slide set (sound on LP record or cassette tape), three programs: 15 minutes, 17 minutes, and 18 minutes, 1974, The Center for Humanities, Inc. Provides excellent discussions and illustrations of the misleading use of language in advertising, violence in the media, and the misleading use of language and images in the media presentation of politics.

Propaganda Techniques. Film, 11 minutes, 1950, Coronet Instructional Media. Deals with methods of recognizing and evaluating propaganda; rather outdated.

Truth and the Dragon. Film, 10 minutes, 1969, Indiana University Audio-Visual Center. Illustrates use of misleading language to confuse.

Effective Writing: Learning from Advertising Language. Film, 11 minutes, 1973, Coronet Instructional Media. Examines use of connotations in advertising with application to student writing.

Language of Advertising, The. Film, part of *Language in Action Series,* 30 minutes, 1959, Indiana University Audio-Visual Center. Focuses on misleading language in advertising.

Print

Communication Is Power: A Book of Activities by Jeffrey Schrank. Suggests activities for students studying units on language in advertising, violence and the media, and politics and the media; to be used with *Communication Is Power: Mass Media and Mass Persuasion* sound-slide set. Paperbound, The Center for Humanities, Inc., 1976.

"Weasel Words: God's Little Helpers," by Paul Stevens, pp. 155-172 in *Language Awareness,* edited by Paul A. Eschholz et al. Examines misleading language in advertising. Paperbound, St. Martin's Press, 1974.

"The Principles of Newspeak," by George Orwell, pp. 243-253 in *Language Awareness,* edited by Paul A. Eschholz et al. Shows in this excerpt from *1984* how language can be manipulated to force persons to think in prescribed molds and to make certain thoughts impossible. Paperbound, St. Martin's Press, 1974.

"Exploring the Persuasive Power of Words," pp. 95-104 in *A Contemporary Rhetoric* by Maxine Hairston. Discusses the use of connotations in persuasion with clear illustrative examples. Hardcover, Houghton Mifflin, 1974.

"The Language of Law," by David Mellinkoff, pp. 65-69 in *Language Awareness,* edited by Paul A. Eschholz et al. Translates the language of lawyers into plain English and explains what the language of the law is designed to conceal. Paperbound, St. Martin's Press, 1974.

"Gobbledygook," by Stuart Chase, pp. 89-98 in *Language Awareness,* edited by Paul A. Eschholz et al. Shows the use of purposefully confusing language in government, law, and education. Paperbound, St. Martin's Press, 1974.

"Selection, Slanting, and Charged Language," by Newman P. Birk and Genevieve B. Birk, pp. 335-345 in *Language: An Introductory Reader,* edited by J. Burl Hogins and Robert E. Yarber. Shows how a speaker's or a writer's bias is reflected in his choice of words and illustrates objectionable extremes in such choices. Paperbound, Harper and Row, 1969.

"Politics and the English Language," by George Orwell, pp. 22-34 in *Language Awareness,* edited by Paul A. Eschholz et al. Shows how pretentious and meaningless words may be used to fool the public. Paperbound, St. Martin's Press, 1974.

"Words and Behavior," by Aldous Huxley, pp. 444-455 in *About Language,* edited by Soren F. Cox et al. Shows how words may lead to frequently negative actions because the words disguise harsh realities. Paperbound, Charles Scribner's Sons, 1970.

"Words and Their Meanings," by Aldous Huxley, pp. 161-165 in *Reading About Language,* edited by Charlton Laird and Robert M. Gorrell. Discusses the tendency to objectify and to personify abstractions in the speech of politicians, newspersons, and scientists. Paperbound, Harcourt Brace Jovanovich, 1971.

V. SEMANTICS

Audiovisual Materials

Discovering Language: How Words Get New Meanings. Film, 11 minutes, 1973, Coronet Instructional Media. Shows how meanings of words change through generalization, specialization, amelioration, and pejoration.

Why Do People Misunderstand Each Other? Film, 30 minutes, 1961, Indiana University Audio-Visual Center. Shows how different meanings of the same words cause problems in communication.

Print

"Words and Meanings," pp. 342–361 in *The Origins and Development of the English Language,* 2d ed. by Thomas Pyles. Discusses in simple language the types of semantic change—generalization, specialization, pejoration, and amelioration—as well as taboos and euphemisms. Hardbound, Harcourt Brace Jovanovich, 1971.

"Changing Meanings and Values of Words," pp. 232–273 in *The Development of Modern English,* 2d ed., by Stuart Robertson and Frederic G. Cassidy. Presents a thorough discussion of the types of semantic change—generalization, specialization, elevation, and degradation—and rather outdated discussions of euphemisms, slang, and differences between British and American English. Hardbound, Prentice-Hall, 1954.

"Words," pp. 111–122 in *The English Language: An Introduction for Teachers* by Fred Brengelman. Presents an interesting discussion of semantic features of similar words and how such words may be differentiated. Paperbound, Prentice-Hall, 1970.

"Meaning," pp. 183–232 in *English: An Intro-*

duction to Language by Thomas Pyles and John Algeo. Presents excellent discussions of and exercises on definition, connotation, and changes in meaning. Paperbound, Harcourt, Brace and World, 1970.

"Meaning and Generative-Transformational Grammar," pp. 143–149 in *Introduction to Linguistics* by Ronald Wardhaugh. Explains and illustrates how the meaning of several nouns can be indicated by matrices indicating the presence or absence of certain semantic features. Paperbound, McGraw-Hill, 1972.

"Meaning," pp. 181–188, 191–213 in *Working with Aspects of Language* by Mansoor Alyeshmerni and Paul Taubr. Provides exercises defining English words in terms of matrices of semantic features and matrices for connotational judgments about musical, political, social, and entertainment terms. Paperbound, Harcourt, Brace and World, 1970.

"The Vocabulary of English," pp. 118–129 in *The English Language: An Introduction* by W. Nelson Francis. Discusses the arbitrary nature of meaning and the extension and limitation of the semantic ranges of English words. Paperbound, W. W. Norton and Co., 1965.

"Semantic Change," pp. 271–239 in *Aspects of the History of English* by John C. McLaughlin. Presents a very sophisticated and theoretical discussion of semantic theory and historical semantic change in English. Hardbound, Holt, Rinehart and Winston, 1970.

"Early Semantics" and "The First Complete Model," pp. 109–134 in *Guide to Tranformational Grammar* by John T. Grinder and Suzette Haden Elgin. Provides a sophisticated discussion of the beginnings of semantic speculation by the early transformational generative grammarians. Hardbound, Holt, Rinehart and Winston, 1973.

3

The Sound System of English

This chapter identifies the segmental phonemes or significant sounds of English; introduces and identifies the suprasegmental English phonemes of stress, pitch, and junctions; explains the concept of allophones or nonsignificant differences in sound; and concludes with an examination of the sequences of sounds that are permitted by English structure. A practical result of this unit may be that students will develop an understanding of why they have particular spelling problems. Another probable result is that students will develop an awareness of their own pronunciations of words. Yet another practical result of the students' learning something about the complex patterning of the English sound system is that the students are likely to develop an understanding of the problems they have in learning to speak a foreign language without having an accent and the problems a non-native speaker has in learning to speak English without having an accent.

First, the students should be introduced to the significant sounds of English. Since English spelling gives such a poor representation of the sounds of the language, this introduction will require the introduction of phonemic symbols to represent these significant sounds. The articulatory production of the various segmental phonemes is not included in the content overview of this chapter in the interest of saving space and to avoid duplicating material usually present in modern classroom texts. The most difficulty with this particular topic will be encountered when dealing with the suprasegmental phonemes of stress, pitch, and juncture, since the English writing system generally does not represent them at all.

Then, the concept of allophones or nonsignificant variations within each phoneme may be introduced. With a little help, students will be able to hear the phonetic differences among sounds that they have previously considered the same sounds because of the structural patterning of these different sounds.

Finally, the combinations of sounds that may occur in English words may be examined. Students will discover that there is also patterning at this level of language. They may then understand the changes that English makes in the pronunciation of words borrowed from other languages with different phonotactical patterns than English.

The first topic in this chapter must be taught before the other two, but either the second or third topic may be omitted at the teacher's discretion. The second topic is probably the most difficult of the three to teach. The third topic is probably the easiest to teach but the least crucial to the students' understanding of the English sound system.

OBJECTIVES

If all three topics in the chapter are taught by the teacher, the students should, at the end of the unit, be able to:

1. Define *phoneme* and *allophone*
2. Transcribe English words into phonemic symbols
3. Translate phonemic representation of English words back into conventional writing
4. Demonstrate familiarity with suprasegmental phonemes of stress, pitch, and juncture
5. Illustrate the pattern of complementary distribution or free variation for the allophones of a particular English phoneme
6. Explain why allophonic differences within a phoneme can be ignored by native speakers of English
7. Identify permissible and impermissible phonemic sequences in English

---

CONTENT OVERVIEW

Phonemes or Significant Units of Sound

The English language, like all other languages, is made up of sounds emitted from the mouth and interpreted by a person who hears these sounds. While the sounds that different speakers of English may make may differ slightly from speaker to speaker, these differences are usually ignored by other speakers of English who hear these slightly different sounds as if they were the "same" sound. A group of sounds that sound the same to speakers of English is called a phoneme, which may be defined as the smallest significant unit of sound. One way to identify the smallest significant units of sound in English is to find the pairs of words that differ from each other in only one sound each, such as *pat* and *bat* or *tap* and *tab;* such pairs of words are called minimal pairs. The pairs of words in the previous sentence identify /p/ and /b/ as two phonemes in English because native speakers of English will hear each word in each pair as different from the other, yet the sounds in each pair are identical except for the /p/ and the /b/.

It is important to notice that phonemes are not just letters in the alphabet but are significant units of sound. Indeed, the same phoneme may be spelled with different letters of the English alphabet or even combinations of letters; for example, the /s/ phoneme is spelled with an ⟨s⟩ initially in *sense,* but with a ⟨c⟩ in *cents,* and with ⟨sc⟩ in *scents.* Conversely, the same writing symbol may stand for different phonemes in different words; for example, the ⟨g⟩ writing symbol stands for the /g/ phoneme initially in *gun,* the /ǰ/ phoneme in *gene,* and the /ž/ phoneme medially in *regime.* It is quite clear that conventional English spelling is a very poor guide to identifying the phonemes of the English language.

Instead of using English spelling to study the pattern of significant units of sound in English, it is necessary to transcribe English words into a phonemic alphabet. Although there are several phonemic alphabets used in America to transcribe the phonemes of English, the two most commonly used are a modification of the International Phonetic Alphabet (IPA) and the Trager-Smith system. The following symbols for the segmental phonemes of English are those commonly used by those linguists who follow the

PHONEMIC SYMBOLS FOR ENGLISH CONSONANTS

/p/ The first sound in *pin*, second in *spin*, last in *nip*
/t/ The first sound in *tick*, second in *stick*, last in *kit*
/k/ The first sound in *cat*, second in *scat*, last (ck) in *tack*
/b/ The first sound in *ban*, last in *nab*
/d/ The first sound in *dog*, last in *mad*
/g/ The first sound in *go*, last in *lag*
/č/ The first sound (ch) in *chin*, last (tch) in *watch*
/ǰ/ The first sound in *Jim* or *gym*, last (dge) in *fudge*
/f/ The first sound in *fall*, last (gh) in *laugh*
/θ/ The first sound (th) in *thick*, last (th) in *breath*
/s/ The first sound in *sin*, last (ss) in *hiss*
/š/ The first sound (sh) in *shake*, last (sh) in *smash*
/v/ The first sound in *vine*, last (ve) in *love*
/ð/ The first sound (th) in *then*, last (the) in *breathe*
/z/ The first sound in *zeal*, last in *his*
/ž/ The medial consonant in *vision*, last sound (ge) in *rouge*
/m/ The first sound in *man*, second in *smear*, last (mb) in *crumb*
/n/ The first sound (kn) in *know*, second in *snip*, last in *mean*
/ŋ/ The last sound (ngue) in *tongue*
/l/ The first sound in *laugh*, second in *slice*, last (ll) in *fall*
/r/ The first sound (wr) in *write*, last in *door*
/j/ The first sound in *you* or *ewe*
/w/ The first sound in *woo* or *one*
/h/ The first sound in *his* or (wh) *whole*

PHONEMIC SYMBOLS FOR ENGLISH VOWELS AND DIPHTHONGS

/i/ The vowel sound in *he* and *sneak*
/ɪ/ The vowel sound in *pit* and *bin*
/e/ The vowel sound in *way* and *plain*
/ɛ/ The vowel sound in *pet* and *dead*
/æ/ The vowel sound in *nap* and *laugh*
/u/ The vowel sound in *who* and *boot*
/ʊ/ The vowel sound in *put* and *look*
/o/ The vowel sound in *go* and *moan*
/ɔ/ The vowel sound in *law* and *bought*
/ʌ/ The vowel sound in *but* and *tough*
/a/ The vowel sound in *rob* and *father* (first syllable)
/ə/ The unstressed vowel sound in the first syllable of *above* and the second syllable of *sofa*
/aɪ/ The diphthong in *my* and *kind*
/aʊ/ The diphthong in *out* and *cow*
/ɔɪ/ The diphthong in *boy* and *coin*

IPA system. They are duplicated on Reproduction Page 3 for reproduction for class use. Some of the resources listed in the annotated bibliography, however, use Trager-Smith symbols.

Symbols for English Consonant Phonemes

/p/   The first sound in *pin*, second, in *spin*, last in *nip*

/t/   The first sound in *tick*, second in *stick*, last in *kit*

/k/   The first sound in *cat*, second in *scat*, last (ck) in *tack*

/b/   The first sound in *ban*, last in *nab*

/d/   The first sound in *dog*, last in *mad*

/g/   The first sound in *go*, last in *lag*

/č/   The first sound (ch) in *chin*, last (tch) in *watch*

/ǰ/   The first sound in *Jim* or *gym*, last (dge) in *fudge*

/f/   The first sound in *fall*, last (gh) in *laugh*

/θ/   The first sound (th) in *thick*, last (th) in *breath*

/s/   The first sound in *sin*, last (ss) in *hiss*

/š/   The first sound (sh) in *shake*, last (sh) in *smash*

/v/   The first sound in *vine*, last (ve) in *love*

/ð/   The first sound (th) in *then*, last (the) in *breathe*

/z/   The first sound in *zeal*, last in *his*

/ž/   The medial consonant in *vision*, last sound (ge) in *rouge*

/m/   The first sound in *man*, second in *smear*, last (mb) in *crumb*

/n/   The first sound (kn) in *know*, second in *snip*, last in *mean*

/ŋ/   The last sound (ngue) in *tongue*

/l/   The first sound in *laugh*, second in *slice*, last (ll) in *fall*

/r/   The first sound (wr) in *write*, last in *door*

/j/   The first sound in *you* or *ewe*

/w/   The first sound in *woo* or *one*

/h/   The first sound in *his* or (wh) *whole*

Some speakers of English do not use the /ž/ phoneme in final position as in *rouge* above and on Reproduction Page 3; instead they use the /ǰ/ phoneme, the last sound of *grudge*. It will, thus, be necessary for the teacher to determine whether *rouge* is an appropriate example to illustrate the /ž/ phoneme for his or her students. A further qualification of the list of consonant phonemic symbols above is that some linguists who otherwise use IPA symbols will use the symbol *y* rather than *j* for the /j/ phoneme.

Symbols for English Vowels and Diphthongs

/i/   The vowel sound in *he* and *sneak*

/ɪ/   The vowel sound in *pit* and *bin*

/e/   The vowel sound in *way* and *plain*

/ɛ/   The vowel sound in *pet* and *dead*

/æ/   The vowel sound in *nap* and *laugh*

/u/   The vowel sound in *who* and *boot*

/ʊ/   The vowel sound in *put* and *look*

/o/   The vowel sound in *go* and *moan*

/ɔ/   The vowel sound in *law* and *bought*

/ʌ/   The vowel sound in *but* and *tough*

/a/   The vowel sound in *rob* and *father* (first syllable)

/ə/   The unstressed vowel sound in the first syllable of *above* and the second syllable of *sofa*

/aɪ/   The diphthong in *my* and *kind*

/aʊ/   The diphthong in *out* and *cow*

/ɔɪ/   The diphthong in *boy* and *coin*

Some speakers of English may not use the /ɔ/ phoneme in *bought* or occasionally not in *law* above and on Reproduction Page 3; they may have /a/ as the vowel phoneme in one or both of these words. Thus, the teacher will have to determine whether either or both of these words are appropriate examples to illustrate this phoneme for his or her students. It should also be noted that the IPA symbol for the sequence of the vowel +/r/ in words like *bird, herd, word,* and *hurt* is /ɜ/ and is not included above; most linguists believe that this symbol is unnecessary and prefer to represent the sequence of vowel +/r/ in these words with two symbols such as /ʊr/.

In addition to the segmental phonemes (vowels, consonants, and diphthongs) above, English has suprasegmental phonemes of stress, pitch, and juncture that co-occur with the segmental phonemes anytime a word is said. Stress phonemes are the easiest of the suprasegmental phonemes for most people to hear, and there are four phonemic or significant stresses in English: /ˊ/ primary, /ˆ/ secondary, /ˋ/ tertiary, and /ˇ/ weak or unstressed. Any word pronounced in isolation will have a primary stress, even words like *the* /ðʌ́/ which in the normal stream of speech has an unstressed vowel /ðə̌/. A word like *observation* /âbzùrvésǎn/ illustrates all four stresses within one word: the third syllable has the greatest or primary stress; the first syllable has the next greatest or secondary stress; the second syllable has a lesser or tertiary stress; and the last syllable has the weakest stress. It should be noted that in phonemic transcription the stress phonemes are written above the vowel or diphthong that serves as the center or nucleus of the syllable. In Chapter 4, we will see how stress is used to differentiate pairs of nouns and verbs like *cóndùct* (noun) vs. *cŏndúct* (verb) and *súspèct* (noun) vs. *sŭspéct* (verb) on the basis of stress. It should also be noted that since stress is a matter of relative loudness or softness with which a syllable is said, the four stress phonemes indicate only the stress *pattern* of speakers of English and not an absolute measure of volume; in other words, a quiet person's primary stress will not be as loud as a loud person's primary stress, but both will have the same contrasts among primary, secondary, tertiary, and weak stress within their speech.

The second type of suprasegmental phoneme is pitch caused by the frequency of vibration of the vocal chords. Again, there are four phonemic or significant pitches in English. Although some linguists number the pitches in descending order, the most common system of indicating pitch is in ascending order: /[1]/ for low pitch, /[2]/ for normal pitch, /[3]/ for high pitch, and /[4]/ for highest pitch. If one speaks in a monotone without changing pitch at all, one is using pitch level 2. Obviously, people have different-pitched voices, men generally having lower voices than women, so pitch is again a matter of relative contrasts within a person's speech rather than an absolute. Pitch level 3 normally coincides with primary stress, since the suprasegmentals are intrinsically related in a stream of speech. For example, in a sentence like [2]*He wants some* [3]*candy*[1], the normal pitch pattern is to use pitch level 2 until the first syllable of *candy,* which also gets the primary stress. It should be noted that the voice drops to a pitch lower than 2 on the last syllable of *candy,* indicating that the sentence is a statement and that it is completed. One might shift the primary stress to one of the other three words in the sentence (to contrast the word with something else; e.g., *he* not *she, some* not *a lot*) to notice how the pitch level 3 also shifts to the newly stressed syllable. Pitch level 4 or highest pitch also is used with the onset of the primarily stressed syllable, although speakers of English do not use pitch 4 except to indicate some extreme degree of emotion. Incidentally, this use of pitch level 4 by speakers of other languages as part of their normal pitch range helps to contribute the stereotypes of speakers of certain languages as highly emotional by speakers of English. In phonemic transcription, the suprasegmental pitch numbers are indicated at the beginning and end of an utterance and any place between where a change of pitch occurs. Pitch differences are easiest to hear for speakers of English when pitch patterns are used to differentiate sentences with the same segmental phonemes, such as the statement *This is the book* /[2]ðîs ìz ðə̌ [3]búk[1]/ from the question *This is the book?* /[2] ðîs ìz ðə̌[3] búk[3]/; these two sentences illustrate the most common pitch patterns for statements and for questions not marked as questions by either a question word like *why* or an inversion of part of the predicate like *Is this the book?*

The last type of suprasegmental phoneme is the juncture phoneme. Juncture is simply the way a segmental phoneme is ended within a sentence or at the end of a sentence. Close juncture between two segmental phonemes involves no discernible pause between the segmental phonemes as in the way the segmental phonemes of *plan* /plæn/ are said together. In phonemic transcription as shown in the transcription of *plan* (or *observation* above), close juncture is indicated by writing the segmental phonemes close together. Close juncture contrasts with open juncture, which is a slight retardation of one segmental phoneme before the next segmental phoneme is begun as in the contrast between the preposition *about* /əbaʊt/ and the phrase *a bout* (fight) /ə baʊt/. Open juncture is indicated in transcription by leaving a space between segmental phonemes as in the transcription of *a bout* (or *This is the book* above) or by putting a plus sign /+/ between the segmental phonemes.

       Three types of juncture are known as terminal junctures because they occur at the ends of sentences or the ends of phrases. As stated before, the suprasegmentals are intrinsically related; therefore, it is useful to describe the terminal junctures not only in terms of how the preceding segmental phoneme is ended but also in terms of the pitch patterns that surround these terminal junctures. A sustained terminal juncture is the result of cutting off the production of a segmental phoneme sharply with the same pitch being used both before and after the juncture (usually pitch 2) such as occurs before and after the appositive in *John, my son, slept* /ǰan | maɪ sʌn | slɛpt/ or in other places where commas are used in writing such as *Since he's asleep, let's read* /sɪns hiz əslip | lɛts rid/. In transcription, the sustained terminal juncture is indicated by one perpendicular line /|/. The rising terminal juncture is the pause between segmental phonemes after the segmental phoneme before the pause has been cut off, but not as sharply as for a sustained terminal juncture; the rising terminal juncture is also preceded by a slight rise in pitch, a rise in pitch not significant enough to change the pitch from one phonemic level to another. The rising terminal juncture normally occurs between items in a series such as when one is going through the ABCs /e||bi||si||di||i/ or at the end of a question marked as a question by a high pitch at the end as in *He is here?* /²hi ɪz ³hɪr³ ||/ or *This is the book?* above. In transcription, the rising terminal juncture is indicated by two parallel perpendicular lines /||/. The falling terminal juncture is the pause that occurs when the previous segmental phoneme is not cut off at all but allowed to trail off into silence, usually with pitch level 1, the low pitch. It normally occurs after individual words pronounced in isolation or at the end of statements like *It's five o'clock* /²its faɪv³ əklak¹#// or *John, my son, slept,* above.

Allophones or Nonsignificant Sound Differences

One of the ways that a phoneme was defined above is that it is a group of sounds that sound the same to speakers of English. This group of sounds within a particular phoneme consists of allophones. Each allophone includes phonetically identical sounds, but when one compares different allophones of the same phoneme, one discovers that the allophones themselves are only phonetically similar. The sounds that are identical and within a particular allophone are called phones. In reality, what one speaks is phones. However, each phone is part of an allophone (of phonetically identical phones), and each allophone is part of a phoneme (of phonetically similar allophones). The reason speakers of English do not notice allophonic differences is that the allophones of any particular phoneme are in complementary distribution most of the time or in free variation occasionally; in other words, the phonetic differences among allophones are never used to differentiate a particular word from another one. An analysis of some English phonemes should make these concepts clear.

       The /p/ phoneme (as well as all of the other consonant phonemes) has several allophones which can be illustrated by the /p/ sounds in the words: *peat, peek, peep, peach; speed, speak, spear, spirit; leaped, reaped, beeped,* and *heaped.* If one says each of the first four words, one may notice that an audible puff of air is released after each /p/ sound; thus one could represent each of the phones that begins the first four words with a symbol like [pʰ]. (Notice that phonetic symbols are enclosed in brackets in contrast to the virgules that enclose phonemic symbols.) The puff of air that accompanies each of the [pʰ] phones, called an aspirated [pʰ], is usually sufficient to move a piece of paper held up to the lips when one says the word. In contrast, the /p/ sounds in each of the next four words do not have this aspiration or audible air released when they are produced; they will not cause a paper held next to the lips to move when they are said. One might use a symbol such as [pˈ] to represent each of these unaspirated [pˈ] phones. In the last four words, the /p/ sounds are not only not aspirated, but unlike the [pˈ]s in the second four words, they are not even released. When one says *leaped,* for example, a closure of the lips is made in order to make a /p/ sound, but no air escapes after the closure of the lips until the following /t/ sound is produced. Phonetically, the word would be written [lip̚t̚], using the symbol [p̚] for an unreleased [p̚] sound. The same symbol [p̚] would be used to represent the /p/ sounds in the last three words, since the /p/s in each of these words are also unreleased.

The complementary distribution of these different allophones of /p/ become apparent when the words with [pʰ] phones, [pʳ] phones, and [p̚] phones are grouped like this:

[pʰitʳ]	[spʳid]	[lip̚t̚]
[pʰikʳ]	[spʳikʳ]	[rip̚t̚]
[pʰip̚]	[spʳɪr]	[bip̚t̚]
[pʰič̆]	[sp ɪrətʳ]	[hip̚t̚]

As these examples illustrate, the aspirated [pʰ] phones occur initially before a vowel, the unaspirated [pʳ] phones after an initial /s/ and before a vowel, and the unreleased [p̚] phones after a vowel and before a /t/. The aspirated [pʰ] phones can be considered part of an aspirated [pʰ] allophone, since they are phonetically identical. Similarly, the unaspirated [pʳ] phones can be considered part of an unaspirated [pʳ] allophone, and the unreleased [p̚] phones part of an unreleased [p̚] allophone. The three allophones, then, are in complementary distribution in these three environments. Only phones belonging to the [pʰ] allophone occur in the first position, while only phones belonging to the [pʳ] allophone and the [p̚] allophone occur in the second and third positions, respectively. One would never find an unaspirated [pʳ] occurring initially before a vowel in an English word, nor would one find an aspirated [pʰ] occurring after an initial /s/ and before a vowel in an English word. There is no overlap in the environments of the three different allophones of /p/ in these environments, and there is no minimal pair such as [pʰitʳ] and [pʳitʳ] that is differentiated from each other as separate words in English on the basis of a different allophone.

It was necessary to say "in English" in these last generalizations because there are languages in the world in which /pʰ/ and /pʳ/ are separate phonemes, not allophones of the same phoneme. Other languages that have only one /p/ phoneme may have a different set of allophones and a different complementary distribution of those allophones, so it is again necessary to stress that we are talking only about the complementary distribution of the allophones of /p/ in English. For example, the /p/ phoneme in French does not have an aspirated [pʰ] in initial position before a vowel, but uses an unaspirated [pʳ] allophone in that position. Often the "accent" that a person is said to have when speaking a foreign language is only the result of failing to learn the complementary distribution of the allophones of particular phonemes in the foreign language and instead transferring the pattern of allophonic distribution of corresponding phonemes in his native language to the foreign language.

As mentioned above, allophones of a particular phoneme may also be in free variation in certain positions or environments. This is true of the three allophones of /p/ identified above. In utterance final position (the last phone in the last word in a sentence), it is impossible to predict which kind of a /p/ phone will be used. For example, in the command *Stop!* /stap/, the /p/ may be represented by a phone from each of the three allophones: [stʳapʰ]; [stʳapʳ]; or, particularly if the speaker is angry, [stʳap̚]. The point is, however, that the native speaker of English hears these three pronunciations as the "same" word since the allophonic differences in the /p/ allophones are nonsignificant in English.

The /e/ phoneme (as well as the other vowel and diphthong phonemes) also has several allophones, which can be illustrated by the /e/ sounds in the words: *say, play, way; grade, graze, grave; great, grace, grape; grain, same,* and *pane.* Here the phonetic differences are in length and in the presence or absence of nasalization. The /e/ sounds in each of the first three words are longer than those in the second three words, and the /e/ sounds in the second three words are longer than those in the third three words. One could indicate these phonetic differences by using [e:] to represent the very long /e/s in the first three words, by using [e·] to indicate the long /e/s in the next three words, and by using [e] to represent the nonlong /e/s in the third set of three words. The /e/s in the fourth set of three words are long like those of the second set, but they also have a nasal quality to them. The /e/s in the fourth set of three words might then be represented by a symbol such as [ẽ·].

The complementary distribution of these different allophones of /e/ becomes apparent when the words with [e:] phones, [e.] phones, [e] phones, and [ẽ.] phones are grouped like this:

[se:]	[gre.d]	[gretʳ]	[grẽ.n.]
[ple:]	[gre.z.]	[gres.]	[sẽ.m.]
[we:]	[gre.v.]	[grepʳ]	[pʰẽ.n.]

As these examples illustrate, the very long [e:] phones occur at the end of a word; the long [e.] phones before a voiced consonant (one produced with vibration of the vocal chords); the nonlong [e] phones before a voiceless consonant (one produced with no vibration of the vocal chords); and the long, nasalized [ẽ.] phones occur before nasal consonants (those in which part of the sound comes through the nose). The very long [e:] phones are part of an [e:] allophone, since they are phonetically identical. The long [e.] phones, the nonlong [e] phones, and the long, nasalized [ẽ.] phones can be grouped into an [e.] allophone, an [e] allophone, and an [ẽ.] allophone, respectively, for the same reason. These four allophones of /e/ are thus in complementary distribution in these four environments. Only phones belonging to the [e:] allophone will occur at the end of a word, while only phones belonging to the [e.] allophone will occur before voiced consonants except nasals, and the like. There is no overlap in the environments of the four allophones of /e/ identified above, and there is no minimal pair such as [se:] and [se.] that are differentiated from each other as separate words in English on the basis of a different /e/ allophone. There appear to be no environments in English where these different allophones of /e/ are in free variation.

Sequences of Sound in English

Since English has thirty-nine segmental phonemes (identified above), the number of potential sequences of sound combinations for words of even four or five phonemes in length is astronomical, let alone for words of twenty or twenty-five phonemes in length. However, English, like all other languages, permits only certain sequences of phonemes to be used together in a series. This distribution of the permissible sequences of sound in English is called phonotactics. Other languages will have different phonotactic patterns from English, so when English borrows a word from another language and the word does not conform to English phonotactics, there are two choices to be made in pronouncing the word in English. The first is to keep the foreign pronunciation and use a sequence of phonemes that does not normally occur in English, such as the initial /ts/ in Russian *tsar, tzar,* or *czar;* the second is to change the pronunciation to conform to English phonotactics, such as the common English pronunciation of the variously spelled word above as /zar/ with an initial /z/ instead of /ts/.

Very little has been determined concerning the phonotactics of English vowels, but the general rule seems to be that no more than two vowels or diphthongs may occur next to each other in the same word and that most frequently a vowel or diphthong will not be preceded by a vowel or diphthong in the same word. Two vowels or diphthongs may occur in sequence in a word initially as in *aorta* /eɔrta/, medially as in *chaotic* /keatək/, and finally as in *idea* /aɪdiə/, however.

English permits a maximum of three consonant phonemes initially in a word, but there are severe restrictions on this maximum initial consonant cluster. To begin with, the first consonant phoneme must always be /s/. The second consonant must always be a /p/, /t/, or /k/, and the third consonant must always be an /l/, /r/, /w/, or /j/. Thus, sequences like /spl-/ as in *splash,* /str-/ as in *strike,* /skw-/ as in *squash,* and /skj-/ as in *skew* represent the largest initial consonant clusters.

There are also restrictions on the permissible sequences of two initial consonants in English words. One pattern always involves /s/ as the first consonant and permits only /p/, /t/, /k/, /m/, /n/, /f/, /l/, or /w/ as the second consonant. Examples of words with consonant sequences are *spare, steak, score, smell, snare, sphere, slow,* and *swim.* The other permissible pattern of two initial consonants permits variety in the first consonant, /p/, /t/, /k/, /b/, /d/, /g/, /f/, /θ/, /š/ (only before /r/), or /h/ (only before /w/ or /j/), but restricts the second consonant in the cluster to /l/, /r/, /w/, or /j/. Examples are *please, trash, queen, blue, dwell, grow, feud, threw, shred,* and *when.* Some dialects of English have accepted a Germanic phonotactic pattern which permits an initial /š/ followed by /l/, /w/, /m/, or /n/ as in *schlock, schwa, schmaltz,* and *schnook,* but these sequences only occur in obviously borrowed words from German and Yiddish.

All single consonants may occur initially in an English word except /ŋ/, but /ž/ occurs only in borrowed words such as the originally French *genre.*

Medially, English allows a maximum of four consonant sounds in sequence as in *temptress.* However, these four consonants are always split between two syllables with the second syllable being a derivational suffix. Since there are many such derivational suffixes, the possible combinations of consonants medially is large and rather unrestricted.

In final position, English words have a maximum of three consonant phonemes in uninflected words or four consonant phonemes, including inflectional /s/, /z/, /t/, or /d/. When an uninflected word in English ends in three consonants, the first of the three consonants may be either /r/, /m/, /n/, /k/, or /l/. The /r/ is followed only by the sequences /ps/ as in *corpse,* /st/ as in *thirst,* or /ts/ as in *quartz.* The /m/ must be followed by /p/ and either /t/ as in *attempt,* /s/ as in *glimpse* or in some people's pronunciation of words like *nymph,* /f/. The /n/ can be followed only by /ts/ as in *chintz;* the /k/ can be followed only by /st/ as in *text* or /sθ/ as in *sixth;* the /l/ can be followed only by /fθ/ in *twelfth.*

Final consonant clusters involving two phonemes, except for the inflectional phonemes mentioned above, are restricted to those beginning with /p/, /t/, /k/, /s/, /f/, /m/, /n/, /ŋ/, /d/, /l/, and /r/. The consonants that may follow /p/ and /k/ are restricted to /s/ and /t/ as in *lapse* and *script,* and in *mix* and *tract.* Only one consonant may follow /t/, the /θ/ as in *eighth.* The /s/ may be followed only by /p/, /t/, or /k/ as in *crisp, mist,* and *risk.* The /f/ may be followed by either /t/ or /θ/ as in *craft* and *eighth.* The /m/ may be followed only by /p/ or /f/ as in *lamp* and *triumph,* the /n/ only by /t/, /d/, /ǰ/, /č/, and /θ/ as in *tint, bank, change, hunch,* and *tenth,* the /ŋ/ only by /k/ as in *bank.* The /d/ may be followed only by /z/ and /θ/ as in *adze* and *width.* The /l/ and the /r/ may be followed by most other consonant phonemes.

All English consonant phonemes may occur singly in final position in a word except for /j/, /w/, and /h/, those consonants which some linguists identify as semivowels to differentiate them from the other consonants.

REPRODUCTION PAGE 4

TRANSCRIBING FROM PHONEMIC SYMBOLS

Directions: *Use the list of Phonemic Symbols to help you write the words below in current English spelling.*

1. /dɪp/ _____	26. /kaʊ/ _____	51. /hæf/ _____
2. /dip/ _____	27. /šev/ _____	52. /tu/ _____
3. /šɛl/ _____	28. /gʊd/ _____	53. /ju/ _____
4. /šek/ _____	29. /tɔl/ _____	54. /skɔld/ _____
5. /ful/ _____	30. /praɪz/ _____	55. /saɪ/ _____
6. /wʊl/ _____	31. /fjud/ _____	56. /ek/ _____
7. /sop/ _____	32. /pɪg/ _____	57. /luz/ _____
8. /sɔ/ _____	33. /ɛb/ _____	58. /lus/ _____
9. /pæd/ _____	34. /mun/ _____	59. /aʊr/ _____
10. /hʌg/ _____	35. /tæks/ _____	60. /bam/ _____
11. /waɪf/ _____	36. /čæf/ _____	61. /wʊrk/ _____
12. /ǰab/ _____	37. /ðe/ _____	62. /əbaʊt/ _____
13. /slavč/ _____	38. /wo/ _____	63. /sofə/ _____
14. mɔɪst/ _____	39. /hɔk/ _____	64. /šʊrt/ _____
15. /pju/ _____	40. /taʊn/ _____	65. /grop/ _____
16. /tič/ _____	41. /ǰʌǰ/ _____	66. /skrim/ _____
17. /pæθ/ _____	42. /θru/ _____	67. /splæš/ _____
18. /ǰæm/ _____	43. /rɔŋ/ _____	68. /strɛč/ _____
19. /jæm/ _____	44. /saɪn/ _____	69. /əraʊnd/ _____
20. /pamp/ _____	45. /vju/ _____	70. /smak/ _____
21. /juθ/ _____	46. /hɪm/ _____	71. /snɔr/ _____
22. /pʊl/ _____	47. /bɪld/ _____	72. /pliz/ _____
23. /ðoz/ _____	48. /bʌŋk/ _____	73. /slɪk/ _____
24. /θɪŋ/ _____	49. /flu/ _____	74. /trʌbəl/ _____
25. /gloz/ _____	50. /mjul/ _____	75. /rɪtən/ _____

LEARNING EXPERIENCES

Topic I: Phonemes or Significant Units of Sound

- Have the students use the symbols on Reproduction Page 3 to write the phonemically written words below and on Reproduction Page 4 in conventional spelling. The answers are indicated below in parentheses but not on Reproduction Page 4.

1.	/dɪp/	(dip)	39.	/hɔk/	(hawk)
2.	/dip/	(deep)	40.	/taʊn/	(town)
3.	/šɛl/	(shell)	41.	/ǰʌǰ/	(judge)
4.	/šek/	(shake)	42.	/Θru/	(through or threw)
5.	/ful/	(fool)	43.	/rɔŋ/	(wrong)
6.	/wʊl/	(wool)	44.	/saɪn/	(sign)
7.	/sop/	(soap)	45.	/vju/	(view)
8.	/sɔ/	(saw)	46.	/hɪm/	(him or hymn)
9.	/pæd/	(pad)	47.	/bɪld/	(build)
10.	/hʌg/	(hug)	48.	/bʌŋk/	(bunk)
11.	/waɪf/	(wife)	49.	/flu/	(flew or flu(e))
12.	/ǰab/	(job)	50.	/mjul/	(mule)
13.	/slaʊč/	(slouch)	51.	/hæf/	(half)
14.	/mɔɪst/	(moist)	52.	/tu/	(two or to(o))
15.	/pju/	(pew)	53.	/ju/	(you or ewe)
16.	/tič/	(teach)	54.	/skɔld/	(scald)
17.	/pæΘ/	(path)	55.	/saɪ/	(sigh)
18.	/ǰæm/	(jam)	56.	/ek/	(ache)
19.	/jæm/	(yam)	57.	/luz/	(lose)
20.	/pamp/	(pomp)	58.	/lus/	(loose)
21.	/juΘ/	(youth)	59.	/aʊr/	((h)our)
22.	/pʊl/	(pull)	60.	/bam/	(bomb)
23.	/ðoz/	(those)	61.	/wʊrk/	(work)
24.	/Θiŋ/	(thing)	62.	/əbaʊt/	(about)
25.	/gloz/	(glows)	63.	/sofə/	(sofa)
26.	/kaʊ/	(cow)	64.	/šʊrt/	(shirt)
27.	/šev/	(shave)	65.	/grop/	(grope)
28.	/gʊd/	(good)	66.	/skrim/	(scream)
29.	/tɔl/	(tall)	67.	/splæš/	(splash)
30.	/praɪz/	(prize)	68.	/strɛč/	(stretch)
31.	/fjud/	(feud)	69.	/əraʊnd/	(around)
32.	/pɪg/	(pig)	70.	/smak/	(smock)
33.	/ɛb/	(ebb)	71.	/snɔr/	(snore)
34.	/mun/	(moon)	72.	/pliz/	(pleas(e))
35.	/tæks/	(tax or tacks)	73.	/slɪk/	(slick)
36.	/čæf/	(chaff)	74.	/trʌbəl/	(trouble)
37.	/ðe/	(they)	75.	/rɪtən/	(written)
38.	/wo/	(woe or whoa)			

- Have the students use the symbols on Reproduction Page 3 to transcribe the words below (and on Reproduction Page 5) into phonemic transcription. The answers are

TRANSCRIBING INTO PHONEMIC SYMBOLS

Directions: *Use the list of Phonemic Symbols to help you write the following words in phonemic transcription.*

1. sick	21. rest	41. caps
2. dig	22. tooth	42. cads
3. fad	23. cat	43. picks
4. hive	24. sail	44. pigs
5. rough	25. crutch	45. wreaths
6. shun	26. brick	46. times
7. thick	27. love	47. rakes
8. this	28. shout	48. pails
9. rang	29. child	49. toes
10. saw	30. tribe	50. walks
11. hot	31. these	51. things
12. stand	32. cheat	52. gives
13. would	33. wretch	53. robs
14. book	34. which	54. robbed
15. wait	35. wild	55. popped
16. grow	36. ouch	56. dreamed
17. toil	37. brain	57. banged
18. brief	38. match	58. raced
19. sheet	39. sign	59. rushed
20. drive	40. wood	60. missed

indicated below but not on the Reproduction Page. Keep in mind, however, that because of dialect differences, the students' answers may be correct even when they differ from the answer below.

1. sick /sɪk/	21. rest /rɛst/	41. caps /kæps/
2. dig /dɪg/	22. tooth /tuθ/	42. cads /kædz/
3. fad /fæd/	23. cat /kæt/	43. picks /pɪks/
4. hive /haɪv/	24. sail /sel/	44. pigs /pɪgz/
5. rough /rʌf/	25. crutch /krʌč/	45. wreaths /riθs/ or /riðz/
6. shun /šʌn/	26. brick /brɪk/	46. times /taɪmz/
7. thick /θɪk/	27. love /lʌv/	47. rakes /reks/
8. this /ðɪs/	28. shout /šaʊt/	48. pails /pelz/
9. rang /ræŋ/	29. child /čaɪld/	49. toes /toz/
10. saw /sɔ/	30. tribe /traɪb/	50. walks /wɔks/
11. hot /hat/	31. these /ðiz/	51. things /θɪŋz/
12. stand /stand/	32. cheat /čit/	52. gives /gɪvz/
13. would /wʊd/	33. wretch /rɛč/	53. robs /rabz/
14. book /bʊk/	34. which /(h)wɪc/	54. robbed /rabd/
15. wait /wet/	35. wild /waɪld/	55. popped /papt/
16. grow /gro/	36. ouch /aʊč/	56. dreamed /drimd/
17. toil /tɔɪl/	37. brain /bren/	57. banged /bæŋd/
18. brief /brif/	38. match /mæč/	58. raced /rest/
19. sheet /šit/	39. sign /saɪn/	59. rushed /rʌšt/
20. drive /draɪv/	40. wood /wʊd/	60. missed /mɪst/

• Using Reproduction Page 6, have the students indicate the primary stress on the words below. The stress marks are indicated below but not on the Reproduction Page. The students are also asked on the Reproduction Page what generalizations they can draw about the stress patterns of nouns and verbs that are spelled alike (1–12). The generalizations are that the nouns in each pair have a primary stress on

INDICATING PRIMARY STRESS

Directions: Indicate which syllable is stressed in the words below by marking over the vowel that is the center of the stressed syllable. What generalizations can you draw about the stress patterns of nouns and verbs that are spelled alike (1–12)?

1. conflict (verb)
2. conflict (noun)
3. pervert (verb)
4. pervert (noun)
5. suspect (noun)
6. suspect (verb)
7. contract (noun)
8. contract (verb)
9. permit (verb)
10. permit (noun)
11. relay (verb)
12. relay (noun)
13. belief
14. differ
15. phoneme
16. window
17. utilize
18. operate
19. operation
20. silly

the first syllable and that the verbs in the pairs have the primary stress on the second syllable. You might also point out that the nouns in these pairs have a tertiary stress on the second syllable, while the first syllables of the verbs in these pairs have weak stress. You should also point out that this pattern applies only to two-syllable noun and verb pairs and not to all two-syllable nouns and verbs.

1. conflíct (verb)
2. cónflict (noun)
3. pervért (verb)
4. pérvert (noun)
5. súspect (noun)
6. suspéct (verb)
7. cóntract (noun)
8. contráct (verb)
9. permít (verb)
10. pérmit (noun)
11. reláy (verb)
12. rélay (noun)
13. belíef
14. díffer
15. phóneme
16. window
17. útilize
18. óperate
19. operátion
20. sílly

- Using Reproduction Page 7, have the students answer the following questions about sentences *a* through *j* on which pitch patterns have been indicated. The answers have been given in parentheses below but not on the Reproduction Page.

1. Which sentence is a question? (b) Which sentence might indicate fear? (c) Which sentence is just an average statement? (a)

   a.   [2]I failed the [3]test[1]

   b.   [2]I failed the [3]test[3]

   c.   [2]I failed the [4]test[1]

2. Which of the following would you expect to be followed by "but he is leaving soon"? (e) Which of the following is a question? (f) Which of the following is a statement *and* the end of the sentence? (d)

   d.   [2]He is [3]here[1]

PITCH AND MEANING

Directions: Answer the questions below about the meanings of the sentences for which pitch patterns are indicated by putting the letter of the sentence in the space after each question.

1. Which sentence is a question? _____ Which sentence might indicate fear? _____ Which sentence is just an average statement? _____
   a. ^{2}I failed the ^{3} test^1
   b. ^{2}I failed the ^{3} test^3
   c. ^{2}I failed the ^{4} test^1

2. Which of the following would you expect to be followed by "but he is leaving soon"? _____ Which of the following is a question? _____ Which of the following is a statement *and* the end of the sentence? _____
   d. ^{2}He is ^{3} here^1
   e. ^{2}He is ^{3} here^2
   f. ^{2}He is ^{3} here^3

3. Which of the following should you respond to with "Yes" or "No"? _____ Which of the following should you respond to with "Pie" or "Cake"? _____
   g. ^{2}Do you want ^{3} pie^3 ^{2}or ^{3} cake^1?
   h. ^{2}Do you want ^{3} pie^3 ^{2}or ^{3} cake^3?

4. Which of the following could be either a command to a dog or a response to the question "Where is your brother?" _____ Which of the following is a question? _____
   i. ^{3}Home^1
   j. ^{3}Home^3

---

e. ^{2}He is ^{3}here^2

f. ^{2}He is ^{3}here^3

3. Which of the following should you respond to with "Yes" or "No"? (h) Which of the following should you respond to with "Pie" or "Cake"? (g)

g. ^{2}Do you want ^{3}pie^3 ^{2}or ^{3} cake^1?

h. ^{2}Do you want ^{3}pie^3 ^{2}or ^{3} cake^3?

4. Which of the following could be either a command to a dog or a response to the question, "Where is your brother?" (i) Which of the following is a question? (j)

i. ^{3}Home^1

j. ^{3}Home^3

- Using Reproduction Page 8, have the students indicate where open juncture /+/ occurs in *a* through *f* below and where sustained terminal juncture /|/, rising terminal juncture /|||/, and falling terminal juncture /#/ occur in *g* through *l* below. Open juncture occurs between word boundaries in *a* through *f*. The terminal junctures in *g* through *l* are indicated below for each sentence, but not on the Reproduction Page.

a. yellowed rug vs. yellow drug

b. nitrate vs. night rate

c. a board vs. aboard

d. an ale vs. a nail

e. I scream vs. ice cream

f. That's tough vs. that stuff

JUNCTURE PHONEMIC SYMBOLS

Directions: Supply the appropriate juncture phoneme symbols to differentiate among the following words and phrases:

1. Indicate where open juncture /+/ occurs in the following phrases that have the same segmental phonemes:
   a. yellowed rug vs. yellow drug
   b. nitrate vs. night rate
   c. a board vs. aboard
   d. an ale vs. a nail
   e. I scream vs. ice cream
   f. That's tough vs. that stuff

2. Indicate where a sustained terminal juncture /|/, a rising terminal juncture /||/, and a falling terminal juncture /#/ would be used in the following sentences:
   g. He has gone, hasn't he?
   h. "He is gone," I thought.
   i. She brought two books, a pencil, and a notebook.
   j. Our dog, Abby, is sick.
   k. If you'll wait, I'll get some for you.
   l. These are the ones you wanted?

g.   He has gone, /||/ hasn't he? /||/

h.   "He is gone," /||/ I thought. /#/

i.   She brought two books, /||/ a pencil, /||/ and a notebook. /#/

j.   Our dog, /||/ Abby, /||/ is sick. /#/

k.   If you'll wait, /|||/ I'll get some for you. /#/

l.   These are the ones you wanted? /||/

Topic II: Allophones or Nonsignificant Sound Differences

• Using Reproduction Page 9, have the students determine whether the allophones of the consonant phonemes used initially and finally in the words below are long or short. The students are asked to draw a general conclusion about the distribution of long and short allophones for these consonant phonemes: that generalization is that each of the phonemes has a shorter allophone that occurs initially in a word and a longer allophone that occurs finally in a word (as indicated below but not on the Reproduction Page).

/r/	/s/
rear /rɪr/	cease /sis/
roar /rɔr/	Sis /sɪs/
rare /rɛr/	sass /sæs/
initially: short	initially: short
finally: long	finally: long

REPRODUCTION PAGE 9

LONG OR SHORT ALLOPHONES

Directions: *Indicate whether the allophones of the consonant phonemes used at the beginning and end of the words below are long or short by writing the words* long *or* short *after* initially *and* finally *below. Can you draw any general conclusion about the distribution of long and short allophones of these consonant phonemes? The generalization will also hold true for the allophones of /v/, /θ/, /ð/, and /ž/.*

/r/
rear /rɪr/
roar /rɔr/
rare /rɛr/
initially:
finally:

/s/
cease /sis/
Sis /sɪs/
sass /sæs/
initially:
finally:

/n/
noon /nun/
nun /nʌn/
Nan /næn/
known /non/
noun /naʊn/
nine /naɪn/
initially:
finally:

/m/
mum /mʌm/
Mom /mam/
mime /maɪm/
maim /mem/
initially:
finally:

/l/
lull /lʌl/
Lil /lɪl/
initially:
finally:

/f/
fife /faɪf/
initially:
finally:

/z/
zoos /zuz/
initially:
finally:

/š/
shush /šʌš/
initially:
finally:

/č/
church /čʊrč/
initially:
finally:

/ǰ/
judge /ǰʌǰ/
initially:
finally:

/n/
noon /nun/
nun /nʌn/
Nan /næn/
known /non/
noun /naʊn/
nine /naɪn/
initially: short
finally: long

/m/
mum /mʌm/
Mom /mam/
mime /maɪm/
maim /mem/
initially: short
finally: long

/l/
lull /lʌl/
Lil /lɪl/
initially: short
finally: long

/f/
fife /faɪf/
initially: short
finally: long

/z/
zoos /zuz/
initially: short
finally: long

/š/
shush /šʌš/
initially: short
finally: long

/č/

church /čʊrč/
initially: short
finally: long

/ǰ/

judge /ǰʌǰ/
initially: short
finally: long

- Using Reproduction Page 10, have the students determine the complementary distribution and free variation pattern of the aspirated [kʰ] allophone, the unaspirated [kʳ] allophone, and the unreleased [k˺] allophone of the /k/ phoneme in the words below by identifying the environment in which each of the allophones occurs in complementary distribution and the environment where all three allophones occur in free variation. The environments are identified below but not on the Reproduction Page.

[kʰæp]	[skʳæmp]	[læk˺t]	[lʊkʰ]
[kʰip]	[skʳi]	[lik˺t]	[lʊkʳ]
[kʰʌp]	[skʳʌm]	[plʌk˺t]	[lʊk˺]
[kʰep]	[skʳet]	[ek˺t]	

Complementary Distribution:

The [kʰ] allophone occurs initially before a vowel.

The [kʳ] allophone occurs after an initial /s/ and before a vowel.

The [k˺] allophone occurs before a /t/.

Free Variation:

The [kʰ] allophone, the [kʳ] allophone, and the [k˺] allophone may all occur finally in a word.

REPRODUCTION PAGE 10

ASPIRATED, UNASPIRATED, AND UNRELEASED ALLOPHONES

Directions: *Determine the complementary distribution and free variation pattern of the aspirated* [kʰ] *allophone, the unaspirated* [kʳ] *allophone, and the unreleased* [k˺] *allophone of the /k/ phoneme in the words below by identifying the environment in which each of the allophones occurs in complementary distribution and the environment where all three allophones occur in free variation. Indicate your conclusions by completing the sentences that follow:*

[kʰæp]	[skʳæmp]	[læk˺t]	[lʊkʰ]
[kʰip]	[skʳi]	[lik˺t]	[lʊkʳ]
[kʰʌp]	[skʳʌm]	[plʌk˺t]	[lʊk˺]
[kʰep]	[skʳet]	[ek˺t]	

Complementary Distribution:
The [kʰ] allophone occurs . . .

The [kʳ] allophone occurs . . .

The [k˺] allophone occurs . . .

Free Variation:
The [kʰ] allophone, the [kʳ] allophone, and the [k˺] allophone may all occur . . .

ALLOPHONE DISTRIBUTION

Directions: *Determine the complementary distribution pattern of the very long* [i:] *allophone, the long* [i.] *allophone, the nonlong* [i] *allophone, and the long, nasalized* [ĩ.] *allophone of the* /i/ *phoneme in the words below by identifying the environment in which each of the allophones occurs in complementary distribution. Indicate your conclusions by completing the sentences which follow.*

[ti:]	[ti.z]	[šit]	[sĩ.m]
[si:]	[si.d]	[sit]	[sĩ.n]
[ski:]	[li.g]	[bič]	[krĩ.m]
[tri:]	[li.v]	[lik]	[lĩ.n]

Complementary Distribution:
The [i:] allophone occurs . . .

The [i.] allophone occurs . . .

The [i] allophone occurs . . .

The [ĩ.] allophone occurs . . .

- Using Reproduction Page 11, have the students determine the complementary distribution pattern of the very long [i:] allophone, the long [i.] allophone, the nonlong [i] allophone, and the long, nasalized [ĩ.] allophone of the /i/ phoneme in the words below by identifying the environment in which each of the allophones occurs in complementary distribution. The environments are identified below but not on the Reproduction Page.

[ti:]	[ti.z]	[šit]	[sĩ.m]
[si:]	[si.d]	[sit]	[sĩ.n]
[ski:]	[li.g]	[bič]	[krĩ.m]
[tri:]	[li.v]	[lik]	[lĩ.n]

Complementary Distribution:

The [i:] allophone occurs in final position.

The [i.] allophone occurs before a voiced sound (except nasals).

The [i] allophone occurs before a voiceless sound.

The [ĩ.] allophone occurs before nasals.

- Using Reproduction Page 12, have the students write the complementary distribution pattern for the allophones of the /h/ phoneme in the words below for which phonetic transcriptions are given. The vowel symbols with ˳ under them stand phonetically for voiceless vowels. The complementary distribution is given below but not on the Reproduction Page.

he [i̥i]	his [ɪ̥z]
hit [ɪ̥t]	hoot [u̥ut]
hate [e̥et]	hoe [o̥o]
head [ɛ̥ɛd]	hide [ḁaɪd]

ALLOPHONE PATTERNS

Directions: *The allophones of the /h/ phoneme that occur before vowels are themselves corresponding voiceless vowels. You may test by saying the initial /h/ as if you were going to say each of the words below. You are given the phonetic transcription for each of the words below. Write the complementary distribution pattern for the allophones of the /h/ phoneme below the words. Note that a vowel symbol with a . below it indicates a voiceless vowel.*

he [i̥i]   his [ɪ̥ɪz]
hit [ɪ̥ɪt]   hoot [u̥ut]
hate [e̥et]   hoe [o̥o]
head [ɛ̥ɛd]   hide [ḁaɪd]
hat [æ̥æt]   has [æ̥æz]
who [u̥u]   house [ḁaʊs]
hurt [ʊ̥ʊrt]   hill [ɪ̥ɪl]
hold [o̥old]   heard [ʊ̥ʊrd]
halt [ɔ̥ɔlt]   hop [ḁap]
hot [ḁat]   home [o̥om]
height [ḁaɪt]   hick [ɪ̥ɪk]
hound [ḁaʊnd]   hike [ḁaɪk]
hoist [ɔ̥ɔɪst]   haze [e̥ez]
hut [ʌ̥ʌt]   hum [ʌ̥ʌm]

Complementary Distribution:
The [u̥] allophone occurs . . .

The [ʊ̥] allophone occurs . . .

The [o̥] allophone occurs . . .

The [ɔ̥] allophone occurs . . .

The [ḁ] allophone occurs . . .

The [ʌ̥] allophone occurs . . .

The [i̥] allophone occurs . . .

The [ɪ̥] allophone occurs . . .

The [e̥] allophone occurs . . .

The [ɛ̥] allophone occurs . . .

The [æ̥] allophone occurs . . .

hat [æ̦æt]   has [æ̦æz]
who [u̦u]   house [a̦avs]
hurt [y̦vrt]   hill [ɪ̦ɪl]
hold [o̦old]   heard [y̦vrd]
halt [ɔ̦ɔlt]   hop [a̦ap]
hot [a̦at]   home [o̦om]
height [a̦aɪt]   hick [ɪ̦ɪk]
hound [a̦avnd]   hike [a̦aɪk]
hoist [ɔ̦ɔɪst]   haze [e̦ez]
hut [ʌ̦ʌt]   hum [ʌ̦ʌm]

Complementary Distribution:

The [u̦] allophone occurs before /u/.

The [y̦] allophone occurs before /v/.

The [o̦] allophone occurs before /o/.

The [ɔ̦] allophone occurs before /ɔ/ and /ɔɪ/.

The [a̦] allophone occurs before /a/, /aɪ/, and /av/.

The [ʌ̦] allophone occurs before /ʌ/.

The [i̦] allophone occurs before /i/.

The [ɪ̦] allophone occurs before /ɪ/.

The [e̦] allophone occurs before /e/.

The [ɛ̦] allophone occurs before /ɛ/.

The [æ̦] allophone occurs before /æ/.

Topic III: Sequences of Sound in English

- Using Reproduction Page 13, have the students write English words with the following initial consonant clusters. The students are told that three of the following clusters are not permitted initially in English. Sample answers are given below, but not on the Reproduction Page. Other answers are obviously acceptable.

1.	/skr-/	scratch		11.	/fl-/	flea
2.	/spl-/	splash		12.	/šw-/	*impossible*
3.	/skw-/	squash		13.	/sl-/	slow
4.	/stn-/	*impossible*		14.	/fr-/	freeze
5.	/str-/	strike		15.	/šr-/	shred
6.	/sf-/	sphere		16.	/st-/	stone
7.	/pr-/	prune		17.	/Ɵr-/	throw
8.	/sm-/	small		18.	/sn-/	sneeze
9.	/ky-/	cube		19.	/sŋ-/	*impossible*
10.	/tw-/	twice		20.	/pl-/	place

- Using Reproduction Page 14, have the students write English words with the following final consonant clusters. The students are told that three of the following

INITIAL CONSONANT CLUSTERS

Directions: *Write an English word that begins with each of the following initial consonant clusters. Three of the consonant clusters do not occur in English, so do not get frustrated when you cannot think of words that begin with some of these sequences of sound.*

1. /skr-/
2. /spl-/
3. /skw-/
4. /stn-/
5. /str-/
6. /sf-/
7. /pr-/
8. /sm-/
9. /ky-/
10. /tw-/
11. /fl-/
12. /šw-/
13. /sl-/
14. /fr-/
15. /šr-/
16. /st-/
17. /θr-/
18. /sn-/
19. /sŋ-/
20. /pl-/

FINAL CONSONANT CLUSTERS

Directions: *Write an English word that ends with each of the following final consonant clusters. Three of the consonant clusters do not occur in English, so do not get frustrated when you cannot think of words that end with some of these sequences of sound.*

1. /-mps/
2. /-ksθ/
3. /-rst/
4. /-lfθ/
5. /-plt/
6. /-nč/
7. /-lǰ/
8. /-st/
9. /-ŋk/
10. /-ks/
11. /-ls/
12. /-sk/
13. /-hm/
14. /-lθ/
15. /-mp/
16. /-fθ/
17. /-st/
18. /-sp/
19. /-sŋ/
20. /-nt/

clusters are not permitted finally in English. Sample answers are given below, but not on the Reproduction Page. Other answers are obviously acceptable.

1.	/-mps/	glimpse	7.	/-lǰ/	bulge
2.	/-ksθ/	sixth	8.	/-st/	twist
3.	/-rst/	burst	9.	/-ŋk/	junk
4.	/-lfθ/	twelfth	10.	/-ks/	fix
5.	/-plt/	*impossible*	11.	/-ls/	else
6.	/-nč/	hunch	12.	/-sk/	ask

CONSONANT-VOWEL PATTERNS

Directions: *In the formulas for English words below, C stands for any consonant phoneme and V stands for any vowel or diphthong phoneme. Write an English word that has the consonant-vowel pattern indicated in the formulas below. One of the formulas is not a possible formula for an English word, so you will not be able to find a word with that sound pattern in it.*

1. VC
2. CV
3. CVC
4. VCC
5. CCV
6. CCVC
7. CVCC
8. CCVCC
9. CVCCC
10. CCCVCC
11. CCVCCC
12. CCCVCCC
13. CCCCVCC
14. VCV
15. VCVC
16. VCCVC
17. CVCVC
18. CCVCVC
19. CVCCV
20. CCVCVC

13.	/-hm/	*impossible*	17.	/-st/	ghost
14.	/-lθ/	wealth	18.	/-sp/	gasp
15.	/-mp/	bump	19.	/-sŋ/	*impossible*
16.	/-fθ/	fifth	20.	/-nt/	punt

- Using Reproduction Page 15, have the students write an English word with the following patterns of consonant and vowel or diphthong phonemes. In the formulas, *C* stands for any consonant phoneme, and *V* stands for any vowel or diphthong phoneme. The students are told that one of the formulas stands for a consonant-vowel pattern that does not occur in English. Sample answers are given below, but not on the Reproduction Page. Other answers are also possible, of course.

1.	VC	at	8.	CCVCC	crunch	15.	VCVC	orate
2.	CV	go	9.	CVCCC	thirst	16.	VCCVC	oyster
3.	CVC	cat	10.	CCCVCC	strange	17.	CVCVC	unit
4.	VCC	act	11.	CCVCCC	glimpse	18.	CCVCVC	driven
5.	CCV	glow	12.	CCCVCCC	strength	19.	CVCC	window
6.	CCVC	crash	13.	CCCCVCC	*impossible*	20.	CCVCVC	stable
7.	CVCC	hard	14.	VCV	away			

ASSESSING ACHIEVEMENT OF OBJECTIVES

Ongoing Evaluation

The extent to which students have mastered the concepts covered under each topic can be measured by any of the activities assigned to the class as individuals.

Final Evaluation

For an overall evaluation of the students' mastery of the concepts in this chapter, if all topics in the chapter have been taught, a test constructed from among the following test items may be used:

1. Write each of the following English words which have been written phonemically in conventional English spelling:

    A. /čit/

    B. /šip/

    C. /gret/

    D. /brɛd/

    E. /klæs/

    F. /dop/

    G. /buθ/

    H. /raʊnd/

    I. /ǰɔz/

    J. /faɪnd/

    K. /trʌbəl/

2. Transcribe each of the following English words in phonemic symbols:

    A. battle

    B. pull

    C. choice

    D. teeth

    E. bathe

    F. vine

    G. shed

    H. road

    I. ring

    J. frown

    K. under

3. Mark the primarily, secondarily, tertially, and weakly stressed syllables in the word *education.*

4. Mark the pitch patterns on the two sentences below.

    A. Tom is my brother.

    B. You are not feeling well?

5. Indicate the juncture phonemes that occur at the end of the two sentences below.

   A. I live in a white house.

   B. You ate the whole pie?

6. Explain and show with examples the complementary distribution pattern of at least two allophones of a particular phoneme.

7. Give an example of an English word that begins with three consonant phonemes.

8. Give an example of an English word that ends with three consonant phonemes.

9. Give an example of a consonant cluster that does *not* occur initially in English words.

10. Give an example of a consonant cluster that does *not* occur finally in English words.

RESOURCES FOR TEACHING ABOUT THE SOUND SYSTEM OF ENGLISH

Below is a selected and annotated list of resources useful for teaching the topics in this chapter and arranged in order of ascending difficulty. Special strengths and weaknesses are mentioned in the annotations. Addresses of publishers or distributors can be found in the alphabetical list on pages 263–265 in Appendix A. Films are black and white unless otherwise indicated.

I. PHONEMES OR SIGNIFICANT UNITS OF SOUND

Audiovisual Materials

Sounds of Language, The. Film, part of *Language and Linguistics* Series, 30 minutes, 1958, Indiana University Audio-Visual Center. Explains how the phonemes of a language are identified and how various English phonemes are produced.

Print

"The Phoneme," etc., pp. 11–28 in *An Introductory English Grammar,* 2d ed., by Norman C. Stageberg. Identifies the segmental phonemes of English in articulatory terms using modified IPA symbols. Provides simple exercises. Paperbound, Holt, Rinehart and Winston, 1971.

"Stress," "Pitch Levels and Terminals," and "Internal Open Juncture," pp. 45–74 in *An Introductory English Grammar,* 2d ed., by Norman C. Stageberg. Explains the stress, pitch, and junc-

ture phonemes of English. Provides copious exercises. Paperbound, Holt, Rinehart and Winston, 1971.

"The Phonology of English," pp. 77–88 in *A Survey of Modern Grammars,* 2d ed., by Jeanne H. Herndon. Lists and explains the phonemes of English in articulatory terms using the Trager-Smith system. Paperbound, Holt, Rinehart and Winston, 1976.

"The Vowels of English," "The Consonants of English," and "Prosodic Features," pp. 56–69 in *English: An Introduction to Language* by Thomas Pyles and John Algeo. Uses IPA symbols to identify the segmental and suprasegmental phonemes of English. Provides simple exercises. Paperbound, Harcourt, Brace and World, 1970.

"Transcription for Reading Practice," etc., pp. 30–42 in *Problems in the Origins and Development of the English Language,* 2d ed., by John Algeo. Provides exercises using IPA symbols for transcription and reading, and exercises explaining the articulation of English segmental phonemes. Paperbound, Harcourt Brace Jovanovich, 1972.

"Phonological Systems," pp. 145-155 in *Language and Its Structure,* 2d ed., by Ronald W. Langacker. Identifies the segmental phonemes (but does not use the term) of English in articulatory terms using IPA symbols. Paperbound, Harcourt Brace Jovanovich, 1973.

"Suprasegmental Units," pp. 63-66 in *Introduction to Linguistics* by Ronald Wardhaugh. Identifies the suprasegmental phonemes of stress, pitch, and juncture in English. Paperbound, McGraw-Hill, 1972.

Exercises, pp. 39-47 in *Workbook to Accompany Introduction to Linguistics* by Ronald Wardhaugh. Provides phonemic transcription exercises. Paperbound, McGraw-Hill, 1972.

"Suprasegmental Phonemes," pp. 150-157 in *The Structure of American English* by W. Nelson Francis. Identifies and illustrates the stress, pitch, and juncture phonemes of American English. Hardbound, The Ronald Press Co., 1958.

"Sounds and Letters," pp. 88-91, 94-106 in *Linguistics, English, and the Language Arts* by Carl A. Lefevre. Identifies the segmental phonemes of English using the Trager-Smith phonemic symbols. Has teaching suggestions. Paperbound, Teachers College Press, 1970.

"Language as Sound," pp. L33-L65 in *Persuasion and Pattern* by Albert R. Kitzhaber et al. Explains the phonemes of English in terms of distinctive features. Not recommended for students, but provides exercises. Hardbound, Holt, Rinehart and Winston, 1974.

II. ALLOPHONES OR NONSIGNIFICANT SOUND DIFFERENCES

Audiovisual Materials

Sounds of Language, The. Film, part of *Principles and Methods of Teaching a Second Language* Series, 31 minutes, 1961, Indiana University Audio-Visual Center. Explains the phoneme and allophones and contrasts the sound patterns of English and Spanish.

Print

"The Phoneme as a Class of Sounds: Allophones," pp. 92-94 in *Linguistics, English, and the Language Arts* by Carl A. Lefevre. Illustrates the concept of allophones by discussing the allophones of English /p/, /t/, and /k/. Paperbound, Teachers College Press, 1970.

"Distinctive Sounds," pp. 54-55 in *English: An Introduction to Language* by Thomas Pyles and John Algeo. Identifies allophones of some English consonants. Paperbound, Harcourt, Brace and World, 1970.

"16.6" to "16.12," pp. 261-266 in *An Introduction to Descriptive Linguistics,* rev. ed., by H. A. Gleason, Jr. Illustrates how allophones of English phonemes are phonetically similar and either in complementary distribution or free variation. Hardbound, Holt, Rinehart and Winston, 1961.

"Allophones: Complementary Distribution of Sounds" and "Classifying Allophones as Members of the Same Phoneme," pp. 37-41 in *An Introduction to General Linguistics* by Francis P. Dinneen. Illustrates allophones of English phonemes and identifies criteria for grouping allophones into phonemes. Hardbound, Holt, Rinehart and Winston, 1967.

"The Significant Sounds of Speech: Phonemics," pp. 119-150 in *The Structure of American English* by W. Nelson Francis. Provides a comprehensive description of the allophones of the segmental phonemes of English using the Trager-Smith system. Recommended for teachers. Hardbound, The Ronald Press Co., 1958.

III. SEQUENCES OF SOUND IN ENGLISH

Print

"Phonotactics," pp. 61–63 in *English: An Introduction to Language* by Thomas Pyles and John Algeo. Discusses initial and final consonant clusters in English. Provides simple exercises. Paperbound, Harcourt, Brace and World, 1970.

"Phonotactics," pp. 75–82 in *An Introductory English Grammar,* 2d ed., by Norman C. Stageberg. Identifies the permissible consonant sequences and positions of segmental phonemes within English words. Paperbound, Holt, Rinehart and Winston, 1971.

"Contrastive Units" and "English Consonants," pp. 49–55 in *Introduction to Linguistics* by Ronald Wardhaugh. Shows which consonants occur initially, medially, and finally, as well as permissible English consonant clusters. Paperbound, McGraw-Hill, 1972.

Exercises, pp. 47–49 in *Workbook to Accompany Introduction to Linguistics* by Ronald Wardhaugh. Provides exercises dealing with English phonotactics. Paperbound, McGraw-Hill, 1972.

"The Sounds: Understanding and Producing the 'Stream of Speech,'" pp. 16–20 in *Teaching and Learning English as a Foreign Language* by Charles C. Fries. Identifies and illustrates the permissible initial and final consonant clusters in English. Paperbound, University of Michigan Press, 1945.

"The Sound-System: Consonant Sequences," pp. 6–7 in *Problems in the Origins and Development of the English Language,* 2d ed., by John Algeo. Provides exercises dealing with the phonotactics of English initial consonant sequences and what English does with words borrowed from other languages with different phonotactical patterns. Paperbound, Harcourt Brace Jovanovich, 1972.

4

The Way Words Are Made in English

This chapter introduces the concepts of morphemes as abstract meanings and allomorphs as the different ways these abstract meanings are reflected in the language. It also introduces the concepts of inflections and derivational affixes necessary to analyze the component parts of individual words and to create new words in the language. Finally, it identifies the four parts of speech and some of the classes of function words in English.

A practical result of this unit should be that the students will become aware that words do have identifiable meaningful components and that words cannot be used loosely. A more concrete practical result of the study of this material is that the students will be able to analyze unfamiliar words and to create new words using the structural devices of English grammar. A final practical result is that students will develop an understanding of what the various parts of speech in English really are.

Initially, the students should be introduced to the concepts of morphemes, allomorphs, and morphs. These concepts will indicate both how meaning is reflected in the English language and also that a word is not necessarily a single unit of meaning.

Then, derivational and inflectional affixes should be studied. These affixes are particular kinds of morphemes that are added to other morphemes to form new words. This topic will make clear that words often have specific components, each of which has a specific meaning.

Finally, the students will be ready to examine the different classes of words or parts of speech of the English language. Traditional definitions which have not been helpful to students trying to learn the different kinds of words in English can be discarded. The traditional definitions can then be replaced with definitions of the various parts of speech based upon structural characteristics of these classes of words.

While it is not impossible to teach the third topic in this chapter without teaching the first two first or to teach the second topic without having first taught the first topic, it would be difficult to do so. More importantly, it would deprive the students of the theoretical backgrounds necessary to understand the structure of English words and the English parts of speech clearly.

OBJECTIVES

If all three topics in this chapter are taught by the teacher, the students should, at the end of the unit, be able to:

1. Define *morph, allomorph,* and *morpheme*
2. Show the complementary distribution of the allomorphs of morphemes like {Plural} and {Past}
3. Explain the differences between inflectional and derivational suffixes
4. Define and give examples of *homophones*
5. Illustrate nouns marked as such by determiners, inflections, derivational affixes, word order, and stress
6. Illustrate verbs marked as such by auxiliaries, inflections, derivational affixes, word order, and stress
7. Illustrate adjectives marked as such by qualifiers, inflections, derivational affixes, and word order
8. Illustrate adverbs marked as such by qualifiers, inflections, derivational affixes, and word order
9. Explain the differences between function words and the four parts of speech
10. Derive a noun, an adverb, and a verb from a base adjective like *tight*

CONTENT OVERVIEW

Morphemes and Allomorphs

The English language, like all other languages, contains abstract, meaningful concepts called morphemes. These morphemes may be grammatical concepts like {Plural}, which may be associated with nouns or with specific lexical concepts like the noun {book} or the adjective {clear}. Notice that morphemes are written between braces. However, morphemes are manifested within the language by individual occurrences of a morpheme that are called morphs; for example, the word *paths* consists of two morphs: /pæɵ/ being a morph belonging to a {path} morpheme, and /z/ (spelled ⟨s⟩) being a morph belonging to the {Plural} morpheme. It is best to begin the discussion of morphemes and allomorphs, then, with the definition of a morph, which is the smallest meaningful unit of sound.

The smallest meaningful unit of sound refers to the sound or sequence of sounds in a word to which a particular meaning may be assigned. The word *glimpsed* /glɪmpst/ contains two morphs: /glɪmps/, which means something like "view partially or incompletely," and /t/, which means "past tense." Notice that the first morph contains six sounds (phonemes) while the second contains only one. It is true that /glɪmps/ contains the sequence /ɪmp/, which is also a morph in English, but the meaning of /ɪmp/ has no relationship to the meaning of /glɪmps/. It is only coincidence that they share some of the same sounds in the same sequence, so the morph /glɪmps/ cannot be broken down further into /gl/ with some part of the meaning of /glɪmps/ assigned to it, /ɪmp/ meaning "a small, mischievous person," and /s/ with some part of the meaning of /glɪmps/ assigned to it.

It should be noted that some morphs like /glɪmps/ may occur by themselves and still have meaning; they are called free morphs because their occurrence is not limited to their appearing with another morph. Other morphs like /t/ in /glɪmpst/ only have meaning, past tense in this case, when bound to another morph like /glɪmps/ or /lʊk/ (*look*) or /slæp/ (*slap*); these are called bound morphs. In the words *cats* and *unkind,* /kæt/ and /kaɪnd/ are free morphs because they can occur without the final /s/ and the initial /ʌn/, respectively, but the final /s/ and initial /ʌn/ are bound morphs, since the former can mean "plural" only when attached to a base morph like /kæt/ or /pɛt/ (*pet*) and the latter can only mean "negative" when attached to a base morph like /kaɪnd/ or /tru/ (*true*).

Obviously, certain morphs occur rather frequently in English, and it would be cumbersome to talk about the /s/ morphs meaning plural at the end of the words *cats, books, cups, desks,* and all other nouns forming their plural by adding an /s/ sound. Instead, it is common to refer to the /s/ allomorph of the noun plural morpheme. An allomorph consists of phonemically and semantically identical morphs. Thus, the /s/ allomorph of the noun plural morpheme encompasses the /s/s at the end of the words *cats, books, cups,* and *desks* above as well as all of the other /s/s used to pluralize nouns in English because each of these /s/s sounds the same to a speaker of English and means plural. The /s/ allomorph will also include the /s/ added to form the plural of new nouns in English such as /glɪp/, should such a word ever be added to the English language.

The reason that it was assumed that the plural of a non-existent English noun like /glɪp/ would be an /s/ morph which was part of the /s/ allomorph of the noun plural morpheme is that the allomorphs of a particular morpheme always occur in a particular patterned relationship with each other. This relationship is shown by the definition of a morpheme as a group of semantically identical allomorphs in complementary distribution (or rarely in free variation). Notice that this definition specifically does not say that the allomorphs of a morpheme will be phonemically identical (sound the same to a native speaker). All the definition says is that allomorphs of the same morpheme must mean the same thing and occur in a particular pattern. The concept of a morpheme can be illustrated by the following plural nouns in English which are written in both conventional spelling and phonemic transcription:

cats /kæts/	dogs /dɔgz/	dishes /dɪsəz/
packs /pæks/	stoves /stovz/	places /plesəz/
cups /kʌps/	stars /starz/	noises /nɔɪzəz/
caps /kæps/	dabs /dæbz/	judges /ǰʌǰəz/
books /bʊks/	pencils /pɛnsəlz/	matches /mæčəz/
picks /pɪks/	nuns /nʌnz/	garages /gəražəz/

In the first column, each of the nouns forms its plural by adding an /s/ morph to the singular form. Thus, it may be said that each of the final /s/s belongs to an /s/ allomorph of the noun plural morpheme, since each of them is an /s/ (phonemically identical) and means plural (semantically identical). Each of the nouns in the second column forms its plural by adding a /z/ allomorph of the noun plural morpheme, since they are all /z/s (phonemically identical) and mean plural (semantically identical). In the third column, each of the singular forms has been pluralized by adding a /əz/ morph, an unstressed vowel plus /z/, to the singular form. Then, each /əz/ morph belongs to a /əz/ allomorph, since they are phonemically identical /əz/s, and they all mean plural.

The three allomorphs just identified—the /s/ allomorph, the /z/ allomorph, and the /əz/ allomorph—can be shown to be allomorphs of the same morpheme if they can be shown to be semantically identical and in complementary distribution (or possibly in free variation). The three allomorphs are clearly semantically identical, since all of the morphs in each allomorph mean plural. Showing that they are in complementary distribution is only a little more difficult. The singular forms of the nouns in the third column end in six different sounds identified in phonemic transcription as /s/, /š/, /č/, /z/, /ž/, and /ǰ/. If one thinks of other nouns ending in these sounds such as *wish, crash, watch, nose,* and *badge* and pluralizes them, one will always add /əz/ to the singular form rather than adding an /s/ or just a /z/. This phenomenon occurs because the structure of English requires that nouns ending in one of these six sounds will always form their plurals using morphs belonging to the /əz/ allomorph. The singular forms of the nouns in the first column end in voiceless sounds (sounds produced without vibration of the vocal chords). In English, nouns ending in voiceless sounds, except for /s/, /š/, and /č/, which are also voiceless, form their plurals by adding morphs from the /s/ allomorph of the noun plural morpheme. This generalization can be checked by forming the plural of other words ending in voiceless sounds such as *sock, envelope, apricot,* and *strike* and noticing that morphs from the /s/ allomorph are added in each case rather than from the /əz/ or /z/ allomorphs. The nouns in the second column, however, end in voiced sounds (sounds produced with vibration of the vocal chords). In English, nouns ending in voiced sounds, except for /z/, /ž/, and /ǰ/, which are also voiced, form their plurals by adding morphs from the /z/ allomorph of the noun plural morpheme. This generalization may be checked by forming the plural of other words ending in voiced sounds such as *door, wall, gum,* and *banana* and noticing that morphs from the /z/ allomorph are added to each of these words instead of morphs from the /s/ or /əz/ allomorphs. Thus, the complementary distribution of these three allomorphs is established: morphs from the /s/ allomorph are added to nouns ending in voiceless sounds except /s/, /š/, and /č/ but never to nouns ending in voiced sounds or in /s/, /š/, or /č/: morphs from the /z/ allomorph are added to nouns ending in voiced sounds except /z/, /ž/; and /ǰ/ but never to nouns ending in voiceless sounds or in /z/, /ž/, or /ǰ/; and morphs from the /əz/ allomorph are added to nouns ending in /s/, /š/, /č/, /z/, /ž/, and /ǰ/ but never to nouns ending in other sounds.

Of course, not all of the allomorphs of the noun plural morpheme have been identified. The three allomorphs of {Plural} identified above are the phonologically conditioned allomorphs, that is, their complementary distribution is determined by the last sound in the singular form of the noun. If English were an orderly language like Turkish or if adults started imitating children who learn these "regular" allomorphs of {Plural} first and extend them to irregular nouns, like *tooths* and *foots,* we would have determined all of the allomorphs of {Plural}. However, there are morphologically conditioned allomorphs of {Plural} as well that are also in complementary distribution with the three phonologically conditioned allomorphs. Morphologically conditioned allomorphs are distributed on the basis of the singular base morphs that they are added to and must be learned by children as exceptions to the general pattern of phonologically conditioned allomorphs. Although morphologically conditioned allomorphs will be examined in greater detail under the section "Parts of Speech," some examples of morphologically conditioned allomorphs of {Plural} are: /ən/ added to the base morph /aks/ (*ox*) /Ø/ (no phonemic addition) to base morphs like /šip/ (*sheep*) and /dɪr/ (*deer*), and /aʊ→aɪ/ (replacive allomorph) added to bases like /maʊs/ (*mouse*) and /laʊs/ (*louse*).

The reason the phrase "or rarely in free variation" was added parenthetically to the definition of a morpheme is that very occasionally more than one allomorph of a morpheme may be added to the same base, depending upon a speaker's dialect. With {Plural}, for example, some speakers of English may add the phonologically conditioned /əz/ allomorph to form the plural of *mongoose,* while others will use the morphologically conditioned /u→i/ allomorph by analogy with *goose-geese.* Indeed, the same speaker may alternate in use between both allomorphs, thus using free variation. More commonly, two different allomorphs of {Past}, the verb past tense morpheme, are used by speakers of different dialects of English to form the past tense of *dive.* Some speakers will add the phonologically conditioned /d/ to /daɪv/, while others will use the morphologically conditioned replacive allomorph /aɪ→o/.

It is necessary when discussing morphology to point out that a certain sequence of sounds is not always a member of a particular allomorph of a particular morpheme just because it belongs to that allomorph in certain places in the language. The key requirement is that it must represent the meaning of that particular morpheme. For example, the /s/ morph occurring at the end of /kæts/ (*cats*) clearly belongs to the /s/ allomorph of {Plural}, but the /s/ morph at the end of /kæts/ (*cat's*) belongs to the /s/ allomorph of another morpheme, {Possessive}, while the /s/ morph at the end of /dɛkərets/ (*decorates*) belongs to an /s/ allomorph of a verb suffix {Present} and means third person singular present tense. These are homophones that may be defined as phonemically identical allomorphs of different morphemes. Some morphemes that have only one allomorph may even be said to be homophonous morphemes such as {well_N} in *The well is dry,* {well_Adj} in *He is well now,* and {well_Adv} in *She did her work well.*

Inflectional and Derivational Affixes

Affixes are special kinds of morphemes which are always bound to other morphemes. In English, there are only two kinds of affixes, prefixes and suffixes. Other languages such as Old Irish have infixes, affixes not added to the front or back of other morphemes but within other morphemes such as the ⟨i⟩ in the nickname of the legendary Irish hero Cu Chulainn (literally, "dog of Culann") that is infixed to show possession in the man's name Culann (the ⟨h⟩ is added due to lenition caused by the vowel in Cu). In English, the suffixes must be further divided into inflectional and derivational suffixes.

Inflectional suffixes are morphemes added to base morphemes that do not change the part of speech of the base morpheme; the native speaker of English also considers the base morpheme to which an inflectional suffix has been added to be still somehow the same word as the base morpheme without the inflection. In addition, with a few exceptions, an inflectional suffix may not be followed by another suffix in the same word. For example, the base morpheme {agree} may have a /z/ added to it: /əgriz/. Notice that *agree* and *agrees* are still the same part of speech and still considered the "same" word in *I agree with you* and *He agrees with you* and that no other suffixes may be added after /z/ since /əgrizd/ (*agreesed*) and /əgrizmənt/ (*agreesment*) are not English words. These generalizations are true because the /z/ morph meaning third person singular present tense is part of the /z/ allomorph of the verb inflection {Present} mentioned above. Similarly, we may add a /d/ suffix to {agree} producing /əgrid/. Notice again that *agree* and *agreed* are still the same part of speech and still considered the "same" word in *I agree with you* and *I agreed with you* and that no other suffixes may be added after /d/, since /əgridz/ (*agreeds*) and /əgridəbəl/ (*agreedable*) are not English words. Again, these generalizations are true because the /d/ morph meaning past tense is part of the /z/ allomorph of the verb inflection {Past} mentioned above.

There are only eight inflectional suffixes in modern English: {Plural} and {Possessive} occurring with nouns; {Present}, {Past}, {Past Participle}, and {Present Participle} occurring with verbs; and {Comparative} and {Superlative} occurring with many adjectives and a few adverbs. The morphemic representations given here for these morphemes will not necessarily be those used in other sources one might consult, since there is no agreement among linguists about how to write grammatical morphemes. For example, instead of {Plural}, many linguists use {-S₁}, {-Z₁}, {-es}, or {Pl} to represent the same concept. About all that is generally agreed upon is that the morphemes are to be written between braces. Since there are only these eight inflectional morphemes in modern English, it should be obvious from the concepts they represent that each of these inflections is used with very high frequency in the English language.

Derivational suffixes are morphemes added to base morphemes that usually change the part of speech of the base morpheme. Even if the derivational suffix does not change the part of speech of the base morpheme, the native speaker recognizes that the base morpheme and the base morpheme plus the derivational affix are not the same word as in *friend* and *friendship,* both being nouns but the second noun being derived from the base morpheme {friend} by adding the derivational suffix {-ship}. Derivational suffixes may also be followed by other suffixes. These features of derivational suffixes may be illustrated by using the base morpheme {careₙ} and adding the suffix {-ful}. Notice that *care* and *careful* are not only not the same word, but they are also different parts of speech. *He showed great care* is grammatical, but *He showed great careful* is not. This is because an adjective *careful* has been derived from the noun *care.* Notice also that another suffix {-ly_Adv} can be added after the adjective derivational suffix {-ful}, giving *carefully* and showing that derivational suffixes may be followed by other suffixes. Of course, suffixes added to words ending in derivational suffixes need not be other derivational suffixes. If one goes back to the base morpheme {agree} and adds the noun derivational suffix {-ment} producing *agreement,* one may also add an inflectional suffix /s/ belonging to the /s/ allomorph of {Plural} to the derived noun *agreement* to produce *agreements.*

All prefixes in English are derivational. Although they may not change a base morpheme to another part of speech when they are added, the word formed by adding a prefix to a base morpheme is always considered a different word from the base morpheme itself. For example, *like* and *dislike* (formed by adding the derivational prefix {dis-} to the base morpheme {like}), and *sure* and *unsure* (formed by adding the derivational prefix {un-} to the base morpheme sure) are recognized not only as different words but even as opposites.

Parts of Speech

There are many kinds of words in English but only four that can be identified as parts of speech by formal characteristics such as inflections, derivational affixes, characteristic word order positions, co-occurrence with other types of words called function words, and characteristic stress patterns. These four which form classes or parts of speech are nouns, verbs, adjectives, and adverbs. The other kinds of words called function words in the previous sentence include types of words called determiners, auxiliaries, qualifiers, prepositions, coordinators, relatives, and so on. The four parts of speech include the vast majority of the words in a dictionary, while there are only a few hundred function words in English. It follows logically, then, that the function words like *the* (a determiner), *shall* (an auxiliary), and *very* (a qualifier) will each be used with much greater frequency than individual nouns like *gnu*, verbs like *obfuscate*, or adjectives like *tender*. It should also be noted that function words tend to have grammatical meaning but very little lexical meaning (as shown by definitions in a dictionary), while words belonging to the four parts of speech are loaded with lexical meanings as can be seen by looking at a dictionary for the meaning of words like *train* or *dog*. A further distinction between function words and parts of speech is that function words are a closed class with no new ones being made up or borrowed from other languages, while the four parts of speech are added to both by creation of new words and by borrowings from other languages. English may create a new noun like *astronaut* or borrow nouns like the French *détente,* the German *Gestalt,* and the Spanish *sombrero,* but it does not make up new determiners or borrow the French *la,* the German *die,* or the Spanish *el* to modify them; *the* works nicely for both the created and the borrowed nouns.

The preceding paragraph flies in the face of much of what has been taught about parts of speech in traditional grammar, and it was meant to do so. The traditional eight parts of speech were based on an inaccurate description of the English language by analogy with the traditional inaccurate description of Latin, which was based on the late classical analysis of Greek. Classical Greek was said to have eight parts of speech: nouns, verbs, adverbs, pronouns, prepositions, conjunctions, articles, and participles (evidently including adjectives). Roman grammarians writing grammars of Latin noticed that Latin did not have an article but felt that Latin should have as many parts of speech as Greek and added interjections to make eight parts of speech for Latin. The authors of the first traditional English grammars, being familiar with Latin grammar, kept eight parts of speech for the same reason. Of course, if one thinks about the interjections one uses in English such as *darn* or *goodness,* one will notice that they tend really to be nouns or verbs. In other words, the traditional parts of speech ignore certain real differences in English word classes and create some artificial ones.

The traditional definitions of the various parts of speech were frequently vague or even downright wrong, too. For instance, if one defines a noun as "the name of a person, place, or thing," the word "thing" is no clearer than the word "noun" that is being defined. If one says *She has an idea, idea* is clearly a noun, and presumably a thing rather than a person or a place. However, *idea* is certainly not a thing in the same sense that *dog* is in *She has a dog.* Without getting into theology, it is clear that *God* is a noun, but is it a person or a place or a thing? The traditional definition of an adjective is that it is a "word that modifies a noun." Yet in *the interesting story, the talking dog, the reading room,* and *the people here, interesting, talking, reading,* and *here* all modify nouns but are different kinds of words. *Interesting* is an adjective; it can form a comparative like *more interesting. Talking* is a verb; it cannot form a comparative *more talking,* but, unlike the adjective *interesting,* it may also follow the noun it modifies: *the dog talking. Reading* is a noun; of course, it cannot form a comparative *more reading,* but it gets a greater stress than the noun *room* which it modifies. Notice that in *the interesting story, story* gets the greatest stress; if one stresses *room* rather than *reading* in *the reading room,* one has the logical absurdity of a room which is in the process of reading. *Here* is an adverb; besides not being capable of forming a comparative *more here,* it follows the noun it modifies and cannot precede it, while the adjective *interesting* precedes the noun it modifies and cannot follow it.

One reason that the nonsensical traditional definitions of the parts of speech have been accepted for so long, aside from the fact that students are smart enough not to take teachers seriously when what they say makes no sense, is that everyone already knows what nouns, verbs, adjectives, and adverbs are anyway before he or she begins formal schooling. A child hearing a sentence like *The glarphers arrived yesterday* would not know what a *glarpher* was (since the word does not exist in English), but the child would know that *glarpher* was a noun because of certain formal devices. Most obviously, *glarphers* is a noun because it has a final /z/ meaning plural, part of the /z/ allomorph of {Plural}, and only nouns form plurals in English. Similarly, the child would be aware that the {-er} derivational suffix marked certain derived nouns like *singer, sitter,* and *grocer.* The child would also be aware, although probably no one ever even mentioned the word *noun,* that nouns followed certain function words like the determiner *the* and that they normally came before verbs like *arrived* in statements in English. The point is that children learn the various types of words or parts of speech by context, that is, the formal devices used in English, rather than by being taught definitions of the parts of speech when the definitions make little sense anyway.

In reality, a noun in English is marked as a noun by function words called determiners, the ability to take two noun inflections, certain characteristic derivational suffixes, predictable word order relationships with verbs, and occasionally by characteristic stress patterns that differentiate them from other otherwise homophonous words belonging to other parts of speech.

Noun determiners include words like *the, a, an, both, all, my, his,* and numbers like *one, twenty-eight,* and so on. Notice that determiners include what have traditionally been identified as possessive forms of personal pronouns. Because numbers are determiners, this class of function words has more individual morphemes than other function word classes do. The point of determiners is that they signal that a noun will follow shortly and help to identify the noun. If one says *I saw a* or *She has my,* a speaker of English naturally knows that a noun modified by these determiners must follow shortly. From the examples of determiners given here, it should be evident that, as stated before, function words have grammatical meaning and little lexical meaning.

Nouns as a part of speech also have the ability to inflect with the {Plural} and {Possessive} morphemes being added to the base noun. The {Plural} inflection has three phonologically conditioned allomorphs: /s/, /z/, and /əz/; and many morphologically conditioned allomorphs including the following:

/s/ after base morphemes ending in voiceless sounds except /s/, /š/, and /č/ as in *books*

/z/ after base morphemes ending in voiced sounds except /z/, /ž/, and /ǰ/ as in *walls*

/əz/ after base morphemes ending in /s/, /š/, /č/, /z/, /ž/, and /ǰ/ as in *watches*

/ən/ after {ox} as in *oxen*

/Ø/ after {sheep}, {deer}, {trout}, etc., as in *deer*

/u→i/ after {goose} and {tooth} as in *geese*

/æ→ɛ/ after {man} as in *men*

/ʊ→i/ after {foot} as in *feet*

/aʊ→aɪ/ after {mouse} and {louse} as in *mice*

There are other replacive allomorphs like the last four as well as morphologically conditioned allomorphs reflecting foreign ways of pluralizing nouns that have been borrowed into English that are still maintained by speakers of English. Examples of such foreign plural forms are /əm/ added to {cherub} to produce *cherubim,* /m→Ø/ added to {datum} to produce *data,* and /n→Ø/ added to {phenomenon} to produce *phenomena.* Sometimes the speakers of English have gotten a little confused while using foreign plurals so that words like the originally Latin {alumnus} has a plural spelled the Latin way *alumni* but pronounced the way the Latin *alumnae* (the feminine version of *alumni*) is pronounced. The height of such confusion is the English borrowing of the Latin verb form *ignoramus* ("we do not know") as an English noun inflected for plurality by the phonologically conditioned /əz/ allomorph of {Plural}.

The {Possessive} morpheme, which is the other noun inflection, has three phonologically conditioned allomorphs, /s/, /z/, and /əz/, which are homophonous with the three phonologically conditioned allomorphs of {Plural}. {Possessive} also has one morphologically conditioned allomorph /Ø/ that is used after a phonologically conditioned allomorph of {Plural}. It was stated above that inflectional suffixes, with a few exceptions, could not be followed by other suffixes. The exceptions involve the {Possessive} inflection whose allomorphs may follow the allomorphs of the {Plural} inflection as follows. If a phonologically conditioned allomorph of {Plural} is added to a base morpheme such as /kæt/ + /s/ /cats/, /dɔg/ + /z/ (*dogs*), and /ǰʌǰ/ + /əz/ (*judges*), then the morphologically conditioned /Ø/ allomorph (which represents a concept but no sound) of {Possessive} may be added as in /kæt/ + /z/ of {Plural} + /Ø/ of {Possessive} (*cats'*). Also, if a morphologically conditioned allomorph of {Plural} is added to a base morpheme such as /aks/ + /ən/ (*oxen*) or /fʊt/ + /ʊ→i/ (*feet*), the phonologically conditioned allomorphs of {Possessive} may be added as in

/aks/ + /ən/ of {Plural} + /z/ of {Possessive} (*oxen's*) or /fʊt/ + /ʊ→i/ of {Plural} + /s/ of {Possessive} (*feet's*).

Not all nouns have derivational affixes, but many nouns are identifiable as such by characteristic derivational suffixes. Common noun derivational suffixes include {-ness} as in *kindness,* {-ment} as in *agreement,* {-ity} as in *hostility,* and {-ist} as in *violinist,* but there are about twenty other noun derivational suffixes. Sometimes, these derivational suffixes have alternate spellings such as {-ance}, which may be spelled either *-ance* as in *grievance* or *-ence* as in *dependence,* and {-er}, which is spelled *-er* in *teacher, -or* in *sailor, -ar* in *liar,* and *-yer* in *lawyer.* The first three spellings of the {-er} noun derivational suffix all represent the /ər/ allomorph of this derivational morpheme, but the *-yer* spelling represents the /jər/ allomorph that occurs only when added to the base morpheme {law} and historically to the base morphemes {coal} and {saw}, producing nouns which survive only as proper nouns in American English: *Collier* and *Sawyer.*

Nouns are also marked in English by characteristic word orders in sentences. In sentences like *Glarphs are funny* and *She hates blicks, glarphs* and *blicks* are marked as nouns, in addition to their plural inflections, by the fact that *glarphs* occurs before a verb as a subject and *blicks* occurs after a verb as a direct object. Other common word order positions for nouns include after another noun inflected with {Possessive} as in *John's book,* before another noun following a verb as an indirect object as in *give dogs candy,* after another noun following a verb as an object complement as in *elected Tom president,* and after a linking verb as a subject complement as in *became a father.*

Some nouns are also identified as nouns by stress patterns that differentiate them from other parts of speech. The stress pattern of primary stress on the first syllable and tertiary stress on the second syllable differentiates some two-syllable nouns like *suspect, conduct,* and *permit* from otherwise homophonous verbs that have their primary stress on the second syllable and a weakly stressed first syllable. Nouns used as noun adjuncts (modifiers of following nouns and not inflected with the {Possessive} morpheme) receive a greater stress than the nouns they modify, but other parts of speech modifying nouns receive a lesser stress than the nouns they modify. As a result, *orderly* in *the órderly room* (a room for orderlies) is identified as a noun, but *orderly* in *the orderly róom* (a neat room) is identified as not being a noun but, in this case, as an adjective.

Verbs are marked in English by the same five devices that identified nouns. Specifically, verbs may take four verb inflections, occur after function words called auxiliaries, have characteristic derivational suffixes and prefixes, occur in predictable word order relationships with nouns, and occasionally be differentiated from otherwise homophonous parts of speech by stress patterns.

The four verb inflections are {Present}, {Past}, {Past Participle}, and {Present Participle}. {Present} means that the verb is present tense and that its subject is third person singular. This inflectional morpheme has only three allomorphs: /s/, /z/ and /əz/; these are phonologically conditioned and have the same pattern of complementary distribution as the homophonous allomorphs of {Plural} and {Possessive}. For example, the /s/ allomorph occurs after verb bases ending in voiceless sounds except /s/, /š/, and /č/ like /stap/ + /s/ (*stops*); the /z/ allomorph occurs after verb bases ending in voiced sounds except /z/, /ž/, and /ĵ/ like /lɪsən/ + /z/ (*listens*); the /əz/ allomorph occurs after verb bases ending in /s/, /š/, /č/, /z/, /ž/, and /ĵ/ like /wač/ + /əz/ (*watches*).

{Past} is simply the past tense morpheme. It has three phonologically conditioned allomorphs, /t/, /d/, and /əd/, and many morphologically conditioned allomorphs including the following:

/t/ after base morphemes ending in voiceless sounds except /t/ as in *walked*

/d/ after base morphemes ending in voiced sounds except /d/ as in *lived*

/əd/ after base morphemes ending in /t/ or /d/ as in *waited*

/Ø/ after {hit}, {bet}, {burst}, etc. as in *hit*

/i→o/ after {freeze} as in *froze*

/ɪ→æ/ after {sing} and {ring} as in *sang*

/ʌ→æ/ after {run} as in *ran*

There are, of course, other replacive allomorphs like the last three. There are also some instances in English where the /t/ allomorph is morphologically conditioned rather than phonologically conditioned; for example, in some dialects, the past tense form of *spill* is not /spɪld/ using the phonologically conditioned /d/ but /spɪlt/ where the /t/ has been added because of the particular base morpheme {spill}.

The {Past Participle} morpheme is misnamed, since it has nothing to do with past tense. The auxiliary in front of a verb inflected with {Past Participle} carries the tense: *He has walked* is present and *He had walked* is past. However, the Latinate phrase is maintained because of its familiarity. This inflectional morpheme has the same three phonologically conditioned allomorphs as {Past}, but it has a different distribution of morphologically conditioned allomorphs as shown in the following explanation of complementary distribution:

/t/ after base morphemes ending in voiceless sounds except /t/ as in *have walked*

/d/ after base morphemes ending in voiced sounds except /d/ as in *have lived*

/əd/ after base morphemes ending in /t/ or /d/ as in *have waited*

/Ø/ after {come}, {hit}, {bet}, etc., as in *have come*

/n/ after {see}, etc., as in *have seen*

/ən/ after {give}, etc., as in *have given*

/ɪ→ʌ/ after {sing} and {ring} as in *have sung*

Notice that the examples have been given following the auxiliary *have;* the ability to follow the auxiliary *have* is an easy way to differentiate verbs inflected with the {Past Participle} morpheme from those inflected with the {Past} inflection, since most verbs have homophonous past and past participle forms. Another way to differentiate the two is that verbs inflected with {Past Participle} may modify nouns as in *the driven snow,* but verbs inflected with {Past} may not; for example, *the drove snow* is not grammatical in English.

The final verb inflection, {Present Participle}, is also misnamed, since it does not carry present tense meaning or any tense meaning at all. The auxiliary in front of a verb inflected with {Present Participle} carries the tense: *He is walking* is present tense and *He was walking* is past tense. While the {Present Participle} morpheme has at least two allomorphs /əŋ/ and /ən/, one need not worry about their complementary distribution, since they are distributed along two parameters unrelated to the particular verb they are added to; they are distributed along geographic dialect lines and by the formality or informality of the situation. There may be some confusion among verbs with this inflection, however, and nouns ending in the homophonous {ing_N} derivational suffix and adjectives ending in the homophonous {ing_Adj} derivational suffix. Of course, context usually resolves the ambiguity. *Breathing* is marked as a verb in *Jim is breathing oxygen* by the auxiliary *is* as well as by word order, following a noun subject and being followed by a noun direct object. When a verb inflected with a {Present Participle} appears before a noun and modifies it as in *a moving truck,* it is distinguished from a noun ending in the derivational {-ing_N} by not having a greater stress than the noun it modifies and from an adjective in the derivational {-ing_Adj} by not being able to have a qualifier like *very* placed in front of it like *the very interesting book.*

Auxiliaries have already been mentioned in passing, but they are the kind of function words that help to identify verbs as verbs. Certain kinds of auxiliaries appear with verbs that have no inflectional suffixes like *can* in *She can sing well* and *ought to* in *She ought to study harder.* The various forms of the auxiliary *be* occur with verbs inflected with {Present Participle} as in *The boys were singing.* The various forms of the auxiliary *be* and of the auxiliary *have* occur with verbs inflected with the {Past Participle} as in *It was given* and *They had given.* No auxiliaries occur with verbs inflected with {Past}.

Derivational suffixes and prefixes mark derived verbs as verbs, although not all verbs are derived verbs. Common derivational suffixes marking verbs are {-en} as in *brighten* and *lengthen* and {-ize} as in *criticize* and *modernize.* Common derivational prefixes occurring with verbs are {en-} as in *enlarge* and *endanger* and {de-} as in *demean* and *dethrone.* There are many other verb derivational affixes, however.

Sometimes verbs are also marked by both derivational prefixes and suffixes such as *enlighten* and *declassify*.

Verbs also appear in characteristic word order positions in sentences. In commands, they usually occur first in a sentence as in *Give that pen to me*. In declarative statements, they usually occur after noun subjects as in *The girls arranged the party* and frequently before noun objects as in the previous example.

Occasionally, verbs are differentiated from otherwise homophonous disyllabic nouns as mentioned above by having the primary stress on the second syllable as in *suspect* and *conduct*. Some verbs marked by the $\{$-ate$_V\}$ derivational suffix like *syndicate* are differentiated from otherwise homophonous trisyllabic nouns like *syndicate* by having a tertiary stress on the third syllable of the verb, whereas the third syllable of the corresponding noun is unstressed.

Adjectives are also identifiable by the formal criteria of derivational affixes, two inflections, appearance after function words called qualifiers, characteristic word order positions, and occasionally by the absence of primary stress.

There are approximately twenty suffixes that added to other parts of speech or to bound base morphemes to form adjectives. Examples are $\{$-ful$\}$ as in *helpful*, $\{$-less$\}$ as in *helpless*, and $\{$-y$\}$ as in *leafy*. Some derivational suffixes like $\{$-able$\}$ have alternate spellings in English such as *-able* in *remarkable* and *-ible* in *horrible*. The $\{$-ly$_{Adj}\}$ derivational suffix has a homophone in the $\{$-ly$_{Adv}\}$ derivational suffix. However, the $\{$-ly$_{Adj}\}$ derivational suffix is generally added to base morphemes that are nouns like $\{$friend$\}$ giving *friendly* or bound forms like $\{$ug-$\}$ giving *ugly*, while the $\{$-ly$_{Adv}\}$ derivational suffix is generally added to bases that are adjectives like *quickly* and *carefully*.

The most common adjective derivational prefixes are the negative morphemes $\{$un-$\}$ as in *uncooperative* and $\{$in-$\}$ as in *inconsiderate*. The $\{$in-$\}$ morpheme actually has four allomorphs, all of which are phonologically conditioned as follows:

/ɪl/ before bases beginning with /l/ as in *illegal*

/ɪr/ before bases beginning with /r/ as in *irrelevant*

/ɪm/ before bases beginning with /m/, /p/, and /b/ as in *impossible*

/ɪn/ before bases beginning with sounds other than /l/, /r/, /m/, /p/, and /b/ as in *inaccurate*

The two adjective inflections are $\{$Comparative$\}$ and $\{$Superlative$\}$. The $\{$Comparative$\}$ has only two allomorphs: /s/ occurring after the bound allomorph /wʊr/ of the adjective base morpheme $\{$bad$\}$ giving *worse* and /ər/ occurring after other bases as in *wider*. The $\{$Superlative$\}$ also has only two allomorphs, /st/ appearing after the bound allomorph /wʊr/ of the adjective base morpheme $\{$bad$\}$ and the bound allomorph /bɛ/ of the adjective base morpheme $\{$good$\}$ giving *worst* and *best*, respectively, and /əst/ appearing after other bases as in *kindest*. Actually, the comparative and superlative forms of *bad* and *good* are really the result of the historical process of suppletion by which two or more words with the same lexical meaning are combined into one paradigm.

There are some problems with using the inflections to identify adjectives. To begin with, not all adjectives form their comparative and superlative forms by adding inflections. In general, only those adjectives that are not marked as adjectives by derivational suffixes like *sweet* take the inflections, that is, *sweeter* and *sweetest*. *Friendly* is an exception in that it will also take the inflections despite having a derivational suffix, giving *friendlier* and *friendliest*. Another problem is that a few adverbs take the same $\{$Comparative$\}$ and $\{$Superlative$\}$ inflections. These adverbs that inflect are homophonous with certain adjectives. For example, *hard, harder,* and *hardest* are adjectives in *This is a hard rock, This is a harder rock,* and *This is the hardest rock,* but they are adverbs in *He works hard, He works harder,* and *He works hardest*. There is also the noun derivational suffix $\{$-er$\}$ that is homophonous with the prevalent allomorph of $\{$Comparative$\}$. In isolation, it is impossible to tell whether *cleaner* is an adjective inflected with $\{$Comparative$\}$ or a noun with the $\{$-er$\}$ derivational suffix. Of course, context resolves the ambiguity; *cleaner* is an adjective marked by the qualifier *much* as well as other devices in *The room is much cleaner* and a noun marked by the determiner *this* as well as other devices in *This cleaner will remove any spot*.

Qualifiers are the type of function word that helps to identify adjectives as such. There are about twenty qualifiers that mark adjectives; *very, quite, rather, too, more,* and *most* are common qualifiers. Qualifiers are sometimes identified as adverbs of degree in traditional grammar, but they differ from adverbs in their function as well as in their lack of much lexical meaning. For instance, *very* and *extremely* might at first appear to be the same kind of word in *He talks very rapidly* and *He talks extremely rapidly,* but *very* requires that a word like *rapidly* follow it. *He talks extremely* is grammatical, but *He talks very* is not. In general, adjectives marked as such by derivational affixes like *careful* form their comparative and superlative degrees, not with the inflections {Comparative} and {Superlative}, but with the qualifiers *more* and *most* as in *more careful* and *most careful.*

Word order marks adjectives as adjectives definitely only when an adjective occurs after a qualifier and before a noun as in *the rather lucky team.* Both the qualifier and the noun are necessary to identify an adjective by word order, since words other than adjectives may appear before and modify nouns as in *the football team,* but these other parts of speech cannot follow a qualifier, that is, *the rather football team* is not grammatical. Adjectives, of course, may also appear in other word order positions such as after a linking verb as a subject complement as in *She was nice,* but other parts of speech may also occur there such as nouns as in *She was a teacher* and adverbs as in *She was there.*

Stress is rarely used to identify adjectives, but occasionally the absence of stress on a word modifying a noun indicates that the word is an adjective rather than a homophonous noun, as was shown with the adjective *orderly* and the noun *orderly* above. Another example shows that *Spanish* is an adjective in *Srta. Rocha is a Spánish teacher* (she may teach English) but that *Spanish* is a noun in *Mr. Smith is a Spanish téacher* (he teaches Spanish although he is English or American).

Adverbs may also be identified by derivational affixes, inflections, qualifiers, word order, and occasionally by stress.

The derivational affixes that identify adverbs are {-ly$_{Adv}$}, {-wards}, {-wise}, and {a-}; {-ly$_{Adv}$} is the most frequently used as in *clearly* and *hopelessly,* but it does have a homophone {-ly$_{Adj}$} identified above. {-wards} has two allomorphs, /-wərdz/ and /-wərd/, which are complementarily distributed dialectally or may be in free variations in some persons' dialect as in *The child walks backwards* or *The child walks backward.* The /wərd/ allomorph of the {-wards} morpheme is homophonous with the /wərd/ allomorph of the {-ward} adjective derivational suffix as used in *That backward child needs extra help.* There is no problem with homophones for the {-wise} derivational suffix as in *lengthwise,* but many English teachers have a prejudice against adverbs derived using this derivational suffix such as *teacher-wise.* The {a-} derivational prefix is phonemically an unstressed vowel /ə/ in adverbs like *aloud* or *abroad,* so it is not confused with the similarly spelled adjective derivational prefix {a-}, phonemically /e/, in adjectives like *amoral* and *atypical.*

As mentioned above, a few adverbs that are homophonous with adjectives also inflect with {Comparative} and {Superlative}. Examples are *fast* and *hard,* which are adverbs in *He works hard (harder) (hardest)* and *She ran fast (faster) (fastest).*

Adverbs are also generally marked by the same qualifiers that mark adjectives such as *very, rather,* and *quite* in *very happily, rather strangely,* and *quite rapidly.* A few qualifiers like *right* in *right away* modify adverbs but not adjectives in some dialects. However, my native dialect allows *right* to occur before adjectives as in *right interesting* as well as before adverbs.

Word order does identify an adverb as an adverb absolutely when an adverb occurs after a noun or nouns used as complements of a verb such as in *The man sent the family a bill hesitantly* or *yesterday* or *abroad,* and so on. Unfortunately, adverbs are movable and do not always appear in that word order position. For example, the sentence above could be said, *The man hesitantly sent the family a bill* or *Hesitantly, the man sent the family a bill.*

The only adverbs that are identified by stress are adverbs like *over, out, in,* and *under* that have homophonous prepositions, another type of function word. Notice that *down* gets a primary stress in *Tom fell down* where *down* is an adverb, but that *down* is stressed less in *He fell down the hill* where *down* is a preposition. Usually, of course, adverbs like this occur last in a sentence, whereas prepositions, as *preposition* implies, occur before their objects rather than last in a sentence. In the event that a preposition does occur last in a sentence such as *This is the cliff which he drove over,* the preposition *over* in this case will still receive a lesser stress than the adverb *over* in *He told the story over.*

DIVIDING WORDS INTO MORPHS

Directions: *Divide the words below into the morphs (meaningful units of sound) that make up the various parts of words.*

1. resharpen
2. quickly
3. watches
4. clarify
5. multicolored
6. unresponsive
7. inactive
8. waited
9. players
10. snowy
11. prettier
12. scholarship
13. clearance
14. policeman
15. duckling
16. idolize
17. biology
18. troublesome
19. orange
20. unfolding

LEARNING EXPERIENCES

Topic I: Morphemes and Allomorphs

- Using Reproduction Page 16, have the students divide the words below into the various morphs that make up each word. The morphs making up each word are separated by hyphens in parentheses below, but not on the Reproduction Page.

  1. resharpen (re-sharp-en)
  2. quickly (quick-ly)
  3. watches (watch-es)
  4. clarify (clar-ify)
  5. multicolored (multi-color-ed)
  6. unresponsive (un-respons-ive)
  7. inactive (in-act-ive)
  8. waited (wait-ed)
  9. players (play-er-s)
  10. snowy (snow-y)
  11. prettier (pretti-er)
  12. scholarship (schol-ar-ship)
  13. clearance (clear-ance)
  14. policeman (police-man)
  15. duckling (duck-ling)
  16. idolize (idol-ize)
  17. biology (bio-logy)
  18. troublesome (trouble-some)
  19. orange (only one morph)
  20. unfolding (un-fold-ing)

- Divide the class into small groups and ask each group to make a list of the different ways English nouns are made plural. Then compare the lists in class and add any allomorphs of {Plural} that the groups have omitted. It may be necessary to point out the ⟨s⟩ at the ends of nouns is sometimes pronounced /s/ and sometimes /z/.

- Divide the class into small groups and ask each group to make a list of as many different forms of verbs as possible that can follow the auxiliary *have*. Then compare the lists in class and add any allomorphs of {Past Participle} that the groups have omitted. It may be necessary to point out that *-ed* is pronounced /t/, /d/ and /əd/ after different words.

ADDING -ED

Directions: *The past tense of verbs is often indicated by adding -ed to the simple form of a verb, but the -ed may be pronounced as a /t/, a /d/, or /əd/. After the past tense forms listed below, indicate whether the -ed is pronounced /t/, /d/, or /əd/. Then indicate what kinds of sounds the different pronunciations of -ed follow. As a clue, notice which sounds are voiced and which are voiceless.*

1. snowed
2. rained
3. patted
4. wished
5. hoped
6. hated
7. played
8. copied
9. screamed
10. clapped
11. folded
12. tricked
13. missed
14. raised
15. needed
16. breathed
17. groaned
18. laughed
19. cried
20. shoveled

- Using Reproduction Page 17, have the students indicate whether the /t/, /d/, or /əd/ allomorph of {Past} is used in each of the verbs below. The answers are given below but not on the Reproduction Page. The students are also asked to indicate what kinds of sounds before the -ed are followed by each of these allomorphs. That information is given in the overview for this chapter.

1. snowed /d/		11. folded /əd/	
2. rained /d/		12. tricked /t/	
3. patted /əd/		13. missed /t/	
4. wished /t/		14. raised /d/	
5. hoped /t/		15. needed /əd/	
6. hated /əd/		16. breathed /d/	
7. played /d/		17. groaned /d/	
8. copied /d/		18. laughed /t/	
9. screamed /d/		19. cried /d/	
10. clapped /t/		20. shoveled /d/	

- In order to teach the concept of homophones, use Reproduction Page 18 and have the students decide how many parts of speech each of the words below can be used as. The students are also asked to use each word in a sentence illustrating its use as each of these parts of speech. The answers (in parentheses) and sample sentences are given below but not on the Reproduction Page.

1. treasure	(2: noun and verb)	The treasure was finally found.
		I will treasure this gift forever.
2. kind	(2: noun and adjective)	That kind tastes sour.
		The kind man comforted her.
3. relay	(2: noun and verb)	They ran a relay.
		I will relay your message.

PARTS OF SPEECH

Directions: *Indicate how many different parts of speech each of the words below can be and then use each word in a sentence illustrating its use as each of these parts of speech.*

1. treasure

2. kind

3. .ela

4. group

5. orderly

6. bear

7. trains

8. bored

9. flies

10. cooler

AFFIXES

Directions: *Indicate whether the prefixes and suffixes underlined in the words below are inflectional or derivational affixes.*

1. fool<u>ish</u>
2. <u>anti</u>social
3. teach<u>er</u>
4. teacher<u>s</u>
5. watch<u>ed</u>
6. tall<u>er</u>
7. care<u>ful</u>
8. careful<u>ly</u>
9. <u>re</u>assess
10. deep<u>est</u>
11. activ<u>ate</u>
12. coach<u>es</u>
13. conventio<u>nal</u>
14. <u>un</u>conventional
15. music<u>ian</u>
16. musician<u>'s</u>
17. driv<u>en</u>
18. man<u>ly</u>
19. <u>im</u>practical
20. king<u>dom</u>

4. group   (2: noun and verb)   The entire group is ready.
                                            They will group us by height.

5. orderly   (2: noun and adjective)   That orderly brought the message.
                                            A neat room is an orderly room.

6. bear   (2: noun and verb)   The bear frightened him.
                                            He can bear the responsibility.

7. trains   (2: noun and verb)   The trains ran on time.
                                            He trains seals for the circus.

8. bored   (2: verb and adjective)   That story bored me.
                                            I was very bored.

9. flies   (2: noun and verb)   The flies swarmed around the carcass.
                                            He flies a large jet.

10. cooler   (2: noun and adjective)   The picnic cooler was lost.
                                            The nights are cooler now.

- Have each student write a short essay with examples explaining how morphs are parts of an allomorph and how allomorphs are parts of morphemes.

Topic II: Inflectional and Derivational Affixes

- Using Reproduction Page 19, have the students indicate whether the prefixes and suffixes underlined in the words below are inflectional or derivational affixes. The answers are given below in parentheses but not on the Reproduction Page.

1. foolish (derivational)
2. antisocial (derivational)
3. teacher (derivational)
4. teachers (inflectional)
5. watched (inflectional)
6. taller (inflectional)
7. careful (derivational)
8. carefully (derivational)
9. reassess (derivational)
10. deepest (inflectional)
11. activate (derivational)
12. coaches (inflectional)
13. conventional (derivational)
14. unconventional (derivational)
15. musician (derivational)
16. musician's (inflectional)
17. driven (inflectional)
18. manly (derivational)
19. impractical (derivational)
20. kingdom (derivational)

- Using Reproduction Page 20, have the students add the inflections indicated to each word below and then use the word in its inflected form in a sentence. Sample sentences are given below but not on the Reproduction Page.

1. girl (a noun)

    A. With the {Plural} inflection: The girls left early.

    B. With the {Possessive} inflection: The girl's work was superior.

2. talk (a verb)

    A. With the {Present} inflection: Tom talks nonsense.

    B. With the {Past} inflection: They talked too loudly.

    C. With the {Past Participle} inflection: They have talked together previously.

    D. With the {Present Participle} inflection: Mary is talking to Sue.

INFLECTIONS

Directions: *Add each of the inflections indicated to each word below and then use the word in its inflected form in a sentence.*

1. girl (a noun)
    A. With the {Plural} inflection:

    B. With the {Possessive} inflection:

2. talk (a verb)
    A. With the {Present} inflection:

    B. With the {Past} inflection:

    C. With the {Past Participle} inflection:

    D. With the {Present Participle} inflection:

3. sick (an adjective)
    A. With the {Comparative} inflection:

    B. With the {Superlative} inflection:

4. fast (an adverb)
    A. With the {Comparative} inflection:

    B. With the {Superlative} inflection:

---

3. sick (an adjective)

    A. With the {Comparative} inflection: I was sicker yesterday than I am now.

    B. With the {Superlative} inflection: Don was the sickest person in the group.

4. fast (an adverb)

    A. With the {Comparative} inflection: He drove the car much faster.

    B. With the {Superlative} inflection: The winner ran the race fastest.

- Divide the class into small groups, and using Reproduction Page 21, have each group write down as many words as possible ending in the following derivational suffixes or beginning with the following derivational prefixes. Sample answers are given below (although many others are possible) but not on the Reproduction Page.

    1. nouns ending in -*ness:* happiness, sadness, truthfulness, meanness

    2. nouns ending in -*ism:* fatalism, communism, mysticism, Catholicism

REPRODUCTION PAGE 21

PREFIXES AND SUFFIXES

Directions: *Write down as many words as possible ending in the following derivational suffixes or beginning with the following derivational prefixes:*

1. nouns ending in -*ness*
2. nouns ending in -*ism*
3. nouns ending in -*ity*
4. nouns ending in -*er*
5. nouns ending in -*ment*
6. nouns ending in -*ance*
7. verbs beginning with *re-*
8. verbs beginning with *dis-*
9. verbs ending in -*ate*
10. verbs ending in -*ify*
11. verbs ending in -*en*
12. verbs ending in -*ize*
13. adjectives beginning with *un-*
14. adjectives ending in -*ful*
15. adjectives ending in -*less*
16. adjectives ending in -*ive*
17. adjectives ending in -*able*
18. adjectives ending in -*al*
19. adverbs ending in -*ly*
20. adverbs ending in -*wise*

3. nouns ending in -*ity:* hostility, reality, facility, duplicity

4. nouns ending in -*er:* runner, plumber, retailer

5. nouns ending in -*ment:* assignment, refinement, argument, agreement

6. nouns ending in -*ance:* deliverance, abundance, conveyance, reliance

7. verbs beginning with *re-:* replay, retort, reassign, rewrite

8. verbs beginning with *dis-:* disassociate, disrupt, disappoint, displease

9. verbs ending in -*ate:* operate, orchestrate, extrapolate, duplicate

10. verbs ending in -*ify:* beautify, clarify, simplify, classify

11. verbs ending in -*en:* darken, lighten, blacken, sharpen

12. verbs ending in -*ize:* socialize, moralize, criticize, modernize

13. adjectives beginning with *un-:* unkind, uncommon, uncertain, unhappy

14. adjectives ending in -*ful:* beautiful, helpful, hopeful, careful

15. adjectives ending in -*less:* careless, hopeless, hairless, meatless

16. adjectives ending in -*ive:* attractive, active, creative, objective

17. adjectives ending in -*able:* desirable, remarkable, conceivable, believable

18. adjectives ending in -*al:* fatal, moral, annual, national

19. adverbs ending in -*ly:* carelessly, eagerly, respectfully, clearly

20. adverbs ending in -*wise:* lengthwise, otherwise, likewise, book-wise

- Ask each student to write a short essay explaining and illustrating the differences between inflectional suffixes and derivational suffixes.

NOUN IDENTIFIERS

Directions: *Identify the determiners, inflections, derivational suffixes, word order positions, and stress patterns that identify the nouns as nouns in the following sentences. Not all devices will necessarily be used to identify any particular noun.*

1. Some musicians study music seriously.

2. Those children need nourishment.

3. The suspect is a sailor.

4. My nargships are valuable.

Topic III: Parts of Speech

- Have each student write five sentences in which a noun is marked by a determiner and five sentences in which there are no determiners. The first five will be easy, but the second five will be difficult, since determiners occur before most nouns.

- Have each student write five sentences in which nouns occur both before and after verbs.

- Write the following words on the board and ask the students whether the words are nouns or verbs: *conflict, permit, contract,* and *combat.* There should be some disagreement, since each word may be either a noun or a verb. Explain how stress of the first syllable of each word marks it as a noun and stress on the second syllable of each word marks it as a verb.

- Using Reproduction Page 22, have the students identify the determiners, inflections, derivational suffixes, word order positions, and stress patterns that identify the nouns as nouns in the following sentences. The last sentence contains a noun that is a nonsense word in order to emphasize that the structural devices rather than a word's lexical meaning identify it as a noun. The nouns and the devices that mark them are given below but not on the Reproduction Page.

1. Some musicians study music seriously.

    musicians

    1. Determiner—*some*

    2. Inflection—/z/ allomorph of {Plural}

    3. Derivational suffix—{-ian}

    4. Word order—noun before verb

music

    1. Word order—noun after verb

2. Those children need nourishment.

children

    1. Determiner—*those*

    2. Inflection—/rən/ allomorph of {Plural}

    3. Word order—noun before verb

nourishment

    1. Derivational suffix—{-ment}

    2. Word order—noun after verb

3. The suspect is a sailor.

suspect

    1. Determiner—*the*

    2. Stress—primary stress on first syllable

    3. Word order—noun before verb

sailor

    1. Determiner—*a*

    2. Derivational suffix—{-er}

    3. Word order—noun after verb

4. My nargships are valuable.

nargships

    1. Determiner—*my*

    2. Inflection—/s/ allomorph of {Plural}

    3. Derivational suffix—{-ship}

    4. Word order—noun before verb

- Have each student write five sentences in which a verb is marked by an auxiliary and five sentences in which there are no auxiliaries. Then use their sample sentences to show which auxiliaries occur with the various inflected forms of the verbs, which auxiliaries occur with the uninflected form of the verb, and which inflected form of the verb (the one inflected with {Past}) cannot have auxiliaries in front of it.

VERB IDENTIFIERS

Directions: *Identify the auxiliaries, inflections, derivational affixes, word order positions, and stress patterns that identify the verbs as verbs in the following sentences. Not all devices will necessarily be used to identify any particular verb.*

1. Both men had clarified their positions.

2. The new surroundings disoriented the prisoners.

3. Mr. Smith will conduct the investigation.

4. My dog has stricated before.

- Have each student write five sentences in which a verb follows a noun as a subject, five sentences in which a noun follows a verb as an object, and five sentences in which no noun precedes a verb as a subject. Point out that the last five sentences are all commands.

- Using Reproduction Page 23, have the students identify the auxiliaries, inflection, derivational affixes, word order positions, and stress patterns that identify the verbs as verbs in the following sentences. The last sentence contains a verb which is a nonsense word in order to emphasize that the structural devices rather than a word's lexical meaning identify it as a verb. The verbs and the devices that mark them are given below but not on the Reproduction Page.

1. Both men had clarified their positions.

clarified

1. Auxiliary—*had*

2. Inflection—/d/ allomorph of {Past Participle}

3. Derivational suffix—{-ify}

4. Word order—verb after a noun as subject and before a noun as object

2. The new surroundings disoriented the prisoners.

disoriented

1. Inflection—/d/ allomorph of Past

2. Derivational prefix—{dis-}

3. Word order—verb after a noun as subject and before a noun as object

3. Mr. Smith will conduct the investigation.

conduct

1. Auxiliary—*will*

2. Stress—primary stress on second syllable

3. Word order—verb after a noun as subject and before a noun as object

4. My dog has stricated before.

stricated

1. Auxiliary—*has*

2. Inflection—/əd/ allomorph of {Past Participle}

3. Derivational suffix—{-ate}

4. Word order—verb after a noun as subject

- Using Reproduction Page 24, have the students form the comparative and superlative forms of the following adjectives. The forms are given below but not on the reproduction page. The students are asked to draw generalizations about the kinds of adjectives that inflect with {Comparative} and {Superlative} versus those adjectives that take the qualifiers *more* and *most*. Generalizations may include statements that short adjectives inflect and that longer adjectives take *more* and *most* or that adjectives without derivational suffixes inflect and those with derivational suffixes take *more* and *most*. You should point out that a few derived adjectives like *homely* and *friendly* will also inflect, however.

		Comparative Form	Superlative Form
1.	quick	quicker	quickest
2.	lavish	more lavish	most lavish
3.	traditional	more traditional	most traditional
4.	remarkable	more remarkable	most remarkable
5.	strange	stranger	strangest
6.	useful	more useful	most useful
7.	marvelous	more marvelous	most marvelous
8.	small	smaller	smallest
9.	large	larger	largest
10.	significant	more significant	most significant
11.	devoted	more devoted	most devoted
12.	interesting	more interesting	most interesting
13.	sharp	sharper	sharpest
14.	careless	more careless	most careless
15.	hot	hotter	hottest

- Using Reproduction Page 25, have the students determine whether each of the words below is an adjective or not by seeing whether it can appear both before a noun and after a qualifier in the blanks in the sentences below. The answers are given in parentheses below but not on the Reproduction Page.

ADJECTIVES

Directions: *Form the comparative and superlative form of the adjectives below. Some of the adjectives will take the {Comparative} and {Superlative} inflections, but others will form their comparative and superlative forms with the qualifiers* more *and* most. *After you have done the first part of the exercise, see if you can draw any generalizations about the types of adjectives that take the inflections and those that do not.*

	Comparative Form	Superlative Form
1. quick		
2. lavish		
3. traditional		
4. remarkable		
5. strange		
6. useful		
7. marvelous		
8. small		
9. large		
10. significant		
11. devoted		
12. interesting		
13. sharp		
14. careless		
15. hot		

1. That_____person is quite_____.

   A. mysterious (Yes)

   B. fat (Yes)

   C. interesting (Yes)

   D. sleeping (No. It is a verb and will not fit into the second slot.)

   E. murdered (No. It is a verb and will not fit into the second slot.)

   F. tired (Yes)

   G. terrible (Yes)

   H. alone (No. It is an adverb and will not fit into the first slot.)

   I. intelligent (Yes)

   J. foolish (Yes)

2. The_____room was quite_____.

   A. crowded (Yes)

   B. reading (No. It is a noun and will not fit into the second slot.)

   C. dirty (Yes)

   D. cold (Yes)

   E. sun (No. It is a noun and will not fit into the second slot.)

• Have each student write sentences using *fast, hard, quick,* and *slow* as an adjective and then as an adverb. Then have each student write sentences with each of the words as an adjective and an adverb but inflected with {Comparative} and {Superlative}.

IDENTIFYING ADJECTIVES

Directions: *Since not all words that modify nouns are adjectives and since adjectives may be preceded by qualifiers like* quite, *determine which of the words below are adjectives by seeing if they will fit in both blanks in each of the sentences below.*

1. That _____ person is quite _____ .
   A. mysterious
   B. fat
   C. interesting
   D. sleeping
   E. murdered
   F. tired
   G. terrible
   H. alone
   I. intelligent
   J. foolish
2. The _____ room was quite _____ .
   A. crowded
   B. reading
   C. dirty
   D. cold
   E. sun

- Have each student write five sentences with adverbs occurring after nouns used as direct objects of verbs. Then have them rewrite each sentence with the same adverb appearing in a position other than after nouns used as direct objects. The point of this activity is to emphasize that adverbs are marked by word order as adverbs only in one position, but that they may occur in other positions too.

- Using Reproduction Page 26, have the students write appropriate adverbs in the blanks in the following sentences. Sample answers are given below in parentheses but not on the Reproduction Page; other answers may also be correct, of course. The students are asked to identify derivational affixes on the adverbs they used and what derivational suffix is used most frequently. More than likely, adverbs ending in $\{$-ly$_{Adv}\}$ will be used most frequently.

ADVERBS

Directions: *Write appropriate adverbs in the blanks in the following sentences. What derivational affixes mark some of these adverbs as adverbs? What derivational suffix is used most frequently?*

1. The man walked _____ down the road.

2. Those girls _____ eat dinner together.

3. After _____ opening the letter, he began reading it.

4. He told her lies _____ .

5. The _____ famous writer died.

6. He drove the car _____ .

7. Staring _____ at the book, he continued to read.

8. Your hat is _____ where you left it.

9. Mary laughed _____ .

10. The student worked very _____ .

1. The man walked_____ down the road. (slowly, hurriedly, away)

2. Those girls_____ eat dinner together. (usually, frequently, always)

3. After_____ opening the letter, he began reading it. (quickly, carefully)

4. He told her lies_____. (constantly, yesterday, there, occasionally)

5. The_____famous writer died. (extremely, exceedingly, widely)

6. He drove the car_____. (carelessly, there, then, away, fast)

7. Staring_____at the book, he continued to read. (intently, hard)

8. Your hat is_____where you left it. (there, upstairs, here)

9. Mary laughed_____. (hysterically, loudly, then, today)

10. The student worked very_____. (slow[ly], fast, diligently, carefully)

- Ask each student to write a paragraph or a short essay analyzing the parts of speech in a few lines of poetry by Dylan Thomas, e. e. cummings, or some other poet who is creative in his or her use of language.

- Ask each student to write a paper explaining how function words, inflections, derivational affixes, word order, and stress indicate what part of speech an unfamiliar word encountered in reading may be.

- Ask each student to write a paper pointing out the weaknesses of the traditional definitions of the traditional eight parts of speech.

ASSESSING ACHIEVEMENT OF OBJECTIVES

Ongoing Evaluation

The extent to which students have mastered the concepts covered under each topic can be measured by any of the activities assigned to the class as individuals, particularly the writing activities.

Final Evaluation

For an overall evaluation of the student's mastery of the concepts in this chapter, if all topics in the chapter have been taught, a test constructed directly from the list of student objectives for the chapter as listed on page 54 can be used. As an alternative, one might consider a test composed of the following items:

1. Define and give examples of *morphs, allomorphs,* and *morphemes.*

2. Identify five allomorphs of the {Past Participle} inflection, show their comple-

mentary distribution, and give an example of a verb marked as a verb by each of the allomorphs you identified.

3. Identify five inflectional suffixes (other than {Past Participle}) and five derivational suffixes. Then indicate which part of speech each of these suffixes helps to identify and give an example illustrating a word with each of these inflections.

4. Why are words like *walks* and *warmer* ambiguous as to what part of speech they belong to?

5. List the four parts of speech or form classes of words. Then list the kind of function word that helps to identify each part of speech, and give an example of each.

6. Explain what function words are.

7. Give examples of nouns ending in three derivational suffixes.

8. Give examples of verbs beginning or ending with four derivational affixes.

9. Give examples of adjectives beginning or ending with four derivational affixes.

10. Give examples of adverbs beginning or ending with two derivational affixes.

11. Put a ´ over the syllable which gets the greatest stress if the words below are the part of speech indicated in parentheses:

   A. pervert (a verb)

   B. imprint (a noun)

   C. suspect (a noun)

   D. relay (a verb)

12. Write above each word in the sentences below what part of speech or type of function word each word is.

   1. Some very perplexing questions may have rather simple answers.

   2. Other people often have suggested foolish solutions.

   3. That sick person visits a doctor frequently.

RESOURCES FOR TEACHING ABOUT THE WAY WORDS ARE MADE IN ENGLISH

Below is a selected and annotated list of resources useful for teaching the topics in this chapter, divided into audiovisual materials and print materials and arranged in order of ascending difficulty. Special strengths and weaknesses are mentioned in the annotations. Addresses of publishers or distributors can be found in the alphabetical list on pages 263–265 in Appendix A. Films are black and white unless otherwise indicated.

I. MORPHEMES AND ALLOMORPHS

Print

"The Anatomy of Words," pp. L67-L90 in *Persuasion and Pattern* by Albert R. Kitzhaber et al. Explains the concept of words being formed from morphemes being combined. Provides simple exercises. Hardbound, Holt, Rinehart and Winston, 1974.

"Morphology," pp. 68-76 in *Introduction to Linguistics* by Ronald Wardhaugh. Discusses allomorphs and morphemes in an easily understood manner. Paperbound, McGraw-Hill, 1972.

Exercises, pp. 56-63 in *Workbook to Accompany Introduction to Linguistics* by Ronald Wardhaugh. Provides exercises analyzing the morphology of individual words and the complementary distribution of the allomorphs of various derivational prefixes and inflectional suffixes in English. Paperbound, McGraw-Hill, 1972.

"Something of Morphemics," by George P. Faust, pp. 176-181 in *A Linguistic Reader,* edited by Graham Wilson. Provides an easily understood explanation of morphs, allomorphs, and morphemes, including suprasegmental morphemes. Has discussion questions. Paperbound, Harper and Row, 1967.

"The Morphology of English," pp. 89-93 in *A Survey of Modern Grammars,* 2d ed., Jeanne H. Herndon. Gives a short explanation of morphs, allomorphs, and morphemes. Paperbound, Holt, Rinehart and Winston, 1976.

"Morphemes," etc., pp. 85-93, 100-105 in *An Introductory English Grammar,* 2d ed. by Norman C. Stageberg. Defines and illustrates morphemes, allomorphs, bases, and affixes. Has exercises. Paperbound, Holt, Rinehart and Winston, 1971.

"Morphemes" and "Allomorphs," pp. 98-106 in *English: An Introduction to Language* by Thomas Pyles and John Algeo. Identifies and illustrates the concepts of morphemes and allomorphs. Provides simple exercises. Paperbound, Harcourt, Brace and World, 1970.

"The Morpheme," pp. 51-63 in *An Introduction to Descriptive Linguistics,* rev. ed., by H. A. Gleason, Jr. Defines and illustrates the concepts of morphemes, allomorphs, roots, and affixes. Hardbound, Holt, Rinehart and Winston, 1961.

"Building Blocks of Speech: Morphemics," pp. 162-196 in *The Structure of American English* by W. Nelson Francis. Provides the most comprehensive explanation of morphs, allomorphs, morphemes, bases and affixes, bound and free allomorphs, homophones, and superfixes. Recommended for teachers. Hardbound, The Ronald Press Co., 1958.

II. INFLECTIONAL AND DERIVATIONAL AFFIXES

Audiovisual Materials

Grammar, Part 1. Film, part of *Language and Linguistics* Series, 30 minutes, 1958, Indiana University Audio-Visual Center. Discusses noun and verb inflectional and derivational affixes (and stress morphemes).

Print

"Affixes" and "Inflection and Derivation," pp. 76-78 in *Introduction to Linguistics* by Ronald Wardhaugh. Differentiates among derivational prefixes, inflectional suffixes, and derivational suffixes. Paperbound, McGraw-Hill, 1972.

"The Morphology of English," pp. 93-96 in *A Survey of Modern Grammars,* 2d ed., by Jeanne H. Herndon. Explains and illustrates the differences between derivational affixes and inflectional suffixes. Paperbound, Holt, Rinehart and Winston, 1976.

"Inflection and Derivation," pp. 196-200 in *The Structure of American English* by W. Nelson Francis. Identifies derivational prefixes and differentiates derivational from inflectional suffixes. Hardbound, The Ronald Press Co., 1958.

"Derivation," pp. 194-202 in *The Development of Modern English,* 2d ed., by Stuart Robertson and Frederic G. Cassidy. Provides an interesting discussion of both live and dead derivational affixes in English. Hardbound, Prentice-Hall, 1954.

"Inflectional Affixes" etc., pp. 112–118 in *An Introductory English Grammar*, 2d ed., by Norman C. Stageberg. Identifies the eight inflectional suffixes of English and discusses homophones. Provides exercises. Paperbound, Holt, Rinehart and Winston, 1971.

"Prefixes" and "Derivational Suffixes," pp. 92–97 in *An Introductory English Grammar*, 2d ed., by Norman C. Stageberg. Identifies the common derivational affixes of English. Has exercises. Paperbound, Holt, Rinehart and Winston, 1971.

"The Use of Prefixes and Suffixes" and "New Affixes and New Uses of Old Ones," pp. 279–289 in *The Origins and Development of the English Language*, 2d ed., by Thomas Pyles. Provides an interesting and readable discussion of derivational affixes in English, particularly good on new derivational affixes. Hardbound, Harcourt Brace Jovanovich, 1971.

Exercises, pp. 245–247 in *Problems in the Origins and Development of the English Language*, 2d ed., by John Algeo. Presents fairly sophisticated exercises dealing with derivational affixes. Paperbound, Harcourt Brace Jovanovich, 1972.

"Nominals: Surfacing as Nouns," pp. L121–L128 in *Persuasion and Pattern* by Albert R. Kitzhaber et al. Discusses noun derivational affixes. Provides exercises. Hardbound, Holt, Rinehart and Winston, 1974.

"Outline of English Morphology," pp. 92–110 in *An Introduction to Descriptive Linguistics*, rev. ed., by H. A. Gleason, Jr. Gives a comprehensive analysis of inflectional morphemes and their allomorphs but is inadequate in its discussion of derivational morphemes. Hardbound, Holt, Rinehart and Winston, 1961.

III. PARTS OF SPEECH

Audiovisual Materials

Parts of Speech. Set of eight filmstrips, 1955, Encyclopaedia Britannica Educational Corporation. Gives an unsophisticated traditional explanation of the eight parts of speech of traditional grammar.

Speaking of Grammar. Sound filmstrip (sound on LP record or cassette tape), 25 minutes, 1975, Guidance Associates. Provides a good overview of the structural devices marking the four parts of speech, the types of function words, and grammatical functions.

Communication Skills: Who's Afraid of Grammar? Part II. Sound-slide set (sound on LP record or cassette tape), three programs: 19 minutes (dialect and "standard" English); 23 minutes (word order, inflection, and structure words); 24 minutes (syntactic processes of coordination and subordination), 1976, The Center for Humanities, Inc. Uses slides of artworks to teach the importance of word order, inflections, and function words to identify parts of speech and to introduce the concepts of modification and formation of commands and questions from declarative sentences.

Print

"Structural Analysis of English Syntax," pp. 98–105 in *A Survey of Modern English Grammars*, 2d ed., by Jeanne H. Herndon. Provides a short overview of nouns, verbs, adjectives, and adverbs in terms of inflections, derivational affixes, intonation patterns, word order, and function words. Paperbound, Holt, Rinehart and Winston, 1976.

"The Parts of Speech: Positional Approach" etc., pp. 55–60 in *Modern English Grammar for Teachers* by J. N. Hook and Michael G. Crowell. Presents a cursory review of the structural devices used to identify the various parts of speech in English. Hardbound, The Ronald Press Co., 1970.

"Form Classes," pp. 57–62 in *An Introduction to General Linguistics* by Francis P. Dinneen. Defines and identifies parts of speech using formal criteria. Hardbound, Holt, Rinehart and Winston, 1967.

"Inflectional Paradigms," pp. 119–146 in *An Introductory English Grammar*, 2d ed. by Norman C. Stageberg. Identifies the four parts of speech in terms of inflections. Provides exercises. Paperbound, Holt, Rinehart and Winston, 1971.

"Word Classes: Nouns, Verbs, Adjectives, Adverbs," pp. 114–138 in *Linguistics, English, and the Language Arts* by Carl A. Lefevre. Identifies the four parts of speech in terms of inflection and word order. Has teaching suggestions. Paperbound, Teachers College Press, 1970.

"Parts of Speech," pp. 195–223 in *An Introductory English Grammar,* 2d ed., by Norman C. Stageberg. Defines the four parts of speech by identifying their inflectional and derivational affixes and shows other parts of speech and syntactic structures used nominally, verbally, adjectivally, and adverbially. Provides exercises. Paperbound, Holt, Rinehart and Winston, 1971.

"Classification of Derivational Affixes," pp. 149–161 in *Linguistics, English, and the Language Arts* by Carl A. Lefevre. Lists and illustrates the major derivational affixes used to derive nouns, verbs, adjectives, and adverbs in English. Provides teaching suggestions. Paperbound, Teachers College Press, 1970.

"What's in a Word," pp. L81–L106 in *Structure and Plan* by Albert R. Kitzhaber et al. Explains grammatical and semantic features of nouns and verbs using feature matrices in a clear and relatively simple fashion. Provides exercises. Hardbound, Holt, Rinehart and Winston, 1974.

"Noun and Verb Features: Clues to Identify," pp. L65–L85 in *Substance and Process* by Albert R. Kitzhaber et al. Identifies grammatical and semantic features of nouns and verbs in terms of feature matrices. Provides exercises. Hardbound, Holt, Rinehart and Winston, 1974.

"Parts of Speech," pp. 59–111 in *A Short Introduction to English Grammar* by James Sledd. Points out the absurdity of traditional definitions of parts of speech and then defines nouns, verbs, adjectives, and adverbs in terms of their inflectional and derivational affixes, word order, and function words. Provides simple exercises. Hardbound, Scott, Foresman and Co., 1959.

"Grammar—Part I: The Parts of Speech," pp. 222–290 in *The Structure of American English* by W. Nelson Francis. Provides the most complete analysis of English nouns, verbs, adjectives, and adverbs in structural terms of word order, prosody, function words, inflections, and derivational affixes. Strongly recommended for teachers. Hardbound, The Ronald Press Co., 1958.

5

How Words Go Together in English

This chapter shows that there are very few syntactic relationships that occur among words in English. The four syntactic relationships that everyone agrees upon are modification, predication, complementation, and coordination. There are actually three other syntactic relationships, however. The first of these, introduction, will be discussed under modification. The two others, differentiation and equalization, will be discussed under complementation, since they occur only between multiple complements following a transitive verb. A practical application of this unit will be that students will develop an awareness that English is essentially a binary language, that is, that all structures in English sentences consist of two parts (with the occasional exception of structures of coordination), so that English syntax is relatively simple. A further practical application is that students will be able to analyze the structure of their own sentences so that they can write grammatical sentences and correct any ungrammatical sentences they have written. A final practical application of this unit should be that students will develop confidence in their own writing ability by learning that they have already internalized and used the syntax of English when they speak.

First, the students should be introduced to the structure of modification, which consists of a modifier and a head, since this structure is usually used several times in every sentence they speak. While discussing this topic, it will be necessary to use the other syntactic relationships too, since modifiers are often not single words but other syntactic structures as well.

Second, the students should study the structure of predication thoroughly, since most English sentences are a structure of predication. The structure of predication consists of a subject and a predicate. It will be shown that the subject may be a structure of modification, a structure of complementation, a structure of coordination, or another structure of predication, and that the predicate may be a structure of modification, a structure of complementation, or a structure of coordination.

Third, the students should study the structure of complementation, which consists of a verb and a complement or complements. The different kinds of verbs and complements will be examined under this topic.

Finally, the students should study the structure of coordination, which consists of two or more grammatically equivalent units. This syntactic relationship is probably the easiest to understand. It is also the only one which may have more than two constitutents.

While it would be possible to discuss any of the four topics in the unit separately, failure to teach all four topics would lead to a fragmentary understanding of English syntax by the students.

OBJECTIVES

If all four topics in this chapter are taught by the teacher, the students should, at the end of the unit, be able to:

1. Define *modification, predication, complementation,* and *coordination*
2. Give examples of nouns modified by determiners, other nouns, adjectives, verbs, adverbs, prepositional phrases, and included (subordinate) clauses
3. Give examples of verbs modified by auxiliaries, other verbs, adverbs, adjectives, prepositional phrases, and included clauses
4. Give examples of adjectives modified by qualifiers, other adjectives, nouns, verbs, adverbs, prepositional phrases, and included clauses
5. Give examples of adverbs modified by qualifiers, other adverbs, nouns, and included clauses
6. Explain the ambiguity of a sentence like *She runs this way* on the basis of whether *this way* is a modifier or a complement of the verb
7. Write sentences with nouns, adjectives, verbs, adverbs, structures of predication, structures of complementation, and structures of coordination as subjects
8. Write sentences with structures of complementation with direct objects, indirect objects and direct objects, direct objects and object complements, and subject complements as predicates
9. Write sentences with structures of modification and coordination as predicates
10. Explain the ambiguity of sentences like *He called Jane a nurse* in terms of whether the two complements following the verb are an indirect object and a direct object or a direct object and an object complement

---

CONTENT OVERVIEW

Modification

All sentences in English consist of words in a small number of syntactic relationships with each other. The most frequent of these relationships is that of modification. A structure of modification consists of a modifier and a head. Both the modifier and the head may be other syntactic structures rather than individual words, though. The other common syntactic structures that may be used as either modifiers or heads are a structure of predication (subject and predicate), a structure of complementation (a verbal element and a complement or complements), and a structure of coordination (two or more grammatically equivalent units). Each of the parts of speech may also serve as a modifier or a head.

Nouns are the most frequent heads in structures of modification. Of course, nouns may be modified by determiners as in *the book*. Nouns are also modified by nouns in three different kinds of modification. Nouns may be modified by other nouns inflected for possession as in *John's book*. They may also be modified by uninflected nouns as in *soap manufacturer* or by nouns inflected for plurality as in *communications specialist;* these are both noun-adjunct constructions in which the noun modifier gets a greater stress than the noun head. The third type of construction in which a noun may modify another noun is the appositive construction in which the modifying noun follows the head noun it modifies as in *the dog, Lassie.*

Nouns may also be modified by adjectives, verbs, and adverbs. Adjectives usually precede nouns they modify except when the adjectives themselves are modified by prepositional phrases or included clauses; thus, *friendly dog* but *The girl, eager to please, smiled* and *A dog, larger than I had expected, appeared.* Verbs inflected with the present participle and the past participle inflections may appear both before and after nouns they modify as in *The running boy passed me; the boy, running, passed me; The expected person did not appear;* and *The person expected did not appear.* When the modifying verb is part of a more complex structure such as the head of a structure of modification itself, however, the modifying verb always follows the noun as in *The man startled by the noise jumped* or *The water running in the gutter is dirty.* The infinitive is traditionally identified as *to* plus the base form of the verb and is considered a separate verb form, although it is historically a prepositional phrase. In any case, *to* plus the base form of a verb can also modify a noun before it as in *The person to see has gone.* Adverbs always follow nouns they modify as in *the people here* or *the party afterwards.*

Obviously, noun heads may be modified by structures of modification as above or in *the very funny lady* where *very funny* modifies *lady* but *very* by itself does not. However, noun heads may also be modified by structures of coordination involving various parts of speech such as *the pretty but antisocial cat,* by structures of complementation such as *The person chewing gum is my friend,* and by subordinate clauses like *the person who was late* and *the reason that it happened.* The last two examples illustrate two kinds of function words: relatives and includers (traditionally: relative pronouns and subordinating conjunctions). Relatives include *who(m), which, that, whoever,* and so on, and have a syntactic function in the structures of predication they introduce such as subject in *the dog that bit me* or direct object in *the movie that they saw.* Includers include *after, because, since, than, that, unless,* and so on, and do not have a structural function within the structures of predication that they introduce. Instead, they fulfill a fifth syntactic relationship: introduction. They introduce a structure of predication and allow it to modify some word or other structure as in *The fact that it happened is clear* or to allow that structure of predication to serve a nominal function in another structure of predication such as subject in *When it happened is unknown.*

The syntactic relationship of introduction also holds between another type of function word, prepositions, and their objects. Prepositions include words like *at, by, for, from, with,* and the like, and compound prepositions like *back of, due to,* and *together with.* Prepositions serve to introduce their objects so that the objects can modify other words or structures. Examples of prepositional phrases modifying nouns are *the clerk at the store* and *the hole in the wall.*

Verbs and structures of complementation involving verbs are the next most frequent heads in structures of modification. Of course, verbs may be modified by auxiliaries as in *has run,* but they may also be modified by the four parts of speech: nouns, other verbs, adjectives, and adverbs. Traditional grammar was correct when it said that adverbs can modify verbs; adverbs may precede verbs they modify as in *immediately understood,* but they may also follow verbs they modify as in *understood immediately.* However, adjectives may also modify verbs in idiomatic expressions such as *He ran wild;* notice that the meaning of this sentence is not the same as the meaning of *He ran wildly* where *wildly* is an adverb. Verbs may also modify verbs as in *Some people work sitting.* The traditional infinitive (really a prepositional phrase) may also modify verbs as in *They study to learn.* Even nouns may modify verbs as in *She sleeps nights.* However, any time a noun modifies a verb, the sentence is potentially ambiguous in its structure. In the preceding example, *nights* was construed as adverbial like *then* in *She sleeps then.* However, it would also have been possible to interpret *nights* as a direct object. To determine whether a noun following a verb is a modifier or a complement, it is necessary to determine whether *it* or *them* may be substituted for the noun and the same meaning kept; if it can be, the noun is a complement; if not, it is a modifier. A similar substitution test may be required to determine whether an infinitive following a verb is a modifier or a complement as in the ambiguous sentence: *She plans to succeed.* One meaning of the sentence allows the substitution of *it* for *to succeed;* in that case, *to succeed* is a direct object. If the sentence means *She plans so that she will succeed,* *to succeed* cannot be replaced by *it* and is, thus, a modifier.

Verbs may be modified by structures of coordination such as *can and will sing* or *sang loudly and clearly,* by structures of complementation such as *died whistling "Dixie"* or *sat feeling sad,* by structures of predication like *left after he saw Tom,* and by structures of modification such as *left very shortly* where *very shortly* modifies *left* but *very* by itself does not (it modifies *shortly*). Verbs may also be modifed by prepositional phrases like *danced after the game* where the preposition *after* and its object *the game* are in the introduction relationship.

Adjectives may also be heads in structures of modification. Their most common modifiers are qualifiers like *very, too, rather,* and so on, as in *very sweet, too sweet, rather sweet,* and the like. However, adjectives may also be modified by adverbs, nouns, verbs, and other adjectives. Traditional grammar was correct in stating that adverbs modify adjectives as in *remarkably tasty,* but nouns may also modify adjectives in *ice cold, sky blue, rock hard,* and so on. Verbs may modify adjectives in phrases like *freezing cold* and *boiling hot,* and other adjectives may modify adjectives in phrases like *bluish green, pale blue,* and *icy cold.*

Adjectives may be heads modified by structures of coordination as in *surprisingly and remarkably young,* by structures of predication introduced by includers such as *prettier than I had expected* or *as pretty as they said,* and by structures of introduction like prepositional phrases as in *a problem interesting to linguists.* Occasionally, a modifier of an adjective will even be a structure of modification itself as in *much more careful* where *much* does not modify *careful* but *more,* and *much more* modifies *careful.*

Adverbs may also be heads in structures of modification. The most common modifiers of adverbs are qualifiers like *more* in *more carefully,* but adverbs as modifiers of other adverbs are fairly frequent such as *completely successfully* and *totally backwards.* Occasionally a noun will also modify an adverb as in *two feet down* or *miles away.*

Structures with adverbs as heads may also have as modifiers structures of coordination such as *unnecessarily and stupidly carelessly,* structures of predication introduced by includers such as *harder than he should,* and by structures of introduction like prepositional phrases as in *as quietly as possible.* Again, a modifier of an adverb head may be a structure of modification itself as in *very unnecessarily slowly* where *very* modifies *unnecessarily* rather than *slowly* and *very unnecessarily* modifies *slowly.*

Predication

As mentioned above, a structure of predication consists of two parts, a subject and a predicate, which are usually in that order. Both subjects and predicates may be individual words or more complex structures themselves.

Any of the four parts of speech or a structure of modification with one of the four parts of speech as its head may be used as a subject. Nouns (and pronouns as a subclass of nouns) are the most frequent subjects as in *John cried, He cried,* and *Seven silly children cried.* Examples of adjectives used as subjects are *Pretty is as pretty does* and *Fearful of death is a bad way to be.* Although verbs inflected with the present participle inflection may be subjects because similarly inflected verbs as parts of structures of complementation such as *Teaching grammar is fun* are, it is impossible to say definitively that *teaching* in *Teaching is fun* is a verb used as a subject rather than a noun formed from the verb by adding the $\{-ing_N\}$ derivational suffix. However, the traditional infinitive of *to* plus the base form of the verb can be used as a subject as in *To see is to believe.* Adverbs may also be used as subjects in sentences like *Very often is too often* or *Right now is when I want it.*

The other syntactic structures may also serve as subjects in structures of predication. Structures of predication either introduced by relatives as in *Who found it is unknown* or by includers as in *That it will snow tomorrow is clear* may serve as subjects in other structures of predication. So may structures of complementation as in *Shearing sheep is dirty work* or *Being stupid is easy.* Structures of coordination involving any of the parts of speech or other syntactic structures such as *The boy and the girl walked slowly* or *Giving tests and grading them take time* may also serve as subjects. Finally, prepositional phrases also serve occasionally as subjects as in *Over the fence is out* that one might hear in a neighborhood baseball game.

The reason it was stated above that subjects and predicates usually occur in that order is that there are some exceptions to this normal statement order. One exception involves the use of the function word *there* to introduce a sentence like *There is a man here.* This function word is different from the homophonous adverb *there* as shown by the previous example; if *there* were an adverb in that sentence, the sentence would be a logical absurdity saying that a man was both *here* and *there* at the same time. The function word *there* has an introduction function with the structure of predication it introduces and allows a reversal of the subject and part of the predicate for stylistic variation without producing a question.

The second exception to the subject-predicate order involves questions that are marked as questions by the reversal of part of the predicate with the subject either with or without the use of function words called interrogators like *why, when, where,* and the like. With the exception of *be* (and, in some dialects, *have*), which may be placed in front of the subject to form a question such as *Are the girls hungry* or *Have the boys the time,* most verbs require moving only the first auxiliary or, if there are no auxiliaries in front of the verb, adding the auxiliary *do* to the position in front of the subject as in *Can the painters come tomorrow* and *Do the newspapers arrive on time.* Of course, questions marked by a rising terminal junction or by a type of function word traditionally known as an interrogative pronoun such as *who, which, what, whatever,* and so on, as in *The food is ready* or *Who ate the cake* still have the subject before the predicate. Notice that the interrogative pronouns are usually homophonous with the relatives mentioned above and have a structural function (such as subject) within the structures of predication where they appear.

Predicates in structures of predication always involve a verb. This verb may have complements, so the predicate may be a structure of complementation. The verb or the structure of complementation may have modifiers, so the predicate may be a structure of modification. Finally, of course, the predicate may be a structure of coordination involving two or more verbs or two or more structures of complementation with or without modifiers.

The simplest kind of predicate involves only a verb as in *The man slept.* However, the verb may be modified by any of the modifiers of verbs listed above in the section on modification such as auxiliaries as in *has been sleeping* or adverbs as in *slept soundly* or both as in *has been sleeping soundly.* The verb may have a complement or complements: *dinner* in *eats dinner* is a direct object; *his wife* is an indirect object, and *flowers* is a direct object in *sent his wife flowers*; *Carter* is a direct object, and *President* is an object complement in *elected Carter President*; and *a man* is a subject complement in *became a man.* The predicate may also be a structure of coordination involving verbs as in *sang and danced* or involving structures of complementation as in *told jokes and sang folk songs.* Obviously, structures of complementation and of coordination in predicates may serve as heads in structures of modification as in *told jokes until the audience booed* or *has told jokes and sung songs professionally.*

Predicates may also be made negative by the addition of the function word *not,* which has three allomorphs /nat/ spelled *not,* /ənt/ after bases ending in /d/ or /t/ as in *shouldn't,* and /nt/ after bases ending in other sounds as in *don't,* both spelled *n't.* The last two allomorphs are in complementary distribution with each other, and the first allomorph is in free variation with the other two. The function word *not* is added after the first auxiliary modifying the verb as in *will not be coming* or after the verb *be* (and in some dialects after the verb *have* as in *is not here* or *haven't the time*). If no auxiliary appears before the verb (other than *be* or *have*), the auxiliary *do* is added so *not* can appear after an auxiliary and before the verb as in *does not explain clearly.*

Complementation

As indicated above, a structure of complementation involves a verbal element and a complement or complements. There are four major types of complements in English: direct object, subject complement, indirect object, and object complement.

A structure involving a verbal element and a direct object is the most common type of structure of complementation. The most common type of direct object is a noun or a noun-headed structure of modification as in *That student missed two classes.* Notice that the subject in this sentence, *that student,* and the direct object, *two classes,* have different referents, that is, refer to different things. This phenomenon is true for all direct objects (except for the subclass of reflexive pronouns of the pronoun subclass of nouns like *himself*) and is useful in differentiating direct objects from subject complements in structures of complementation.

Other parts of speech than nouns and other syntactic structures than structures of modification may also serve as direct objects, however. An example of an adjective-headed structure of modification as a direct object is *She chose the handsomest.* An example of an adverb as a direct object is *The cat wants out.* In *They like talking,* it is impossible to say definitively whether the direct object, *talking,* is a present participle form of a verb or a derived noun with the $\{ing_N\}$ derivational suffix; however, verbs in their present participle form clearly occur in structures of complementation used as direct objects as in *They like talking nonsense.* The traditional infinitive or *to* plus the base form of the verb may also be used as a direct object as in *The students hate to study.* Any of the parts of speech may be used in a structure of coordination as a direct object as in *The teacher failed two boys and three girls* or *Tom likes to fish and to hunt.* Similarly, *The man saw what happened* and *The woman knows when it happened* illustrate structures of predication beginning with a relative and introduced by an includer, respectively. Structures of complementation used as direct objects in other structures of complementation appear in sentences like *Tom tried giving Mary candy* and *Dogs like smelling bad.*

The other type of single complement following a verb in a structure of complementation is a subject complement. Nouns or noun-headed structures of modification are common subject complements as in *Carter became President* and *Tom is a fool.* Notice that, unlike the direct object, *President* and *a fool* do have the same referents as the subjects in the sentences, that is, refer to the same things. Another way the two kinds of complements may be differentiated is that subject complements follow linking verbs (*be* or verbs that may be replaced by some form of *be*) and that direct objects follow transitive verbs (which may not be replaced by *be* without radically changing the meaning of the sentence). Transitive verbs also have passives, that is, the direct object may be made the subject of the sentence with some form of the auxiliary *be* placed before the verb, the verb inflected with the past participle inflection, and the original subject made the object of the preposition *by*; an example would be to change *The boy ate the cake* where *ate* is a transitive verb into *The cake was eaten by the boy.* Linking verbs have no passive forms, so changing *Carter became President* to *President was become by Carter* would be ungrammatical.

Other parts of speech than nouns and other syntactic structures than structures of modification may also serve as subject complements. Adjectives are fairly common subject complements as in *The woman remained silent* and *Tom is much stranger than I thought at first.* Adverbs may also appear as subject complements after linking verbs as *The time is now* and *Bill remained right there.* Verbs are less frequently subject complements; however, in *Seeing is believing, believing* as a subject complement may be considered a verb inflected with the present participle rather than a derived noun with the $\{-ing_N\}$ derivational suffix, since verbs in the present participle form may appear as the verbal element in a structure of complementation used as a subject complement such as in *His favorite entertainment is reading books.* Of course, the traditional infinitive may be used as a subject complement as in *To cheat is to fail.* Any parts of speech may appear in a structure of coordination as a subject complement as in *The girls are Betty and June* and *He appeared calm but depressed.* As mentioned, structures of complementation may also be subject complements as in *His strong point is remaining silent.* Structures of predication may also be subject complements such as *A disaster is what happened.* Finally, prepositional phrases may be subject complements as in *That woman is out of sight* and *That person is from Indiana.*

The third type of complement that occurs in structures of complementation is the indirect object. It can occur only if a direct object also occurs after it. In *Sally gave Scott a kiss, Scott* is an indirect object, and *a kiss* is a direct object. Notice that the two complements in this structure of complementation, the indirect object and the direct object, have different referents (refer to different things). This phenomenon is useful in differentiating an indirect object plus a direct object from the sequence of direct object and object complement discussed below. The relationship between an indirect object and a direct object is a sixth syntactic relationship because they are not a structure of coordination as one might first think, since they are not grammatically equivalent units. This relationship is generally ignored by structural linguists, so I have taken the liberty of naming it the differentiation relationship.

As the example in the preceding paragraph indicates, nouns and noun-headed structures of modification are the most frequent kinds of indirect objects. However, adjectives used nominally may also be indirect objects as in *The judges awarded the prettiest the first prize.* The other parts of speech are not normally used as indirect objects, although they can be in tour de force sentences. Structures other than structures of modification may be used as indirect objects, however. *Give John and Gene my regards* illustrates the use of coordination as an indirect object. *The child gives watching television his complete attention* illustrates the use of a structure of complementation as an indirect object. *Some people assign whatever happens a strange interpretation* illustrates the use of a structure of predication begun with a relative as an indirect object.

The last major type of complement that occurs in structures of complementation is the object complement. It can occur only if a direct object occurs before it. In *The people elected Smith senator, Smith* is a direct object, and *senator* is an object complement. Notice that the two complements in this structure of complementation, the direct object and the object complement, have the same referents (refer to the same things); the two could be joined by some form of *be* to form a true statement like *Smith is senator.* This fact allows one to differentiate between an indirect object and a direct object versus a direct object and an object complement fairly easily. The relationship between a direct object and an object complement is the seventh syntactic relationship. Since this relationship is generally ignored in analyses of English syntax, I have taken some liberty again and named it the equalization relationship.

As the example in the preceding paragraph indicates, nouns and noun-headed structures of modification are frequently used as object complements. Adjectives are also common object complements as in *Their grades made the students very happy.* Occasionally an adverb will be used as an object complement as in the ambiguous sentence, *The girls found Horace alone.* If this sentence means that the girls had no help in finding Horace, *alone* is a modifier of the structure of complementation *found Horace;* but if it means Horace was alone when the girls found him, *alone* is part of the complement of *found,* an object complement in the equalization relationship with *Horace.*

Several syntactic structures other than structures of modification may also be object complements. *Sarah considers Joe her lord and her master* illustrates the use of a structure of coordination as an object complement. *His mother made Abe what he is* illustrates the use of a structure of predication as an object complement: *what* is a relative and an object complement within the structure of predication *what he is.* Rarely, a structure of complementation may be used as an object complement as in *I call that job taking candy from a baby* (actually, in this case, it is a structure of modification with a structure of complementation as its head that is the object complement). Finally, prepositional phrases may also be used as object complements as in *His family considers Bill beyond hope.*

Coordination

As indicated above, a structure of coordination consists of two or more grammatically equivalent units. The grammatically equivalent units are joined by another type of function word called coordinators such as *and, but, or, as well as, either . . . or, neither . . . nor,* and so on. The last two coordinators in this list are sometimes called correlatives, since they are separated from each other by the first of the grammatically equivalent units they join as in *Neither Bill nor Tom will take responsibility.* The other coordinators simply appear between the grammatically equivalent units they join as in *The boys and the girls argued.*

As the examples in the previous paragraph show, nouns may appear in a structure of coordination used as a subject; however, they may also be joined in a structure of coordination in any other noun function as well, such as direct object as in *The dog chased the cats and the squirrels* or indirect object as in *Their grandparents sent Mary and Bill large packages.* Similarly, adjectives may appear in structures of coordination in various adjective functions such as modification in sentences like *The attractive and intelligent child surprised his elders* or as subject complements in sentences like *The man is either sick or drunk.*

Adverbs can be joined in structures of coordination as a modifying unit such as *Dick eats rapidly and noisily* or as a subject complement such as in *The present is here and now.* Examples of verbs appearing in structures of coordination are *The students studied and passed* where the structure of coordination is the predicate and *The crying and groaning victim was rushed to a hospital* where the structure of coordination is a modifier.

The previous examples show only two grammatically equivalent units in each structure of coordination, but the structures of coordination may involve more than two grammatically equivalent units. *The Romans came, saw, and conquered* shows three grammatically equivalent units joined in a structure of coordination used as a predicate. *Tom, Dick, Harry, Bill, or John will provide transportation for you* illustrates five grammatically equivalent units joined in a structure of coordination used as a subject.

Any of the parts of the other syntactic structures may be structures of coordination, not just those illustrated above showing the various parts of speech in structures of coordination. Both head and modifiers in structures of modification can be structures of coordination: in *the men and women, men and women* is the head in a structure of modification as well as a structure of coordination; in *short and fat people, short and fat* is a modifier in a structure of modification as well as a structure of coordination. Both subjects and predicates in structures of predication can be structures of coordination as shown by the structure of predication, *Dogs and cats run and jump.* Similarly, both verbal elements and complements in structures of complementation may be structures of coordination: in *The woman shot and killed her husband, shot and killed* is a structure of coordination as well as the verbal element in the structure of complementation *shot and killed her husband;* in *Frank eats apples and oranges, apples and oranges* is a structure of coordination as well as the complement (direct object) in the structure of complementation *eats apples and oranges.* Even the elements in a prepositional phrase, the introduction function, may be structures of coordination; in *for and of the people,* the prepositional element *for and of* is a structure of coordination; in *from Mary and Jane,* the object of the preposition *Mary and Jane* is a structure of coordination.

Finally, structures of predication, structures of complementation, and structures of modification may also be joined in structures of coordination. *The team lost eight games, but the school still supports it* illustrates two structures of predication joined in a structure of coordination. *John likes peanuts yet hates peanut butter* shows two structures of complementation joined in a structure of coordination. The subject *pretty girls and handsome boys* in *Pretty girls and handsome boys usually know that they are attractive* illustrates two structures of modification joined in a structure of coordination.

LEARNING EXPERIENCES

Topic I: Modification

- Using Reproduction Page 27, have the students write sentences in which the noun *man* is modified by each of the words or constructions below. Sample answers are given below but not on the Reproduction Page. The students are also asked to write a sentence in which another noun is modified by each of the same kinds of words or constructions.

  1. a (a determiner): A man left this package.

  2. music (a noun): The music man sold musical instruments.

  3. old (an adjective): The old man drank coffee.

  4. singing (a verb): The man singing woke me.

  5. upstairs (an adverb): The man upstairs is sleeping.

  6. in the car (a prepositional phrase): The man in the car stopped.

NOUN MODIFIERS

Directions: *Write a sentence in which the noun* man *is modified by each of the words or constructions below. You may have other modifiers of* man *in each sentence as well. Then write a sentence in which another noun is modified by each of the same kinds of words or constructions.*

1. a   (a determiner)

2. music   (a noun)

3. old   (an adjective)

4. singing   (a verb)

5. upstairs   (an adverb)

6. in the car   (a prepositional phrase)

7. kind and friendly   (a structure of coordination)

8. eating candy   (a structure of complementation)

9. who spoke to me   (a structure of predication—relative clause)

10. wanted by the police   (a structure of modification)

---

7. kind and friendly (a structure of coordination): The kind and friendly man gave us directions.

8. eating candy (a structure of complementation): The man eating candy is fat.

9. who spoke to me (a structure of predication—relative clause): The man who spoke to me was my teacher.

10. wanted by the police (a structure of modification): A man wanted by the police may be dangerous.

- Break the class into small groups and have each group use as many prepositions as possible in making up prepositional phrases modifying nouns. Then compare the lists from the small groups and compile a list of prepositions that introduce phrases that modify nouns.

- Have the students, individually or in groups, find all of the noun-headed structures of modification in a paragraph of one of their texts. If the same paragraph is assigned to all students, compare the results in class.

- Ask each student to write the longest sentence he or she can with the largest number of modifiers of a noun as a subject.

- Ask the students to find two possible meanings to the sentences below. Then explain the ambiguity in terms of whether what follows the verb is a modifier or a complement.

  1. My father works weekends.

  2. The woman lived eighty years.

  3. He hopes to live.

  4. She prays to be spared.

- Using Reproduction Page 28, have the students write sentences in which the verb *run* is modified by each of the words or constructions below. Sample answers are given below but not on the Reproduction Page. The students are also asked to write a sentence in which another verb is modified by the same kinds of words or con-

---

REPRODUCTION PAGE 28

VERB MODIFIERS

Directions: *Write a sentence in which the verb* run *is modified by each of the words or constructions below. You may have other modifiers of* run *in each sentence as well. Then write a sentence in which another verb is modified by each of the same kinds of words or constructions.*

1. should (an auxiliary)

2. often (an adverb)

3. limping (a verb)

4. true (an adjective)

5. miles (a noun)

6. in races (a prepositional phrase)

7. frequently but slowly (a structure of coordination)

8. chasing a ball (a structure of complementation)

9. very rapidly (a structure of modification)

10. when they are frightened (a structure of predication–included clause)

---

structions. Unless they pick verbs like *come* and *go*, they probably will not be able to modify the verb with a noun or an adjective, however.

1. should (an auxiliary): People should run to stay in shape.

2. often (An adverb): Children often run.

3. limping (a verb): Injured athletes may run limping.

4. true (an adjective): Tuned-up cars run true.

5. miles (a noun): Cross-country teams run miles.

6. in races (a prepositional phrase): Thoroughbred horses run in races.

7. frequently but slowly (a structure of coordination): Joggers run frequently but slowly.

8. chasing a ball (a structure of complementation): Outfielders run chasing a ball.

9. very rapidly (a structure of modification): Sprinters run very rapidly.

10. when they are frightened (a structure of predication—included clause): Most animals run when they are frightened.

- Have the students, individually or in groups, find all of the verb-headed structures of modification in a paragraph of one of their texts. If the same paragraph is assigned to all students, compare the results in class.

- Using Reproduction Page 29, have the students write sentences in which the adjective *green* is modified by each of the words or constructions below. Sample answers are given below but not on the Reproduction Page. The students are also asked to write a sentence in which another adjective is modified by the same kinds of words or constructions.

1. very (a qualifier): The trees are very green.

2. unusually (an adverb): Tom turned unusually green.

3. light (an adjective): The light green sweater is attractive.

4. pea (a noun): Pea soup is pea green.

5. to eat (a verb): The apples are too green to eat.

6. as grass (prepositional phrase): Those freshmen are green as grass.

7. pale and sickly (a structure of coordination): The sick person turned pale and sickly green.

8. very dark (a structure of modification): Emerald green is very dark green.

9. than I had seen before (a structure of predication—included clause): Those plants were greener than I had seen before.

- Using Reproduction Page 30, have the students underline the adverb-headed structures of modification in the paragraph below. The adverb-headed structures of modification are underlined below but not on the Reproduction Page.

Some people can write quite rapidly. Other people write unusually slowly. Although no one writes as fast as Superman, some students will have very nearly

ADJECTIVE MODIFIERS

Directions: *Write a sentence in which the adjective* green *is modified by each of the words or constructions below. You may have other modifiers of* green *in each sentence as well, and you may need to use inflected forms of* green. *Then write a sentence in which another adjective is modified by each of the same kinds of words or constructions.*

1. very (a qualifier)

2. unusually (an adverb)

3. light (an adjective)

4. pea (a noun)

5. to eat (a verb)

6. as grass (a prepositional phrase)

7. pale and sickly (a structure of coordination)

8. very dark (a structure of modification)

9. than I had seen before (a structure of predication—included clause)

---

finished a paper when others are <u>pages away from the end</u>. No one should be expected to write <u>faster than he or she can</u>, but students who write habitually and <u>unnecessarily slowly</u> can be shown <u>right away</u> that their lack of speed handicaps them <u>rather greatly academically</u>.

- Ask each student to write a short essay on the types of modifiers of nouns, verbs, adjectives, and adverbs.

FINDING ADVERB-HEADED MODIFIERS

Directions: *Underline the adverb-headed structures of modification in the paragraph below.*

Some people can write quite rapidly. Other people write unusually slowly. Although no one can write as fast as Superman, some students will have very nearly finished a paper while others are pages away from the end. No one should be expected to write faster than he or she can, but students who write habitually and unnecessarily slowly can be shown right away that their lack of speed handicaps them rather greatly academically.

Topic II: Predication

- Have each student find the subjects in all of the structures of predication in a paragraph of one of his or her textbooks. If the same paragraph is assigned to all students, compare the results in class.

- Using Reproduction Page 31, have the students draw a line between the subjects and the predicates in the sentences below. The line is drawn between the subject and predicate below but not on the Reproduction Page.

1. The high school basketball team | has won its last three games.
2. That young man who is waiting for Mary | is her fiancé.
3. Cheating at cards | is dishonest.
4. From here to there | is thirty yards.
5. That the treasure once existed | has been established.
6. The old | deserve some respect.
7. Children | sometimes speak the truth at inappropriate times.
8. Ben, Barry, and Ron | came for dinner.
9. Killing animals | is sadistic.
10. Some people from Alabama | speak with a drawl.
11. Frequently | is too often.
12. Chasing rainbows | seems futile.

REPRODUCTION PAGE 31

DISTINGUISHING SUBJECTS FROM PREDICATES

Directions: *Draw a line between the subjects and the predicates in the sentences below.*

1. The high school basketball team has won its last three games.
2. That young man who is waiting for Mary is her fiancé.
3. Cheating at cards is dishonest.
4. From here to there is thirty yards.
5. That the treasure once existed has been established.
6. The old deserve some respect.
7. Children sometimes speak the truth at inappropriate times.
8. Ben, Barry, and Ron came for dinner.
9. Killing animals is sadistic.
10. Some people from Alabama speak with a drawl.
11. Frequently is too often.
12. Chasing rainbows seems futile.
13. A penny saved won't buy much.
14. Whoever did that should be punished.
15. The kind old man from New York gave Mary his handkerchief.
16. My father's house needs paint.
17. To forgive is divine.
18. Living comfortably requires some money.
19. Whatever happens will happen.
20. Electing him chairman was a terrible mistake.

13. A penny saved | won't buy much.

14. Whoever did that | should be punished.

15. The kind old man from New York | gave Mary his handkerchief.

16. My father's house | needs paint.

17. To forgive | is divine.

18. Living comfortably | requires some money.

19. Whatever happens | will happen.

20. Electing him chairman | was a terrible mistake.

- Using Reproduction Page 32, have the students write a sentence using each of the following words or structures as the subject or as the head in a structure of modification used as the subject. The students are also asked to write another sentence in which the same parts of speech or structures are used as the subjects. Sample sentences are given below but not on the Reproduction Page.

1. girls (a noun): The girls defeated the boys.

2. poor (an adjective): The poor are starving.

3. to tell (a verb): To tell would be wrong.

REPRODUCTION PAGE 32

WRITING SENTENCES WITH SUPPLIED SUBJECTS

Directions: *Write a sentence using each of the following words or structures as the subject or as the head in a structure of modification used as the subject. Then write other sentences in which the same parts of speech or structures are used as the subjects.*

1. girls   (a noun)

2. poor   (an adjective)

3. to tell   (a verb)

4. then   (an adverb)

5. in the water   (a prepositional phrase)

6. who did it   (a structure of predication)

7. reading books   (a structure of complementation)

8. Dick and Jane   (a structure of coordination)

---

4. then (an adverb): Then is when it happened.

5. in the water (a prepositional phrase): In the water is where they found him.

6. who did it (a structure of predication): Who did it is unknown.

7. reading books (a structure of complementation): Reading books broadens the mind.

8. Dick and Jane (a structure of coordination): Dick and Jane are siblings.

- Have each student find the predicates in all of the structures of predication in a paragraph from one of his or her textbooks. If the same paragraph is assigned to all students, compare the results in class.

- Using Reproduction Page 33, have the students write a sentence using the following structures involving verbs within the predicate. Sample answers are given below but not on the Reproduction Page.

1. a verb modified by an auxiliary: Tom has arrived.

2. a verb modified by an adverb: Time passes quickly.

REPRODUCTION PAGE 33

WRITING SENTENCES WITH SUPPLIED PREDICATES

Directions: *Write a sentence using the following structures involving verbs within the predicate. Other elements may also be added to the predicate than just those indicated.*

1. a verb modified by an auxiliary

2. a verb modified by an adverb

3. a verb modified by a prepositional phrase

4. a verb modified by an included clause

5. a verb with a complement

6. a verb with a complement but modified by an adverb

7. a verb with a complement but modified by an auxiliary

8. a verb with a complement but modified by an included clause

9. two verbs in a structure of coordination

10. a verb modified by two auxiliaries

---

3. a verb modified by a prepostional phrase: Most people sleep at night.

4. a verb modified by an included clause. He eats when he is hungry.

5. a verb with a complement: Students like school.

6. a verb with a complement but modified by an adverb: They take tests there.

7. a verb with a complement but modified by an auxiliary: Ed has prepared his assignments.

8. a verb with a complement but modified by an included clause: The kids had a party after the game ended.

9. two verbs in a structure of coordination: Sarah slipped and fell.

10. a verb modified by two auxiliaries: The students may have understood.

- Ask each student to write a short essay on the kinds of subjects that may appear in structures of predication.

Topic III: Complementation

- Using Reproduction Page 34, have the students write sentences using each of the following words or structures as a direct object. Sample answers are given below but not on the Reproduction Page. The students are also asked to write other sentences in which the same parts of speech or structures are used as direct objects.

REPRODUCTION PAGE 34

WRITING SENTENCES WITH SUPPLIED DIRECT OBJECTS

Directions: *Use each of the following words or structures as a direct object in a sentence. Then write other sentences in which the same parts of speech or structures are used as direct objects.*

1. men (a noun)

2. the sick (an adjective-headed structure of modification)

3. out (an adverb)

4. to fly (a verb)

5. taking tests (a structure of complementation)

6. that the pencil should be here (a structure of predication)

7. Debbie and Sue (a structure of coordination)

---

1. men (a noun): They hire men.

2. the sick (an adjective-headed structure of modification): Doctors treat the sick.

3. out (an adverb): The dog wants out.

4. to fly (a verb): Isis likes to fly.

5. taking tests (a structure of complementation): Students dislike taking tests.

6. that the pencil should be here (a structure of predication): I think that the pencil should be here.

7. Debbie and Sue (a structure of coordination): Mary called Debbie and Sue.

- Using Reproduction Page 35, have the students write sentences using each of the following words or structures as a subject complement. Sample answers are given below but not on the Reproduction Page. The students are also asked to write other sentences in which the same parts of speech or structures are used as subject complements.

1. a nut (a noun-headed structure of modification): A pecan is a nut.

2. neat (an adjective): The room seemed neat.

3. here (an adverb): Tom was here.

REPRODUCTION PAGE 35

WRITING SENTENCES WITH SUPPLIED SUBJECT COMPLEMENTS

Directions: *Use each of the following words or structures as a subject complement in a sentence. Then write other sentences in which the same parts of speech or structures are used as subject complements.*

1. a nut (a noun-headed structure of modification)

2. neat (an adjective)

3. here (an adverb)

4. to believe (a verb)

5. from California (a prepositional phrase)

6. winning money (a structure of complementation)

7. wet and dirty (a structure of coordination)

8. what he wanted (a structure of predication)

---

4. to believe (a verb): To see is to believe.

5. from California (a prepositional phrase): The Bergers are from California.

6. winning money (a structure of complementation): His goal is winning money.

7. wet and dirty (a structure of coordination): The dog was wet and dirty.

8. what he wanted (a structure of predication): Harry became what he wanted.

• Using Reproduction Page 36, have the students indicate whether the complements underlined in the sentences below are subject complements, direct objects, indirect objects, or object complements. The answers are written above the complements below but not on the Reproduction Page.

             direct object
1. They opposed <u>his election</u>.

                subject complement
2. Wendy and Kate are <u>upstairs</u>.

            indirect object   direct object
3. Ed supposed <u>Mary</u>   <u>the hostess</u>.

          subject complement
4. Mr. Jones is <u>a teacher</u>.

          subject complement
5. He seems <u>rather tired</u>.

             direct object   object complement
6. The chickens chose <u>Chanticleer</u>   <u>their spokesman</u>.

          subject complement
7. Mark has become <u>an alienated person</u>.

           direct object   object complement
8. Priscilla considered <u>John's proposal</u> <u>a joke</u>.

        subject complement
9. Scott was <u>in the backyard</u>.

           indirect object   direct object
10. The organization sent <u>him</u>   <u>a yellow rose</u>.

        subject complement
11. The styles were <u>quite strange</u>.

        indirect object   direct object
12. I mailed <u>Jane</u>   <u>a love letter</u>.

        direct object
13. The big dog scratched <u>its fleas</u>.

        direct object   object complement
14. They found <u>Walter</u>   <u>quite happy</u>.

        subject complement
15. A wedding is <u>a strange ritual</u>.

REPRODUCTION PAGE 36

IDENTIFYING SENTENCE PARTS

Directions: *Indicate above each complement underlined below whether it is a subject complement, direct object, indirect object, or object complement.*

1. They opposed his election.
2. Wendy and Kate are upstairs.
3. Ed supposed Mary the hostess.
4. Mr. Jones is a teacher.
5. He seems rather tired.
6. The chickens chose Chanticleer their spokesman.
7. Mark has become an alienated person.
8. Priscilla considered John's proposal a joke.
9. Scott was in the backyard.
10. The organization sent him a yellow rose.
11. The styles were quite strange.
12. I mailed Jane a love letter.
13. The big dog scratched its fleas.
14. They found Walter quite happy.
15. A wedding is a strange ritual.
16. A sow's ear remains a sow's ear.
17. The company gave its seven top employees large raises.
18. People eat breakfast in the morning.
19. The class voted Tim the person most likely to succeed.
20. Bernie seemed a nice person.

---

                                     subject complement
16. A sow's ear remains a sow's ear.

                        indirect object   direct object
17. The company gave its seven top employees large raises.

                    direct object
18. People eat breakfast in the morning.

                        direct object   object complement
19. The class voted Tim   the person most likely to succeed.

                    subject complement
20. Bernie seemed a nice person.

- Have each student write a paragraph on how one tells a direct object from a subject complement.

- Have each student write a paragraph on how one tells the sequence of an indirect object and a direct object from the sequence of a direct object and an object complement.

- Ask each student to write a short essay on the parts of speech and syntactic structures that may be used as the different kinds of complements in English.

Topic IV: Coordination

- Ask each student to find all of the structures of coordination on a page of one of his or her textbooks. If the same page is assigned to all students, compare the results in class.

IDENTIFYING COORDINATING STRUCTURES

Directions: *Underline the structures of coordination in the following sentences:*

1. I am studying algebra, biology, English, French, and history this semester.
2. I have traveled far and seen much.
3. Romeo and Juliet were lovers.
4. I like chicken but hate turkey.
5. They watch television sporadically and infrequently.
6. Either Sally or Betty must have broken it.
7. David is a young and innocent child.
8. Tom, Dick, or Harry brought the pickles.
9. She is pretty but dumb.
10. Some people prefer coffee rather than tea.
11. Phil hates chemistry, but Carl likes it.
12. I lost or misplaced my pen.
13. Ben likes sweet-and-sour pork.
14. They are from Poland or Russia.
15. Harry brought Tom and Jim their coats.
16. John is tired, yet he refuses to rest.
17. The Porters raise tomatoes, lettuce, and carrots.
18. Snow and rain are types of precipitation.
19. Mr. Rice teaches mathematics and coaches basketball.
20. I just met Kim and Bruce.

- Using Reproduction Page 37, have the students underline the structures of coordination in the sentences below. The structures of coordination are underlined below but not on the Reproduction Page.

1. I am studying <u>algebra, biology, English, French, and history</u> this semester.

2. I have <u>traveled far and seen much.</u>

3. <u>Romeo and Juliet</u> were lovers.

4. I <u>like chicken but hate turkey.</u>

5. They watch television <u>sporadically and infrequently.</u>

6. <u>Either Sally or Betty</u> must have taken it.

7. David is a <u>young and innocent</u> child.

8. <u>Tom, Dick, or Harry</u> brought the pickles.

9. She is <u>pretty but dumb.</u>

10. Some people prefer <u>coffee rather than tea.</u>

11. <u>Phil hates chemistry, but Carl loves it.</u>

12. I <u>lost or misplaced</u> my pen.

13. Ben likes <u>sweet and sour</u> pork.

14. They are from <u>Poland or Russia.</u>

15. · Harry brought <u>Tom and Jim</u> their coats.

16. <u>John is tired, yet he refuses to rest.</u>

17. The Porters raise <u>tomatoes, lettuce, and carrots.</u>

18. <u>Snow and rain</u> are types of precipitation.

19. Mr. Rice <u>teaches mathematics and coaches basketball</u>.

20. I just met <u>Kim and Bruce</u>.

- Using Reproduction Page 38, ask the students to write sentences using the following structures of coordination. Sample sentences are given below but not on the Reproduction Page. The students are also asked to write other sentences in which the same kinds of words or structures are used in structures of coordination.

1. basketball and football (nouns): Roger plays basketball and football.

2. rich and handsome (adjective): Prince Charmings are usually rich and handsome.

3. cry and eat (verbs): Babies cry and eat.

4. slowly but surely (adverbs): He works slowly but surely.

5. of the people, by the people, and for the people (prepositional phrases): Government of the people, by the people, and for the people shall not perish.

6. who did it and when it happened (structures of predication): Sam Spade knows who did it and when it happened.

7. purple cows and pink elephants (structures of modification): Purple cows and pink elephants are relatively rare.

8 acting the fool and playing the clown (structures of complementation): Dean is acting the fool and playing the clown.

REPRODUCTION PAGE 38

WRITING SENTENCES USING COORDINATION

Directions: *Write sentences in which the following structures of coordination are used. Then write other sentences in which the same kinds of words or structures are used in structures of coordination.*

1. basketball and football (nouns)

2. rich and handsome (adjectives)

3. cry and eat (verbs)

4. slowly but surely (adverbs)

5. of the people, by the people, and for the people (prepositional phrases)

6. who did it and when it happened (structures of predication)

7. purple cows and pink elephants (structures of modification)

8. acting the fool and playing the clown (structures of complementation)

• Ask each student to write a short essay on the uses and composition of structures of coordination in English.

ASSESSING ACHIEVEMENT OF OBJECTIVES

Ongoing Evaluation

The extent to which students have mastered the concepts covered under each topic can be measured by any of the activities assigned to the class as individuals, particularly the writing activities.

Final Evaluation

For an overall evaluation of each student's mastery of the concepts in this chapter, if all topics in the chapter have been taught, a test constructed directly from the list of student objective for the chapter as listed on page 82 can be used. As an alternative, one might compose a test from among the following items:

1. Name the two parts of a structure of modification, the two parts of a structure of predication, the two parts of a structure of complementation, and the two or more parts of a structure of coordination.

2. Modify the noun *man* by a determiner, another noun, an adjective, an adverb, a prepositional phrase, and a relative clause.

3. Modify the verb *run* by an auxiliary, another verb, an adjective, an adverb, a prepositional phrase, and an included (subordinate) clause.

4. Modify the adjective *cold* by a qualifier, another adjective, a noun, a verb, and an adverb.

5. Modify the adverb *quickly* by a qualifier, another adverb, and a prepositional phrase.

6. Explain the ambiguity of a sentence like *The child asks to learn* in terms of whether *to learn* is a modifier or a complement of *asks*.

7. Write a sentence with each of the following as a subject:

   A. a noun

   B. an adjective

   C. an adverb

   D. a structure of complementation

   E. a structure of predication

   F. a structure of coordination

8. Write a sentence with each of the following as a direct object:

   A. a noun

       B. an infinitive

       C. a structure of coordination

       D. a structure of predication

       E. a structure of complementation

9. Write a sentence with the following kinds of complements:

       A. an indirect object and a direct object

       B. a direct object and a noun object complement

       C. a direct object and an adjective object complement

       D. an adjective subject complement

       E. a noun subject complement

       F. an adverb subject complement

10. Explain how one distinguishes between the following:

       A. a noun direct object and a noun subject complement

       B. an indirect object plus a direct object and a direct object and a noun object complement

RESOURCES FOR TEACHING ABOUT HOW WORDS GO TOGETHER IN ENGLISH

Below is a selected and annotated list of resources useful for teaching the topics in this chapter, divided into audiovisual materials and print materials and arranged in order of ascending difficulty. Special strengths and weaknesses are mentioned in the annotations. Addresses of publishers or distributors can be found in the alphabetical list on pages 263-265 in Appendix A. Films are black and white unless otherwise indicated.

I. MODIFICATION

Audiovisual Materials

Communication Skills: Who's Afraid of Grammar, Part III. Sound-slide set (sound on LP record or cassette tape) with three programs: 19 minutes (dialect and "standard" English); 23 minutes (word order, inflection, and structure words); 24 minutes (syntactic processes of coordination and subordination), 1976, The Center for Humanities, Inc. Uses slides of artworks to introduce the concept of transformations to show syntactic relationships of modification by subordinate clauses (and of coordination).

Print

"Expanding with Adverbs" and "Expanding with Adjectives," pp. 250-258 in *Patterns of Communicating* (Grade 8) by Allan A. Glatthorn and Jane Christensen. Shows modification by adverbs, adjectives, and prepositional phrases. Has simple exercises. Hardbound, D. C. Heath and Co., 1975.

"Syntactic Combinations," pp. 107-112 in *A Survey of Modern Grammars,* 2d ed. by Jeanne H. Herndon. Provides a short introduction to syntactic structures with the greatest emphasis on modification. Paperbound, Holt, Rinehart and Winston, 1976.

"Construction Types," pp. 88-91 in *Introduction to Linguistics* by Ronald Wardhaugh. Identifies and provides simple examples of the syntactic relationships of modification, predication, complementation, and coordination. Paperbound, McGraw-Hill, 1972.

Exercises, pp. 77-85 in *Workbook to Accompany Introduction to Linguistics* by Ronald Wardhaugh. Provides sentences (including ambiguous ones) for analysis into structures of modification, predication, complementation, and coordination. Paperbound, McGraw-Hill, 1972.

"The Four Syntactic Structures" and "Structures of Modification," pp. 291-325 in *The Structure of American English* by W. Nelson Francis. Introduces the concepts of modification, predication, complementation, and coordination and provides the most comprehensive, illustrated discussion of the structure of modification. Hardbound, The Ronald Press Co., 1958.

"Prepositions," pp. 155-159 in *An Introductory English Grammar,* 2d ed., by Norman C. Stageberg. Shows the introductory function of prepositions and the modification function of prepositional phrases. Provides exercises. Paperbound, Holt, Rinehart and Winston, 1971.

"Clause Adverbials," pp. 258-260 in *An Introductory English Grammar,* 2d ed., by Norman C. Stageberg. Shows the introductory function of subordinating conjunctions and the modification function of subordinate clauses. Has exercises. Paperbound, Holt, Rinehart and Winston, 1971.

"Included Clauses" and "Sentence Modifiers," pp. 389-409 in *The Structure of American English* by W. Nelson Francis. Illustrates the modifying function of included clauses; differentiates between relative clauses and those introduced by simple includers (subordinate conjunctions); and illustrates the concept of sentence modifiers using included clauses, absolute constructions, infinitives, participles, prepositional phrases, and adverbs. Hardbound, The Ronald Press Co., 1958.

II. PREDICATION

Print

"A Summary of Common Sentence Patterns," etc., pp. 180-196 in *Linguistics, English, and the Language Arts* by Carl A. Lefevre. Provides an analysis of basic sentence patterns (structures of predication) with some attention to structures of modification and complementation. Paperbound, Teachers College Press, 1970.

"Sentence Parts: You Have the Combination," pp. L17-L32 in *Invention and Design* by Albert R. Kitzhaber et al. Illustrates structures of predication (NP+VP) as the basic patterns for English sentences. Provides simple exercises. Hardbound, Holt, Rinehart and Winston, 1974.

"Subjects and Predicates," pp. 137-164 in *A Short Introduction to English Grammar* by James Sledd. Identifies the common types of predication in English and sentence formulas to produce them. Has exercises. Hardbound, Scott, Foresman and Co., 1959.

"Basic Sentence Patterns," pp. 169-192 in *An Introductory English Grammar,* 2d ed., by Norman C. Stageberg. Identifies common subject and predicate structures of English sentences while introducing the basic sentence patterns of English. Provides exercises. Paperbound, Holt, Rinehart and Winston, 1971.

"Structures of Predication," pp. 325-342 in *The Structures of American English* by W. Nelson Francis. Provides a comprehensive, illustrated explanation of the structure of predication although the discussion of verb phrases is rather complex. Hardbound, The Ronald Press Co., 1958.

"A Look at Transformational Grammar," pp. 291-336 in *An Introductory English Grammar,* 2d ed., by Norman C. Stageberg. Gives a reasonably simple transformational-generative model which produces simple structures of predication in English. Has exercises. Paperbound, Holt, Rinehart and Winston, 1971.

III. COMPLEMENTATION

Audiovisual Materials

Language and Meaning. Film, part of *Language and Linguistics* Series, 29 minutes, 1958, Indiana University Audio-Visual Center. Explains how structure plays a part in the meanings of sentences.

Print

"The Predicate," pp. 237–249 in *Patterns of Communicating* (Grade 8) by Allan A. Glatthorn and Jane Christensen. Discusses direct objects and indirect objects as complements of transitive verbs and subject complements as complements of linking verbs. Provides simple exercises. Hardbound, D. C. Heath and Co., 1975.

"Complements," pp. 27–34 in *Warriner's English Grammar and Composition* (complete course) by John E. Warriner and Francis Griffith. Defines the major types of complements in notional terms. Provides exercises. Hardbound, Harcourt Brace Jovanovich, 1973.

"Verbal Sequences," pp. 121–136 in *A Short Introduction to English Grammar* by James Sledd. Illustrates and identifies the major types of complementation in English. Has exercises. Hardbound, Scott, Foresman and Co., 1959.

"Basic Sentence Patterns," pp. 169–192 in *An Introductory English Grammar,* 2d ed., by Norman C. Stageberg. Identifies the major structures of complementation in terms of the basic sentence patterns of English. Provides copious exercises. Paperbound, Holt, Rinehart and Winston, 1971.

"The Verb and Its Complementation," pp. 347–374 in *A Concise Grammar of Contemporary English* by Randolph Quirk and Sidney Greenbaum. Explains the different kinds of complements in structures of complementation and illustrates them clearly. Not recommended for students. Hardbound, Harcourt Brace Jovanovich, 1973.

"Structures of Complementation," pp. 342–355 in *The Structure of American English* by W. Nelson Francis. Provides a good discussion of the structure of complementation but does not explain the relationships between multiple complements of the same verb. Hardbound, The Ronald Press Co., 1958.

"Surface Structure and Transformations: Indirect Objects," pp. 337–341 in *An Introductory English Grammar,* 2d ed., by Norman C. Stageberg. Uses a transformational-generative model to explain how one type of complement, the indirect object, is introduced into English sentences. Has exercises. Not recommended for younger students. Paperbound, Holt, Rinehart and Winston, 1971.

IV. COORDINATION

Audiovisual Materials

Communication Skills: Who's Afraid of Grammar, Part III. Sound-slide set (sound on LP record or cassette tape) with three programs: 19 minutes (dialect and "standard" English); 23 minutes (word order, inflection, and structure words); 24 minutes (syntactic processes of coordination and subordination), 1976, The Center for Humanities, Inc. Uses slides of artworks to introduce the concept of transformations to syntactic relationships of coordination (and of modification by subordinate clauses).

Print

"Compounding," pp. 258–265 in *Patterns of Communicating* (Grade 8) by Allan A. Glatthorn and Jane Christensen. Provides a simple discussion of the structure of coordination. Has simple exercises. Hardbound, D. C. Heath and Co., 1975.

"Coordinates," pp. 42–46 in *The System of English Grammar* by Ralph B. Long and Dorothy R. Long. Explains and illustrates the structure of coordination simply. Hardbound, Scott, Foresman and Co., 1971.

"Coordination," pp. 270-273 in *An Introductory English Grammar,* 2d ed. by Norman C. Stageberg. Gives a simple explanation of the structure of coordination. Has exercises. Paperbound, Holt, Rinehart and Winston, 1971.

"Structures of Coordination," pp. 355-366 in *The Structure of American English* by W. Nelson Francis. Provides a complete but complex illustrated analysis of the structure of coordination. Hardbound, The Ronald Press Co., 1958.

"Coordination," pp. 253-275 in *A Concise Grammar of Contemporary English* by Randolph Quirk and Sidney Greenbaum. Provides a complex but thorough explanation with copious illustrations of the structure of coordination. Not recommended for students. Hardbound, Harcourt Brace Jovanovich, 1973.

6

Regional Dialect Differences

This chapter focuses on vocabulary, pronunciation, morphological, and syntactic differences in the English spoken in various regions of the United States. One practical application of the unit is the development of an awareness that persons who speak English differently from the way in which the student does are not necessarily "wrong"; conversely, the student is also not necessarily "wrong" if he or she speaks English differently from others. Ideally, then, the students should develop not only a tolerance but also an appreciation of their fellow students who speak differently than they do, and the students who speak a regional dialect different from those of their fellow students should develop a positive attitude toward their own speech patterns. Another practical result of this unit will be to teach or to reinforce what has already been taught about the geography and the history of the United States.

The students should first be made aware of the causes of dialect differences in the different regions of the country. This can be achieved by discussing the settlement history of the thirteen original states (where in England the early colonists in each colony came from); the contacts these colonists had with speakers of other languages such as Dutch, German, and various American Indian languages; the geographic restrictions of communication among the various colonies such as rivers, mountain ranges, and swamps; the migration routes westward and which geographic dialect areas contributed the most people to the westward movement; and the various European as well as Indian languages that were spoken in the areas that were added to the United States before English-speaking people moved into them, French and Spanish being the notable examples. Then the student will be prepared to understand the present regional dialect differences within the United States within a coherent framework rather than as isolated facts.

When dealing with specific regional dialect differences, the teacher should probably begin with vocabulary differences, since they are most easily observable and require no knowledge of phonology, morphology, or syntax to discuss. In addition, some of the vocabulary differences may already be familiar to the students. It might be wise to begin with vocabulary differences among groups of geographic dialects like Northern *string beans* versus

Midland *green beans* versus Southern *snap beans* or Northern *pail* versus Midland and Southern *bucket.* Then the teacher can focus on the regional vocabulary items that the students use and contrast them with their counterparts in nearby dialect areas such as the use of *soda* for a "carbonated soft drink" in the Hudson Valley dialect area of New York State in contrast to *pop* in western upstate New York and the well-known *tonic* of the eastern New England dialect area with Boston as its center.

Pronunciation differences in regional dialects should be the next topic of discussion because they are numerous and more likely to be kept as one moves from one geographic dialect area to another than are vocabulary differences which are more obvious and thus more likely to be changed to avoid being considered "different." Again it might be wise to begin with pronunciation differences among broad categories of regional dialects such as the /s/ pronunciation of the medial consonant in *greasy* in Northern and North Midland dialects versus the /z/ pronunciation in the same word in South Midland and Southern dialects or the /u/ (the vowel in *two*) pronunciation of *coop* in the Northern and North Midland dialects versus the /ʋ/ (the vowel in *should*) pronunciation of the same word in South Midland and Southern dialects. Then the teacher can focus on the regional pronunciations of words in the students' own geographic dialect area and contrast these pronunciations with those of nearby regions with which the students may be familiar such as the /a/ (the vowel in *shot*) pronunciation of the middle vowel of *tomato* that often occurs in the speech of New York City, Philadelphia, Virginia, and parts of New England (reflecting the close contact of the areas with England during the colonial period) versus the /e/ (the vowel in *say*) that occurs in most other dialect areas of the United States.

Morphological regional dialect differences may be discussed next, but it should be noted that many morphological regional dialect differences are nonstandard, so some social dialect issues may be raised in their discussion. The suggestion again is that dialect features which separate broad dialect areas be discusssed first such as the Northern standard English *dove* (past form of *dive*) versus the Midland and Southern standard English *dived.* Then the teacher can focus on regional morphological features that differentiate the students' dialect area from surrounding dialect areas such as /klom/ (rhymes with *comb*) as a nonstandard form in eastern Virginia versus the nonstandard /klʌm/ (rhymes with *dumb*) of the Midland dialects directly to the north versus nonstandard /klɪm/ (rhymes with *limb*) of the other Southern dialects to the south versus standard *climbed* everywhere else.

Finally, syntactic regional dialect differences may be introduced. There are really no syntactic features that separate major groups of geographic dialects from each other in the way that the common British way of forming questions with inversion of *have* as in *Have you the time?* differentiates British dialects from all American dialects, which prefer the use of the dummy auxiliary *do* as in *Do you have the time?* Instead, the teacher will have to focus on distinctive features of specific geographic dialect areas like the dialect area encompassing the southern parts of Ohio, Indiana, and Illinois that allow the use of *anymore* in a positive statement like *We like it anymore* in contrast with most other dialects that allow *anymore* only in a negative statement like *We don't like it anymore.*

Any of these topics may be used independently of the others. If the teacher chooses all of them, however, it is suggested that they be presented in the order given.

OBJECTIVES

If all of the topics in this chapter are chosen by the teacher, the student should be able to:

1. Explain how the presence or absence of postvocalic /r/ and the use of *to, till,* or *of* in time expressions in modern American dialects reflects the parts of England from which the early colonists came
2. Identify the major geographic features that perpetuated or increased geographic dialect differences during the colonial period and during the early days of nationhood
3. Identify regional vocabulary items that reflect contact of English-speaking people with people who spoke Dutch, German, French, Spanish, and American Indian languages
4. Give examples of vocabulary items that differentiate one geographic dialect area from another or a major group of dialects from other major groups
5. Identify regional pronunciations that differentiate one geographic dialect area from another or a major group of dialects from other major groups
6. Give examples of morphological regional dialect features and identify which dialects have these features
7. Give examples of syntactic regional dialect features and identify which dialects have these features
8. Explain why one regional dialect is no better or no worse than any other regional dialect

CONTENT OVERVIEW

Causes of Regional Dialect Differences in the United States

American regional dialects reflect the dialects of English brought to America by the colonists, the contacts the speakers of English have had with non-English speakers, the routes of migration (which determine which dialects were carried westward and which dialects of the East Coast were mixed together in western areas), geographical features that isolate speech communities, old political boundaries, and proximity to cultural centers that developed in America.

Dialects on the East Coast tend to differ from each other more than do Western dialects because settlers in the colonies tended to come bringing different British geographic dialects with them and because these differences were maintained in the colonies due to the little travel back and forth among the various colonies. The early colonists of the New England seaboard and of the tidewater region of Virginia and the Carolinas came from the southeastern part of England, which lost postvocalic /r/ before and during the period of colonization. As a result, the dialects of those regions of America still lack postvocalic /r/. Western New England and the Piedmont areas of Virginia, North Carolina, and South Carolina were not settled until the eighteenth century by the Scotch-Irish and settlers from northern England who had kept postvocalic /r/, as do the dialects of those regions today. The settlers in the Middle Atlantic States in 1776 were approximately one-third Scotch-Irish or northern Englanders; one-third Quakers, who were also primarily from the North of England; and one-third German. Since the first two-thirds of the population of the area spoke a Northern British dialect that kept postvocalic /r/, the last third also learned to speak a dialect of English that kept the /r/.

The speech of western New England was carried into upstate New York and from there into northern Pennsylvania, Ohio, Indiana, Illinois, and points northward from which it spread westward. Geography played an obvious part here since eastern New Englanders became tied to the sea economically, and water routes and the absence of mountains enabled western New Englanders and the people of upstate New York to travel westward fairly easily, especially after the Erie Canal was constructed. The speech of the coastal South was hemmed in to the west by the Appalachian Mountains but spread south and then westward into Georgia, Alabama, Mississippi, Louisiana, eastern Texas, and eastern Tennessee once it was possible to cross the rivers and swamps of the tidewater region. The speech of the Middle Atlantic States and the Piedmont area of the South spread westward in an ever-widening band because of water routes (particularly the Ohio River and its tributaries) and because of the friendly relationships that the Quakers of the Middle Atlantic States had with the Indians on the frontiers.

From the first English colonization of America to the final incorporation of land into the continental United States, English speakers have had contact with American Indian languages. The influences of these languages have been primarily in terms of vocabulary like *succotash, wigwam, sagamore;* Indian names for tribes like *Mohawk, Onondaga,* and *Cherokee;* or rivers like *Mississippi* and *Mississinewa.* Since American Indian languages are much more diverse than European languages, it would be well for a teacher to look at a local map to identify the particular Indian influence on the dialect of the area. Of course, the speakers of English encountered the Dutch in New York State, so that the Hudson Valley and New York City dialects have vocabulary like *suppawn* (corn mush), *barrack* (haystack), and *pot cheese* (cottage cheese) not shared by other American dialects. However, place names ending in *−kill* (brook) are a good indication of the area of Dutch influences. As mentioned above, the Middle Atlantic States had a large German population before the Revolutionary War. The Pennsylvania Dutch (who were German, not Dutch) are the most notable example. As a result, the dialects of eastern Pennsylvania still have Germanisms like *fatcake* (doughnut), *spook* (ghost), and *thick-milk* (curdled milk). The area that was part of the Louisiana Purchase was populated rather sparsely with French-speaking people (except for Louisiana), but the place names from Sault Ste. Marie to Des Moines to Baton Rouge show French influence on a large number of American English dialects. *Prairie* in the Midwest and *bayou* and *levee* in Louisiana reveal a greater degree of French influence. Florida, the Southwest, and the Rocky Mountain States reflect the Spanish spoken there before the speakers of English came in such places names as *Florida, California,* and *Colorado.* The Southwest shows the greatest degree of Spanish influence, particularly in terms associated with cattle raising; for example, *lariat* (la riata), *hacienda, ranch(o),* and *chaps.*

More recently, American dialects have been influenced by mass emigration from Europe of Finns into northern Michigan, Germans into Wisconsin, and Norwegians into Minnesota in particular, and in general of Scandinavians and Germans into the upper Midwest. Large influxes of Italians into the New England area and upstate New York as well as urban centers of the Midwest, of Slavs (particularly Poles) into the urban centers of the Northeast and Midwest, and of East European Jews into the urban centers of the Northeast have influenced the dialects of all of these areas. It would be well for the teacher to focus on the influence of the particular foreign-language groups on the dialect of the local area, and foods would be a good place to begin, that is, *kielbasa, manicotti, borscht,* and *rouladen.*

Routes of migration and geographical features that isolate speech communities might well be considered together, since the migration routes westward in the United States were restricted by geographical features like mountain ranges and opened up by other geographical features like rivers and lakes. Students will notice that the line separating Midland dialects from Southern dialects coincides with the Appalachians in Virginia and North Carolina, for example, because the mountains stopped the westward movement of speakers of Southern dialects. The Great Lakes, the Mohawk Valley, and finally the completion of the Erie Canal, on the other hand, facilitated the westward movement of people from the Inland North, just as the Ohio and southern Mississippi River system made the westward movement easier for speakers of South Midland dialects than of other dialects. The completion of the National Road to Indianapolis in the first half of the nineteenth century established a migration route for speakers of North Midland dialects westward, particularly for Pennsylvanians. Deserts in the Southwest encouraged settlers to take other routes of migration.

Old political boundaries have some influence on regional dialects, the areas of French and Spanish conquest in North America being obvious examples. However, even the boundaries between English-speaking colonies furthered geographical dialect differences because trade was usually restricted among the colonies before the Revolutionary War. State lines still reflect dialect differences in the United States, so that what are called *counties* elsewhere in the United States are called *parishes* in Louisiana, what are called *towns* in New York State are called *townships* in the midwestern states, and what are usually called *county seats* elsewhere are called *county sites* in parts of Georgia.

The presence of a large cultural center nearby will often influence the dialects of surrounding areas. In the United States, no one cultural center dominates the country, but several cultural centers dominate smaller areas. What happens linguistically is best explained by the wave theory, which says that if the dialect of a cultural center is perceived as having prestige, it will have a ripple effect on the surrounding areas because people will pick up features of this dialect and incorporate them into their own dialects. Of course, the closer one is to this cultural center, the more features will be picked up; the farther away, the fewer. In the early nineteenth century when the dialect of Boston had greater prestige than it does today, there was greater imitation of it than there is now. However, there are still pronunciations of *aunt* with an /a/ vowel (as in *hot*) rather than an /æ/ vowel (as in *hat*) as far away from eastern New England as Minnesota, and South Carolina and Tennessee among blacks, that reflect the influence of New England teachers in the last century. On the other hand, the use of *tonic* for carbonated soft drink is restricted to a very small area surrounding Boston, specifically those towns that were on the delivery route of a particular soft-drink manufacturer. Similarly the use of *chopped meat* for ground beef has been picked up by the surrounding dialects of northern New Jersey and southwestern Connecticut as well as the Hudson Valley area north of New York City and is not limited to New York City. The dialect of Charleston, South Carolina, was widely perceived as prestigious and imitated in the tidewater area of South Carolina in the past, although its influence and prestige appear to be diminishing. The dialect of Chicago influences the surrounding dialects, but it does not have a large area that it dominates. The same is doubtless true of the dialects of Denver, San Francisco, Dallas, and Atlanta. In general, the presence of a cultural center nearby influences the surrounding dialects less now than it did in the past.

Regional Vocabulary Differences in the United States

Vocabulary items, as indicated above, are frequently indicators of regional dialects. Because of increasing education among the population and of the influence of national media, there is a tendency for speakers to discard regional vocabulary items in favor of more general terms, so it will be necessary for the teacher to use his or her own judgment about the current accuracy of statements made here and in the suggested resources listed later in the chapter. In general, Northern dialects can be identified by their use of *string beans, pail, sweet corn/corn on the cob, angleworm* (earthworm), *buttonball* (sycamore), and so on. Midland dialects generally use *green beans, bucket, roasting ears, fish(ing) worm, sycamore, blinds* (roller shades), and so on. Southern dialects generally use *snap beans, bucket, roasting ears, earthworm, sycamore, shades/curtains,* and so on. More examples are given in the "Learning Experiences" section of this chapter.

Phonological Differences Among Geographic Dialects in the United States

Pronunciations are probably a better indication of regional dialects than are vocabulary items. Postvocalic /r/ has been mentioned above. In general, the /r/ in *barn* will be pronounced in Northern dialects (except for the dialects of eastern New England and New York City) and Midland dialects, but not in Southern dialects. In eastern New England, an intrusive /r/ is frequently added to a word ending in a vowel when the next word begins with a vowel. In the Midland dialects, an intrusive /r/ is frequently added after the vowel in *wash* and *Washington.* Generally, *grease* and *greasy* will have /s/ in Northern dialects (except for the New

York City dialect, which has either /s/ or /z/); have /z/ in Midland dialects (except for the eastern parts of the North Midland area); and have /z/ in Southern dialects. Generally, Midland dialects substitute /ɪ/ (the vowel in *hit*) for /ɛ/ (the vowel in *head*) before nasals so that *pen* and *pin* will be indistinguishable. The Northern and Midland dialects have /s/ in the middle of *Mrs.*, whereas Southern dialects use /z/. In the Midland and Northern dialects (except for eastern New England and to some extent in New York City), *merry* and *Mary* will have the same vowel in the first syllable, that is, the /ɛ/ the vowel in *head*); in Southern dialects and the Northern dialects indicated as exceptions, the two words will have different vowels, *Mary* having the /e/ (the vowel in *hate*). It is impossible to give the pronunciation features that further subdivide the Northern, Midland, and Southern dialects in the overview, but some of them are suggested in the activities under the following section of "Learning Experiences" which the teacher may pursue at greater length.

Morphological Differences Among Geographic Dialects in the United States

Morphological differences among the standard varieties of American regional dialects are rare, Northern *dove* versus Midland and Southern *dived* being the most common one. Other morphological differences in verb forms among regional dialects tend to be in nonstandard usages like the Northern *clim* (preterite of *climb*), Midland *clum*, Eastern Virginia *clome* versus general Southern *clim*; the Northern *see* (preterite of *see*), Midland and Southern *seen*; and South Midland and Southern perfective use of *done* as in *I done did it*. The Southern use of *you-all* for a plural is standard, but the Midland use of *you-uns* and the occasional Northern use of *youse* are nonstandard.

Syntactically, the Midland dialects seem to have the most distinctive dialect features. The Midland use of *all the further* (as far as), *all the better, wait on someone* (wait for someone), *quarter till the hour* rather than *quarter to* or *of*, and elliptical *want off* (want to be let off) are fairly clear dialect markers. The Northern use of *hadn't ought* (oughtn't) and its use in Eastern North Midland dialects, *quarter of* (but not the Northern use of *quarter to*), and *standing on line* (rather than *in line*) shared by some Southern dialects help to mark Northern dialects as such. Southern and South Midland dialects also use *might could* (as does the German-influenced part of eastern Pennsylvania), *use to didn't*, and *I'm not for sure*.

LEARNING EXPERIENCES

Topic I: Causes of Regional Dialect Differences
          in the United States

- Divide the students into small groups and ask each group to use a different dictionary to look up the pronunciation of *aunt, brooch, dais, garage, orange, root, route, suite,* and *wash.* The groups should find more than one pronunciation for some words in the same dictionary and conflicting pronunciations in different dictionaries. This exercise can be used to point out that there may be different pronunciations in different dialects and that they are all "correct" in specific areas.

- Divide the students into small groups and ask each group to use a different dictionary to look up the meanings of *branch* (noun), *carry, run* (noun), *soda,* and *stoop* (noun). The groups may find meanings of these words that they have not encountered before. This exercise can be used to point out that there may be different meanings to words in different dialects and that they are all "correct" in specific areas.

- Provide the students with maps of the local area and ask them to make lists of the place names of cities, towns, rivers, and other topographical phenomena that suggest something about the settlement and migration patterns of your local area. The lists can then be collated to discuss aspects of local history that will have influenced the students' dialect.

- If there are students with clear ethnic identities in the class, ask them to form groups based on these ethnic identities and compile lists of words, pronunciations, grammatical forms, or syntactic structures they have noticed their relatives using that people outside that ethnic group in the area do not use. For example, Finnish-Americans may eat *kahvipulla* and speak sentences with a subject noun last and a postcedent subject pronoun first as in *He was here yesterday, the television man.* These differences can then be used to explain how contact with speakers of other languages may bring about geographic dialect differences as in the Southwest.

- After you have explained the three broad categories of American regional dialects, use maps 1, 2, 3, or 4 below (also on Reproduction Pages 39, 40, and 41) and ask each student to identify which category the local dialect falls into, his or her parents' native dialects fall into, and his or her grandparents' dialects fall into. Then ask the students whose parents or grandparents have dialects that differ from their own

---

REPRODUCTION PAGE 39

MAP 1 WORD GEOGRAPHY OF THE EASTERN STATES

0   50
SCALE IN MILES

THE SPEECH AREAS OF THE EASTERN STATES

The North	The Midland	The South
1. N.E. New England	7. Delaware Valley	14. Delmarva (E. Shore of Maryland and Virginia, and S. Delaware)
2. S.E. New England	8. Susquehanna Valley	
3. S.W. New England	9. Upper Potomac and Shenandoah Valleys	
4. Upstate New York and W. Vermont	10. Upper Ohio Valley	15. Virginia Piedmont
5. Hudson Valley	11. N. West Virginia	16. N.E. No. Carolina (Albemarle Sound and Neuse Valley)
6. Metropolitan New York	12. S. West Virginia	17. Cape Fear and Peedee Valleys
	13. W. No. and W. So. Carolina	18. So. Carolina

Source. Hans Kurath, *A Word Geography of the Eastern United States* (Ann Arbor, Michigan: University of Michigan Press, 1949).

MAP 2 DIALECT AREAS OF THE UNITED STATES

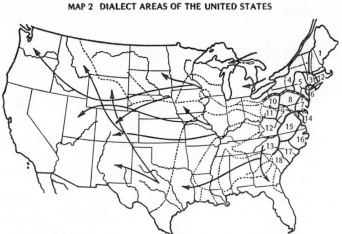

ATLANTIC SEABOARD AREAS (AFTER KURATH). TENTATIVE DIALECT BOUNDARIES.
Arrows indicate direction of migrations.

The North	The Midland	The South
1. Northeastern New England	*North Midland*	14. Delmarva (Eastern
2. Southeastern New England	7. Delaware Valley (Philadelphia)	Shore)
3. Southwestern New England	8. Susquehanna Valley	15. The Virginia Piedmont
4. Inland North (western	9. Upper Ohio Valley (Pittsburgh)	16. Northeastern North
Vermont, Upstate New	11. Northern West Virginia	Carolina (Albemarle
York & derivatives)		Sound & Neuse Valley)
5. The Hudson Valley	*South Midland*	17. Cape Fear & Peedee
6. Metropolitan New York	9. Upper Potomac & Shenandoah	Valleys
	12. Southern West Virginia &	18. The South Carolina
	Eastern Kentucky	Low Country
	13. Western Carolina & Eastern	(Charleston)
	Tennessee	

Source: W. Nelson Francis, *The Structure of American English* (New York: The Ronald Press Co., 1958), pp. 580–581. Reprinted by permission of John Wiley & Sons, Inc.

what differences they have noticed. These differences can then be tied into a discussion of why such differences occur.

• After you have discussed the three broad categories of American regional dialects, use maps 1, 2, 3, or 4 on Reproduction Pages 39–41 and ask each student who was not born in the local area or who has lived in another dialect area to identify the broad dialect category of the place where he or she was born or has lived. Then ask these students what differences they noticed between the local dialect and the dialect of the areas where they were born or have lived. Ask the students who have always lived in the local area what differences they have noticed in the speech of the students who were born or who have lived elsewhere. Again, these differences can be tied in to a discussion of why such differences occur. It will be necessary to repeat the idea that any dialect differences discussed may be "correct" in order to spare hurt feelings.

• After the students have studied the causes of dialect differences, have each student write an essay explaining why the local dialect has the features that it does. It will be necessary to remind the students to consider settlement history, geography, migration routes, contacts with other languages, and proximity to large cultural centers.

REPRODUCTION PAGE 41

MAP 3

DIALECT AREAS
IN THE
GREAT LAKES REGION

NORTHERN

MIDLAND

Small areas indicate
mixed usage

MAP 4

NORTH
DAKOTA

MINNESOTA

SOUTH
DAKOTA

NEBRASKA

IOWA

Source: **Adapted** from **"Dialect Distribution and Settlement Patterns in the Great Lakes Region" by Alva L. Davis,** *Ohio State Archeological and Historical Quarterly,* 60: 48–50 (1951). Reprinted with permission of the Ohio Historical Society.

Topic II: Regional Vocabulary Differences in the United States

- Using Reproduction Page 42, have your students classify their dialect as Northern, Midland, or Southern on the basis of the following vocabulary items:

Northern	Midland	Southern
string beans	green beans	snap beans
pail	bucket	bucket
sweet corn/ corn on the cob	roasting ears	roasting ears
swill "garbage fed to hogs"	slop	slop
corn husks	corn husks (North)/ corn shucks (South)	corn shucks

CLASSIFYING YOUR DIALECT

Directions: *Classify your dialect as primarily Northern, Midland, or Southern on the basis of the following vocabulary items. Do not be surprised if you use some words in more than one column, since dialect mixing is not uncommon, or if you use other words than those in the lists.*

Northern	Midland	Southern
string bean	green beans	snap beans
pail	bucket	bucket
sweet corn/corn on the cob	roasting ears	roasting ears
swill "garbage fed to hogs"	slop	slop
corn husks	corn husk (North)/corn shucks (South)	corn shucks
brook "small stream"	run (North)/branch (South)	branch
clapboards "finished siding"	weatherboards	weatherboards
shades "window covering on roller"	blinds	shades
distance	piece "distance"	distance
escort "take someone someplace"	escort	carry
wishbone "breast bone of chicken"	wishbone (North)/pulley bone (South)	pulley bone
cherry pit	cherry pit (North)/cherry seed (South)	cherry seed

FURTHER CLASSIFYING YOUR DIALECT

Directions: *See if you can classify your dialect even further after you have decided whether it is Northern, Midland, or Southern on the basis of the following vocabulary items, which break the three broad dialect areas down into subdivisions. Do not be surprised if you use some words in more than one column, because dialect mixing is not uncommon, or if you use other words than those in the lists. Not all Southern dialects are represented here.*

Northern Dialects

Eastern New England	Inland North	New York City and Hudson Valley
pigsty "pigpen"	pigpen	pigpen
apple dowdy "deep-dish apple pie"	deep-dish apple pie	deep-dish apple pie
buttonwood	sycamore	sycamore
porch/piazza	porch/stoop	stoop (NYC)/porch (HV)
sour milk cheese/Dutch cheese "cottage cheese"	Dutch cheese	pot cheese
bonny-clabber "curdled milk"	lobbered milk	
haystack	haystack	barrack
ground beef/hamburg	ground beef/hamburg(er)	chopped meat (NYC)/ ground beef/hamburg(er)(HV)

Midland Dialects

North Midland	South Midland	Eastern Pennsylvania	Western Pennsylvania
run "creek"	creek	creek	creek
smearcase "cottage cheese"	cottage cheese	cottage cheese	cottage cheese
baby buggy	baby carriage	baby coach	baby cab
sidewalk	sidewalk	pavement	sidewalk
ghost	ghost	spook	ghost
curdled milk	clabber milk	thick milk	crudded milk
sugar maple	sugar tree	sugar maple	sugar tree

Southern Dialects

Eastern Virginia	South Carolina–Georgia Low Country
evening "afternoon"	evening "afternoon"
batter bread "spoonbread"	awendaw "spoonbread"
goobers "peanuts"	pinders "peanuts"
lumber room "storeroom"	
	savannah "grassland"

brook "small stream"	run (North)/ branch (South)	branch
clapboards "finished siding"	weatherboards	weatherboards
shades "window covering on roller"	blinds	shades
distance	piece "distance"	distance
escort "take someone someplace"	escort	carry
wishbone "breastbone of chicken"	wishbone (North)/ pulley bone (South)	pulley bone
cherry pit	cherry pit (North)/ cherry seed (South)	cherry seed

- Using Reproduction Page 43, after your students have classified their dialect as Northern, Midland, or Southern, have them try to classify their dialect further on the basis of the following vocabulary items:

Northern Dialects

Eastern New England	Inland North	New York City and Hudson Valley
pigsty "pigpen"	pig pen	pigpen
apple dowdy "deep-dish apple pie"	deep-dish apple pie	deep-dish apple pie
buttonwood	sycamore	sycamore
porch/piazza	porch/steep	stoop (NYC)/ porch (HV)
sour milk cheese/Dutch cheese "cottage cheese"	Dutch cheese	pot cheese
bonny-clabber "curdled milk"	lobbered milk	
haystack	haystack	barrack
ground beef/hamburg	ground beef/ hamburg(er)	chopped meat (NYC)/ ground beef/ hamburg(er) (HV)

Midland Dialects

North Midland		South Midland
run "creek"		creek/branch
smearcase "cottage cheese"		cottage cheese
baby buggy		baby carriage
sidewalk		sidewalk
ghost		ghost
curdled milk		clabber milk
sugar maple		sugar tree

Eastern Pennsylvania	Western Pennsylvania
creek	creek
cottage cheese	cottage cheese
baby coach	baby cab
pavement	sidewalk
spook	ghost
thick milk	crudded milk
sugar maple	sugar tree

Southern Dialects

Eastern Virginia	South Carolina-Georgia Low Country
evening "afternoon"	evening "afternoon"
batter bread "spoon bread"	awendaw "spoon bread"
goobers "peanut"	pinders "peanuts"
lumber room "storeroom"	
	savannah "grassland"

- Ask the students for examples of regional vocabulary items they have heard that have not yet been introduced into the class, particularly words used elsewhere in your state. This activity will help the class to differentiate the local dialect from surrounding dialects, distinctions that are usually not made in the discussions of large dialect areas. It would be wise to point out that any of the dialect regions ordinarily mentioned can be broken down into smaller divisions on the basis of a few words not shared throughout a large dialect area that generally shares most dialect features.

- Have your students write a paragraph using the vocabulary of their own dialect and then the same paragraph using the vocabulary of another region.

Topic III: Phonological Differences among Geographic Dialects in the United States

- Using Reproduction Page 44, have your students classify their dialects as primarily Northern, Midland, or Southern on the basis of the following pronunciations:

Northern

different vowels in *horse* and *hoarse* (except for New York City and Hudson Valley)

same vowel in *Mary* and *merry* (except for eastern New England and New York City)

/s/ in *grease* (verb) and *greasy*

/s/ in the middle of *Mrs.*

different vowels in *tin* and *ten*

/r/ not pronounced in *park* (except for Inland North and Hudson Valley)

wash not pronounced with /r/

vowel sound of *put* in *root*

last sound of *breathe* in *with*

CLASSIFYING DIALECTS BY PRONUNCIATION

Directions: *See if you can classify your dialect as primarily Northern, Midland, or Southern on the basis of the following pronunciations. You may have pronunciations from more than one column because of dialect mixing, but your dialect will be classified as predominantly one of three broad categories.*

Northern

different vowels in *horse* and *hoarse* (except for New York City and Hudson Valley)
same vowels in *Mary* and *merry* (except for eastern New England and New York City)
/s/ in *grease* (verb) and *greasy*
/s/ in the middle of *Mrs.*
different vowels in *tin* and *ten*
/r/ not pronounced in *park* (except for Inland North and Hudson Valley)
wash not pronounced with /r/
vowel sound of *put* in *root*
last sound of *breathe* in *with*

Midland

same vowel in *horse* and *hoarse* (except in South Midland)
same vowels in *Mary* and *merry*
/z/ in *grease* and *greasy* (except for Eastern North Midland)
/s/ in the middle of *Mrs.*
same vowels in *tin* and *ten*
/r/ pronounced in *park*
wash pronounced with /r/
vowel sound of *boot* in *root*
last sound of *breath* in *with*

Southern

same vowels in *horse* and *hoarse*
different vowels in *Mary* and *merry*
/z/ in *grease* and *greasy*
/z/ in the middle of *Mrs.*
same vowels in *tin* and *ten*
/r/ not pronounced in *park*
wash not pronounced with /r/
vowel sound of *boot* in *root*
last sound of *breath* in *with*

Midland

same vowels in *horse* and *hoarse* (except in South Midland)

same vowels in *Mary* and *merry*

/z/ in *grease* and *greasy* (except for Eastern North Midland)

/s/ in the middle of *Mrs.*

same vowels in *tin* and *ten*

/r/ pronounced in *park*

wash pronounced with /r/

vowel sound of *boot* in *root*

last sound of *breath* in *with*

Southern

same vowels in *horse* and *hoarse*

different vowels in *Mary* and *merry*

/z/ in *grease* and *greasy*

/z/ in the middle of *Mrs.*

same vowel in *tin* and *ten*

/r/ not pronounced in *park*

wash not pronounced with /r/

vowel sound of *boot* in *root*

last sound of *breath* in *with*

- Using Reproduction Page 45, after your students have classified their dialect as Northern, Midland, or Southern, have them try to classify their dialect further on the basis of the following pronunciations:

Northern Dialects

Eastern New England
/r/ not pronounced in *park*
/r/ added to *idea* of it
different vowels in *Mary* and *merry*
different vowels in *rode* and *road*
different vowels in *coil* and *curl*
vowel sound of *hot* in *aunt*
vowel sound of *fought* in *fog*
/g/ not pronounced in *song*

Inland North
/r/ pronounced in *park*
/r/ not added to *idea* of it
same vowels in *Mary* and *merry*
same vowels in *rode* and *road*
different vowels in *coil* and *curl*
vowel sound of *hat* in *aunt*
vowel sound of *hot* in *fog*
/g/ not pronounced in *song*

New York City and Hudson Valley
/r/ not pronounced in *park* (NYC)//r/ pronounced in *park* (HV)
/r/ added to *idea* of it (NYC)//r/ not add to *idea* of it (HV)
same vowels in *rode* and *road*
same vowels in *coil* and *curl*
vowel sound of *hat* in *aunt*
vowel sound of *hot* in *fog*
/g/ pronounced in *song*

Midland Dialects

North Midland
vowel sound of *thick* in *creek*
vowel sound of *fought* in *fog*
vowel sound of *boot* in *food*
vowel sound of *pie* in *nice*
same vowels in *horse* and *hoarse*
vowel sound of *ooze* in *Tuesday*

South Midland
vowel sound of *eat* in *creek*
vowel sound of *fought* in *fog*
vowel sound of *boot* in *food*
vowel sound of *hot* (lengthened) in *nice*
different vowels in *horse* and *hoarse*
sounds of *you* in *Tuesday*

Eastern Pennsylvania
vowel sound of *eat* in *creek*
vowel sound of *hot* in *fog*
vowel sound of *boot* in *food*
vowel sound of *pie* in *nice*
same vowels in *horse* and *hoarse*

Western Pennsylvania
vowel sound of *eat* in *creek*
vowel sound of *fought* in *fog*
vowel sound of *foot* in *food*
vowel sound of *pie* in *nice*
same vowels in *horse* and *hoarse*

REPRODUCTION PAGE 45

FURTHER CLASSIFYING DIALECTS

Directions: *See if you can classify your dialect even further after you have decided whether it is Northern, Midland, or Southern on the basis of the following pronunciations, which break the three broad dialect areas into subdivisions. Do not be surprised if you use pronunciations in more than one column, because dialect mixing is not uncommon. Not all Southern dialects are represented here.*

Northern Dialects

Eastern New England	Inland North	New York City and Hudson Valley
/r/ not pronounced in *park*	/r/ pronounced in *park*	/r/ not pronounced in *park* (NYC)/ /r/ pronounced in *park* (HV)
/r/ added to *idea* of it	/r/ not added to *idea* of it	/r/ added to *idea* of it (NYC)/ /r/ not added to *idea* of it (HV)
different vowels in *Mary* and *merry*	same vowels in *Mary* and *merry*	
different vowels in *rode* and *road*	same vowels in *rode* and *road*	same vowels in *rode* and *road*
different vowels in *coil* and *curl*	different vowels in *coil* and *curl*	same vowels in *coil* and *curl*
vowel sound of *hot* in *aunt*	vowel sound of *hat* in *aunt*	vowel sound of *hat* in *aunt*
vowel sound of *fought* in *fog*	vowel sound of *hot* in *fog*	vowel sound of *hot* in *fog*
/g/ not pronounced in *song*	/g/ not pronounced in *song*	/g/ pronounced in *song*

Midland Dialects

North Midland	South Midland
vowel sound of *thick* in *creek*	vowel sound of *eat* in *creek*
vowel sound of *fought* in *fog*	vowel sound of *fought* in *fog*
vowel sound of *boot* in *food*	vowel sound of *boot* in *food*
vowel sound of *pie* in *nice*	vowel sound of *hot* (lengthened) in *nice*
same vowels in *horse* and *hoarse*	different vowels in *horse* and *hoarse*
vowel sound of *ooze* in *Tuesday*	sounds of *you* in *Tuesday*

Eastern Pennsylvania	Western Pennsylvania
vowel sound of *eat* in *creek*	vowel sound of *eat* in *creek*
vowel sound of *hot* in *fog*	vowel sound of *fought* in *fog*
vowel sound of *boot* in *food*	vowel sound of *foot* in *food*
vowel sound of *pie* in *nice*	vowel sound of *pie* in *nice*
same vowels in *horse* and *hoarse*	same vowels in *horse* and *hoarse*

Southern Dialects

Eastern Virginia	North Carolina	South Carolina–Georgia Low Country
different vowels in *out* and *loud*	same vowels in *out* and *loud*	different vowels in *out* and *loud*
different vowels in *right* and *ride*	same vowels in *right* and *ride*	same vowels in *right* and *ride*
/hw/ sounds in *why*	/hw/ sounds in *why*	no /h/ before /w/ in *why*
vowel sound of *hot* in *crop*	vowel sound of *hot* in *crop*	vowel sound of *fought* in *crop*
vowel sound of *hot* in *long*	vowel sound of *hot* in *long*	vowel sound of *fought* in *long*
vowel sound of *hit* in *fish*	vowel sound of *heat* in *fish*	vowel sound of *hit* in *fish*
afraid rhymes with *head*	*afraid* rhymes with *made*	*afraid* rhymes with *made*
vowel sound of *put* in *bulk*		vowel sound of *putt* in *bulk*

Southern Dialects

Eastern Virginia

different vowels in *out* and *loud*
different vowels in *right* and *ride*
/hw/ sounds in *why*
vowel sound of *hot* in *crop*
vowel sound of *hit* in *fish*
afraid rhymes with *head*
vowel sound of *put* in *bulk*

North Carolina

same vowels in *out* and *loud*
same vowels in *right* and *ride*
/hw/ sounds in *why*
vowel sound of *hot* in *crop*
vowel sound of *heat* in *fish*
afraid rhymes with *made*

South Carolina–Georgia Low Country

different vowels in *out* and *loud*
same vowels in *right* and *ride*

no /h/ before /w/ in *why*
vowel sound of *fought* in *crop*
vowel sound of *fought* in *long*
vowel sound of *hit* in *fish*
afraid rhymes with *made*
vowel sound of *putt* in *bulk*

- Ask the students for examples of pronunciations they have heard which have not yet been introduced into the class, particularly pronunciations used elsewhere in your state. This activity will help the class to differentiate the local dialect from surrounding dialects, distinctions that are usually not made in the discussion of large dialect areas. It would be wise to mention that any of the dialect regions ordinarily mentioned can be broken down into smaller divisions on the basis of a few pronunciations not shared throughout a large dialect area that generally shares most dialect features.

- Ask the students if they are aware of any pronunciation differences between their speech and that of their classmates who come from a different part of town or a different part of the school district. If differences are identified, have the class try to ascertain why these particular differences occur. This activity will emphasize that dialect boundary lines may be drawn to divide a very small geographic area, perhaps even from block to block.

- Have each student write a short scene depicting a communication problem which might occur between speakers of different dialects. For example, a midlander might ask for a *pen* to write with, but a northerner might bring him a *pin* because *pen* is pronounced differently in Northern and Midland dialects.

Topic IV: Morphological Differences among Geographic Dialects in the United States

- Using Reproduction Page 46, have your students classify their dialects as primarily Northern, Midland, or Southern on the basis of the following grammatical forms:

Northern	Midland	Southern
youse (plural of *you*)	you-uns/you-all (South)	you-all
who (plural of *who*)	who all	who
dove (past tense of *dive*)	dived	dived
clim (past tense of *climb*)	clum	clim/clome (eastern Virginia)
see (past tense of *see*)	seen/seed (South)	seed/see (eastern Virginia)
woke up	woke up/got awake (eastern Pennsylvania)	waked up
have gone	have gone/have went	have gone
have drank	have drunk	have drunk

CLASSIFYING DIALECTS BY GRAMMAR

Directions: *See if you can classify your dialect as primarily Northern, Midland, or Southern on the basis of the following grammatical forms. You may not have some of the distinctive grammatical forms given here because some of them are considered nonstandard or old-fashioned.*

Northern	Midland	Southern
youse (plural of *you*)	you-uns/you-all (South)	you-all
who (plural of *who*)	who all	who
dove (past tense of *dive*)	dived	dived
clim (past tense of *climb*)	clum	clim/clome (eastern Virginia)
see (past tense of *see*)	seen/seed (South)	seed/see (eastern Virginia)
woke up	woke up/got awake (eastern Pennsylvania)	waked up
have gone	have gone/have went	have gone
have drank	have drunk	have drunk

• If your students have Midland or Southern dialects, have them classify their dialects further, using Reproduction Page 47, on the basis of the following morphological forms:

Midland

North Midland	South Midland
you-uns (plural of *you*)	you-uns /you-all
seen (past tense of *see*)	seen/seed
woke up	woke up
did (past tense of *do*)	done did
didn't use to	used to didn't
might be able	might could
not sure	not for sure

Eastern Pennsylvania	Western Pennsylvania
you-uns	you-uns
seen	seen
got awake	woke up
did	did
didn't use to	didn't use to
might could	might be able
not sure	not sure

Southern

Eastern Virginia	South Carolina–Georgia Low Country
clome (past tense of *climb*)	clim
see (past tense of see)	seed

• Ask the students for examples of grammatical forms they have heard which have not yet been introduced into the class, particularly grammatical forms used elsewhere in your state. This activity will help to differentiate the local dialect from surrounding dialects, distinctions not usually made in the discussion of large dialect areas. It would be wise to mention that any of the dialect regions ordinarily mentioned can be broken down into smaller divisions on the basis of a few grammatical forms not shared throughout a large dialect area that generally shares most dialect features.

FURTHER CLASSIFYING BY GRAMMAR

Directions: *If your dialect is Midland or Southern, see if you can classify your dialect further on the basis of the following grammatical forms. Some of these forms are old-fashioned or nonstandard, so do not be upset if you do not use all of the forms indicated for your dialect.*

Midland

North Midland	South Midland
you-uns (plural of *you*)	you-uns/you-all
seen (past tense of *see*)	seen/seed
woke up	woke up
did (past tense of *do*)	done did
didn't use to	use to didn't
might be able	might could
not sure	not for sure

Eastern Pennsylvania	Western Pennsylvania
you-uns	you-uns
seen	seen
got awake	woke up
did	did
didn't use to	didn't use to
might could	might be able
not sure	not sure

Southern

Eastern Virginia	South Carolina—Georgia Low Country
clome (past tense of *climb*)	clim
see (past tense of *see*)	seed

- Ask the students whose grandparents live in the local dialect area if they have noticed their grandparents using different grammatical forms than they do. The point of this activity is to emphasize that grammatical differences between dialects are diminishing because of increased education and exposure to mass media.

- Ask the students if they have noticed any grammatical differences between their speech and that of their classmates. If differences are identified, try to ascertain whether the differences reflect older forms of the local dialect or influence of another dialect because of other areas the students, their parents, or their grandparents have lived in.

Topic V: Syntactic Differences among Geographic Dialects in the United States

- Using Reproduction Page 48, have your students classify their dialects as primarily Northern, Midland, or Southern on the basis of the following syntactic expressions:

Northern	Midland	Southern
as well as	all the better	as well as
as far as	all the further	as far as
all to once/all at once	all at once	all at once
quarter to/quarter of (the hour)	quarter till	quarter to
want to get off	want off	want to get off

CLASSIFYING DIALECTS BY SYNTACTIC DIFFERENCES

Directions: See if you can classify your dialect as primarily Northern, Midland, or Southern on the basis of the following ways of saying things. Although you may say some things in more than one column, the majority of your expressions will be in only one column.

Northern	Midland	Southern
as well as	all the better	as well as
as far as	all the further	as far as
all to once/all at once	all at once	all at once
quarter to/quarter of (the hour)	quarter till	quarter to
want to get off	want off	want to get off
wait for (someone)	wait on (not *serve* someone)	wait for
hadn't out (to do something)	oughtn't (except Eastern North Midland)	oughtn't
sick to one's stomach (except in southeastern New England, New York City, and Hudson Valley)	sick at one's stomach/ sick in one's stomach (eastern Pennsylvania)	sick at one's stomach/ sick in one's stomach (eastern Virginia)

wait for (someone)	wait on (not *serve* someone)	wait for
hadn't ought (to do something)	oughtn't (except Eastern North Midland	oughtn't
sick to one's stomach (except in southeastern New England, New York City, and Hudson Valley)	sick at one's stomach/ sick in one's stomach (eastern Pennsylvania)	sick at one's stomach/ sick in one's stomach (easter Virginia)

- Using Reproduction Page 49, have your students classify their dialect further on the basis of the following syntactic expressions:

Northern

Eastern New England

in line

lives on Pleasant Street

are buttons on the coat

burn coal in the stove

sick to one's stomach/sick at one's stomach (southeastern NE)

Inland North

in line

lives on Pleasant Street

are buttons on the coat/are buttons onto the coat

burn coal into the stove/burn coal in the stove

sick to one's stomach

New York City and Hudson Valley

on line

lives in Pleasant Street

are buttons on the coat

burn coal in the stove

sick at one's stomach

Midland

North Midland	South Midland
didn't use to	use to didn't
bitten by a dog	dog-bit
sick at one's stomach	sick at one's stomach
tire "become tired"	give out
met	met
all gone	all gone
woke up	woke up/waked up (eastern Kentucky)

Eastern Pennsylvania	Western Pennsylvania
didn't use to	didn't use to
bitten by a dog	bitten by a dog
sick on one's stomach	sick at one's stomach
tire	tire
met	ran onto
all "all gone"	all gone
got awake	woke up

Southern

Eastern Virginia	South Carolina–Georgia Low Country
ran up on "met"	met
bitten by a dog	dog-bit
for purpose	on purpose
sick in one's stomach/	sick at one's stomach
sick at one's stomach	

- Ask the students for examples of syntactic expressions they have heard that have not yet been introduced into the class, particularly expressions used elsewhere in your state. This activity will help to differentiate the local dialect from surrounding dialects, distinctions not usually made in the discussion of large dialect areas. It would be wise to mention that any of the dialect regions ordinarily discussed can be broken down into small areas on the basis of a few expressions not shared throughout a large dialect area that generally shares most dialect features.

- Particularly if the students have had trouble with previous activities because they no longer use the dialectal expressions given there, ask them for examples of expressions they have heard older persons in the local area use but they themselves do not use. This activity will reinforce the idea that syntactic dialect differences are decreasing with increased education and exposure to mass media.

FURTHER CLASSIFYING DIALECTS

Directions: *See if you can classify your dialect even further after you have decided whether it is primarily Northern, Midland, or Southern on the basis of the following expressions. Again you may not use all of the expressions in the particular column representing your dialect, because some of them are used only by older persons.*

Northern

Eastern New England	Inland North	New York City and Hudson Valley
in line	in line	on line
lives on Pleasant Street	lives on Pleasant Street	lives in Pleasant Street
are buttons on the coat	are buttons on the coat/are buttons onto the coat	are buttons on the coat
burn coal in the stove	burn coal into the stove/burn coal in the stove	burn coal in the stove
sick to one's stomach/sick at one's stomach (south-eastern New England)	sick to one's stomach	sick at one's stomach

Midland

North Midland	South Midland
didn't use to	use to didn't
bitten by a dog	dog-bit
sick at one's stomach	sick at one's stomach
tire "become tired"	give out
met	met
all gone	all gone
woke up	woke up/waked up (eastern Kentucky)

Eastern Pennsylvania	Western Pennsylvania
didn't use to	didn't use to
bitten by a dog	bitten by a dog
sick on one's stomach	sick at one's stomach
tire	tire
met	ran onto
all "all gone"	all gone
got awake	woke up

Southern

Eastern Virginia	South Carolina–Georgia Low Country
ran up on "met"	met
bitten by a dog	dog-bit
for purpose	on purpose
sick in one's stomach/sick at one's stomach	sick at one's stomach

- If your students are reading any American literature by dialect writers, ask them to compile lists of dialect expressions that they encounter in their reading. Southern writers like William Faulkner, Southwestern writers like J. Frank Dobie and John Steinbeck, or South Midland writers like Jesse Stuart are good authors for this kind of activity.

ASSESSING ACHIEVEMENT OF OBJECTIVES

Ongoing Evaluation

The extent to which students have mastered the concepts covered under the five topics in this chapter can be measured by any of the activities assigned to class members as individuals, particularly the writing activities.

Final Evaluation

For an overall evaluation of the students' grasp of the concepts in this chapter, if all topics in the chapter have been taught, a test constructed directly from the list of student objectives for the chapter as listed on page 109 can be used. In lieu of that option, one might compose a test from among the following items:

1. Identify the broad dialect category of a speaker who uses the words *string beans, pail, corn on the cob,* and *wishbone* (or *green beans, bucket, roasting ears,* and *piece* meaning *distance*) (or *snap beans, bucket, roasting ears, carry* meaning *take* or *escort,* and *pulley bone*).

2. Give three vocabulary items that are part of the dialect vocabulary of your region.

3. Give one example of the vocabulary items of your geographic area that reflects the contact of English speakers with each of the foreign languages that are or have been important in your region.

4. Identify the broad dialect category of a speaker who uses the pronunciations of /s/ in *grease, greasy,* and the middle of *Mrs.,* the vowel of *put* in *root,* and different vowels in *tin* and *ten* (or the same vowels in *Mary* and *merry,* /s/ in the middle of *Mrs.,* /r/ in *park,* and an extra /r/ in *wash*) (or /z/ in *grease, greasy,* and the middle of *Mrs.,* /r/ not pronounced in *park,* and the vowel sound of *boot* in *root*).

5. Give three pronunciations that help to identify your geographic dialect.

6. Identify the broad dialect category of a speaker who says *dove* for the past tense of *dive, woke up,* and *youse* as a plural of *you* (or *dived, have went,* and *you-uns*) (or *dived, waked up, you-all,* but not *who-all*).

7. Give three grammatical forms that occur in your dialect but that may not occur in other regional dialects.

8. Identify the broad dialect category of a speaker who says *quarter to* or *quarter of, hadn't ought,* and *want to get off* (or *quarter till, sick at one's stomach, all the further,* and *want off*) (or *quarter to, oughtn't, want to get off,* and *as well as* rather than *all the better*).

9. Give two expressions of your local dialect that help to identify the region of the country where you live.

10. Give five causes of dialect differences in the United States.

RESOURCES FOR TEACHING ABOUT
REGIONAL DIALECT DIFFERENCES

Below is a selected and annotated list of resources useful for teaching the topics in this chapter, divided into audiovisual materials and print materials and arranged in order of ascending difficulty. Special strengths and weaknesses are mentioned in the annotations. Addresses of publishers or distributors can be found in the alphabetical list on pages 263-265 in Appendix A. Films are black and white unless otherwise indicated.

I. CAUSES OF REGIONAL DIALECT DIFFERENCES IN THE UNITED STATES

Audiovisual Materials

Regional Backgrounds. Set of four sound filmstrips (sound on record or cassette tape) called *New England, The South, The Mid-Atlantic,* and *The Southwest,* Filmstrip House. Provides a settlement history of each region dealing with both English and non-English settlers and the development of regional subcultures.

Settling the New World. Set of six color filmstrips called *Spanish Colonization, French Colonization, New England Colonization, The Middle Colonies, The Southern Colonies,* and *Colonial Government,* Encyclopaedia Brittanica Educational Corporation. Shows differences among settlement groups during colonial period.

U.S. Growth and Expansion. 27 color transparencies of maps with overlay transparencies, Encyclopaedia Brittanica Educational Corporation. Shows European colonization, routes of westward expansion, and transportation.

Print

"Eastern Settlement," pp. 17-19 in *Dialects of American English* by Carroll E. Reed. Provides a general overview of dialect differences caused by settlement patterns in the English colonies in North America. Paperbound, University of Massachusetts Press, 1973.

"The Origin of the Dialectal Differences in Spoken American English," by Hans Kurath, pp. 12-21 in *A Various Language,* edited by Juanita V. Williamson and Virginia M. Burke. Provides the most complete short settlement history and discussion of the westward movement of English-speaking people in America emphasizing where the various groups of settlers came from in England and the rest of the British Isles. Hardbound, Holt, Rinehart, and Winston, 1971.

"Dialect Differences and Their Causes," pp. 480-485 in *The Structure of American English* by W. Nelson Francis. Gives a short general introduction to the various causes of dialect differentiation. Hardbound, The Ronald Press Co., 1958.

"The Westward Movement," pp. 41-44 in *Dialects of American English* by Carroll E. Reed. Provides a general overview of migrations from the East Coast of the United States to the Midwest after the Revolutionary War. Paperbound, University of Massachusetts Press, 1973.

"Forces Underlying Dialect Distribution in America," pp. 500-511 in *The Structure of American English* by W. Nelson Francis. Provides an overview with some specific detail of the pattern of early settlement and westward movement in the United States. Hardbound, The Ronald Press Co., 1958.

"Area Linguistics and the Teacher of English," by Hans Kurath, pp. 90-95 in *A Linguistics Reader,* edited by Graham Wilson. Discusses attitudes teachers should have and actions they should take concerning dialect differences and what they should know about dialect differences. Recommended for teachers. Paperbound, Harper and Row, 1967.

"The Reasons for Dialect Differences," by Roger W. Shuy, pp. 344-349 in *Language* edited by Virginia P. Clark et al. Discusses how patterns of settlement history, population shifts, and physical geography have created dialect differences in the United States. Paperbound, St. Martin's Press, 1972.

"The Influence of Foreign Language Settlements," pp. 527-534 in *The Structure of American English* by W. Nelson Francis. Illustrates influences on American English dialects of German, French, Scandinavian, and African languages, etc. Hardbound, The Ronald Press Co., 1958.

"Language on the American Frontier," by Frederic G. Cassidy, pp. 85-101 in *Aspects of American English*, 2d ed., edited by Elizabeth M. Kerr and Ralph M. Aderman. Discusses early settlement history in the English-speaking colonies and borrowings into American English of words from American Indian languages, French, Spanish, Dutch, and German, and coinage of new words. Provides study questions and exercises. Paperbound, Harcourt Brace Jovanovich, 1971.

"Early American Speech Adoptions from Foreign Tongues," by Thomas Pyles, pp. 69-86 in *A Various Language*, edited by Juanita V. Williamson and Virginia M. Burke. Illustrates with copious examples the influence on American English vocabulary of American Indian languages, African languages, Dutch, German, French, and Spanish. Hardbound, Holt, Rinehart and Winston, 1971.

II. REGIONAL VOCABULARY DIFFERENCES IN THE UNITED STATES

Audiovisual Materials

Dialects. Film, part of *Language and Linguistics* Series, 30 minutes, 1958, Indiana University Audio-Visual Center. Demonstrates regional vocabulary items and how people tend to drop specifically regional words from their vocabulary in favor of more general words as their education increases.

Our Changing Language. Record, National Council of Teachers of English, 1965. Gives readings of twelve regional dialects of the United States as well as Old English, Middle English, and Early Modern English.

Print

"Eastern Words," pp. 21-27 in *Dialects of American English* by Carroll E. Reed. Gives vocabulary items differentiating dialects in the eastern third of the United States. See also maps, pp. 85-93, which illustrate areas in which specific vocabulary items occur. Paperbound, University of Massachusetts Press, 1973.

"Vocabulary Differences," pp. 266-267 in *A Survey of Modern Grammars*, 2d ed., by Jeanne H. Herndon. Provides a short list of vocabulary items to differentiate Northern, Midland, and Southern dialect areas. Paperbound, Holt, Rinehart and Winston, 1976.

"American Dialect Geography," pp. 142-147 in *Aspects of Language* by Dwight Bolinger. Shows principal dialect areas of the eastern third of the United States, vocabulary isoglosses in the Midwest, and dialect mixing in Colorado with clear maps. Paperbound, Harcourt, Brace and World, 1968.

"Regional and Local Words," by Hans Kurath, pp. 182-190 in *Aspects of American English*, 2d ed., edited by Elizabeth M. Kerr and Ralph M. Aderman. Discusses contrasting vocabulary items in the eastern United States. Provides study questions and exercises. Paperbound, Harcourt Brace Jovanovich, 1971.

"What Do You Call It?" by Hans Kurath, pp. 245-254 in *A Various Language*, edited by Juanita V. Williamson and Virginia M. Burke. Discusses contrasting words for the same thing in the various regional dialects of the eastern United States and identifies the geographic boundaries between these dialects. Has two maps showing the occurrences of specific words. Hardbound, Holt, Rinehart and Winston, 1971.

"Sectional Atlas Studies," pp. 45-70 in *Dialects of American English* by Carroll E. Reed. Gives vocabulary differences that distinguish dialects in the Great Lakes area, the upper Middle West, Texas, Colorado, California, the Pacific Northwest, and the Rocky Mountain area with the greatest detail for California and the Pacific Northwest. See also maps, pp. 98-116. Paperbound, University of Massachusetts Press, 1973.

"The Principal Dialect Areas of the United States," pp. 511-527 in *The Structure of American English* by W. Nelson Francis. Gives distinctive vocabulary items of eighteen dialect areas in the eastern United States. See also maps, pp. 584-585. Hardbound, The Ronald Press Co., 1958.

"Principal and Subsidiary Dialect Areas in the North-Central States" by Albert H. Marckwardt, pp. 220-230 in *Readings in Applied English Linguistics,* 2d ed., edited by Harold B. Allen. Discusses and provides six maps showing isoglosses of vocabulary items for the dialect areas of North Dakota, South Dakota, Nebraska, Minnesota, Iowa, Wisconsin, Illinois, Indiana, Ohio, Kentucky, and Michigan. Paperbound, Appleton-Century-Crofts, 1967.

"The Primary Dialect Areas of the Upper Midwest," by Harold B. Allen, pp. 366-378 in *A Various Language,* edited by Juanita V. Williamson and Virginia M. Burke. Defines dialect areas in Iowa, Nebraska, South Dakota, North Dakota, and Minnesota using vocabulary and pronunciation differences and illustrates the areas on a map. Hardbound, Holt, Rinehart and Winston, 1971.

"Dialect Distribution and Settlement Patterns in the Great Lakes Region," by Alva L. Davis, pp. 357-365 in *A Various Language,* edited by Juanita V. Williamson and Virginia M. Burke. Discusses vocabulary to define dialect areas of Michigan, Ohio, Indiana, and Illinois. Hardbound, Holt, Rinehart and Winston, 1971.

"A Southeast Texas Dialect Study," by Arthur Norman, pp. 309-328 in *A Various Language,* edited by Juanita V. Williamson and Virginia M. Burke. Discusses distinctive vocabulary items as well as pronunciations and grammatical forms of the area. Hardbound, Holt, Rinehart and Winston, 1971.

"North Carolina Accents," by Lucia C. Morgan, pp. 268-279 in *A Various Language,* edited by Juanita V. Williamson and Virginia M. Burke. Gives a short settlement history of North Carolina and distinctive vocabulary and pronunciation of the area. Hardbound, Holt, Rinehart and Winston, 1971.

"Notes on the Sounds and Vocabulary of Gullah," by Lorenzo D. Turner, pp. 121-135 in *A Various Language,* edited by Juanita V. Williamson and Virginia M. Burke. Shows influence of West African languages on the vocabulary in the Gullah or Geechee dialect of English spoken by blacks of the Sea Islands and coastal South Carolina and Georgia. Hardbound, Holt, Rinehart and Winston, 1971.

III. PHONOLOGICAL DIFFERENCES AMONG GEOGRAPHIC DIALECTS IN THE UNITED STATES

Audiovisual Materials

Dialects. Film, part of *Language and Linguistics* Series, 30 minutes, 1958, Indiana University Audio-Visual Center. Provides a clear differentiation of regional dialects on the basis of pronunciations and emphasizes that phonological features are the best indicators of regional dialects.

Cassette recording to accompany *Culture, Class, and Language Variety,* edited by A. L. Davis. Casette has recording of passages by four dialect speakers (transcribed in book); book focuses primarily on nonstandard dialects. Paperbound, National Council of Teachers of English, 1972.

Americans Speaking. Record and pamphlet, 1967. Record has speakers from six dialect areas speaking conversationally and reading set passages; pamphlet gives texts of passages and a checklist for listening.

Print

"East Coast Dialects," pp. 214-215 in *Language and Linguistics* by Julia S. Falk. Provides a short, clear discussion of the major pronunciation features separating Northern, Midland, and Southern dialects of the eastern United States. Paperbound, Xerox College Publishing, 1973.

"Grease and Greasy: Geographical Variation," by E. Bagby Atwood, pp. 424-433 in *A Various Language,* edited by Juanita V. Williamson and Virginia M. Burke. Discusses and shows on a map the areas in the eastern third of the United States where the two words are pronounced with /s/ and /z/. Hardbound, Holt, Rinehart and Winston, 1971.

"American Regionalisms," by John Nist, pp. 165-171 in *Aspects of American English,* 2d ed., edited by Elizabeth M. Kerr and Ralph M. Aderman. Divides Northern dialects into three groups,

Midland dialects into six groups, and identifies a general Southern dialect on the basis of specific pronunciations. Provides a map, study questions, and exercises. Paperbound, Harcourt Brace Jovanovich, 1971.

"Sectional Atlas Studies," pp. 45–70 in *Dialects of American English* by Carrroll E. Reed. Gives pronunciation differences that differentiate dialects in the Great Lakes area, Texas, Colorado, and Wisconsin. See also maps, pp. 94, 102. Paperbound, University of Massachusetts Press, 1973.

"The Principal Dialect Areas of the United States," pp. 511–527 in *The Structure of American English* by W. Nelson Francis. Gives distinguishing pronunciation differences of eighteen dialect areas in the eastern United States. See also map, p. 582. Hardbound, The Ronald Press Co., 1958.

"The Primary Dialect Areas of the Upper Midwest," by Harold B. Allen, pp. 366–378 in *A Various Language,* edited by Juanita V. Williamson and Virginia M. Burke. Defines dialect areas in Iowa, Nebraska, South Dakota, North Dakota, and Minnesota using pronunciation and vocabulary differences. Provides a map. Hardbound, Holt, Rinehart and Winston, 1971.

"Pronunciation in the Pacific Northwest," by Carroll E. Reed, pp. 379–386 in *A Various Language,* edited by Juanita V. Williamson and Virginia M. Burke. Discusses most frequent and variant pronunciations in Washington, Idaho, and adjacent sections of Oregon and Montana. Hardbound, Holt, Rinehart and Winston, 1971.

"North Carolina Accents," by Lucia C. Morgan, pp. 268–279 in *A Various Language,* edited by Juanita V. Williamson and Virginia M. Burke. Discusses settlement history of North Carolina and traces distinctive pronunciations back to historical factors. Hardbound, Holt, Rinehart and Winston, 1971.

"A Southeast Texas Dialect Study," by Arthur Norman, pp. 309–328 in *A Various Language,* edited by Juanita V. Williamson and Virginia M. Burke. Discusses distinctive pronunciations as well as vocabulary and grammatical forms of that area. Hardbound, Holt, Rinehart and Winston, 1971.

"Some Eastern Virginia Pronunciation Features," E. Bagby Atwood, pp. 255–267 in *A Various Language,* edited by Juanita V. Williamson and Virginia M. Burke. Provides seven maps showing occurrence of distinctive pronunciations and

discusses these features, which occur in the region. Hardbound, Holt, Rinehart and Winston, 1971.

"Notes on the Sounds and Vocabulary of Gullah," by Lorenzo D. Turner, pp. 121–135 in *A Various Language,* edited by Juanita V. Williamson and Virginia M. Burke. Shows influence of West African languages on pronunciation in the Gullah or Geechee dialect of English spoken by blacks on the Sea Islands and coastal South Carolina and Georgia. Hardbound, Holt, Rinehart and Winston, 1971.

"The Pronunciation of English in Metropolitan Chicago," by Lee A. Pederson, pp. 525–548 in *A Various Language,* edited by Juanita V. Williamson and Virginia M. Burke. Discusses phonological distinctions of the dialect of the Greater Chicago area. Not recommended for students. Hardbound, Holt, Rinehart and Winston, 1971.

"The Pronunciation of English in San Francisco," by David DeCamp, pp. 549–569 in *A Various Language,* edited by Juanita V. Williamson and Virginia M. Burke. Discusses phonological patterns in use in San Francisco. Not recommended for students. Hardbound, Holt, Rinehart and Winston, 1971.

"The Speech of San Antonio, Texas," by Janet B. Sawyer, pp. 570–582 in *A Various Language,* edited by Juanita V. Willimson and Virginia M. Burke. Discusses the pronunciations of English by both Anglo and Chicano speakers of the city. Not recommended for students. Hardbound, Holt, Rinehart and Winston, 1971.

"The Position of the Charleston Dialect," by Raven I. McDavid, pp. 569–606 in *A Various Language,* edited by Juanita V. Williamson and Virginia M. Burke. Discusses distinctive pronunciation and other features of the dialect of Charleston, South Carolina, and their spread into parts of Georgia and other parts of South Carolina. Not recommended for students. Hardbound, Holt, Rinehart and Winston, 1971.

"The Pronunciation of English in Boston, Massachusetts: Vowels and Consonants," by Robert L. Parslow, pp. 610–624 in *A Various Language,* edited by Juanita V. Williamson and Virginia M. Burke. Discusses and illustrates with eight maps the three subdialects of the Greater Boston area. Not recommended for students. Hardbound, Holt, Rinehart and Winston, 1971.

IV. MORPHOLOGICAL DIFFERENCES AMONG GEOGRAPHIC DIALECTS IN THE UNITED STATES

Audiovisual Materials

Regional Variations. Color film, part of *Language . . . the Social Arbiter* Series, 28 minutes, Stuart Finley. Discusses the major regional dialects of the United States. Recommended for teachers.

Print

"Eastern Grammar," pp. 37–39 in *Dialects of American English* by Carroll E. Reed. Shows verb forms characteristic of regional dialect areas. See also maps, pp. 94–96. Paperbound, The World Publishing Co., 1967.

"Differences in Verb Forms," pp. 267–269 in *A Survey of Modern English Grammars,* 2d ed., by Jeanne H. Herndon. Provides a short list of past tense and past participle forms whose distribution varies geographically among Northern, Midland, and Southern dialects. Paperbound, Holt, Rinehart and Winston, 1976.

"The Principal Dialect Areas of the United States," pp. 511–527 in *The Structure of American English* by W. Nelson Francis. Gives distinguish-ing morphological features of eighteen dialect areas in the eastern United States. See also map, p. 583. Hardbound, The Ronald Press Co., 1958.

"Sectional Atlas Studies," pp. 45–70 in *Dialects of American English* by Carroll E. Reed. Gives morphological differences that differentiate dialects in the Great Lakes area, the Rocky Mountain area, and the Pacific Northwest. See also maps, pp. 98, 102, 104, and 113. Paperbound, University of Massachusetts Press, 1973.

"Grammatical Differences in the North Central States," by Raven I. McDavid and Virginia G. McDavid, pp. 341–356 in *A Various Language,* edited by Juanita V. Williamson and Virginia M. Burke. Discusses morphological and syntactic peculiarities within the states of Michigan, Wisconsin, Ohio, Indiana, Illinois, Kentucky, and the southern part of Ontario and illustrates their distribution on four maps. Hardbound, Holt, Rinehart and Winston, 1971.

"A Southeast Texas Dialect Study," by Arthur Nor-man, pp. 309–328 in *A Various Language,* edited by Juanita V. Williamson and Virginia M. Burke. Gives verb forms as well as pronunciation and vocabulary distinctive to the area. Hardbound, Holt, Rinehart and Winston, 1971.

V. SYNTACTIC DIFFERENCES AMONG GEOGRAPHIC DIALECTS IN THE UNITED STATES

Print

"The Principal Dialect Areas of the United States," by Raven I. McDavid, pp. 26–41 in *Contemporary English,* edited by David L. Shores. Gives distin-guishing syntactic and other dialect features of eighteen dialect areas in the eastern United States. Paperbound, J. B. Lippincott Co., 1972.

"The Principal Dialect Areas of the United States," pp. 511–527 in *The Structures of American English* by W. Nelson Francis. Gives distinctive syntactic and other dialect features of eighteen dialect areas in the eastern United States. Hard-bound, The Ronald Press Co., 1958.

"Grammatical Differences in the North Central States," by Raven I. McDavid and Virginia G. McDavid, pp. 341–356 in *A Various Language,* edited by Juanita V. Williamson and Virginia M. Burke. Discusses syntactic and morphological features occurring in Michigan, Wisconsin, Ohio, Illinois, Kentucky, and southern Ontario and illustrates their distribution on four maps. Hard-bound, Holt, Rinehart and Winston, 1971.

"A Note on It Is/There Is," by Juanita V. Williamson, pp. 434–436 in *A Various Language,* edited by Juanita V. Williamson and Virginia M. Burke. Discusses the use of *it is* rather than *there is* in Kentucky, Tennessee, Mississippi, Texas, West Virginia, and the Chesapeake Bay area. Hardbound, Holt, Rinehart and Winston, 1971.

"The Position of the Charleston Dialect," by Raven I. McDavid, pp. 596–609 in *A Various Language,* edited by Juanita V. Williamson and Virginia M. Burke. Discusses syntactic as well as other features of the Charleston, South Carolina, dialect and their spread into parts of Georgia and other parts of South Carolina. Hardbound, Holt, Rinehart and Winston, 1971.

7

Social Dialect Differences

This chapter focuses on the social significance of dialect differences and the various social factors that influence one's dialect. A practical application of this study is the development of an awareness on the part of the students of the judgments they make (usually subconsciously) about others because of the others' use of language; the students may begin to question the accuracy of these judgments once they are aware that they are making them. Another practical application is the development of an awareness on the part of the students of what their language reveals about themselves and the kinds of judgments others make about them from their language.

Initially, the student should learn about the several factors that determine social dialects other than the obvious factor of social class. The factors to be introduced as determinants of social dialect differences include occupation, education, sex, age, religion, politics, leisure-time activities, social group affiliations, and occasion or situation. Many of these factors are interrelated, and occupation and education strongly determine social class itself.

Then the idea that standard English and nonstandard English are indications of social status may be introduced. Since standard English is regionally determined in the United States, a discussion of what is standard and nonstandard can be introduced with an examination of the particular features of regional standards of English. Then the processes by which a regional dialect becomes a social dialect should be introduced.

Later, black English as a social dialect should be examined. Its features can be introduced and discussed. Then the explanations of how and why black English dialects developed may be appropriate. The teacher may anticipate some lively discussion when this topic is being studied.

Finally, the issue of Spanish-flavored English may be introduced as a social dialect. Its distinctive features should be discussed as well as the causes and social meanings of such a dialect. Again, class discussion may become heated with this topic because it raises certain political issues.

Any of the four topics in this chapter may be introduced alone, but the order suggested here is meant to indicate the relative importance of each topic. The last two topics are probably most relevant when the local area has large numbers of persons who speak a dialect of black English or of Spanish-flavored English.

OBJECTIVES

If all of the topics in this chapter are chosen, the student should, at the end of the unit, be able to:

1. Illustrate how occupation or profession enters into one's social dialect
2. Explain the part that education plays in social dialects
3. Give examples of language that reflect the age of a speaker
4. Give examples of language that reflect the sex of a speaker
5. Give examples of how religion, political leanings, social group membership, and interests or hobbies may be reflected in a speaker's dialect
6. Illustrate how his or her language should change in different social circumstances
7. Explain his or her own attitude toward speakers of Southern (or Northern) (or Appalachian) dialects or ethnic dialects
8. Give major features of black English dialects
9. Illustrate that black English has a system like any other dialect
10. Explain why black English dialects have developed and been perpetuated
11. Identify major features of Spanish-flavored English

CONTENT OVERVIEW

How Factors Other Than Class, Region, and Ethnic Background Influence Social Dialects

A social dialect involves more than just those features of a person's speech which identify his or her membership in a particular social class or caste, although those are the most obvious parameters by which social judgments are made about a person's speech. Other social factors that are reflected in a person's speech are occupation or profession, education, sex, age, occasion, religion, political orientation, interest in particular sports or amusements, and social group affiliation.

A person who works on a manufacturing assembly line will obviously have a different vocabulary than an accountant, a farmer, a doctor, or a lawyer because each of these persons deals with different things at work. The Latinate vocabulary of doctors and lawyers, of course, also reflects an educational level and, in the United States, a social class; these professionals are also likely to speak a dialect with identifiable syntactic characteristics. Each profession that requires some kind of educational certification, such as teaching and social work, will have a dialect reflecting the concerns of that profession in its vocabulary and the educational level of the profession in its grammar and syntax. Even such diverse occupations as professional basketball, interior decoration, and garbage collection contribute to the social dialect of persons engaged in those kinds of work.

As has been hinted at already, there is often a correlation between occupation and education. It is common to divide social dialects into three categories on the basis of educational achievement: educated or standard English, vernacular English, and uneducated English. Educated or standard English is that generally used by college-educated persons who have a profession that requires its use or persons who were born into families that speak it. There is usually little variation, except in phonology, in this social dialect from geographic region to geographic region. Vernacular English is that generally used by people with at least high school educations who are employed in service, skilled labor, or white-collar jobs. Vernacular English varies more from geographical region to geographical region than does educated English. Uneducated English, as the name implies, is the social dialect spoken by persons with little education and who generally perform unskilled labor. This dialect reflects regional and nonstandard features more than do the other educational dialects. It is obvious that this classification generally parallels social class distinctions, and, as it is possible to divide the population into more than three social classes, it is also possible to set up more than three classifications of social dialects reflecting educational levels.

Since the educational level in the United States has been increasing, there is also likely to be some correlation between educational level and age, another factor that influences social dialects. In addition to educational differences reflected in social dialects of persons of different ages, it is obvious that older people are more likely to use old-fashioned words like *spider* for *skillet* or archaic expressions like *puts me in the mind of* for *remember* than are younger people. Similarly, teenagers are likely to use the slang of the current generation, while their parents are stuck with the slang which was current when they were growing up. The most obvious examples of age-related social dialects are those of children; very few adults use words like *pee-pee, wee-wee, go potty,* and very few people older than elementary school children use number 1 and number 2 as reasons for going to a restroom except when talking to children.

As these last examples indicate, one talks differently in different social situations, and one of the factors that changes the situation or occasion is the age of the person being spoken to. It is not entirely appropriate for an adult who has been asked by a five-year-old child if one of our four-letter words is a "bad" word to reply, "not intrinsically." Students can be made to understand how the age of the person being spoken to affects their social dialect by pointing out that they talk differently to their grandparents, to their parents, to their age mates, and to little children. Other factors that influence the situation and thus the social dialect they use are the degree of formality or informality and the degree of intimacy. For example, they will probably speak differently to adults who have the different roles in their lives of employer, teacher, and parent. They will certainly speak differently to their girlfriend or boyfriend, to close friends of the same sex, and to strangers their age whom they meet.

Sex, then, is another factor that influences one's social dialect. Although this influence on one's social dialect is weaker now than in the past because women are being removed from the pedestal and are being recognized as fellow human beings, there still is a greater tendency for males to use obscene or profane language than for females (at least in mixed company). Similarly, the occupational vocabulary of jobs that were considered men's jobs or women's jobs in the past such as auto mechanic, truck driver, homemaker, and nurse is becoming less of a social dialect influence now than in the past; however, very few men have the courage to use adjectives like *darling* or *precious* (except when referring to *gems*).

Sports or other amusements that interest a person will influence that person's social dialect, and these may reflect some dichotomy on the basis of sexual differences. Despite some notable exceptions such as famous football players who have taken up needlepoint, males are probably more likely to talk about wing-T formations, full court presses, and hook shots, and women are more likely to talk about cross stitches and latch hooks. The point is that one's interests are reflected in one's speech. We have had some presidents recently, for example, who appeared by their language to be playing football rather than running the country. Card players are likely to talk about trumps, deuces, and bowers or use "according to Hoyle."

Religious affiliations influence social dialects to the extent that phrases like *go to mass* (Catholic), *go to church* (Protestant), and *go to temple, go to shul,* or *go to pray* (Jewish) are likely to identify one as a member of a certain social group. Similarly, only fundamentalist Protestants talk about "being saved"; only Catholics use the phrase "separated brethren"; and only Jews (and, of course, Mormons) talk much about "Gentiles."

Political views or affiliations are also reflected in social dialects. Whether one considers the United States a republic or a democracy is likely to indicate a particular orientation. People who refer to a lot of other people as "communists" are likely to be right wing themselves. Of course, only communists talk much about "the proletariat," "the masses," or "the working classes."

Social group affiliation like religious or political group affiliation tends to be reflected in one's social dialect. Lodge members often refer to other members as "Brother so and so," and people who talk about *worshipful masters, worthy matrons, commanders,* or *tail twisters* clearly reveal their social group connections.

Social Features of Regional Dialects

Many of these parameters of social dialect reflect, to some degree, on the more obvious framework, social class, by which social dialects are defined. Additionally, of course, the use of standard English by the upper class and much of the middle class makes standard English a social dialect and the various forms of nonstandard English social dialects as indications of social class. Of course, what is considered standard English varies from one geographic area to another. For example, the upper class (as well as the lower class) in the tidewater area of South Carolina speak a dialect in which postvocalic /r/ is not pronounced, while the middle class is likely to pronounce it. Thus the absence of postvocalic /r/ can be considered a prestigious factor, and its absence a nonprestigious one. On the other hand, in New York City, the absence of postvocalic /r/ is nonprestigious, and its presence is prestigious. The pronunciation of /ð/ (the voiced *th*) in words like *the, this,* and *then* is everywhere prestigious, and the substitution of /d/ in these words is clearly a lower social class feature. The pronunciation of the word *roof* with the vowel in *put* is standard in most of the Midwest but uneducated in the Northeast and vice versa for the pronunciation of the word with the vowel in *shoot*. The pronunciation of /z/ in *greasy* is associated with the lower class in the North where /s/ is the upper-class and middle-class pronunciation, but the /z/ pronunciation is characteristic of the upper and middle classes of the South where the /s/ pronunciation is nonstandard.

There is a general tendency to view any regional dialect feature in a person's speech as nonstandard whether it was in the region from which the person came or not when that person moves to another geographic dialect area unless the person is clearly identifiable as upper class. When a large number of persons move from one geographic area to another, their regional dialect is quickly viewed as a class dialect. Notable examples of this have occurred in Akron, Ohio, where a large number of West Virginians have migrated to work in the rubber plants, and in a small town in Michigan where half the population is originally from the same area in Mississippi. In large industrial cities of the North, where large numbers of persons from the poor, rural areas of the South have migrated to work in factories, their regional dialects are almost always conceived as social dialects, and generally lower-class social dialects; Detroit is the classic example where this occurs.

This phenomenon of a regional dialect becoming a social dialect is particularly likely to happen if the region of the particular dialect is looked down upon by other regions of the country and, as sometimes happens, the region itself has an inferiority complex. In the latter case, speakers of the regional dialect may claim to be proud of their dialect and extremely defensive about it, but their defensiveness reveals an awareness of how others look at the region. The regional dialects that most frequently evoke a negative social judgment by speakers of other regional dialects are the dialects of rural New England, of the East Midland area known as Appalachia, and of the Deep South. Even John F. Kennedy's dialect which was from urban rather than rural eastern New England evoked ridicule. For a long time, southerners were aware that it was nearly impossible for someone from the Deep South to be elected president. Of course, for an outlander to call an Appalachian a hillbilly is to invite a fight.

Confusing the issue of class dialects in the United States is the problem of caste. While it is true that any dialect of American English that shows much influence of the language of a non-English ethnic group is likely not to be considered upper class, dialects that are identified with so-called racial or ethnic minorities (which function like castes in America) are almost always stigmatized as lower class, regardless of the social class of the person speaking them. The major minority groups which function as castes in America are, obviously, blacks and Spanish-speaking Americans, and their dialects, then, function as social dialects.

Black English as Caste Dialects

A cautionary note is appropriate when dealing with black English. Although many of the studies do not recognize this obvious fact, there is no *one* black English dialect. It is obvious that blacks living in different parts of the country and in different social circumstances will speak different dialects; the same general factors that affect American dialects in general will also affect black dialects in particular. The description of black English that follows, then, will be only of characteristics that many black English dialects share; they may not be characteristics of black English in your local area, and they may be characteristics of the dialect of white speakers in your area as well, particularly if you live in the South or South Midland.

Many black English dialects delete final sounds in words, particularly the /r/, /l/, /t/, /d/, /s/, and /z/ sounds. Since the /s/, /z/, /t/, and /d/ sounds are the most frequent forms of the noun plural inflection, the noun possessive inflection, the verb third person singular inflection, the verb past tense inflection, and the verb past participle inflection, this means that black English dialects often lack these formally marked grammatical concepts and, from the point of view of standard English, frequently lack agreement between subjects and verbs. The consonants /ð/ and /θ/ (the first sounds in *then* and *thin*, respectively) are commonly replaced by /d/ and /t/ initially and by /v/ and /f/ finally as in *de* (the), *ting* (thing), *bave* (bathe), and *trufe* (truth); these substitutions are also common in the dialects of whites in the East Midland mountains and of whites who speak a dialect of English that is colored by some other European languages.

Some black English dialects have the following nonstandard morphological and syntactic features. The absence of the copula *be* (and all its forms) before subject complements (*he the teacher, he mean*) and before locatives (*he over here*) and the absence of the auxiliary *be* (in all its forms) before present participles (*he working today* and before *gonna,* that is, *going to* (*he gonna get hurt*), is characteristic of many black English dialects in the present tense. In the past tense, the verb *was* is often used to indicate actions completed in the past (perfect) as in *you was a good baby* in contrast to *been* to indicate past actions continuing to the present or not being completed at a definite time in the past (imperfect) as in *he been there a long time*; with other verbs, the auxiliary *done* indicates the perfect aspect as in *I done went there* in contrast to the auxiliary *been,* which indicates the imperfect aspect as in *she been had a sickness for a long time.* The auxiliaries *will* and *would* are usually deleted in black English (rather than contracted as in most white dialects), so that simple future statements will have an uninflected verb form and no auxiliary as in *I be back* or *I come back tomorrow*; this simple future contrasts with the intentional future, which is marked by *gonna* before the verb as in *things gonna change now.*

These features of black English are considered features of a lower-class dialect. However, at least one-fifth of American blacks have none of the features of black English in their speech, and many others have only a few. It is interesting to note that all of the features said to be characteristic of black English are found in the speech of whites (although generally lower class) in the South, so one can make a strong case for black English being a regional dialect that is perpetuated by blacks who live in other geographic areas. However, these features of alleged black English have been shown to occur with higher frequency in the speech of blacks of the South than of whites in the South. Even in areas other than the South, black English may be spoken by people other than blacks. Whites who live in largely black areas may speak black English, and Puerto Ricans in New York City frequently learn black English. In the past, several Indian tribes did so too. Therefore, one cannot make a perfect fit at all between "black" skin and black English.

The origins of black English are controversial just as a few years ago the now rejected idea that black English and English were two different languages was controversial. The two diametrically opposed explanations of how black English developed are probably both right in that they explain one of the causes and wrong in that they do not include both causes. The older explanation is that black English simply reflects the dialect of the whites that black Americans learned English from during slave times and that black English perpetuates that form of English while the whites have changed their dialects somewhat. The newer explanation is that black English is a creolized language that developed from the pidgin English spoken in Africa by slave traders and learned by slaves themselves so they could communicate with each other (since slaves from Africa spoke many different West African languages before they were enslaved and it was a common practice not to put slaves who spoke the same language together) and with their masters. Pidgin languages always simplify sound patterns and morphological endings, so that when children were born into the slave community and learned to speak, they learned a simplified language (now a creolized language similar to modern black English) as their native language. The creolists argue that black English has become more like the white English dialects since then because of contacts between speakers of black English and speakers of white English dialects. It would have to follow, then, that the speakers of white dialects with black English features have borrowed those features from black English just as black English has borrowed more and more features of white English dialects. Since historical evidence supports both the older and newer explanations, it logically follows that both explanations of the origins of black English have *some* truth to them. Like the old argument over the relative influence of heredity and environment in determining a child's intelligence and personality traits, the relative influence of early English dialect features and a creolized black English that developed from pidgin English remains to be determined.

Spanish-Flavored English as Caste Dialects

The English of Spanish-speaking Americans can be considered caste dialects because of American racism toward people with dark complexions, which most Spanish-speaking persons have, and its attendant pattern of housing segregation. Spanish-speaking people in the United States differ from other foreign language groups in their greater number and in their continuing to speak a non-English language (as well as frequently learning English). As with black English, Spanish-flavored English is not one dialect but many dialects, about which little is known in detail. It is obvious that there will be regional differences in Spanish-flavored English because Spanish-speaking people live in widespread geographic areas in the United States. In addition, they do not all speak the same kind of Spanish, so the interference from their first language will be different on their dialects of English. In the Southwest, most Spanish-speaking persons speak a dialect of Mexican English, but there are areas of Spanish speech as far north and east as Colorado where the Spanish spoken is an older indigenous form that does not reflect Mexican-American culture at all. Of course, the largest concentration of Puerto Rican Spanish speakers on the mainland is in New York City and environs. The largest concentration of speakers of Cuban Spanish is in Dade County, Florida, but there is also a large Cuban and Cuban-American population in Jersey City, New Jersey. The description of Spanish-flavored English which follows, then, may not be completely accurate for the dialect spoken in your particular area.

In general, because the vowel contrasts are not contrasts in Spanish, Spanish-flavored English dialects may not distinguish between /i/ and /ɪ/ (the vowel sounds of *heat* and *hit*), /e/ and /ɛ/ (the vowel sounds of *hate* and *head*), /æ/, /ʌ/ and /a/ (the vowel sounds of *hat, hut,* and *hot*), /u/ and /ʋ/ (the vowel sounds of *cooed* and *could*), or /o/ and /ɔ/ (the vowel sounds of *loafed* and *loft*). The Spanish bilabial stop /β/ is regularly substituted for the similar English sounds /b/ and /v/, although Puerto Rican Spanish-influenced English may use /f/ for /v/ in final position. The /d/ is regularly used for both English /d/ and /ð/ (the first sound of *the*) since Spanish does not have a /ð/, and /n/ is used for both English /n/ and /ŋ/ (the last sound in *sing*) for the same reason. The major pervasive phonological features of Spanish-flavored English are the use of the Spanish three-pitch system instead of the English four-pitch system and the use of stressed syllables where standard English uses the unstressed vowel /ə/ (the first vowel in *about*). There is also some tendency to add an initial /ɛ/ (the vowel in *head*) to English words beginning with /sk/, /sl/, /sn/, /sm/, /st/, /spr/, /str/, and /skr/, since these consonant clusters never begin words in Spanish.

Grammatically, Spanish-flavored English may use or omit the articles *a/an* and *the* where standard English does the opposite, and use Spanish grammatical gender rather than English natural gender in pronouns, that is, *the table is over there; she is covered with dirty dishes.* Since Spanish regularly inserts *no* before the verb in a negative sentence even when other negative words follow the verb, the practice of double negation may also occur in Spanish-colored English as in *I no tell nobody.* Literal translation of Spanish idioms that are comparable to English idioms may introduce non-English prepositional uses in Spanish-colored English such as *to marry with Maria* rather than *to marry Maria* because the Spanish idiom is *casarse con* "marry oneself with."

LEARNING EXPERIENCES

Topic I: How Factors Other Than Class, Region, and
Ethnic Background Influence Social Dialects

- Have the students break up into groups of the same sex and compile two lists of words or expressions, the first list to be of things they would say to members of the same sex but not to members of the opposite sex, and the second list to be of things they would not expect members of the opposite sex to say in front of them. This activity should indicate to what degree there is still a linguistic sexual double standard. It may be that there is none, but the lists may also reveal a difference in the expectations of the students about what is inappropriate for a person of the opposite sex to say.

- Have each student analyze a page from one of his parent's professional, occupational, or union publications or a publication focusing on one of his parent's leisure-time interests for specialized vocabulary or expressions that not everyone will be familiar with. This activity will make apparent the occupational or personal-interest aspects of social dialects. For students whose parents take no such publications, the teacher should be prepared to make appropriate referrals to the school library or his or her own library.

- Ask each student to make lists of things that only little children say, only their parents say, and only their grandparents say. This activity will emphasize the age factor in social dialects.

- Have the students break into small groups on the basis of their religious affiliation, their parents' political persuasion, or their parents' or their own social group membership. Ask each group to compile a list of words or expressions that is used by their group with which the other groups may not be familiar and report back to the class.

- Have the students make a list of slang expressions which they use and another list of slang expressions that are no longer "in" or "cool" that are used by older people. This activity will emphasize the factor of age as an influence on social dialects.

- Ask the students to write how they might relate an incident that happened to them to a member of the same sex and to a member of the opposite sex. This exercise should make them aware that the sex of a person spoken to is part of the situation they react to socially when they speak.

- Have the students write how they might tell the same story about themselves to a small child, to someone their own age, and to an older person. This exercise should make them aware that the age of a person spoken to is part of the situation they react to socially when they speak.

- Have the students write a letter to a close friend and to one of their teachers saying essentially the same thing but in language that recognizes the different degrees of formality of their relationship with the person written to.

- Have each student write a formal speech to be made before a large audience and calling for them to adopt a certain position on an issue and then write how he or she would make the same argument in a conversation with one person his or her own age. This activity emphasizes how the degree of formality in a situation influences one's social dialect.

- Ask the students to write a dialogue using the language expected of each person about the following situations for the following people:

    1. A policeman and a burglar whom he has just arrested

    2. A wealthy lady and a gardener working on her lawn

    3. An auto salesman and a prospective car buyer looking at a car

    4. A doctor and a patient with stomach pains in an examination room

    5. A mother serving spinach to a child who does not like spinach

    6. An auto mechanic working on a lawyer's car to the lawyer

Topic II: Social Features of Regional Dialects

- Have the students break into small groups and have each group compile a list of words or ways of saying things that they would not want a date to say in front of their parents whom he or she was trying to impress. Compare the lists and see if there is agreement in your area about the linguistic features that are looked down on.

- Ask the students for examples of language features they have noticed in the local area that are used by persons from a higher or lower class than their own class. This exercise may present some difficulty, since all Americans like to consider themselves middle class, so it might be necessary, if responses are slow, to ask about the language used by persons whose occupations are fairly clear clues to their social status. This activity should help to identify language features that correlate with class in your local area.

- Ask the students what they think about people who come from specific other geographic areas, like the North, the South, or certain states. After pointing out how the regional dialects of these areas identify a person's origin and thus evoke the stereotypes about people from that area, ask if they know anyone from that area for whom the stereotype is inappropriate. This activity should make the students aware and wary of their linguistic prejudices.

- Ask students who have moved to the local area from another geographic dialect area what their first impressions were of people who talked the way the people in the local area do. See if they have changed their opinion now. If they haven't, you should do some explaining about how dialect features that indicate one thing in one dialect area may indicate something quite different in another area.

- Ask students who have traveled to other dialect areas if the people in those areas made fun of your students' speech and if your students thought the way the people in the other dialect areas talked was silly.

- Ask students who have always lived in the local area what they first thought of any of their fellow students who came from another dialect region. See if their opinions have changed. If not, an explanation that dialect features that indicate one thing in one dialect may indicate something quite different in another is in order again.

- If your community is heterogeneous, ask the students to identify the major groups to see if any of them are identifiable as emigrants from another dialect region. If so, ask the students for examples of language characteristics that mark this group or these groups. Possible examples of such groups are northerners who have come to the South or Appalachia when a manufacturing plant relocated, West Virginians or Kentuckians who moved to Indiana or Ohio for manufacturing jobs, southerners who moved North during or after World War II, midlanders or "Okies" who moved to southern California during the Great Depression, or faculty members' families who moved to the local area when one of the parents took a job at a local college.

- Break the class into small groups and assign each group to study a different recent presidential election to see how close a connection there is between a candidate's regional dialect and whether he carried the states in that region. If information is available on the results of primary elections where there were several candidates for a party's nomination, the correlations may be more obvious.

- Ask each student to write a short essay on a particular instance, which he or she is familiar with, of stereotyping because of a regional dialect or because of social class differences within the local dialect.

Topic III: Black English as Caste Dialects

- Have the students break up into small groups on the basis of "blackness" or "whiteness" and have each group compile lists of things that blacks and whites say differently in your area. See if the lists agree on the features that differentiate the speech of local blacks and whites. Then see if *all* the black students actually say all of the things that blacks allegedly say and if *none* of the whites say them. This activity (while potentially dangerous) may help to identify the features that are locally identified as black English, to show the degree that they are actually used by blacks, and to show the degree to which alleged black English features are shared by local whites.

- If you are brave and students understand you well enough to know that you are not making fun of them, ask both black and white students to tell jokes that are normally told within their group about the other group. This activity will help to identify linguistic differences between blacks and whites, since some of the jokes will make use of dialect differences, but it will also reveal the stereotypes people have of others who speak a different social dialect and reveal to what extent black English is a caste dialect in your area.

- If your students are reading any literature written by black American writers, have them compile an inventory of black English features in the writing of those authors. You will need to point out that "eye dialect," that is, the use of nonstandard spelling, may or may not indicate a real dialect difference. The poetry of Paul Dunbar or the prose of Richard Wright, James Baldwin, or Ralph Ellison would be good literature for this exercise.

- If your students are reading literature by American authors who write about blacks, have them compile an inventory of black English features in the writings of those authors as in the previous activity. White authors are likely to be less accurate than blacks in writing black dialogue, but William Faulkner and Robert Penn Warren would be reasonable authors to use for this exercise.

- Have your students watch one of the popular "black" television shows like "Good Times," "The Jeffersons," or "What's Happening?" and record features of black English used by characters on these shows.

- Have black students in your class carry on a conversation using black English idioms or meanings to words which they think the nonblack students will not understand. If they are successful in not being understood by the nonblacks, point out that one of the functions of some dialects of black English is to serve as concealment dialects. If they are unsuccessful and are understood, emphasize the fact that all dialects in a given area will influence each other.

- After you have discussed how the sound system of some black English dialects differs from the sound system of other American English dialects, use Reproduction Page 50 and have your students indicate which sounds would be left out and which sounds would be changed to other sounds in contrasting the way most people in your area would say the following sentences and the way they might be said in black English. Then ask them whether the black English in your area would really make all of these changes and whether some nonblack speakers would make the same changes in their dialect.

Sentences		Black English
1. The test was hard.	1.	
2. Three tests in one day are too many.	2.	
3. Four tests are even worse.	3.	
4. Bathe the dog.	4.	

REPRODUCTION PAGE 50

SOUNDS OF BLACK ENGLISH

Directions: *From what you have learned in class about the sound system of some black English dialects, indicate which sounds would be left out and which sounds would be changed to other sounds in contrasting the way most people would say these sentences in your area and the way they might be said in black English. Then decide whether the black English of your area would really make all of these changes and whether some nonblack speakers would make the same changes in their dialect.*

Sentences		Black English
1. The test was hard.	1.	
2. Three tests in one day are too many.	2.	
3. Four tests are even worse.	3.	
4. Bathe the dog.	4.	
5. Both pencils are sharpened.	5.	
6. Whose fault is that?	6.	
7. Help me with this problem.	7.	
8. I laughed during the whole class.	8.	
9. She glimpsed the truth.	9.	
10. He called the police.	10.	
11. I know that he's here.	11.	
12. She told the teacher a lie.	12.	
13. She is going to fail.	13.	
14. Their cats scratched him.	14.	
15. What's the length of this room?	15.	

5. Both pencils are sharpened.   5.
6. Whose fault is that?   6.
7. Help me with this problem.   7.
8. I laughed during the whole class.   8.
9. She glimpsed the truth.   9.
10. He called the police.   10.
11. I know that he's here.   11.
12. She told the teacher a lie.   12.
13. She is going to fail.   13.
14. Their cats scratched him.   14.
15. What's the length of this room?   15.

• After you have discussed how the grammatical system of some black English dialects differs from the grammatical system of other American English dialects, use Reproduction Page 51 and have your students indicate what changes would be made in the following sentences if they were translating them into black English. Then ask them whether the black English speakers in your area would really make all of these changes and whether some nonblack speakers would make the same changes in their dialect.

Sentences		Black English
1. I didn't do anything.	1.	
2. He doesn't have his books.	2.	
3. There is a bug on the floor.	3.	
4. He is her boyfriend.	4.	
5. She is fat.	5.	
6. He looked tired yesterday.	6.	
7. She'll do it later.	7.	
8. He'd rather not go.	8.	
9. He always is on time.	9.	
10. They were sleeping in class.	10.	

REPRODUCTION PAGE 51

GRAMMAR OF BLACK ENGLISH

Directions: *From what you have learned in class about grammatical features of some black English dialects, indicate what changes would be made in the following sentences if you were translating them into black English. Then decide whether the black English of your area would really make all of these changes and whether some nonblack speakers would make the same changes in their dialect.*

Sentences		Black English
1. I didn't do anything.	1.	
2. He doesn't have his books.	2.	
3. There is a bug on the floor.	3.	
4. He is her boyfriend.	4.	
5. She is fat.	5.	
6. He looked tired yesterday.	6.	
7. She'll do it later.	7.	
8. He'd rather not go.	8.	
9. He always is on time.	9.	
10. They were sleeping in class.	10.	
11. They have been winning for years.	11.	
12. She talks too much.	12.	
13. I haven't seen her.	13.	
14. I already did it.	14.	
15. She's forgotten their lunch.	15.	

---

11. They have been winning for years.   11.
12. She talks too much.   12.
13. I haven't seen her.   13.
14. I already did it.   14.
15. She's forgotten their lunch.   15.

- Play popular records by black singers in class and ask the students to pick out features of black English in their songs. Be careful to avoid records by black singers who do not use black English like Johnny Mathis or The Fifth Dimension unless, of course, you want to make the point that not all American blacks speak black English.

- Have your black students make a list of vocabulary items and idioms used in the local black dialect that they do not expect nonblacks to understand. Then ask the nonblack students what the items on the list mean. If they can explain the items on the list, focus on the similarities among all dialects in a region. If they cannot, raise the question about whether standardized tests in standard English like IQ tests measure what they purport to measure for students who speak different dialects.

Topic IV: Spanish-Flavored English as Caste Dialects

- Have the students break up into small groups on the basis of Spanish-language background or no Spanish-language background and have each group compile lists of things that *hispanoparlantes* and Anglos say differently in your area. See if the lists agree on the features that differentiate the local English dialects of Spanish-speaking people and non-Spanish-speaking people. Then see if *all* the Spanish-speaking students actually say all of the things that Spanish-speaking people are alleged to say and if *none* of the Anglos say them. This activity may help to identify the features that are locally identified as Spanish-flavored English, to show the degree that they are actually used by Spanish-speaking persons, and to show the degree to which alleged Spanish-English features are shared by Anglos.

- If you are brave and students understand you well enough to know that you are not making fun of them, ask both Spanish-speaking and non-Spanish-speaking students to tell jokes that are normally told within their group about the other group. This activity will help to identify linguistic differences between the dialects of the Spanish-speaking and the non-Spanish-speaking, since some of the jokes will make use of dialect differences, but it will also reveal the stereotypes people have of others who speak a different social dialect and reveal to what extent Spanish-flavored English is a caste dialect in your area.

- If your students are reading any literature by American authors of Spanish descent, have them compile an inventory of Spanish-English features in the writing of those authors.

- If your students are reading literature by American authors who write about Spanish-speaking Americans, have them compile an inventory of Spanish-English features in the writings of those authors as in the previous activity. Authors who are not of Spanish-speaking ancestry may be less accurate in their representation of the features of Spanish-flavored English than authors who are actually Spanish-speaking, however.

- Have your students watch one of the popular television shows portraying Spanish-speaking Americans such as "Chico and the Man" and record features of Spanish-flavored English used by characters on these shows.

- After you have discussed how the sound system of some Spanish-flavored English dialects differs from the sound system of most Anglo dialects, use Reproduction Page 52 and have your students indicate what sounds would be omitted or added and which sounds would be changed if the following sentences were spoken in Spanish-flavored English. Then ask whether the people with Spanish surnames in your area would actually make all of these changes and whether the same changes would be made by anyone else in your community.

Sentences	Spanish-flavored English
1. She beat him.	1.
2. They made an arrest.	2.
3. The strike is over.	3.
4. His suit is tan.	4.
5. John cut his finger.	5.
6. He saw the roses.	6.
7. The pool was empty.	7.
8. Both valves are stuck.	8.
9. Snow is cold.	9.
10. Can George sing?	10.
11. Have you seen Spain?	11.
12. The garage was full.	12.
13. The sheets were dirty.	13.
14. A funny thing happened.	14.
15. Their shares disappeared.	15.

- After you have discussed how the grammatical and syntactic system of some Spanish-flavored English dialects differs from the system of other English dialects,

---

REPRODUCTION PAGE 52

SOUNDS OF SPANISH-FLAVORED ENGLISH

Directions: *From what you have learned in class about Spanish-flavored English, indicate what sounds would be omitted or added and which sounds would be changed if the following sentences were spoken in Spanish-flavored English. Then decide whether the people with Spanish surnames in your area would actually make all of these changes and whether the same changes would be made by anyone else in your community.*

Sentences	Spanish-flavored English
1. She beat him.	1.
2. They made an arrest.	2.
3. The strike is over.	3.
4. His suit is tan.	4.
5. John cut his finger.	5.
6. He saw the roses.	6.
7. The pool was empty.	7.
8. Both valves were stuck.	8.
9. Snow is cold.	9.
10. Can George sing?	10.
11. Have you seen Spain?	11.
12. The garage was full.	12.
13. The sheets were dirty.	13.
14. A funny thing happened.	14.
15. Their shares disappeared.	15.

GRAMMAR OF SPANISH-FLAVORED ENGLISH

Directions: *From what you have learned in class about Spanish-flavored English, indicate what grammatical and idiomatic changes would be made in changing the following sentences into Spanish-flavored English. Then decide whether the people with Spanish surnames in your area would actually make all of these changes.*

Sentences		Spanish-flavored English
1. The table cannot clean itself.	1.	
2. Juan married Maria	2.	
3. He understood nothing.	3.	
4. The pretty house appeared clean.	4.	
5. I want some cotton shirts for men.	5.	
6. You are a student?	6.	
7. He wanted two red apples.	7.	
8. Bring it (the book) here.	8.	
9. I sat on the chair yesterday.	9.	
10. Is he here?	10.	

use Reproduction Page 53 and have your students indicate what changes would be made in the following sentences if they were translating them into Spanish-flavored English. Then ask them whether people with Spanish surnames in your area would really make all of these changes

Sentences		Spanish-flavored English
1. The table cannot clean itself.	1.	
2. Juan married Maria.	2.	
3. He understood nothing.	3.	
4. The pretty house appeared clean.	4.	
5. I want some cotton shirts for men.	5.	
6. You are a student?	6.	
7. He wanted two red apples.	7.	
8. Bring it (the book) here.	8.	
9. I sat on the chair yesterday.	9.	
10. Is he here?	10.	

ASSESSING ACHIEVEMENT OF OBJECTIVES

Ongoing Evaluation

The extent to which students have mastered the concepts covered under each topic can be measured by any of the activities assigned to the class as individuals, particularly the writing activities.

Final Evaluation

For an overall evaluation of the students' mastery of the concepts in this chapter, if all the topics in the chapter have been taught, a test constructed directly from the list of student objectives for the chapter as listed on page 136 can be used. As an alternative, one might consider a test composed of the following items:

1. Give examples of the specialized vocabulary of three different occupations or professions.

2. Illustrate how the same thing might be said by an adult with a college education, a high school education, and an eighth grade education.

3. Give some grammatical differences in the dialects you would expect to be used by the president of General Motors and a person working on an assembly line at a General Motors plant.

4. Give an example of the type of language used in your area by each of these three groups that is not used by the other two: an old person; someone your age; a small child.

5. Give one example of something you would say that you would not expect a person of the opposite sex to say.

6. Give examples of words or phrases that are peculiar to your religion or a club or organization that you or your parents belong to.

7. Describe another student in the class the way you would describe him or her to someone your own age and then in the way that you would describe that person to one of your parents.

8. Identify one regional dialect that is looked down upon in your area.

9. Identify one sound difference and one grammatical difference between black English and the standard English dialect of your area.

10. Identify one sound difference and one grammatical difference between Spanish-flavored English and the standard English dialect of your area.

RESOURCES FOR TEACHING ABOUT SOCIAL DIALECT DIFFERENCES

Below is a selected and annotated list of resources useful for teaching the topics in this chapter, divided into audiovisual materials and print materials and arranged in order of ascending difficulty. Special strengths and weaknesses are mentioned in the annotations. Addresses of publishers or distributors can be found in the alphabetical list on pages 263–265 in Appendix A. Films are black and white unless otherwise indicated.

I. HOW FACTORS OTHER THAN CLASS, REGION, AND ETHNIC BACKGROUND INFLUENCE SOCIAL DIALECTS

Audiovisual Materials

Communication Skills: Who's Afraid of Grammar, Part I. Sound-slide set (sound on LP record or cassette tape) with three programs: 19 minutes (dialect and "standard" English); 23 minutes (word order, inflection, and structure words); 24 minutes (syntactic processes of coordination and subordination), 1976, The Center for Humanities, Inc. Uses slides of photographs and artworks to explain causes of dialect differences, introduces the concept of dialect, and explores the social implications of the use of "standard" English.

What Are the English Language? Film, part of the *English—Fact and Fancy* Series, 30 minutes, 1967, Indiana University Audio-Visual Center. Discusses the social significance of language behavior and the idea of appropriate language for the occasion.

Social Variations. Color film, part of the *Language . . . the Social Arbiter* Series, 27 minutes, Stuart Finley. Discusses how social differences are revealed by persons' speech patterns. Recommended for teachers.

Print

"Kinds of Dialect," pp. 136–139 in *Aspects of Language* by Dwight Bolinger. Provides a good overview of social factors that influence one's dialect such as sex, occupation, age, occasion, religion, politics, lodge affiliation, and interest in particular sports or amusements as well as social class. Paperbound, Harcourt, Brace and World, 1968.

"Social Dialects," pp. 219–228 in *Linguistics and Language* by Julia S. Falk. Provides an introductory overview of the factors that influence social dialect. Paperbound, Xerox College Publishing, 1973.

"Some Varieties of Language," pp. 189–190 in *Introduction to Linguistics* by Ronald Wardhaugh. Discusses how age, sex, occupation, and function influence social dialects. Paperbound, McGraw-Hill, 1972.

"The Traveler's Guide to Hash-House Greek," by Dan Carlinsky, pp. 56–60 in *Language Awareness*, edited by Paul A. Eschholz et al. Provides a glossary of terms used by persons who work in roadside diners. Has discussion questions. Paperbound, St. Martin's Press, 1974.

"Police Have a Slanguage of Their Own," by David Burnham, pp. 82–85 in *Language Awareness,* edited by Paul A. Eschholz et al. Discusses and provides a glossary of slang terms used by the police. Has discussion questions. Paperbound, St. Martin's Press, 1974.

"The Language of Jazz Musicians," by Norman D. Hinton, pp. 286–289 in *Reading About Language,* edited by Charlton Laird and Robert M. Gorrell. Provides a glossary of occupational terms used by jazz musicians. Paperbound, Harcourt Brace Jovanovich, 1971.

"Cultural Levels and Functional Varieties of English," by John S. Kenyon, pp. 294–306 in *Readings in Applied English Linguistics*, 2d ed., edited by Harold B. Allen. Shows that all speakers, regardless of cultural background, have different functional varieties of speech depending on the particular situation, particularly its degree of formality or informality. Paperbound, Appleton-Century-Crofts, 1967.

"Functional Variety in English," by W. Nelson Francis, pp. 249–257 in *Aspects of American English*, 2d ed., edited by Elizabeth M. Kerr and Ralph M. Aderman. Discusses the five styles of language proposed by Martin Joos: casual, intimate, consultative, formal, and frozen (literary). Provides study questions and exercises. Paperbound, Harcourt Brace Jovanovich, 1971.

"Slang and Its Relatives," by Paul Roberts, pp. 258–268 in *Aspects of American English*, 2d ed., edited by Elizabeth M. Kerr and Ralph M. Aderman. Discusses the social implications of slang, specialized vocabulary of different occupations, and colloquial or conversational English. Provides study questions and exercises. Paperbound, Harcourt Brace Jovanovich, 1971.

"Social and Educational Varieties in English," by W. Nelson Francis, pp. 326–335 in *Aspects of American English*, 2d ed., edited by Elizabeth M. Kerr and Ralph M. Aderman. Discusses the social implications of educated or standard, vernacular, and uneducated English dialects. Provides study questions and exercises. Paperbound, Harcourt Brace Jovanovich, 1971.

"How Many Clocks?" by Martin Joos, pp. 244–248 in *Aspects of American English*, 2d ed., edited by Elizabeth M. Kerr and Ralph M. Aderman. Points out that the social aspects of language are tied to a person's age, style, breadth of experience, and the responsibility of one's position in the community. Provides study questions and exercises. Paperbound, Harcourt Brace Jovanovich, 1971.

"Social Influences on the Choice of a Linguistic Variant," by John L. Fisher, pp. 307–315 in *Readings in Applied English Linguistics*, 2d ed., edited by Harold B. Allen. Shows how sex, family status, and degree of formality in a situation influence the pronunciation of *-ing* words among schoolchildren and how teachers stereotype the children on the basis of this pronunciation. Paperbound, Appleton-Century-Crofts, 1967.

"The Language of the Law," by David Mellinkoff, pp. 65–70 in *Language Awareness*, edited by Paul A. Eschholz et al. Illustrates the confusing language style of the legal profession. Has discussion questions. Paperbound, St. Martin's Press, 1974.

II. SOCIAL FEATURES OF REGIONAL DIALECTS

Audiovisual Materials

Dialects. Film, part of *Language and Linguistics* Series, 30 minutes, 1958, Indiana University Audio-Visual Center. Demonstrates regional pronunciation and vocabulary and shows how regional vocabulary is dropped in favor of more general terms as one's education increases (and one's social class is raised).

Print

"Some Social Differences in Pronunciation," by Raven I. McDavid, pp. 42-52 in *Contemporary English*, edited by David L. Shores. Discusses pronunciation differences in certain regional dialects that have or do not have prestige in those regions and points out that prestigious pronunciations in one area may be considered lower class in another area and vice versa. Paperbound, J. B. Lippincott Co., 1972.

"The Language of the City," by Raven I. McDavid, pp. 511-524 in *A Various Language*, edited by Juanita V. Williamson and Virginia M. Burke. Shows how patterns of housing in cities create social dialects out of ethnic or regional dialects. Hardbound, Holt, Rinehart and Winston, 1971.

"White and Negro Listeners' Reactions to Various American-English Dialects," by G. Richard Tucker and Wallace E. Lambert, pp. 293-302 in *Varieties of Present-Day English*, edited by Richard W. Bailey and Jay L. Robinson. Shows favorable and unfavorable reactions of both black and white listeners from the North and South to various Northern and Southern dialects spoken by blacks and whites. Provides study questions. Paperbound, The Macmillan Co., 1973.

"Go Slow in Ethnic Attribution: Geographic Mobility and Dialect Prejudice," by Raven I. McDavid, pp. 258-273 in *Varieties of Present-Day English*, edited by Richard W. Bailey and Jay L. Robinson. Discusses the social attitudes that speakers of one regional dialect have toward speakers of other dialects. Provides study questions. Paperbound, The Macmillan Co., 1973.

"The Non-Standard Vernacular of the Negro Community: Some Practical Suggestions," by William Labov, pp. 336-343 in *Aspects of American English*, 2d ed., edited by Elizabeth M. Kerr and

Ralph M. Aderman. Points out that many features of black English in the North are Southern regional dialect features that have a social rather than a regional meaning in the North, and discusses the problem of social dialects in the schools. Paperbound, Harcourt Brace Jovanovich, 1971.

"Speech Communities," by Paul Roberts, pp. 317-325 in *Aspects of American English*, 2d ed., edited by Elizabeth M. Kerr and Ralph M. Aderman. Points out that people usually assume that the best English is that spoken by groups of persons with whom they associate and are at ease, and discusses education and occupation as factors in social dialects. Paperbound, Harcourt Brace Jovanovich, 1971.

"Language and Communication Problems in Southern Appalachia," by William A. Stewart, pp. 107-122 in *Contemporary English*, edited by David L. Shores. Discusses attitudes toward, and features of, the dialects of both blacks and whites in West Virginia; Kentucky; Tennessee; and parts of Pennsylvania, Ohio, Maryland, Virginia, North Carolina, Georgia, and Alabama. Paperbound, J. B. Lippincott Co., 1972.

"Language and Success: Who Are the Judges?" by Roger W. Shuy, pp. 303-316 in *Varieties of Present-Day English*, edited by Richard W. Bailey and Jay L. Robinson. Shows how employers decide whether or not to employ a person and that what kind of a job a person receives depends upon social judgments made about that person's dialect. Paperbound, The Macmillan Co., 1973.

"General Attitudes towards the Speech of New York City," by William Labov, pp. 274-292 in *Varieties of Present-Day English*, edited by Richard W. Bailey and Jay L. Robinson. Shows the negative attitude that whites in New York City have toward their regional dialect, an attitude not shared by black New Yorkers. Provides study questions. Paperbound, The Macmillan Co., 1973.

"The Social Motivation of a Sound Change," pp. 1-42 in *Sociolinguistic Patterns* by William Labov. Shows correlation between attitudes toward mainlanders and the pronunciation of natives of Martha's Vineyard, Massachusetts. Paperbound, University of Pennsylvania Press, 1972.

"The Effect of Social Mobility on Linguistic Behavior," by William Labov, pp. 640-659 in *A Various Language*, edited by Juanita V. Williamson and Virginia M. Burke. Discusses the differences in pronunciations among five social classes and the effect of upward or downward social movement on pronunciation (or vice versa) on the Lower East Side of New York City. Hardbound, Holt, Rinehart and Winston, 1971.

"The Social Stratification of (r) in New York City Department Stores," pp. 43–69 in *Sociolinguistic*

Patterns by William Labov. Shows the correlation between the presence or absence of postvocalic /r/ in the speech of employees of Saks, Macy's, and Kleins and the social classes each of the stores caters to. Paperbound, University of Pennsylvania Press, 1972.

III. BLACK ENGLISH AS CASTE DIALECTS

Audiovisual Materials

English Language: Patterns of Usage. Film, 11 minutes, 1970, Coronet Instructional Media. Shows variations of language styles among various groups and in various situations.

Print

"Some Linguistic Features of Negro Dialect," by Ralph W. Fasold and Walter A. Wolfram, pp. 53–85 in *Contemporary English*, edited by David L. Shores. Provides the most complete descriptions of distinctive phonological, morphological, and syntactic features of black English dialects. Paperbound, J. B. Lippincott Co., 1972.

"Nonstandard English," pp. 199–209 in *The Science of Language and the Art of Teaching* by Henry F. Beechhold and John L. Behling, Jr. Describes the major phonological and grammatical features of black English dialects. Paperbound, Charles Scribner's Sons, 1972.

"Some Features of the English of Black Americans," by William Labov, pp. 236–257 in *Varieties of Present-Day English*, edited by Richard W. Bailey and Jay L. Robinson. Provides one of the sanest and most complete discussions of phonological and grammatical features of black English dialects. Has study questions. Paperbound, The Macmillan Co., 1973.

"A Dialect of Washington, D.C.," pp. 117–123 in *Working with Aspects of Language* by Mansoor Alyeshmerni and Paul Taubr. Provides a transcription of, and exercises dealing with, a black English dialect showing differences resulting from the ages of speakers and the formality of the situation. Paperbound, Harcourt, Brace and World, 1970.

"Black English Dialects," pp. 270–271 in *A Survey*

of Modern Grammars, 2d ed., by Jeanne H. Herndon. Lists in table format the major phonological and syntactic differences alleged between black English and standard English. Paperbound, Holt, Rinehart and Winston, 1976.

"Dialect Differences and Black English," by Philip S. Dale, pp. 164–170 in *Current Topics in Linguistics*, edited by Nancy Ainsworth Johnson. Discusses major syntactic and phonemic differences between black English and standard English dialects. Paperbound, Winthrop Publishers, 1976.

"Selected Features of Speech: Black and White," by Juanita V. Williamson, pp. 496–507 in *A Various Language*, edited by Juanita V. Williamson and Virginia M. Burke. Shows that the grammatical features alleged to be characteristic of black English are characteristic of the speech of both black and white southern speakers. Hardbound, Holt, Rinehart and Winston, 1971.

A Sociolinguistic Description of Detroit Negro Speech by Walter A. Wolfram. Studies structural characteristics of the speech of Detroit blacks; correlates them with age, sex, and class differences; and contrasts them with the usage of Detroit whites and blacks of other cities. Paperbound, Center for Applied Linguistics, 1969.

"Black English in New York," by J. L. Dillard, pp. 114–120 in *Studies in English to Speakers of Other Languages and Standard English to Speakers of a Non-Standard Dialect*, edited by Rudolpho Jacobson. Traces the history of black English in New York City and argues that it existed there as a separate dialect prior to the mass migration of southern blacks to northern cities after 1940. Paperbound, National Council of Teachers of English, 1971.

"A Phonological and Morphological Study of the Speech of the Negro of Memphis, Tennessee," by Juanita V. Williamson, pp. 583–595 in *A Various*

Language, edited by Juanita V. Williamson and Virginia M. Burke. Describes the morphological systems that result from the phonological systems of black speakers of various social classes, educational levels, and ages in Memphis. Hardbound, Holt, Rinehart and Winston, 1971.

"The Logic of Nonstandard English," by William Labov, pp. 319-355 in *Varieties of Present-Day English*, edited by Richard W. Bailey and Jay L. Robinson. Shows that nonstandard black English does not reflect cognitive deficiency in its speakers but only a different grammatical system. Paperbound, The Macmillan Co., 1973.

"Is the Black English Vernacular a Separate System?" pp. 36-64 in *Language in the Inner City* by William Labov. Proves that black English is not a separate language from standard English but that it only has surface structure differences. Not recommended for students. Paperbound, University of Pennsylvania Press, 1972.

"Should Ghettoese Be Accepted?" by William Raspberry, pp. 412-417 in *Language*, edited by Virginia P. Clark et al. Points out that black English is consistent in syntax and suggests that it be used as a vehicle for teaching reading to students who speak it before they are asked to learn to read in standard English. Paperbound, St. Martin's Press, 1972.

"Black Views of Language Use: Rules of Decorum, Conflict, and Men-of-Words," by Roger D. Abrahams, pp. 183-195 in *Current Topics in Language*, edited by Nancy Ainsworth Johnson.

Demonstrates complex uses of language in the black community that have no counterpart in nonblack communities. Paperbound, Winthrop Publishers, 1976.

"Rules for Ritual Insults," pp. 297-353 in *Language in the Inner City* by William Labov. Analyzes the complex system of *signifying* or *cutting* in black English. Paperbound, University of Pennsylvania Press, 1972.

"The Language of Soul," by Claude Brown, pp. 347-352 in *Aspects of American English*, 2d ed., edited by Elizabeth M. Kerr and Ralph M. Aderman. Presents a very subjective interpretation and evaluation of black idioms. Paperbound, Harcourt Brace Jovanovich, 1971.

"The Functional Nature of Social Dialects: Social Change and the Teaching of Black English," by Robert E. Cromack, pp. 74-82 in *Studies in English to Speakers of Other Languages and Standard English to Speakers of a Non-Standard Dialect*, edited by Rudolpho Jacobson. Discusses the importance of the teacher's attitude toward black English in teaching standard English to speakers of black English. Recommended for teachers. Paperbound, National Council of Teachers of English, 1971.

Black English, by J. L. Dillard. Provides the definitive explanation of the structure of black English, its history and its origin, and discusses most of the social issues surrounding black English. Paperbound, Vintage Books, 1972.

IV. SPANISH-FLAVORED ENGLISH AS CASTE DIALECTS

Audiovisual Materials

Sounds of Language. Film, part of *Principles and Methods of Teaching a Second Language* Series, 32 minutes, 1961, Indiana University Audio-Visual Center. Shows sound features of several languages and problems of learning a second language because of negative transfer, especially for English speakers learning Spanish.

Print

"Spanish-Influenced English," pp. 272-273 in *A Survey of Modern English Grammars*, 2d ed., by Jeanne H. Herndon. Provides in table format

some major pronunciation and syntactic differences between Spanish-influenced English and standard English. Paperbound, Holt, Rinehart and Winston, 1976.

"Puerto Rican English (PRE)," pp. 209-211 in *The Science of Language and the Art of Teaching* by Henry F. Beechhold and John L. Behling, Jr. Describes major phonological and syntactic differences between Puerto Rican English and standard English. Paperbound, Charles Scribner's Sons, 1972.

"English Problems of Spanish Speakers," by A. L. Davis, pp. 123-133 in *Contemporary English*, edited by David L. Shores. Discusses differences between Spanish and English phonology and grammar and how these differences may influence the English spoken by a person whose first language is Spanish. Paperbound, J. B. Lippincott Co., 1972.

"English and the Bilingual Child," by Rudolph C. Troike, pp. 306-318 in *Contemporary English*, edited by David L. Shores. Explains how the differences in the phonological systems of Spanish and English influence the pronunciation of English by a person whose first language is Spanish. Paperbound, J. B. Lippincott, Co., 1972.

"First Language Influences on Ethnic Dialects: Spanish and Navajo," by Muriel R. Saville, pp. 157-163 in *Current Topics in Language*, edited by Nancy Ainsworth Johnson. Explains major differences between Spanish and English

and Navajo and English and where the person speaking Spanish or Navajo as a first language will be likely to carry over features of his or her first language to English. Paperbound, Winthrop Publishers. 1976.

"Social Aspects of Bilingualism in San Antonio, Texas," by Janet B. Sawyer, pp. 226-235 in *Varieties of Present-Day English*, edited by Richard W. Bailey and Jay L. Robinson. Discusses characteristics of the English spoken by Spanish-speaking persons in San Antonio and the attitudes both Anglos and Chicanos have toward English, Spanish, and Spanish-flavored English. Provides study questions. Paperbound, The Macmillan Co., 1973.

8

Writing Systems

This chapter deals with the different writing systems used in the world, the development of the alphabet, changes within the English writing system, and the modern English writing system. A practical application is an awareness that a language can be written in more than one way if there is agreement among the members of the language community on conventional symbols and thus that any writing system is arbitrary and changeable. Furthermore, students should develop an awareness of the writing system they use every day, in both reading and writing, since they probably have not thought about it at all since they were in the primary grades. Additionally, they may become more aware of some of the reasons they have problems in spelling or expressing themselves clearly on paper without the conventional punctuation marks.

Initially, the student should learn that the writing system he or she uses is the result of evolution from earlier writing systems. This can be illustrated with work with picture writing, syllabaries, and transliteration from non-Roman alphabets.

Next, the student should become acquainted with changes in the English writing system over the years. From this knowledge, the student will develop an awareness of the conventional nature of the English writing system, that is, he or she must follow the writing conventions of his or her society in order to be able to communicate graphically because those conventions are arrived at only by the agreement of all members of the society.

Finally, the student will be ready to examine the modern English writing system in detail. This examination should focus on its strengths and weaknesses as well as on the permissible variations within the system.

It would be possible for the teacher to omit the second topic when teaching this chapter. However, it would be impossible to teach about the ways the alphabetic principle of modern English writing is augmented by other writing principles in the third topic unless the first topic has been taught.

OBJECTIVES

If the three topics in this chapter are chosen by the teacher, the student should be able to:

1. Explain the stages in the development from the earliest writing systems to the development of the Roman alphabet
2. Transliterate from one writing system to another provided a key is given
3. Write a simple message in both the conventional English alphabetic system and a non-alphabetic system
4. Identify changes within the English writing system since the first adoption of the Roman alphabet
5. Illustrate remnants of non-alphabetic writing principles still used in the world around him or her
6. Illustrate conventional variations of the alphabetic writing system that are acceptable in his or her culture
7. Discuss strengths and weaknesses of the modern English writing system

---

CONTENT OVERVIEW

Writing Systems of the World and Development of the Alphabet

The precursor of writing was picture drawing such as still occurs in some modern cartoons that have no words. Of course, the figures in the pictures more or less had to resemble the man or the buffalo or whatever it was the intention to represent, and the pictures were always subject to possible misinterpretation. Nearly all cultures developed picture writing, and some never progressed beyond it.

The first step toward modern writing was the standardization of certain picture symbols into ideograms or ideographic writing. Two places where this occurred were China and Sumeria about 3000 B.C. In China, writing did not develop beyond the ideographic stage. The modern Chinese writing system still uses stylized ideographic symbols to stand for each separate idea. As a result, learning to write in Chinese is a time-consuming process, and most Chinese do not learn to write much beyond a basic vocabulary, which is also used in newspapers. The system does have advantages in China, however, because there are many Chinese languages that can use the same writing system. It would be parallel to having Indo-European languages written in ideograms, so that a stick figure representing the idea of "man" would be read as *man* by speakers of English, as *hombre* by speakers of Spanish, and as *adam* by speakers of Iranian. It is the Sumerian development of ideographic writing, however, which is the first step in the development of modern writing.

The ancient Egyptians borrowed the ideographic writing system from the Sumerians, but they also added some symbols called phonograms to indicate partially how the word representing the idea was to be pronounced and other symbols called logograms to indicate the pronunciation of entire short words. Early Egyptian writing involved the combination of three writing principles: a symbol could stand for an idea, a partial pronunciation, or an entire pronunciation.

The Phoenicians, a Semitic people from what is now Lebanon, borrowed the Egyptian writing system, but between 1500 and 1000 B.C. they discarded the ideographic symbols and used the phonograms and logograms to represent sequences of sound as they had done in the Egyptian writing system. Specifically, the symbols which were kept were used to represent a sequence of a consonant plus a vowel. Since the syllables of the Phoenician language usually consisted of a consonant plus a vowel, each symbol stood for a syllable in a word, and the collection of writing symbols was a syllabary.

Since the Phoenicians were seafaring traders, the Greeks came in contact with them and borrowed their writing system. Early Greek records have been found written in a syllabary or syllable-writing system.

However, in the ninth century B.C., the Greeks had created a new writing system, the alphabet, by taking the Phoenician symbols for syllables and using most of the symbols to stand only for the consonant part of the consonant-plus-vowel sequence and leftover symbols to stand for vowels..In other words, they developed a system whereby each sound of the language was represented by a separate writing symbol.

The alphabetic writing principle and many of the Greek writing symbols or modifications of them were borrowed by the other peoples in Europe. The Romans borrowed the Greek symbols and modified them in order to write Latin. The Germanic tribes did the same thing and developed the runic alphabet. When writing was introduced to the Slavic peoples by Saints Cyril and Methodius, they modified the Greek alphabet to record the sounds of Russian and other Slavic languages. Of course, because of the influence of Rome, many peoples, like the English and the Poles, have adopted the Roman alphabet and discarded forms of the alphabets that had been used earlier.

Changes in the English Writing System

The English, like the other Germanic tribes, used the runic alphabet until the early seventh century, at which time they adopted the Roman alphabet with some modifications. The Roman letters: ⟨a, b, c, d, e, f, g, h, i, l, m, n, o, p, r, s, t, u, and x⟩ were adopted to represent Old English sounds that corresponded to the sounds these letters represented in Latin. Two symbols were created by modifying Roman letters: ⟨æ and ð⟩, and the Greek symbols ⟨k and z⟩, which were rarely used in Latin, were also borrowed but also rarely used in English. The Old English writing system retained two of the early runic symbols as well: ⟨þ and ƿ⟩. To represent Old English diphthongs that had no counterpart in Latin, Old English used Latin vowel symbols in combination: ⟨eo, io, ea, and ie⟩. Similarly, sequences of consonants were used to stand for Old English consonants that did not exist in Latin: ⟨sc and cg⟩, the first sequence for /š/ (the first sound in *sheep*) and the second sequence for /ǰ/ (the last sound in *bridge*).

Some further modifications of Old English writing symbols were made in late Old English (the tenth and eleventh centuries), but most of the further writing symbol changes occurred during the Middle English period (roughly 1100–1500 A.D.). The Roman ⟨g⟩ was first used to represent /y/ (the first sound in *yet*), but the Irish modification of ⟨g⟩, the ⟨ȝ⟩ was used in late Old English for the sound. A further modification ⟨ȝ⟩ was used in Middle English before the modern symbol ⟨y⟩ was developed in late Middle English. Although ⟨th⟩ had occasionally been used in Old English, the regular modern use did not begin until about 1400 as a result of the Norman French influence in England. Similarly, the Norman occupation of England introduced the modern uses of ⟨ch, sh, and qu (for /kw/)⟩ during the Middle English period. The use of the elongated ⟨i⟩, that is, ⟨j⟩ began in the Middle English period but did not become regular until the modern English period.

The Modern English Writing System

The modern English writing system is alphabetic except for some few carry-overs of early writing systems. There are thirty-seven writing symbols that all may have variant forms: the twenty-six letters of the alphabet and eleven punctuation marks. The punctuation marks are the period, question mark, exclamation point, comma, colon, semicolon, dash, apostrophe, hyphen, quotation marks, and parentheses. Following the conventional system for the analysis of a language, it is possible to analyze each of these symbols as a grapheme and its variants as allographs. For example, the letter ⟨e⟩ has both capital and small letter forms as well as print and script variants: ⟨E, e, ℰ, ℯ⟩. One could add further allographs to the print forms given by taking into consideration italicized forms and different styles of print used by different printers.

The alphabetic system of modern English writing is augmented by other writing systems. Of course, children still use something approaching picture writing. Traffic signs are often ideographic, or partially so:

. The use of capital and small letters to differentiate *Polish* from *polish* can be construed as the use of phonograms to indicate pronunciation. The use of mathematical symbols to stand for words is logographic; in $2 \times 4 = 8$, each symbol stands for an English word. Other logographic symbols are the ampersand, the percent sign, and the paragraph symbol used by writers, publishers, and English teachers. Syllable writing in English is generally restricted to rebus puzzles in the comic sections of newspapers, brand names like *My-T-Fine,* or spellings like *O.K.* and *bar-b-q.*

LEARNING EXPERIENCES

Topic I: Writing Systems of the World and the Development of the Alphabet

- Draw a pictographic message, either of your own creation or one of the American Indian pictographs from the resources listed below, on the blackboard and have the class decipher it. It may be necessary to provide clues. Discuss how it is difficult to be specific using pictographs.

- Have each member of the class write a pictographic message to another member of the class and have the second member try to decode it. This exercise should enhance the modern English writing system in the eyes of the students.

- In order to illustrate syllable writing and logograms, use rebus writing to write a message on the blackboard and let the class decipher it. Emphasize how this method of writing is easier to understand than pictographic writing, but difficult if the language has more than one word for the same thing. Examples are provided in the resources below.

- Have each student write a rebus-style message to another member of the class, and have the second student decipher it. This exercise should also help develop an appreciation of the alphabetic writing system.

- Have each student write a short paragraph in English omitting all of the vowels from the words. Explain that Hebrew was traditionally written this way (it may also be written with added symbols to indicate vowels now). Point out that this is not a very satisfactory way to write English because English has more vowels (although not very many vowel symbols) than Hebrew.

- Put the following runic key and message on the board and have the class transliterate the message. Point out that the shape of letters in the runic alphabet is the result of the fact that they were carved on wood, since the Germanic tribes did not have paper and pens. Also point out that this shows that we could write modern English using any alphabet.

Key:	ᚺ = c	ᚴ = k	*Message:*
	ᛗ = e	ᛁ = l	
	ᚠ = f	ᚺ = s	ᛁ ᚠᛗᛗᛁ ᚢᛁᚺᚴ
	ᛁ = i		

- Put the following Cyrillic key and message on the blackboard and have the students transliterate the message.

Key:

е	= e	с	= s
и	= i	ш	= sh
к	= k	у	= u
л	= l	ы	= y
о	= o		

Message:

ше ликес бιоу

- In order to show that a syllabary would not be a very efficient way to write English, ask the class to think of as many syllables as they can in English for which a separate symbol would have to be devised. Since the structure of English syllables involves the range of sound combinations from one to at least seven, that is, *I* and *glimpsed*, the number of different syllables the class comes up with should increase rapidly. Rather than making up new symbols for the syllables, giving each new syllable a number will illustrate the point.

- If you or a member of the class writes a language not written in the Roman alphabet (such as Russian, Greek, Hebrew, Arabic, Chinese, or Japanese), have that person write some simple sentences on the blackboard using that writing system and explain how that writing system works by comparing it with the English writing system.

- If any of your students study the common foreign languages taught in secondary schools like French or Spanish, ask them to contrast the spelling system of that language with that of English for silent letters, one writing symbol for one sound, one sound represented by one writing symbol, and other differences.

Topic II: Changes in the English Writing System

- Reproduce the following Old English version of the Lord's Prayer or the Our Father and distribute it to the class to illustrate the difference between the Old English and the modern English writing system. Besides different symbols, the student will also probably comment on the differences in the language such as word order and spelling of familiar words. In order to explain the latter point, it should be pointed out that the words were also pronounced differently.

> Fæder ure þu þe eart on heofonum
> si pin nama gehalgod   to-becume þin rice
> gewurþe pin willa on eorðan swa swa on heofonum
> urne gedæ ghwamlican hlaf syle us to dæg
> and forgyf us ure gyltas swa swa we forgyfað
> urum gyltendum
> and ne gelæd þu us on costnunge
> ac alys us of yfele   soþlice

- Reproduce the following late Middle English version of the same prayer to illustrate the changes in the English writing system due to the influence of the Middle French writing practices. Ask the students to point out the changes.

Oure fadir that art in heuenes
halowid be thi name   thi kyngdom come to
be thi wille don in erthe as in heuene
yeue to us to-day oure eche dayes bred
and foryeue to us oure dettis   as we foryeuen
to oure dettouris
and lede us not in-to temptacion
but deliuer us from yuel   amen

- Reproduce the Early Modern English version of the same prayer below. It is about one hundred years earlier than either the King James or Douay versions with which your students may be familiar. Since the writing symbols are the same as those used today, ask the students to change the spelling of the words to modern spelling.

O oure father which arte in heven
halowed be thy name   Let thy kyngdome come
Thy wyll be fulfilled as well in erth as it ys in heven
Geve vs thisdaye oure dayly breede
and forgeve ve our treaspases even as we forgeve
them which trespas vs.
and leade vs not into temptacion
but delyver vs from evell.
For thyne is the kyngedome and the power, and the
glorye for ever.   Amen

Topic III: The Modern English Writing System

- Ask your students to find examples of pictographic and ideographic writing on road and traffic signs and draw pictures of them to bring to class. In most states, the shapes of the various types of signs can be considered ideographs, that is, danger and warning signs are likely to be of one shape and speed limit signs another. That should be pointed out if it is true in your state. You should also point out that road and traffic signs often combine alphabetic writing with the picture writing and ideographic principles.

- Have the students examine mathematics texts and advertisements for evidence of logographic writing in modern English.

- Ask your students to find as many ways as they can in which a specific English letter may be represented in handwriting and in different kinds of print.

- Have your students write a short paragraph omitting all of the conventional English punctuation and then have the class exchange paragraphs. Ask each student to identify the problems he or she has in reading the paragraph he or she has just received.

- Have the students examine the graphic symbols used in advertisements to see how they are used to catch the reader's eye and have them cut out effective examples for the whole class. In class, point out the different type faces, different colors, different size of letters, different graphic symbols, unusual spellings, and position on the pages that have been used.

- Ask the students to make lists of words with "silent" letters. From the lists, point out which letters are most likely to be silent and where they are most likely to occur.

- Ask the students to find words that have been borrowed from other languages and which are spelled with modifications of the regular English letters such as accent marks, dots over vowels, or modifications of consonant symbols, that is, *cliché* and *façade*.

- Have the students make a list of combinations of letters which are conventionally used to stand for only one sound in English spelling, that is, ⟨ch⟩ in *child* or *chorus*.

- As a class, make a list of homonyms in English to illustrate how many sets of words there are in English that are pronounced alike but spelled differently such as *right, rite, write,* and *wright* or *there, their,* and *they're*.

- Ask each student to make a list as long as he or she can in which a particular vowel writing symbol is pronounced differently like ⟨a⟩ in *cat, father, hate,* and *machine.* Then point out how this phenomenon makes it difficult to spell English words that a person has only heard but has never seen written.

- Ask each student to make a list as long as he or she can in which a particular consonant writing symbol is pronounced differently like ⟨s⟩ in *his, sit,* and *vision.* Again point out how this makes spelling difficult in English.

- Collect the common spelling mistakes from your students' papers and let the class explain why particular words were misspelled in terms of homonyms, silent letters, or letters that are pronounced in these misspelled words in ways other than their most common pronunciation.

- Have each student make lists of words in which the vowel sounds in the following words are spelled differently: *beat, bit, bait, bet, bat, boot, put, boat, bought, box, putt, bite, bout,* and *boil.* For example, the vowel sound in *bait* is spelled differently in *hate, weight, way, maid, croquet,* and so on. This exercise will emphasize how far modern English spelling has gotten away from the alphabetic principle.

ASSESSING ACHIEVEMENT OF OBJECTIVES

Ongoing Evaluation

The extent to which students have mastered the concepts covered in this chapter can be measured by collecting any of the activities assigned individually.

Final Evaluation

For an overall evaluation of the students' mastery of the concepts in the chapter, if all topics in the chapter have been taught, a test constructed directly from the list of student objectives for the chapter as listed on page 156 can be used. As an alternative, depending upon how specific the lectures have been, one might consider a test constructed from the following list of items.

1. Place a *T* in front of each statement below that is true and an *F* in front of each statement that is false.

   _____ A. Before the development of the Cherokee Indian syllabary, the writing system of the North American Indian was essentially pictographic.

   _____ B. The Germanic Futhore was a syllabary.

   _____ C. The symbols in the Japanese syllabary are called runes.

   _____ D. Russian is written in the Cyrillic alphabet.

   _____ E. The Phoenicians developed an ideographic writing system.

   _____ F. The speakers of Old English adopted the Roman alphabet in the seventh century without modifying it.

   _____ G. Egyptian hieroglyphics combined ideographic and phonogrammic writing principles.

   _____ H. In a truly alphabetic writing system, each writing symbol represents only one sound, and each sound is represented by only one writing symbol.

   _____ I. Transliteration means writing in opposite directions on alternating lines.

   _____ J. The modern English use of two consonant symbols to represent one sound like ⟨sh⟩ was borrowed from French writing practices during the Middle English period.

2. Identify or define the following terms:

   A. rune

   B. alphabet

   C. Katakana

   D. pictograph

   E. syllabary

   F. ideograph

   G. Cyrillic alphabet

   H. transliteration

   I. grapheme

   J. digraph

3. Write essays on the following topics:

   A. Most cultures developed a prewriting system called picture writing or pictographs. Trace the stages of development from pictographs to the alphabets of Europe by identifying the different stages as they developed historically as well as the peoples who introduced each stage or modified the previous system.

   B. We know that the Old English adopted the Roman alphabet with modifications in the seventh century. Begin there and give the history of the English writing system to its modern state by indicating what was adopted, changed, or added in the thirteen hundred years.

C. We know that the basis of the modern English writing system is the alphabet. However, there are remnants of earlier writing principles that are used to augment the alphabetic principle. Using examples, discuss how the modern alphabet is supplemented by pictographic, ideographic, and other writing principles.

D. Explain the variations in the acceptable form of letters of the alphabet in terms of the grapheme-allograph pattern.

E. Discuss the strengths and weaknesses of the modern English writing system.

RESOURCES FOR TEACHING ABOUT WRITING SYSTEMS

Below is a selected and annotated list of resources useful for teaching the topics in this chapter, divided into audiovisual materials and print materials and arranged in order of ascending difficulty. Special strengths and weaknesses are mentioned in the annotations. Addresses of publishers or distributors can be found in the alphabetic list on pages 263-265 in Appendix A. Films are black and white unless otherwise indicated.

I. WRITING SYSTEMS OF THE WORLD AND DEVELOPMENT OF THE ALPHABET

Audiovisual Materials

Origin of Writing, The. Filmstrip, part of *Our Literary Heritage* Series, 1970, Educational Filmstrips. Gives fairly complete history of writing systems in use before the development of the alphabet.

Origin of the Alphabet, The. Filmstrip, part of *Our Literary Heritage* Series, 1970, Educational Filmstrips. Provides a simple history of the development of the modern English alphabet from the time of hieroglyphics and cuneiform writing.

Discovering Language: Alphabet Story. Film, 14 minutes, 1973, Coronet Instructional Media. Presents the history of writing systems to the development of alphabets.

Alphabet, The. Film, part of *Language and Linguistics* Series, 30 minutes, 1958, Indiana University Audio-Visual Center. Discusses the origin, development, and spread of the alphabet; illustrates other writing systems; and analyzes the English writing system.

Print

"The History of Writing," pp. 48-61 in *Patterns of Communicating* (Grade 8) by Allan A. Glatthorn and June Christensen. Presents a simple but fairly complete history of the development of writing systems from pictographs to alphabets. Hardbound, D. C. Heath and Co., 1975.

"Writing: Language on Paper," pp. L221-L240 in *Purpose and Change* by Albert R. Kitzhaber et al. Provides a short discussion of and simple exercises using pictographs, ideographs, logographs, rebus writing, syllabaries, and the development of the alphabet. Hardbound, Holt, Rinehart and Winston, 1974.

"Writing Systems," pp. 123-133 in *Linguistics and Language* by Julia S. Falk. Discusses development from logographic to alphabetic writing systems during the last 5,000 years and has a table showing the Japanese hiragana syllabary. Paperbound, Xerox College Publishing, 1973.

"The Growth of Writing," pp. 164-171 in *Aspects of Language* by Dwight Bolinger. Discusses development from ideographic to alphabetic writing systems in the last 5,000 years and has tables illustrating the Cherokee and the Japanese katakana syllabaries. Paperbound, Harcourt, Brace and World, 1968.

"Writing," pp. 199-210 in *The Way of Language* by Fred West. Has a good discussion of the development of writing with illustrative examples, particularly good on hieroglyphics. Paperbound, Harcourt Brace Jovanovich, 1975.

"Table of Alphabetic Development," pp. 203-204 in *Invitation to Linguistics* by Mario Pei. Shows stages in development from Semitic syllabary to Roman and Cyrillic alphabets. Paperbound, Henry Regnery Co., 1965.

"Letters and Sounds," pp. 50-56 in *The Origins and Development of the English Language,* 2d ed., by Thomas Pyles. Has a short discussion of the development of writing with emphasis on the development of the alphabet from the Semitic syllabary. Hardbound, Harcourt Brace Jovanovich, 1971.

"Writing," pp. 133-139 in *Working With Aspects of Language* by Mansoor Alyeshmerni and Paul Taubr. Consists of exercises dealing with a Passamaquoddy Indian pictograph; the Cherokee syllabary; the Hebrew writing system; and English exercises using pictographs, rebus writing, and an analogy to the Chinese writing system. The best resource for exercises on this topic.

Paperbound, Harcourt, Brace and World, 1970.

"Letters and Sounds: A Brief History of Writing," pp. 54-67 in *Problems in the Origins and Development of the English Language,* 2d ed., by John Algeo. Consists of exercises dealing with two American Indian pictographs, Sumerian cuneiform, Egyptian hieroglyphics, Hebrew writing, the Cherokee and Japanese katakana syllabaries, and the Cyrillic and runic alphabets. The most comprehensive set of exercises dealing with this topic, but some are rather difficult. Paperbound, Harcourt Brace Jovanovich, 1972.

"Phonemes and Graphemes," by Joseph H. Friend, pp. 187-191 in *Reading About Language,* edited by Charlton Laird and Robert M. Gorrell. Has a table showing changed shape of letters from Egypt ca. 2000 B.C. to early Roman period. Paperbound, Harcourt Brace Jovanovich, 1971.

"Writing Systems," pp. 408-424 in *An Introduction to Descriptive Linguistics,* rev. ed., by H. A. Gleason, Jr. Discusses the relationships between various writing systems of the world; illustrates the Cherokee and Japanese syllabaries; and discusses alphabetic, morphemic, and ideographic aspects of the modern English writing system. Hardbound, Holt, Rinehart and Winston, 1961.

"The Use of Written Records," pp. 59-73 in *Historical Linguistics,* 2d ed., by Winfred P. Lehman. Presents a particularly good discussion of Egyptian hieroglyphics, Sumerian cuneiform, and the Chinese ideographic writing system. Hardbound, Holt, Rinehart and Winston, 1973.

II. CHANGES IN THE ENGLISH WRITING SYSTEM

Audiovisual Materials

Alphabet, The. Film, part of *Milestones in Writing* Series, 10 minutes, 1957, Syracuse University. Traces part of English alphabet from Greek and Roman alphabets. Too elementary for advanced secondary school students.

Print

"Writing," pp. 210-218 in *The Way of Language* by Fred West. Discusses changes made in the Roman alphabet by the Old English and subsequent changes in the English writing system. Paperbound, Harcourt Brace Jovanovich, 1975.

"Letters and Sounds," pp. 56-77 in *The Origins and Development of the English Language,* 2d ed., by Thomas Pyles. Gives the most comprehensive explanation of writing-symbol changes in English since the Old English adoption of the Roman alphabet to the present. Probably too advanced for most students. Hardbound, Harcourt Brace Jovanovich, 1971.

"Changes in the English Writing System," pp. 74-75 in *Problems in the Origins and Development of the English Language,* 2d ed., by John Algeo. Gives an exercise dealing with the writing-symbol changes in the history of English. Probably more useful to teachers than to students. Paperbound, Harcourt Brace Jovanovich, 1972.

III. THE MODERN ENGLISH WRITING SYSTEM

Audiovisual Materials

Language and Writing. Film, part of *Language and Linguistics* Series, 29 minutes, 1958, Indiana University Audio-Visual Center. Explains misconceptions about language and writing and the connection between the two, with the focus on modern English writing.

Print

"Speech and Writing," pp. 70–94 in *English: An Introduction to Language* by Thomas Pyles and John Algeo. Has a good discussion of the regular-ities and exceptions to the use of English writing symbols. Paperbound, Harcourt, Brace and World, 1970.

"Modern Spelling Reform," pp. 356–373 in *The Development of Modern English,* 2d ed., by Stuart Robertson and Frederic G. Cassidy. Surveys attempts to reform English spelling over the last century. Hardbound, Prentice-Hall, 1953.

"Writing It Down: Graphics," pp. 430–479 in *The Structure of American English* by W. Nelson Francis. Gives the most thorough analysis of the modern English writing system. Highly recommended for teachers but too advanced for most students. Hardbound, The Ronald Press Co., 1958.

9

Language Families of the World

This chapter deals with the major language families of the world, particularly the Indo-European language family of which English is a member, and the vocabulary enrichment of English as the result of borrowing from the other Indo-European languages and non-Indo-European languages. A practical application of this unit is to show the position of English in relationship to other languages and thus dispel the notions of linguistic purity and linguistic superiority. Another practical application is that students may develop some awareness of how their ancestral ethnic groups have contributed to the development of English. In addition, this unit should reinforce what the students already know or teach them a little bit about world geography.

The students should first be made aware of how English developed historically and its relationship to the other Indo-European languages. This can be illustrated by pointing out cognate words in other Indo-European languages with which students might be familiar such as: *foot*, German *Fuss*, French *pied*, Spanish *pie*, Greek *podos*; *mother*, German *Mutter*, French *mère*, Spanish *madre*, Latin *mater*; and the numbers from one to ten.

Then the students can be introduced to the fact that English has borrowed extensively from the other Indo-European languages. It might be useful to point out that these borrowings have two results. The first is that cultural phenomena that were not native to English have been borrowed into English with certain words such as *piano, sauerkraut, tacos, wine, curry,* and *countess.* The second is that English has a multiplicity of vocabulary items for the same things such as *raise* and *rear, cows* and *cattle, ease* and *facility, sea* and *ocean,* and *statute* and *law.*

Next the students may be made aware of the large number of languages and language families of the world in addition to the Indo-European languages with which they may be more familiar. They may be shown that these language families have importance in the world too in order to counter the students' natural Indo-European ethnocentricity.

Finally, the degree to which English has borrowed from non-Indo-European languages may be examined. The vocabulary borrowed will show the degree to which English-speaking people are indebted to other cultures for the contributions those other cultures have made to what most students are likely to have believed was originally English or American culture.

The borrowed vocabulary can also be used to show something of the history of the contacts by speakers of English with speakers of non-Indo-European languages.

The first two topics are related, and the second two also form a unit. Whether all four topics are chosen is up to the teacher. The last two topics will probably be taught most successfully to classes with several students with non-Indo-European ancestry.

OBJECTIVES

If all four topics are chosen by the teacher, the student, at the end of the chapter, should be able to:

1. Identify the place of English in the Indo-European family tree
2. Identify the places of the languages of his or her ancestors in the Indo-European or other language families
3. Name the other Indo-European languages from which English has borrowed vocabulary extensively and the major types of vocabulary borrowed from each
4. Locate on a map the geographic areas where languages belonging to the various branches of Indo-European are spoken
5. List the major language families other than Indo-European and major languages belonging to each
6. Identify on a map the geographic areas where languages belonging to the non-Indo-European languages are spoken
7. Give examples of vocabulary borrowed by English from other Indo-European languages
8. Give examples of vocabulary borrowed by English from non-Indo-European languages
9. Refute the statement that English is a "pure" language and call into question the idea that there can be such a thing as a pure language

---

CONTENT OVERVIEW

The Indo-European Language Family

The Indo-European language family is a group of related languages of which most of the modern languages of Europe (including English) as well as west central Asia and the Indian subcontinent are members. Although there are no records of a language now designated Indo-European, Indo-European has been reconstructed from the forms of its descendants because languages change regularly and the Indo-European languages are related to each other by a series of regular sound changes. In other words, the features of the parent have been hypothesized by looking at the features of the children.

Since "family" is being used here metaphorically, it may be necessary to point out that both it and its "family tree" development are not really accurate descriptive metaphors to explain relationships among related languages, but no better metaphor has been suggested. In a family relationship there are always more than one parent, yet all language families are hypothesized to derive from only one parent. In a natural family, the siblings age at the same rate. Yet in a language family, some members may change very little over a thousand years, and other members will change into various new languages, which themselves will change into other languages. The family tree was devised to account for this latter phenomenon, but it too has major flaws as a metaphor. The most obvious and trivial flaw is that, like geology charts and pedigrees of animals, the language family tree analogy might more appropriately be called a family root system in that it starts from a base and branches off and spreads *downward* as it grows. The major flaw is that the metaphor does not provide a way to show the influence of another related language on a language when both of them derive from different branches on the language family. For instance, English is conventionally shown as deriving from Anglo-Frisian, which is a branch of West Germanic, which is itself a branch of Germanic, one of the major centum branches of Indo-European. Yet, historically English was heavily influenced by Old Norse, which is the western branch of another branch of Germanic, that is, North Germanic, which is parallel with, but different from, West Germanic. More importantly, French influenced English greatly during the Middle English period, but there is no way to show this on a family tree diagram, since French derives from Latin, which itself derives from Italic, another of the major centum branches of Indo-European. With these caveats in mind, we will continue to use the metaphors.

The Indo-European language family originated somewhere in the central part of northern Europe or western Asia from which it began spreading out approximately five thousand years ago or longer. The population was probably large enough for there already to be dialects of Indo-European before groups began migrating from the homeland. All of the living branches of Indo-European (but not the recorded but extinct Tocharian and Hittite) to the east of the homeland are called *satem* languages because the Indo-European palatal /k/ became a sibilant fricative or affricate like /s/, /š/ (the first sound of *she*), of /č/ (the first sound of *cheese*) in these languages. On the other hand, in the languages generally to the west of the homeland called *centum* languages, the Indo-European palatal /k/ fell in with the velar /k/. The words *satem* and *centum* used to indicate the basic dichotomy in Indo-European languages derive from the Avestan and Latin words for "hundred," respectively, Avestan being a development of the Iranian branch of Indo-European and Latin being a development of the Italic branch, both of which are, respectively, members of the satem and centum groups of Indo-European.

The Indo-European homeland is posited where it is on the basis of cognate words (words that mean the same thing and are related to each other by regular sound correspondences) in the various Indo-European languages, by the absence of cognate words for certain things, and by historical references to the areas occupied by various groups at different times. Cognate words in the Indo-European languages for *snow, beech, wolf, bear,* and *mead* (a fermented drink made with honey) indicate the general area of the homeland, since there are *beeches* and *bees* in only parts of Europe and Asia, and *snow* and *bear* suggest a northern latitude. The absence of cognate words for *sea, camel,* and *palm tree* suggests that the homeland was inland and not at a southern latitude.

Cognates also tell something about the stage of civilization reached by Indo-Europeans before they began migrating. Cognate words for *mother, father, sister, brother,* and *nephew* indicate a sense of family organization and relationships. Cognate words for *hound, yoke, wheel, axel,* and *corn* indicate that they were farmers with domesticated animals and that they tilled the soil. Cognate words for *sew* and *weave* indicate domesticity. Cognate words for various gods indicate a sense of religion in their lives.

Probably most of the first Indo-Europeans to leave the original homeland were speakers of the satem branches of the language: Indic, Iranian, Armenian, Albanian, Slavic, and Baltic. Indic and Iranian are sometimes considered one branch, Indo-Iranian, which split into two parts; the same is true for Slavic and Baltic, which are sometimes grouped together as Balto-Slavic.

The earliest records in an Indic language are hymns in Vedic from 1500–1000 B.C. *Sanskrit* developed from Vedic as the cultivated language of the Hindu religion and the literary language of India from 400 B.C. to 1100 A.D. At the same time, various Prakrits or commonly spoken Indic languages were used by uneducated people primarily, but Pali, a Prakrit, also served as the written language for the Buddhist religious writings as well as for inscriptions on monuments. The modern Indic languages are developed from Sanskrit with, no doubt, some influence by the various Prakrits. The major modern Indic languages include: Hindi (spoken by the largest number of people in India), the closely related Hindustani, the closely related Urdu (spoken in Pakistan), Bengali (spoken in Bangladesh and adjacent India), Singhalese (spoken in Ceylon), Romany (the language of the Gypsies), Gujerati, Marathi, and Punjabi.

The earliest attested Iranic languages are Old Persian (with inscriptions from around 500 B.C.) and Avestan, the language of the Zoroastrian scriptures of about 600 B.C. Pehlavi which developed from Old Persian was the official language of the Persian Empire from 300 B.C. to 900 A.D. It is the major ancestor of modern Persian, Kurdish (spoken in western Iran, Iraq, and Turkey by linguistic minorities), Balochi (spoken in Western Pakistan), Afghan (spoken in Afghanistan), and Ossetic (spoken in the northern Caucasus Mountains).

Armenian is recorded from only the fifth century of the modern era, but the Armenians occupied their territory before the birth of Christ. It has borrowed vocabulary extensively from Persian and to a lesser extent from Arabic and Greek. Armenia no longer exists as a separate country, having been taken over by Turkey, Iran, and the Soviet Union. The two branches of modern Armenian reflect this political division, Eastern Armenian being spoken in the parts of Armenia within Iran and the Soviet Union, and Western Armenian being spoken in the part claimed by Turkey.

Albanian is recorded from only the fourteenth century of this era and, like Armenian, has borrowed vocabulary heavily, in Albanian's case from Latin, Greek, Slavic, and Turkish. The two branches of Albanian are *Geg* in northern Albania and *Tosk* in southern Albania and adjacent parts of Greece.

Slavic records exist only from the ninth century, but Slavs inhabited southeastern Poland and western Russia during the time of the Roman Empire. The South Slavic branch includes modern Bulgarian, Serbo-Croatian, and Slovenian as well as Old Church Slavic. West Slavic includes Polish, Czech, Slovak, and Wendish (spoken in eastern Germany). East Slavic includes Russian, White Russian, and Ukrainian.

The Baltic branch of Indo-European is recorded only from the sixteenth century and includes only two modern languages: Lithuanian and Latvian, or Lettish. A third language, Old Prussian, became extinct at the end of the seventeenth century, its speakers having been conquered and absorbed by Germans.

The speakers of the centum branches of Indo-European generally moved southward and eastward from the Indo-European homeland. The exceptions are the now extinct Tocharian and Anatolian branches. Tocharian records in two dialects were found in Chinese Turkestan in the nineteenth century; they are Buddhist writings from the sixth to eighth centuries of the era. Anatolian records were found in the twentieth century in Turkey. Most of the records are in Hittite from the Hittite Empire of 1700–1200 B.C., but there are also records in Luwian and Palaic. The extant centum branches of Indo-European are Hellenic, Italic, Celtic, and Germanic, with Italic and Celtic sometimes considered one branch that split into two parts.

Speakers of the Hellenic branch of Indo-European moved into Greece and Asia Minor early in the second millennium B.C. Hellenic was initially divided into Aeolic, Doric, and Ionic, but the Ionic of Athens spread over the territory of the other branches during the time of Alexander the Great. Modern Greek dialects all descend from Ionic-Attic except for the Tsaconian dialect, which is a remnant of the development of Doric Greek.

Italic speakers entered the Italian peninsula somewhat later than the movement of Hellenic speakers into Greece. Italic was initially divided into two groups: Oscan and Umbrian, and Latin, Faliscan, and Venetic. Oscan inscriptions from the second century B.C., Umbrian records, Faliscan inscriptions, Venetic inscriptions from the first century B.C., and a Latin inscription from about 600 B.C. are the earliest Italic records. Of course, Latin displaced all of the other early Italic languages and is the source of the modern Romance languages. The Italic languages include Portuguese, Spanish, Catalan (spoken in northern Spain), Galician (spoken in northwestern Spain), French, Walloon (spoken in western Belgium), Rhaeto-Romance (spoken in Switzerland), Italian, Sardinian, and Rumanian. In addition, Norman-French is sometimes considered a language separate from French. Provençal spoken in southern France has been replaced by Parisian French, and Dalmatian became extinct in the last century.

Celtic speakers inhabited central Europe and spread from there as far away as Spain, the British Isles, and Asia Minor after 500 B.C., but their area of dominance has shrunk constantly during the modern era. Celtic is divided into two groups: Brythonic and Goidelic or Gaelic. Brythonic Celtic includes the now extinct Gaulish (spoken in continental Europe), the now extinct Pictish (spoken in Scotland), Cornish (extinct in England since 1700), Welsh, and Breton (spoken in Brittany in France by descendants of British Celts who fled across the English Channel to escape Germanic invaders of England in the fifth century). Goedelic Celtic barely survives as Irish, Scots Gaelic (from mass migrations of Irish to Scotland during the first centuries of this era), and Manx (spoken in the Isle of Man). With the exception of some Irish inscriptions of the fifth century, most of the early Celtic records date only from the eighth century.

The first Germanic speakers were located in an area around and including Denmark a couple of centuries B.C. and expanded their area of linguistic dominance greatly for over a thousand years. Germanic is traditionally divided into East Germanic, North Germanic, and West Germanic branches, although East and North Germanic are sometimes combined as one branch. All East Germanic languages are extinct, Burgundians having been destroyed in the fifth century and Vandals and Goths having spread themselves so thinly among the peoples in Spain and North Africa after they conquered them that they were absorbed into the native populations. There is a fifth-century copy of a fourth-century translation of the Bible in Gothic, which is the first extensive record of a Germanic language; however, North Germanic inscriptions exist from the third century. North Germanic is commonly divided into Eastern North Germanic, consisting of Swedish and Danish; and Western North Germanic, consisting of Norwegian, Icelandic, and Faroese.

West Germanic may be divided into three branches: High German, Low German, and Anglo-Frisian; however, Low German is sometimes grouped with either of the other two branches. High German has records in several dialects from the eighth century, and many of these dialects, like Bavarian, are still spoken in addition to standard High German and Yiddish. Low German records exist from the ninth century in Old Low Franconian, the ancestor of modern Dutch, Flemish (spoken in part of Belgium), and Afrikaans (spoken by descendants of Dutch settlers in South Africa), and in Old Saxon, the ancestor of the nearly extinct Plattdeutsch (spoken in some rural areas of northern Germany by older people). Anglo-Frisian, of course, is the ancestor of Frisian, with records from the thirteenth century, and English, with records from the eighth century.

The Germanic branch of Indo-European has undergone a major sound change from the other Indo-European languages called the First Consonant Shift, or Grimm's Law. As a result, cognate words in Germanic languages and in the other Indo-European languages usually have predictably different consonants. For example, words that have /p/, /t/, or /k/ sounds in other Indo-European languages generally have /f/, /Ɵ/ (the first sound of *thin*), or /h/ in Germanic languages. Compare: Latin *pater* and Spanish *padre* with English *father* and German *Vater*; Latin *tres* and French *trois* with English *three*; Latin *centum* with English *hundred* and German *hundert*. Similarly, words that have /b/, /d/, or /g/ in other Indo-European languages usually have /p/, /t/, or /k/ in Germanic languages. Compare: Lithuanian *bala* ("swamp") with English *pool* and Greek *kannabis* with English *hemp*; Latin *duo* and Spanish *dos* with English *two*; Latin *granum* ("grain") with English *corn*. Indo-European /bh/, /dh/, and /gh/ changed to Latin /f/, /f/, and /h/ and Germanic /b/, /d/, and /g/, respectively. Compare Sanskrit *bhrata*, Latin *frater*, and English *brother*; Sanskrit *dha* ("do"), Latin *feci* ("did"), and English *do* and *did*; Latin *hostis* and English *guest.*

As mentioned above, the family tree diagrams do not show how various branches which split from each other in the past may continue to influence each other. Yet there have been a great many such influences on English by other Indo-European languages. The Indo-European languages that have had the greatest influence on English are Latin (during several different periods); Celtic; North Germanic or Old Norse; French (in two dialects); and, to a lesser extent, Greek during and after the Renaissance.

The Germanic languages on the Continent borrowed about two hundred words from Latin before the English language came into existence. These words reflected parts of Roman culture that were new to Germanic speakers. These included foods like *cheese* and *wine*, utensils like *dish* and *kettle*, agricultural terms like *sickle* and *flail*, trade terms like *market* and *cheap*, architectural terms like *wall* and *kitchen*, governmental terms like *tribute* and *toll*, military terms like *camp* and *sign* ("banner"), and other indications of advanced Roman culture like *pipe* and *copper*.

English Borrowings from Other Indo-European Languages

After the ancestors of the English invaded England in the fifth century, they borrowed somewhat from the Brythonic Celts who were already there, but primarily only place names such as *London* and *Kent*, river names such as *Thames* and *Avon*, and names of hills like *Bredon Hill* and *Bryn Mawr*. They also borrowed place names from the Celts that were originally Latin in origin and borrowed by the Celts themselves such as those ending in *-caster* like *Lancaster*, in *-chester* like *Winchester* (both coming from Latin *castra* ["camp"]), in *-wick* like *Harwick* (from Latin *vicus* ["village"]), and in *-coln* like *Lincoln* (from Latin *colonia*). *Cross* and *ass* were also originally Latin but borrowed into English through Celtic during the Old

English period (449–1100). The only other Celtic borrowings into English occurred shortly before or during the Early Modern English period (beginning about 1500). These words are almost exclusively words dealing with aspects of Celtic culture or "quaint" words like *shamrock* and *shillelagh* from Irish Gaelic; *plaid*, *clan*, and *loch* from Scots Gaelic; and *crag* and *penguin* ("head-white") from Welsh.

During the Old English period, the English borrowed about three hundred and fifty words directly from Latin, largely due to the Christianization of England begun at the end of the sixth century and to the establishment of schools. During this time the English borrowed many religious terms like *abbot*, *altar*, *disciple*, *mass*, and *priest*. Educational terms such as *school*, *master*, and *grammatical* were also borrowed. There was a tendency by the Old English to translate Latin words into English equivalents rather than to borrow Latin words, so that *high-father* was used instead of *patriarch*, and *tungol-witega* ("star-wise men") was used instead of *Magi*.

The Old English were much more willing to borrow words from the North Germanic or Old Norse invaders and settlers during the Old English period than they were from Latin because Old English and Old Norse were closely related and cognate words were easily recognizable. Everyday words like *bull*, *egg*, *leg*, *root*, *sister*, and *skull* are Scandinavian in origin, having completely replaced their English cognates in English. Common verbs like *call*, *die*, *drown*, *get*, *give*, and *take* are also originally Old Norse words. Sometimes both the Old Norse and the Old English cognates were kept in English but with a semantic change, so that the two words now have different meanings; originally Old Norse *dike*, *garden*, *hale*, *rear*, *skin*, and *skirt* now have different meanings from the originally Old English cognates: *ditch*, *yard*, *whole*, *raise*, *shin*, and *shirt*.

Of course, as with Celtic, English borrowed many place names from Old Norse. These include those ending in *-by* ("town") like *Derby* and *Rugby*; in *-thorpe* ("village") like *Bishopsthorpe*; in *-thwaite* ("isolated piece of land") like *Applethwaite* and *Satterthwaite*; and in *-toft* ("piece of land") like *Brimtoft* and *Eastoft*. Additionally, the use of the patronymic *-son* in *Johnson* and *Stevenson* comes from the Old Norse way of identifying persons by their father's name.

The most significant influence of Old Norse on English did not appear until the Middle English Period (1100–1500), although these features had to have been borrowed during the late Old English period in northern England where the heaviest settlements of Scandinavians were. Articles like *both*, prepositions like *till* and *with*, and subordinating conjunctions like *though* are all of Old Norse origin. The third person plural pronouns *they*, *them*, and *their* are Old Norse forms; the Old English forms all began with /h/. The *are* form of *be* is Old Norse in origin, as is the *-s* third person singular present tense inflection on verbs as in *he walks* (the Old English inflection still survives as far into Early Modern English as in Chaucerian Middle English *he walketh*).

Modern North Germanic borrowings into English, like the Celtic ones, are either esoteric or reflect something peculiar to Scandinavian culture. Examples are the general Scandinavian *skoal* and *troll*, Norwegian *ski*, Icelandic *geyser* and *saga*, and Swedish *omsbudsman* and *smorgasbord*.

Although the Norman Conquest of England occurred in 1066, the first French words were not recorded in English documents until 1154, though they must have been borrowed earlier. There were two periods and sources of French borrowing during the Middle English period: Norman-French until the end of the thirteenth century and Parisian French until the end of the fifteenth century (and beyond). Altogether, some ten thousand French words were borrowed into the English of the period. The Norman words dealt with religion, warfare, and government primarily. Religious terms like *confession*, *faith*, *hermit*, *mercy*, *novice*, *pastor*, *penance*, *pray*, *temptation*, and *virtue* are from this period. So are military terms like *armor*, *assault*, *navy*, *sergeant*, *soldier*, and *war*. *Administer*, *bailiff*, *councilor*, *countess*, *duke*, *government*, *mayor*, *parliament*, *prince*, *sovereign*, *statute*, and *tax* are examples of the government terms. Norman-French words were also borrowed for cooked meats like *beef*, *mutton*, *pork*, and *veal* as well as cooking processes like *boil*, *broil*, *fry*, and *roast*.

Parisian French borrowing tended to reflect the advanced culture of Paris and frequently involved the language of professions. Businessmen used *contract*, *debt*, and *import*. Lawyers talked about *criminals*, *felonies*, and *judges*. Doctors talked about *medicine* and *ointment* and may have been *surgeons*. Architects and builders used *buttress*, *chamber*, *portal*, and *vault*. Some words were borrowed again from Parisian French even though they had already been borrowed from Norman French. Parisian French *chattel*, *chase*, *chef, guardian,* and *regard* originally meant the same as Norman French *cattle, catch, chief, warden,* and *reward.* Of course, Parisian French has served as a source of English words all through the Modern English period up to the currently out-of-favor *détente.* Other French borrowings during the modern period include *chauffeur, croquet, colonel, denim, corduroy, bourgeois, brochure, garage, renaissance, restaurant,* and *reveille.*

During the Renaissance in England in the Early Modern English period, a new wave of borrowing of Latin terms into English began, many of them cognate with earlier French borrowing or serving as learned synonyms for English words of Germanic origin. Examples include *abdomen, data, education, fortitude, penetrate, splendid, superintendent, urban,* and *vindicate.* Other words that had been borrowed from French were respelled to reflect their original Latin origin. The ⟨b⟩s in *debt* and *doubt,* the ⟨c⟩ in *indict,* and the ⟨b⟩ in *subtle* are examples. At the same time, Greek words were borrowed into English. Examples are *agnostic, autocracy, idiosyncrasy, pathos, telephone, threnody,* and *xylophone.*

During the Early Modern and Modern English periods, English borrowing from other Indo-European languages has continued. Two Italic languages, Spanish and Italian, have been major contributors. Spanish borrowings frequently reflect things from the New World and often have been adopted into American English only. Spanish loanwords into English include *adobe, alligator, avocado, canyon, cargo, corral, flotilla, junta, mesa, mosquito, pueblo, ranch, sombrero, sierra, tornado,* and *vanilla.* Italian loanwords have dealt primarily with music and foods. Musical terms include *allegro, finale, forte, cantata, concerto, opera, piano, viola,* and *violin.* Food names include *artichoke, lasagna, maraschino, pizza, ravioli,* and *spaghetti.*

Borrowings from other Germanic languages since 1500 have come primarily from German, Yiddish, Dutch, and Afrikaans. German words have frequently dealt with geology and, of course, food. Examples of German borrowings are *cobalt, feldspar, gneiss, meerschaum, quartz, zinc,* and *bock* (beer), *delicatessen, lager* (beer), *liverwurst, knockwurst, pretzel, pumpernickel, sauerbraten,* and *sauerkraut.* Yiddishisms include *kibbitz, schmaltz, shnook,* and *shtick.* Dutch borrowings have been more frequent, particularly sailing terms like *buoy, cruise, deck, sloop,* and *yacht.* Other Dutch borrowings include *booze, pickle, isinglass,* and *wiseacre.* Afrikaans is the source of *apartheid, commandeer,* and *trek.*

Because of the British policy of expansion of trade and empire-building, some words from the satem Indo-European languages have also been borrowed into English since 1500. Persian loanwords include *azure, bazaar, caravan, cummerbund, lilac, paradise, scarlet, shawl, taffeta,* and *tiger.* From the Indic languages, *avatar, suttee, svarabhakti* (a linguistic term), and *yoga* are borrowed from Sanskrit, *bandanna, bungalow, dinghy, dungaree, jungle, maharaja, pajamas, shampoo,* and *thug* from Hindustani, and *pal* from Romany. Russian has contributed *bolshevik, pogrom, samovar, steppe, troika,* and *vodka.*

Other Language Families of the World

The Hamitic language family consists of languages indigenous to the northern third of Africa. It is some-times grouped with Semitic as the Hamito-Semitic language family. Much of the original area of Hamitic languages now speaks Arabic, a Semitic language, as the result of the Moslem conquest of North Africa during this era. The four divisions of Hamitic corresponding to the various branches of Indo-European are Berber, Cushitic, Chad, and Egyptian. Berber languages are still spoken in areas of North Africa where Arabic is not spoken; these include Tuareg and Kabyle. Cushitic languages are spoken south of Egypt along the Red Sea and include Somali, Bogo, Tambaru, and Galla. The Chad branch of Hamitic consists of languages spoken south and west of Lake Chad; these include Hausa, Gabin, Mandara, and Ngala. Egyptian is the only branch with extensive written records, going back to the fourth millennium B.C. The only surviving Egyptian language is Coptic, which is the liturgical language of the Coptic Christian church in Egypt.

The Semitic language family consists of three branches: East Semitic, South Semitic, and West Semitic. East Semitic is extinct, but records exist of Akkadian from 2800 B.C. Babylonian and Assyrian were dialects of Akkadian. South Semitic is recorded only from this era, but the major language in this group, Arabic, is now spoken throughout northern Africa and Asia Minor. South Semitic also includes Geez, the liturgical language of the Coptic Christian church in Ethiopia, and Amharic, the learned or scholarly language of Ethiopia. West Semitic included Phoenician (originally spoken in the area of

Lebanon), which was called Punic when it was carried to Carthage in North Africa where it was spoken into the sixth century of this era. West Semitic also includes Hebrew, which is recorded as early as 1100 B.C. and survived only as a liturgical language until its revival with the founding of Israel in this century. It had largely been replaced as a spoken language in Palestine by another West Semitic language, Aramaic, after the sixth century B.C. The fourth West Semitic language is Moabitic, which was spoken in the area that is now Jordan.

South of the Hamitic and Semitic language families in Africa to the equator, the Sudanese or Chari-Nile languages are spoken. These include Dinka and Shilluk. The Sudanese language family is sometimes grouped with the Bantu language family (spoken south of the equator in Africa) into the Niger-Congo family. The most important Bantu language is, of course, Swahili, which is widely used as a trade language in East Africa. The family also includes Wolof in West Africa, Yoruba and Ibo in Nigeria, and Zulu and Xhosa in southeast Africa. The other language family in Africa, the Khoisan family, has only two members, Bushman and Hottentot, spoken in southern Africa.

The Dravidian language family consists of related languages spoken in India before the Indo-European invasion and still spoken primarily in southern India. It includes Telugu with the largest number of speakers in India next to Hindi, Tamil with nearly as many speakers, and Kannada and Malayalam. It also includes Brahui spoken in northern India.

The Finno-Ugric language family contains three languages spoken in Europe: Hungarian, Finnish, and Lappish, and several languages spoken in northern Asia including Samoyedic. It is sometimes classed with the Altaic language family as Ural-Altaic.

The Altaic language family includes Osmanli, the official language of Turkey, and about twenty other Turkic languages spoken chiefly in the Soviet Union including Uzbek, Azerbaijani, and Kazakh. Eastern Altaic includes the Mongol languages, Khalkha and Dagur, and the Gunguz languages, Manchu and Evenki.

The Caucasian language family spoken in the Caucasus Mountains includes many languages about which little is known. Northern Caucasian includes Circassian and Lezgian. Southern Caucasian includes Georgian, Laz, and Mingrelian.

The Sino-Tibetan language family has the largest number of speakers in Asia. It consists of two main branches: Tibeto-Burman and Sinitic. Tibeto-Burman includes several minor languages like Lolo and Kachin, but the two major languages are Tibetan (with records from the seventh century) and Burmese. Sinitic includes all of the branches of Chinese, which despite a common ideographic writing system are mutually unintelligible separate languages. The Chinese languages include: Cantonese (in Canton and Hong Kong); Wu (spoken in Shanghai); the Min dialects of Kan-Hakka, Amoy-Swatow, and Foochow; Northern Mandarin (spoken in Peking) and Manchurian; Southwestern Mandarin (spoken in Szechuan); and Southeastern Mandarin (spoken in Nanking). Chinese records exist from 1300 B.C. Some scholars group the Thai language family as part of the Sinitic branch of Sino-Tibetan. Thai and Laotian are the major languages in the Thai family.

The Mon-Khmer language family consists of languages also spoken in Indochina. Mon is spoken in parts of Burma and Thailand, and Khmer is the language of Cambodia. Vietnamese or Annamite may be part of the same family, but it has borrowed from various surrounding languages.

The Malayo-Polynesian family has the widest geographic distribution of any language family except for Indo-European. The Polynesian subgroup includes Maori (spoken in New Zealand), Samoan, Fijian, and Hawaiian. The Malayan subgroup includes Malagasy (spoken in Madagascar); Javanese, Sundanese, and Bahasa Indonesia (all spoken in Indonesia); Malay (spoken in Malaysia); and Tagalog as well as many other languages of the Philippines. The Melanesian and Micronesian subgroups consist of languages spoken on groups of small Pacific islands.

The Australian language family consists of dying languages, all related to each other. In New Guinea, the languages are identified as Papuan, but they include many unrelated language families. So little is known about Papuan languages that estimates of their numbers range from about one hundred to several hundred.

In addition to these language families of the Eastern Hemisphere, there are various isolated languages and remnants of other language families. Basque, spoken in the Pyrenees of Spain and France, is probably a remnant of a language family spoken in Europe before the Indo-European expansion. The same is true of

Etruscan, which exists only in inscriptions in the Italic peninsula. Sumerian records exist from about 4000 B.C. in Mesopotamia, but it was not related to the Semitic languages of the area. Also in Asia, Japanese, Korean, and Ainu (spoken by Caucasians in the northern Japanese islands) are unrelated to other languages or to each other (except through borrowing). There are also scattered remnants of a Miao-Yao language family of China before the expansion of the Sino-Tibetan family.

In the New World, the number of languages and language families is much larger than that of the Old World. At various times, there have been fifty-four language families proposed for North America, twenty-three language families for Central America, and approximately seventy-five language families for South America. Edward Sapir proposed six major linguistics stocks for North America, each consisting of several related language families, in order to make the discussion of native American language families manageable. There are, however, other classifications as well.

There is general agreement on an Eskimo-Aleut language grouping spoken around the Arctic Ocean. The Athabascan language grouping consists of languages spoken south of Eskimo-Aleut in Alaska and western Canada, but it also includes languages of northern California and the Southwest, including Apache and Navajo. Athabascan is sometimes grouped with some languages southwest of the Athabascan languages in Alaska and Canada as Na-Dene. The Algonquian grouping includes most of the languages of eastern and central Canada as well as those of the northeast coast, the Great Lakes and eastern Midwest, and part of the western plains area in the United States. Algonquian and Delaware on the East Coast, Ojibwa and Cree in the Great Lakes area, and Arapaho and Cheyenne in the plains are examples of Algonquian languages. The Iroquoian language grouping includes Mohawk and Oneida in New York state and Canada, Cherokee and Tuscarora in Tennessee and the Carolinas, and Choctaw, Creek, and Seminole in the southeast; the southeastern grouping is also sometimes identified as Muskogean. The Sioux language grouping consists of languages spoken in the Great Plains area and the southern Midwest, most notably Dakota and Crow. Uto-Aztecan, the language grouping of the Southwest (and much of Mexico), includes Shoshone, Paiute, and Hopi in the United States and Nahuatl in Mexico. Smaller language groupings in the United States are Caddoan (spoken in the central states), Salishan (spoken in the Pacific Northwest), Hokan (spoken in the Southwest and sometimes grouped with Sioux as Hokan-Souian), and Penutian (spoken in California). There are also isolated languages like Zuni that are not related to any of the language families.

In Central America, in addition to the Uto-Aztecan grouping, the Mayan language family is the other major language family, having at least twenty members including Yucatec, Tzeltal, and Tzotzil. The four most important language families of South America are Quechua (in Peru and Bolivia), Guarani (in Paraguay and parts of Brazil), Carib (in northern South America), and Arawak (from the West Indies to central South America).

English Borrowings from Non-Indo-European Languages

English has not borrowed extensively from the indigenous language families of Africa. In fact, it appears not to have borrowed at all from the Hamitic, Sudanese, or Khoisan language families. What African borrowings have occurred all come from the various Bantu languages. Bantu words in common use (although sometimes borrowed through Spanish and Portuguese) include *banana, banjo, benné,* ("sesame"), *buck(ra)* ("man"), *chimpanzee, cooter* ("turtle"), *gnu, goober* ("peanut"), *gorilla, guinea, gumbo, hoodoo, juke*(box), *okra, pinder* ("peanut"), *tote, voodoo, yam,* and *zebra. Cush* and *cala* are used by some blacks in the South for "cornmeal cake" and "rice cake," respectively, and are of Bantu origin. Of course, the Gullah dialect contains a great many words of Bantu origin as Lorenzo Turner has shown, but these are not used by speakers of other English dialects.

The Semitic language family has contributed many more vocabulary items through the two major languages, Arabic and Hebrew. During the Middle English period, English borrowed Arabic terms through French or Italian such as *admiral, alkali, almanac, antimony, bedoin, camphor, cotton, hazard, henna, lemon, mattress, mosque, orange, saffron, sumac, syrup,* and *zenith. Alchemy* and *elixir,* although originally

Greek, were borrowed from Arabic through French at this time, and *cipher* was borrowed through Spanish. During the Early Modern English period, further Arabic borrowings through French and Italian include *alcohol, alcove, alfalfa, algebra, apricot, arsenal, assassin, coffee, emir, fakir, gazelle, giraffe, harem, hashish, jar, minaret, monsoon, sash, sirocco,* and *zero.* Modern English borrowings from Arabic include *Allah, hookah, genie, ghoul, safari, sheik,* and *sultan.* Hebrew words borrowed into English usually through Latin, Greek, or French as intermediaries are *amen, babel, behemoth, cabal, camel, cherub, cinnamon, hosanna, hyssop, jubilee, leviathan, manna, rabbi, sabbath, Satan, seraph, sapphire,* and *shibboleth.* Modern English borrowings include *kibbutz, kosher,* and *Torah.*

English borrowings from Dravidian languages are few. Most of these come through the intermediary of Portuguese such as *atoll, calico, coolie, copra, mango,* and *teak. Curry* and *pariah* are direct borrowings from Tamil, however.

The Finno-Ugric language family has contributed little to English vocabulary, *sauna* being the only example from Finnish. Hungarian borrowings into English include *coach, goulash,* and *paprika.*

Only the Turkic languages of the Altaic language family have served as sources for English vocabulary. *Bey, caftan, fez, horde, janissary, kiosk, odalisque, shish kebab, tulip, turban, turquoise,* and *vampire* are examples. *Coffee* and *kismet,* although originally Arabic, were borrowed into English through Turkish too.

The only Sino-Tibetan languages to have contributed much to English are the Chinese languages. Chinese borrowings (outside of Chinese restaurants) include *catsup, chow, ginseng, kowtow, kumquat, mandarin, oolong, pekoe, serge, tea,* and *tong. Judo, jujitsu,* and *tycoon* are ultimately Chinese, but were borrowed into English from Japanese. *Lama* seems to be the only English word of Tibetan origin.

The Malayo-Polynesian language family has contributed some words to English, but mostly words reflecting regional flora and fauna or cultural phenomena. Malay words borrowed through other European languages into English include *amok, bamboo, bantam, cockatoo, gingham, gong, junk, launch, mangrove,* and *sarong. Rattan* was borrowed directly from Malay into English. Polynesian borrowings include *luau, taboo, tattoo,* and *ukulele.*

Australian language borrowings into English are all words describing Australian phenomena for which English had no other words. Examples are *boomerang, dingo, kangaroo,* and *wombat.*

Japanese words borrowed into English, with the exception of *soy,* are still felt to be Japanese words. Examples are *banzai, geisha, hara-kiri, kamikaze, karate, kimono, rickshaw, sake, samurai, sukiyaki,* and *zen.*

Outside of place names, nearly all of the borrowings into English from the American Indian languages are from the Algonquian grouping. *Igloo* and *kayak,* of course, are from Eskimo-Aleut. Iroquian has contributed *catalpa* and *sequoia,* Athabascan (specifically Navajo) *hogan,* Sioux *tepee,* Uto-Aztecan (specifically Nahuatl) *peyote,* and Penutian *chinook* and *pot latch.* Algonquian has contributed a much larger number of words including *chipmunk, hickory, mackinaw, moose, muskrat, pecan, persimmon, raccoon, squash, succotash, wampum, wigwam,* and *woodchuck.* It is worth noting that nearly all of these English words from American Indian languages have been shortened or otherwise changed to conform to English phonotactics, however.

LEARNING EXPERIENCES

Topic I: The Indo-European Language Family

- Use the Indo-European family tree diagram on Reproduction Page 54 to have each student circle the language or languages that his or her ancestors spoke before they learned English.

- Use the map on Reproduction Page 55 to have each student mark the areas from which his or her ancestors who spoke Indo-European languages came.

REPRODUCTION PAGE 54

THE INDO-EUROPEAN LANGUAGE FAMILY

Directions: *Circle the language or languages your ancestors spoke other than English. From how many branches of Indo-European have you circled languages?*

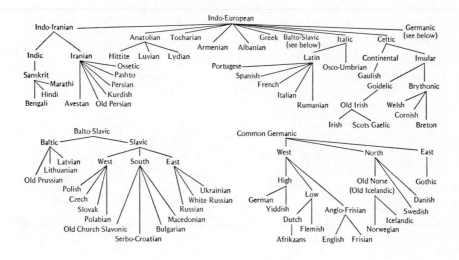

Source: Anthony Arlotto, *Introduction to Historical Linguistics* (Boston: Houghton Mifflin Co., 1977), p. 107.

- Use the map on Reproduction Page 56 to have the students identify the areas of Europe and western Asia where the different branches of Indo-European and non-Indo-European languages are spoken.

Topic II: English Borrowings from Other Indo-European Languages

- Break the students into groups based upon the Indo-European languages their ancestors spoke or an Indo-European language that they are interested in. Many students could fit into more than one group, so they should be grouped in a way to form the largest possible number of groups interested in different languages. Then ask each group to compile a vocabulary list of items borrowed into English from the language of their interest or of their ancestors. Have the groups report to the class.

- Use the same groups as in the previous activity and ask them to compile lists of words their relatives use that come from another Indo-European language but that are not used by speakers of English who do not have the same ethnic background. This activity will show that English is still continuing to borrow vocabulary from

THE INDO-EUROPEAN LANGUAGES IN PRESENT-DAY EUROPE

Directions: *Place an* X *on each place on the map below from which you have ancestors. Which branches of Indo-European do you have represented?*

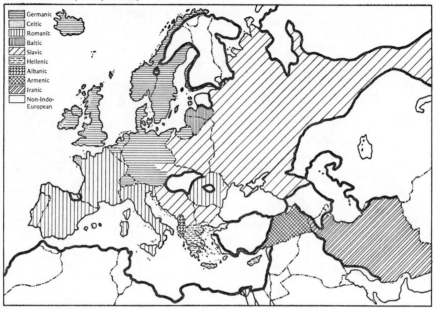

Source: Stuart Robertson and Frederick G. Cassidy, *The Development of Modern English*, 2d ed. (Englewood Cliffs, N.J.: Prentice-Hall, 1954), p. 21. Adapted by permission of Prentice-Hall, Inc., Englewood Cliffs, New Jersey.

other Indo-European languages and the nature of such borrowings, generally ethnic foods.

- Using Reproduction Page 57, have the students identify the source language and the Indo-European branch from which each of the following words was borrowed into English. The sources may be found in most dictionaries.

1. clan	13. innumerable
2. street	14. slogan
3. egg	15. poverty
4. history	16. spinach
5. adventure	17. cypress
6. tundra	18. army
7. bishop	19. plum
8. pajamas	20. bungalow
9. law	21. sister
10. schooner	22. idiosyncrasy
11. angel	23. curse
12. knife	24. obedient

REPRODUCTION PAGE 56

LOCATING INDO-EUROPEAN LANGUAGES

Directions: *Match the numbers in the areas of the map below with the branches of Indo-European spoken in those areas. The non-Indo-European languages spoken in the area have already been marked for you.*

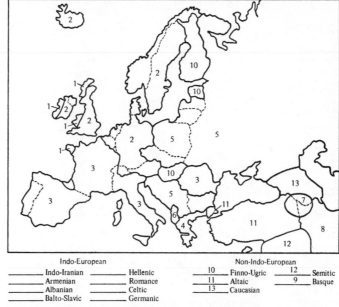

Indo-European		Non-Indo-European	
_____ Indo-Iranian	_____ Hellenic	10 ___ Finno-Ugric	12 ___ Semitic
_____ Armenian	_____ Romance	11 ___ Altaic	9 ___ Basque
_____ Albanian	_____ Celtic	13 ___ Caucasian	
_____ Balto-Slavic	_____ Germanic		

Source: John Algeo, *Problems in the Origins and Development of the English Language*, 2d ed. (New York: Harcourt Brace Jovanovich, 1966 and 1972), p. 84. Redrawn by permission of Harcourt Brace Jovanovich, Inc.

25. radish		28. tiger	
26. violin		29. mosquito	
27. paraffin		30. splint	

- Have each student write a short essay on how English has been augmented by borrowing vocabulary from the other Indo-European languages.

Topic III: Other Language Families of the World

- After the various language families of the world have been discussed, ask each student to identify the non-Indo-European language family, if any, to which the languages of his ancestors belong, and if possible, the specific languages.

- Using Reproduction Pages 58 and 59, have students with African and Asiatic ancestry identify for the class the geographic areas from which their ancestors came and the language families to which the languages of their ancestors belonged.

- Using Reproduction Page 60, have students identify the language families spoken in the different geographic areas of the Eastern Hemisphere.

- Using Reproduction Page 61, have students identify the native American grouping of languages that was originally spoken in your area. If possible, ascertain which particular languages from that grouping were (or are) spoken in your area.

REPRODUCTION PAGE 57

ORIGINS OF WORDS

Directions: *Identify the source language from which English borrowed these words and then identify to which Indo-European branch that source language belongs. You will need to use your dictionary for this exercise.*

		Source Language	Indo-European Branch
1.	clan		
2.	street		
3.	egg		
4.	history		
5.	adventure		
6.	tundra		
7.	bishop		
8.	pajamas		
9.	law		
10.	schooner		
11.	angel		
12.	knife		
13.	innumerable		
14.	slogan		
15.	poverty		
16.	spinach		
17.	cypress		
18.	army		
19.	plum		
20.	bungalow		
21.	sister		
22.	idiosyncrasy		
23.	curse		
24.	obedient		
25.	radish		
26.	violin		
27.	paraffin		
28.	tiger		
29.	mosquito		
30.	splint		

REPRODUCTION PAGE 58

MAJOR LANGUAGE GROUPS OF AFRICA

Directions: *Place an X in each place on the map below from which you have ancestors.*

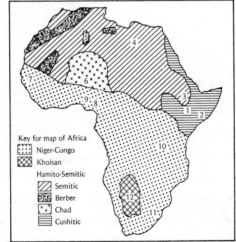

Key for map of Africa
- Niger-Congo
- Khoisan

Hamito-Semitic
- Semitic
- Berber
- Chad
- Cushitic

Familiar Languages

1.	Gulla	5.	Tuareg	9.	Yoruba
2.	Somali	6.	Hausa	10.	Swahili
3.	Amharic	7.	Wolof	11.	Zulu
4.	Arabic	8.	Ibo	12.	Bushman

Source: Anthony Arlotto, *Introduction to Historical Linguistics* (Boston: Houghton Mifflin Co., 1972), p. 56.

MAJOR LANGUAGE GROUPS OF ASIA

Directions: *Place an X in each place on the map below from which you have ancestors.*

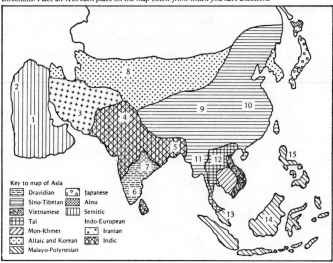

Key to map of Asia
Dravidian   Japanese
Sino-Tibetan   Ainu
Vietnamese   Semitic
Tai   Indo-European
Mon-Khmer   Iranian
Altaic and Korean Indic
Malayo-Polynesian

Familiar Languages

1. Arabic	6. Tamil	11. Burmese
2. Hebrew	7. Telegu	12. Thai
3. Persian	8. Uzbek	13. Malay
4. Hindi	9. Tibetan	14. Dayak
5. Bengali	10. Chinese	15. Tagalog

Source: Anthony Arlotto, *Introduction to Historical Linguistics* (Boston: Houghton Mifflin Co., 1972), p. 51.

LANGUAGE FAMILIES OF THE EASTERN HEMISPHERE

Directions: *Match the numbers in the areas of the map below with the families of languages spoken in those areas.*

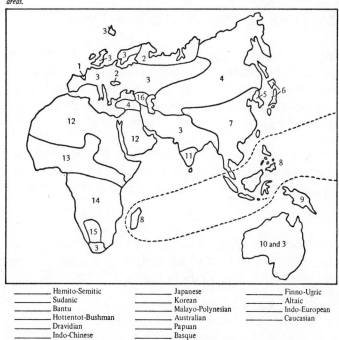

_____ Hamito-Semitic	_____ Japanese	_____ Finno-Ugric
_____ Sudanic	_____ Korean	_____ Altaic
_____ Bantu	_____ Malayo-Polynesian	_____ Indo-European
_____ Hottentot-Bushman	_____ Australian	_____ Caucasian
_____ Dravidian	_____ Papuan	
_____ Indo-Chinese	_____ Basque	

Source: John Algeo, *Problems in the Origins and Development of the English Language,* 2d ed. (New York: Harcourt Brace Jovanovich, 1966 and 1972), p. 83. Redrawn by permission of Harcourt Brace Jovanovich, Inc.

MAJOR LANGUAGE GROUPS OF AMERICA NORTH OF MEXICO

Directions: *From the map below, find the native American language grouping which was originally spoken in your area. What particular language or languages from that group were spoken in your area? Do you know of others that are not listed below?*

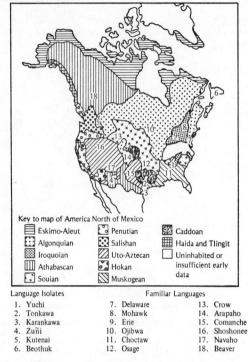

Key to map of America North of Mexico

Eskimo-Aleut	Penutian	Caddoan
Algonquian	Salishan	Haida and Tlingit
Iroquoian	Uto-Aztecan	Uninhabited or insufficient early data
Athabascan	Hokan	
Souian	Muskogean	

Language Isolates	Familiar Languages	
1. Yuchi	7. Delaware	13. Crow
2. Tonkawa	8. Mohawk	14. Arapaho
3. Karankawa	9. Erie	15. Comanche
4. Zuñi	10. Ojibwa	16. Shoshonee
5. Kutenai	11. Choctaw	17. Navaho
6. Beothuk	12. Osage	18. Beaver

Source: Anthony Arlotto, *Introduction to Historical Linguistics,* (Boston: Houghton Mifflin Co., 1972), p. 59,

Topic IV: English Borrowings from Non-Indo-European Languages

- Break the students into groups based upon the non-Indo-European languages or language families that include the languages their ancestors spoke or in which they are interested. Try to form as many groups as possible. Then ask each group to compile a vocabulary list of items borrowed into English from the language or language families of their ancestors or interest.

- Have the students compile a list of vocabulary items borrowed from the native American languages indigenous to your area. Unless your area is within the area where Algonquian languages were spoken, the majority of the vocabulary items will be place names.

- Using Reproduction Page 62, have the students identify the source language and the language family from which each of the following words was borrowed into English. The sources may be found in most dictionaries.

1.	safari	5.	mango
2.	vampire	6.	judo
3.	cinnamon	7.	tea
4.	mugwump	8.	bamboo

SOURCES OF ENGLISH WORDS

Directions: *Use your dictionary to find the source language from which English borrowed the following words and then identify the non-Indo-European language family to which that source language belongs.*

	Source Language	Language Family
1. safari		
2. vampire		
3. cinnamon		
4. mugwump		
5. mango		
6. judo		
7. tea		
8. bamboo		
9. kangaroo		
10. khaki		
11. harem		
12. goulash		
13. pariah		
14. hogan		
15. okra		
16. coffee		
17. chipmunk		
18. giraffe		
19. karate		
20. kibbutz		
21. squash		
22. tycoon		
23. ukulele		
24. banjo		
25. geisha		
26. raccoon		
27. horde		
28. taboo		
29. yam		
30. almanac		

9. kangaroo
10. khaki
11. harem
12. goulash
13. pariah
14. hogan
15. okra
16. coffee
17. chipmunk
18. giraffe
19. karate

20. kibbutz
21. squash
22. tycoon
23. ukulele
24. banjo
25. geisha
26. raccoon
27. horde
28. taboo
29. yam
30. almanac

- Have each student write a short essay on how English has been augmented by vocabulary borrowings from non-Indo-European languages of the world.

ASSESSING ACHIEVEMENT OF OBJECTIVES

Ongoing Evaluation

The extent to which students have mastered the material in this chapter can be measured by collecting any of the activities assigned individually, particularly the writing activities.

Final Evaluation

For an overall evaluation of the students' mastery of the material in this chapter, if all the topics in the chapter have been taught, a test constructed directly from the list of student objectives for the chapter as listed on page 168 can be used. As an alternative, one might use a test composed of the following items, which may be augmented by map questions using the maps from the Reproduction Pages.

1. Show the relationship of English to the other Germanic languages by reconstructing a family tree of the Germanic branch of Indo-European.

2. From what branch of Indo-European (other than Germanic) has English borrowed vocabulary most extensively?

3. Identify the major branches of the Indo-European language family.

4. From what three Indo-European languages did English borrow vocabulary most extensively during the Old English period? Give examples of words borrowed from each language.

5. From what Italic or Romance languages did English borrow vocabulary most extensively during the Middle English period? Give examples of the types of borrowing involved.

6. Give examples of English vocabulary borrowing from four non-Germanic and non-Italic Indo-European languages.

7. Name five major language families of the world other than Indo-European.

8. Give three vocabulary words in English that were borrowed from African languages and three that were borrowed from American Indian languages.

9. Identify four Asia languages from which English has borrowed vocabulary and list two words borrowed from each language.

10. Identify the language family from which at least five of the following words were borrowed into English: *banjo, assassin, calico, sabbath, turban, mandarin, sarong, tattoo, kangaroo, karate, hickory,* and *woodchuck.*

RESOURCES FOR TEACHING
ABOUT LANGUAGE FAMILIES OF THE WORLD

Below is a selected and annotated list of resources useful to teaching the topics in this chapter, divided into audiovisual materials and print materials and arranged in order of ascending difficulty. Special strengths and weaknesses are mentioned in the annotations. Addresses of publishers or distributors can be found in the alphabetical list on pages 263–265 in Appendix A. Films are black and white unless otherwise indicated.

I. THE INDO-EUROPEAN LANGUAGE FAMILY

Audiovisual Materials

History of the Indo-European Language Family. Film, part of *Language and Linguistics* Series, 29 minutes, Indiana University Audio-Visual Center. Discusses the history of the Indo-European languages and interrelationships among them.

Print

"Siblings Cousins and Ancestors," pp. 1–29 in *The Story of British English* by J. N. Hook. Provides a complete but simple discussion of the Indo-European language family. Lists suggested activities. Paperbound, Scott, Foresman and Co., 1974.

"Words: All in the Family," pp. 61–68 in *Words, Words, Words* by Charlton Laird. Provides a superficial overview of the Indo-European language family. Gives exercises. Paperbound, Harcourt Brace Jovanovich, 1972.

"Words: Their Family Traits," pp. 69–74 in *Words, Words, Words* by Charlton Laird. Gives a simple explanation of the relationships between English and the other Indo-European languages in terms of Grimm's Law. Has exercises. Paperbound, Harcourt Brace Jovanovich, 1972.

"Indo-European and Its Branches," pp. 24–38 in *A History of the English Language* by Garland Cannon. Provides a fairly complete short description of the Indo-European language family. Has suggested activities. Paperbound, Harcourt Brace Jovanovich, 1972.

"Indo-European," pp. 10–17 in *The English Language* by Charles B. Martin and Curt M. Rulon. Identifies the Indo-European branches and the differences between Germanic and the other branches clearly. Hardbound, Allyn and Bacon, 1973.

"The Ancestry of English," pp. 15–23 in *The Development of Modern English*, 2d ed., by Stuart Robertson and Frederic G. Cassidy. Discusses the language family and branches of Indo-European in rather conservative terms. Hardbound, Prentice-Hall, 1954.

"The Indo-European Languages," pp. 103–109 in *Introduction to Historical Linguistics* by Anthony Arlotto. Provides a rather terse description of the various branches of Indo-European. Hardbound, Houghton Mifflin, 1972.

Exercises, pp. 84–87 in *Problems in the Origins and Development of the English Language*, 2d ed. by John Algeo. Provides exercises dealing with the location of the various Indo-European branches geographically and with the relationships of individual languages to the other Indo-European languages. Paperbound, Harcourt Brace Jovanovich, 1972.

"The Backgrounds of English," pp. 85–112 in *The Origins and Development of the English Language*, 2d ed., by Thomas Pyles. Identifies the relationships among the various Indo-European languages with good detail and focuses on how Germanic languages differ from the other Indo-European languages. Hardbound, Harcourt Brace Jovanovich, 1971.

"The Major Changes from Indo-European to Germanic," pp. 97–98 in *Problems in the Origins and Development of the English Language*, 2d ed., by John Algeo. Gives an exercise illustrating the seven major changes that separate Germanic from the other Indo-European branches. Paperbound, Harcourt Brace Jovanovich, 1972.

"The Indo-European Family of Languages," pp. 17–45 in *A History of the English Language*, 2d ed., by Albert C. Baugh. Provides a rather scholarly explanation of the Indo-European language family. Hardbound, Appleton-Century-Crofts, 1957.

"The Indo-European Language Family," pp. 21–37 in *Historical Linguistics*, 2d ed., by Winifred P. Lehmann. Describes the Indo-European language family in the best detail of any readily available source. Hardbound, Holt, Rinehart and Winston, 1973.

"Cognate Words in the Indo-European Languages," pp. 90–96 in *Problems in the Origins and Development of the English Language,* 2d ed., by John Algeo. Provides two fairly difficult exercises dealing with related words in various Indo-European languages from the same Indo-European roots. Paperbound, Harcourt Brace Jovanovich, 1972.

II. ENGLISH BORROWINGS
FROM OTHER INDO-EUROPEAN LANGUAGES

Audiovisual Materials

English Language: Story of Its Development. Film, 11 minutes, Coronet Instructional Media, 1952. Relates the external history of English and focuses on various influences on the language.

Discovering Language: How English Borrowed Words. Film, 11 minutes, Coronet Instructional Media, 1973. Shows major influences on English vocabulary.

Print

"Old English," pp. 51-59 in *A History of the English Language* by Garland Cannon. Provides a short, readable explanation of Celtic, Latin, and Scandinavian borrowing during the Old English period. Paperbound, Harcourt Brace Jovanovich, 1972.

"Loanwords," pp. 96-99 in *A History of the English Language* by Garland Cannon. Gives some examples of loanwords from Latin, French, and Scandinavian during the Middle English period. Paperbound, Harcourt Brace Jovanovich, 1972.

"Loanwords," pp. 133-140 in *A History of the English Language* by Garland Cannon. Gives examples of English loanwords from the other Indo-European languages and Arabic. Paperbound, Harcourt Brace Jovanovich, 1972.

"The True-Born Englishman," pp. 31-56 in *The Story of British English* by J. N. Hook. Provides a summary of the types of vocabulary borrowing from different sources during the history of English. Lists activities. Paperbound, Scott, Foresman and Co., 1974.

"Sources of Vocabulary," pp. 146-171 in *The Development of Modern English*, 2d ed., by Stuart Robertson and Frederic G. Cassidy. Discusses English loanwords from other Indo-European languages. Hardbound, Prentice-Hall, 1954.

"Foreign Elements in the English Word Stock," pp. 313-337, 339 in *The Origins and Development of the English Language*, 2d ed., by Thomas Pyles. Discusses the major and minor Indo-European sources of borrowed English vocabulary in great detail and the periods of the various borrowings. Hardbound, Harcourt Brace Jovanovich, 1971.

"Foreign Influences on Old English," pp. 83-124 in *A History of the English Language*, 2d ed., by Albert C. Baugh. Gives a detailed explanation of the Celtic, Latin, and Scandinavian borrowings into English during the Old English period. Hardbound, Appleton-Century-Crofts, 1957.

"Middle English," pp. 200-218, 222-227 in *A History of the English Language*, 2d ed., by Albert C. Baugh. Gives a detailed explanation of the French, Latin, and Low German vocabulary borrowings into English during the Middle English period. Hardbound, Appleton-Century-Crofts, 1957.

"The Renaissance," pp. 267-275 in *A History of the English Language*, 2d ed., by Albert C. Baugh. Gives a detailed explanation of English borrowing from Latin, Greek, French, Italian, and Spanish during the Early Modern English period. Hardbound, Appleton-Century-Crofts, 1957.

"Early American Speech: Adoptions from Foreign Tongues," pp. 48-55 in *Words and Ways of American English* by Thomas Pyles. Provides a simple discussion of early vocabulary borrowings from Dutch, German, French, and Spanish into American English. Paperbound, Random House, 1952.

"Later American Speech: Adoptions from Foreign Tongues," pp. 195-213 in *Words and Ways of American English* by Thomas Pyles. Provides a simple discussion of later American English borrowings from French, Spanish, German, Yiddish, Italian, and Irish. Paperbound, Random House, 1952.

"The Melting Pot," pp. 33-58 in *American English* by Albert H. Marckwardt. Discusses American English vocabulary borrowed from French, Spanish, German, and Dutch. Paperbound, Oxford University Press, 1958.

"Celtic and Latin Influences," pp. 88-90 in *A Structural History of English* by John Nist. Explains and lists borrowings from Latin and Celtic in pre-Christian Old English. Hardbound, St. Martin's Press, 1966.

"Scandinavian Influence," pp. 99-103 in *A Structural History of English* by John Nist. Gives the most comprehensive short discussion of Scandinavian borrowings into late Old English. Hardbound, St. Martin's Press, 1966.

"French Influence," pp. 160–166 in *A Structural History of English* by John Nist. Gives the most comprehensive short discussion of French borrowing into English during the Middle English period. Hardbound, St. Martin's Press, 1966.

"Problems 3.10, 3.11, 3.12, 3.15," pp. 50–51, 54–55, 57, 61 in *Origins of the English Language* by Joseph M. Williams. Provides lists of words borrowed from Latin during the Old English period and words borrowed from Danish during the Old English period and asks what the borrowings reflect about the cultures borrowing and borrowed from. Hardbound, The Free Press, 1975.

"Problems 4.10, 4.11, 4.13," pp. 81–82, 87 in *Origins of the English Language* by Joseph M. Williams. Provides lists of words borrowed from French and Latin during the Middle English period and asks what the borrowings reflect about the cultures borrowing and borrowed from. Hardbound, The Free Press, 1975.

"Problem 5.4" pp. 100–102 in *Origins of the English Language* by Joseph M. Williams. Provides lists of words borrowed during various time periods from Italian, Spanish, Low German languages, German, Slavic, Persian, and Indic languages (as well as non-Indo-European languages), and asks what the borrowed words tell about the relationship of English culture to the cultures of these languages. Hardbound, The Free Press, 1975.

Exercises, pp. 266–272 in *Problems in the Origins and Development of the English Language*, 2d ed., by John Algeo. Provides several fairly difficult exercises dealing with English borrowings from Latin and French. Paperbound, Harcourt Brace Jovanovich, 1972.

III. OTHER LANGUAGE FAMILIES OF THE WORLD

Print

"The Non-Indo-European Languages," pp. 82–85 in *The Origins and Development of the English Language*, 2d ed., by Thomas Pyles. Gives a short overview of the language families of the world other than Indo-European. Hardbound, Harcourt Brace Jovanovich, 1971.

"The World's Languages," pp. 82–83 in *Problems in the Origins and Development of the English Language*, 2d ed., by John Algeo. Provides two exercises dealing with non-Indo-European languages of the Eastern Hemisphere, one dealing with families and one dealing with individual members of families. Paperbound, Harcourt Brace Jovanovich, 1972.

"Language Families," pp. 45–62 in *Introduction to Historical Linguistics* by Anthony Arlotto. Gives a very detailed discussion of the major language families of the world other than Indo-European. Hardbound, Houghton Mifflin, 1972.

"The Afro-Asiatic Language Family, Other Language Families of Africa, Other Language Families of Asia," pp. 38–42 in *Historical Linguistics*, 2d ed., by Winfred P. Lehmann. Presents one of the best short discussions of the language families of Africa and Asia. Hardbound, Holt, Rinehart and Winston, 1973.

IV. ENGLISH BORROWINGS FROM NON-INDO-EUROPEAN LANGUAGES

Audiovisual Materials

English Language: Story of Its Development. Film, 11 minutes, Coronet Instructional Media, 1952. Shows vocabulary contributions of various language groups to English during the history of English.

Print

"Early American Speech: Adoptions from Foreign Tongues," pp. 28–48 in *Words and Ways of American English* by Thomas Pyles. Provides a simple discussion of early American English borrowings from American Indian and African languages. Paperbound, Random House, 1952.

"Later American Speech: Adoptions from Foreign Tongues," pp. 191–195 in *Words and Ways of American English* by Thomas Pyles. Provides a simple discussion of later borrowings from native American languages into American English. Paperbound, Random House, 1952.

"Indian Influence," pp. 22–33 in *American English* by Albert H. Marckwardt. Discusses borrowing of vocabulary into American English from American Indian languages. Paperbound, Oxford University Press, 1958.

"Sources of Vocabulary," pp. 167–169, 171 in *The Development of Modern English*, 2d ed., by Stuart Robertson and Frederic G. Cassidy. Discusses English vocabulary borrowed from Arabic, Hebrew, Indic languages, Malay, Chinese, Japanese, Turkish, and American Indian languages. Hardbound, Prentice-Hall, 1954.

"Foreign Elements in the English Word Stock," pp. 337–339 in *The Origins and Development of the English Language*, 2d ed., by Thomas Pyles. Identifies many of the vocabulary borrowings into English from the non-Indo-European languages of the Old World. Hardbound, Harcourt Brace Jovanovich, 1971.

"Loan-Words from Japanese," p. 273 in *Problems in the Origins and Development of the English Language*, 2d ed., by John Algeo. Provides an exercise dealing with twenty-nine Japanese loanwords in English. Paperbound, Harcourt Brace Jovanovich, 1972.

"Problem 5.4," pp. 100–102 in *Origins of the English Language* by Joseph M. Williams. Lists words borrowed into English at various times from Arabic, Hebrew, Turkic, Dravidian, Tibeto-Chinese, Japanese, Malayo-Polynesian, and Australian (as well as various branches of Indo-European) and asks what these borrowings reflect about the relationship of speakers of English to speakers of these languages. Hardbound, The Free Press, 1975.

10

Old English

This chapter focuses on the history of England during the Old English period, the influence of Latin and Old Norse on the English language of the period, and the structure of the Old English language. A practical application of this study should be the development of awareness of how English-speaking culture began and developed. Another practical application can be the development of an understanding of grammatical concepts of Modern English by comparing and contrasting them with those of Old English.

First, the student should be introduced to the history of Britain before the arrival of the ancestors of the English. Next, the story of how the Angles, Saxons, and Jutes came to occupy Britain should be told. Finally, the processes by which the Anglo-Saxons became the English including the Christianization process and the Viking raids and settlement should be related to the student.

If the teacher wishes, the topic of Latin and Old Norse influence on Old English can be taught then. Latin's influence on Old English was that of the language of a superior culture reflecting the influence of that culture on an inferior culture. The Old Norse borrowings into Old English, on the other hand, reflect the amalgamation of two closely related and equal cultures, those of the Vikings and the Old English.

Finally, the Old English language itself may be examined. It will strike students as a very difficult language because it uses grammatical devices that are different from those of Modern English. If the teacher or some of the students are familiar with a highly inflected language like Latin or Modern German, it might be useful to draw parallels between the grammatical system of Old English and one of those languages. Discussion of the pronunciation of Old English has been omitted from the overview because it would not be an appropriate study for secondary school students; however, the annotated bibliography does list Old English readings on records, so the students can be introduced to how Old English sounds.

The first topic will be the most interesting to students, and the last topic will be the most difficult. The teacher will need to decide on whether the second topic should be introduced or not; one consideration should be whether the topic of English borrowing from other Indo-European langues in Chapter 9 has been taught and, if so, how thoroughly borrowings from Latin and Scandinavian languages were discussed then.

OBJECTIVES

If the three topics in this chapter are chosen for study by the teacher, the students should, at the end of the unit, be able to:

1. Identify the occupants of Britain before the ancestors of the English arrived
2. Identify the ancestors of the English and match up each group with its corresponding kingdoms in the Anglo-Saxon heptarchy
3. Name the four major Old English dialects
4. Identify major figures connected with the Christianization of England
5. Identify the major sources of our knowledge of the history of the Old English period
6. Explain the relationship between the Danes and the Old English during the Old English period and identify major historical figures from both groups
7. Identify the types of English borrowing from Latin and Old Norse and give illustrative examples
8. Identify major differences between the grammatical concepts and devices of Old English nouns and adjectives and those of Modern English
9. Identify major differences between the grammatical concepts and devices associated with Old English verbs and those of Modern English
10. Name the Old English sources of Modern English noun and verb inflections

CONTENT OVERVIEW

The External History of the Old English Period

The best source for the pre-English and early Old English history is the work of the greatest historian of the Dark Ages, the Venerable Bede, a monk who began his scholarly career at the monastery of St. Paul at Wearmouth but spent most of his life at the twin monastery of St. Paul at Jarrow, both in Northumbria. Although he wrote many scholarly works, his most important historically is *The Ecclesiastical History of the English People*, completed around 730 A.D.

Besides being the first reputable historian of the English, Bede made several major contributions to the study of history. In his preface to the *Ecclesiastical History*, he defended and justified the study of history; the defense suggests that educated people in the Dark Ages were suspicious of any study that was not biblical. He also fixed and popularized the idea of dating from the birth of Jesus, our present system with the use of A.D. (*Anno Domini*). This uniform system of dating replaced the Roman practice of dating by regnal years of emperors or popes, the Greek practice of dating in terms of the Olympiad, and the general European practice of dating in terms of the reigns of kings. Bede was also the first historian to consider the English to be one people, although the church had earlier come to the same conclusion in its plans to convert the Anglo-Saxons.

According to Bede, Brittania was inhabited at the beginning of the historical period by Celtic peoples— Britons in the South, and Picts and Scots, the latter having come from Ireland, in the North. Julius Caesar, having conquered the Celts in Gaul, led his Roman army across the English Channel to attack the Celts in Brittania in 55–54 B.C. with less success. The Romans did conquer Brittania except for Scotland and Wales under the emperor Claudius from 43–46 A.D., and the Roman government of Brittania lasted until 410 when the Roman legions were withdrawn because of the need to protect lands closer to Rome from barbarian attacks.

During the nearly four centuries of Roman occupation, the Roman army had protected the Britons from the attacks of the still warlike Scots and Picts to the north and from the occasional incursions by Germanic-speaking Saxons into the southeastern corner of Brittania. As a result, the Britons had become less adept at the martial skills needed to defend themselves. Thus, after the Roman withdrawal, the Britons were unable to defend themselves from the northern Celts, and their king, Vortigern, made the fatal mistake of asking for help from mercenaries from the various West Germanic tribes in Europe. Bede says the Jutes under the brothers Hengest and Horsa were the first to come in 449, but the Saxons and Angles followed shortly. These ancestors of the English were successful in driving back the Scots and Picts. However, instead of being satisfied with the lands the Britons were willing to reward them with, these Germanic mercenaries decided they could just as well take all of the British lands.

After sending home for friends and relatives as reinforcements, the Angles, Saxons, and Jutes proceeded to conquer nearly all of what is now England. The British Celts, who could not defend themselves from the Scots and Picts, could hardly be expected to fare well against their erstwhile protectors. Thus, the British Celts were either killed, assimilated into the Germanic peoples, or forced to withdraw into Cornwall, Wales, or across the English Channel into Brittany in northern France.

Bede detailed the settlement pattern of the Germanic tribes to account for the seven Old English kingdoms, the Anglo-Saxon heptarchy, as follows: the Jutes settled in Kent (including the Isle of Wight); the Saxons settled in Essex, Sussex, and Wessex; the Angles settled in East Anglia, Northumbria, and Mercia. Since he was writing nearly three centuries after the fact, however, Bede may not be completely accurate. Certainly, it is likely that the Germanic invaders of Brittania included people from tribes other than those he mentioned, notably the Frisians.

By tradition, the Jutes came from the northern half of the Danish peninsula, Jutland. However, archaeological and linguistic evidence suggests that they had migrated south and west into the areas of the Frisians and Franks before invading Brittania. If this hypothesis is true, Bede's Jutes certainly included Frisians and probably Franks. The Angles are associated with southern Denmark and Schleswig-Holstein in northern Germany. The Saxons are said to have come from the area south and west of the Angles in Germany, btween the Elbe and Ems. However, they had moved westward absorbing other tribes including the Angarii, Bructeri, Cherusci, and some of the Chauci and mingling with the Frisians before invading the island of Brittania.

The kingdoms within the Anglo-Saxon heptarchy were never of equal strength; they constantly warred against each other, with first one kingdom, then another gaining ascendancy over the others. Bede recorded the early dominance of Kent over the other kingdoms and the shift of hegemony to Northumbria in the seventh and eight centuries. Since he died in 735, he could not relate the rise later in the century of Mercia, due in part no doubt to the harassment of Northumbria later in the eighth century by Vikings (speakers of North Germanic languages and often identified as Danes but no doubt including Swedes and Norwegians as well). Wessex became the dominant Anglo-Saxon kingdom in 825 when the West Saxon king, Egbert, overthrew the Mercian king. Wessex remained the dominant kingdom throughout the rest of the Old English period; in fact, the king of Wessex was called the king of England after 899 until 1016, and again between 1042 and 1066. A Viking or Danish king ruled England during the intervening years of the eleventh century.

Latin and Viking Influence on Old English

Since the *Ecclesiastical History* is concerned with church history primarily, a great deal of it relates to the conversion of the English to Christianity. While the modern reader may find Bede gullible because of the many miracles he reports, one must remember the ambience of Bede's time. Bede strove for accuracy, however, and often indicated sources in the margin opposite his text and cited people who related particular events to him, indicating that he was not always totally convinced of what he was told. Whenever possible, he also incorporated any documents he could procure to support his facts.

According to Bede, St. Augustine and other monks were ordered by Pope Gregory in 596 to go to Brittania to convert the Anglo-Saxons, but they refused at first. Finally obeying the pope, they landed on the Isle of Thanet in 597, where they were greeted more or less hospitably by King Ethelbert of Kent, who shortly thereafter converted to Christianity, having no doubt already been made receptive by his Christian queen, a former princess of the Franks. Bede included a great deal of correspondence between Gregory and

Augustine, who was forever asking Gregory's advice about what to do. One example concerned what to do with the pagan churches after the English converted to Christianity. Gregory's reply was that since the English were already used to worshiping in them, pagan churches could be consecrated as Christian churches and the English allowed to continue to worship in them. Gregory added that any pagan festivals that the English were used to celebrating could be incorporated into the liturgical calendar as a saint's feast day and still celebrated. Easter, for example (the word is cognate with *Istar* and *Astarte*, eastern Mediterranean names for the earth-mother goddess), still retains the trappings of fertility symbols, that is, eggs, rabbits, plants, associated with earlier fertility-rite religions.

Bede recorded the gradual conversion of England during the next century or so. He had little sympathy for the Irish monks who were also converting the English in the North to Christianity, however. When the Italian-converted English of the South of England encountered the Irish-converted English of the North, each group considered the other group heretical, and they frequently killed each other. The major reason for the heresy charges was that the Irish church still operated on the Jewish calendar, a lunar calendar, and thus celebrated Easter on a different date than the Italian church, which had adopted the Julian calendar, a solar calendar. The two groups also disagreed about the shape of the tonsure—the shaving of a priest's head upon ordination. The Roman tradition was that the tonsure should be round; the Irish tonsure consisted of shaving the top of the head from the front straight back. Bede considered it admirable of the Irish monks and their converts when they gave in on both points at a council in 716.

There are many famous stories recorded in Bede's *Ecclesiastical History*. These include Gregory's puns and confusion about Angles and Angels; the story of Caedmon, the first English poet; the conversion of Edwin, king of Northumbria, with the statement by Edwin's high priest, Coifi, that they might as well try Christianity since the old religion did not work anyway; and the comparison by Edwin's nameless thane of a man's life to a sparrow's passage through a warm, lighted room, having entered from the darkness and leaving into darkness.

As indicated in the overview and the annotated bibliography of Chapter 9, a great deal of English vocabulary was borrowed from Latin during this period of Christianization.

Bede's *Ecclesiastical History* was the source for the early entries of the other great document relating the history of the Old English period, *The Anglo-Saxon Chronicle*. This document, which was the source of most other early histories of England, was begun during the reign of Alfred the Great of Wessex, probably around 891.

The *Chronicle* lists the first raid on England by the Vikings (identified as *Danes*) in the entry for 787. The early raids seem to have been primarily looting expeditions in which the Danes burned what they could not carry away. These raids were concentrated in the northern and eastern parts of England, and the monasteries at Lindisfarne and Jarrow were sacked in the last decade of the eighth century. However, the entry for 835 relates the defeat by King Egbert of Wessex of the combined forces of the Danes and the Celts of Cornwall; this suggests that the Vikings were no longer only raiding but had also mounted an expeditionary army. It is about this time that strange entries begin to appear in the *Chronicle* recounting battles in which the English win but that leave the Danes in possession of the battlefield. One would probably call those English defeats now; one surmises a certain pro-English interpretation of these battles on the part of the scribe who made the entries.

From the middle of the ninth century on, the Vikings were clearly bent on colonization in England. From 865 to 878, the Danes conquered and occupied East Anglia, nearly all of Northumbria, and much of Mercia, giving them control of the northeastern half of England. After 870, Wessex was the center of opposition to the Danes. King Alfred the Great, who succeeded his brother Ethered in 871, defeated the Danish forces led by King Guthrum in a major battle in 878, after which under their peace treaty, the Treaty of Wedmore, England was divided into two parts along an old Roman road called Watling Street. Alfred was to rule all of the English parts west of Watling Street, and Guthrun was to rule all of the Danish parts, the Danelaw, which was east of Watling Street. Guthrun shortly thereafter accepted Christianity and Alfred was his godfather.

There was sporadic fighting between the English and the Danes for several decades afterward. During the reign of Alfred, his son, and grandsons, the power of the king of Wessex, who was considered the king of England, gradually extended over the Danelaw as well as the English part of England, and the Danes began to consider themselves English and were assimilated into Anglo-Saxon culture by 959. This assimilation could be accomplished easily because of the similarity between the West Germanic Old English and the North Germanic Old Norse languages. As indicated in the overview and the annotated bibliography of Chapter 9, a great deal of English vocabulary was borrowed from Scandinavian in late Old English.

Once the original Vikings had become English, however, a new wave of Viking attacks on England began when Olaf Tryggvason led ninety-three ships up the Thames and defeated the English forces in 991 as recorded in the poem, "The Battle of Maldon." Other Viking attacks, victories, and acceptances of tribute from the English continued until 1013. In that year the Vikings under King Svein of Sweden decided to keep the territory they conquered; by 1014, Svein had control of all of England and called himself the king of England before he died within the year. He was succeeded on the throne of England by his son, Canute, who consolidated his power by marrying Emma of Normandy, the widow of the last English king, Æthelred. Canute ruled the English who followed him in his wars from 1017 to 1036 against his fellow Vikings. In 1028 and 1029, Canute defeated Olaf Tryggvason, who had become king of Norway, and Canute became the king of Norway as well as of England. Canute was succeeded at his death by his son Harald who was in turn succeeded by Canute's son by Emma of Normandy, Hardecanute.

The English line of Alfred was restored to the throne upon the death of Hardecanute who was succeeded by his half brother (the son of Æthelred and Emma), Edward the Confessor, who was forced to leave the monastic life of a Norman monastery to assume the throne. When he died in 1066 with no heir, the throne of England was up for grabs.

The Old English Language

There were four principal dialects of Old English. Kentish was spoken in the area supposedly settled by the Jutes, that is, Kent. West Saxon was spoken in Wessex and Sussex. Mercian was spoken in Mercia, East Anglia, and Essex (despite the fact that the last name comes from East Saxon). Finally, Northumbrian was spoken in Northumbria, that is, north of the Humber River. Nearly all of the surviving Old English texts are in West Saxon, although many of them are West Saxon copies of manuscripts originally written in other dialects that were made by the scholars Alfred gathered at his court after he established peace with the Danes. Also, the Old English that is studied is usually late West Saxon, since earlier manuscripts had often been destroyed by the Vikings or had otherwise disappeared.

Old English was a highly inflected language like Latin. Nouns had five cases depending upon the grammatical function of the noun. The nominative case was used primarily for nouns used as subjects. The accusative case was used for nouns used as direct objects. The genitive case was used primarily to show possession. The dative case was used for, among other things, nouns used as indirect objects. The rarely used instrumental case is usually translated as "by means of" or "with" the particular noun in Modern English. In addition, as in Modern English, nouns were marked either singular or plural. The masculine a-stem noun declension illustrated below is the source of the regular forms of the two Modern English noun inflections: the plural and the possessive.

Old English Masculine a-stem Noun

	Singular	Plural
Nominative	stān "stone"	stānas "stones"
Accusative	stān	stānas
Genitive	stānes	stāna
Dative	stāne	stānum
Instrumental	stāne	stānum

The nominative and accusative plural forms ending in -as are the source of (e)s plural, now generalized to most other noun declensions as well. The -es genitive singular inflection (which was also shared by neuter a-stem and other noun declensions) is the source of the Modern English 's possessive inflection, which has been generalized to all nouns in Modern English. The irregular noun plurals in Modern English of originally Old English nouns that do not take the *(e)s* plural ending are survivals of the nominative-accusative plural forms of other Old English declensions. *Geese* and *teeth* come from the Old English radical consonant declension nominative-accusative forms *gēs* and *tēð* in which the root vowel differs from that of the singular *gōs* and *tōð* because of a sound change known as umlaut. *Sheep* as a plural identical to the singular comes from Old English *scēap*, the unchanged nominative-accusative plural form of the neuter a-stem noun *scēap*. *Oxen* as the plural of *ox* reflects the Old English masculine n-stem nominative-accusative form *oxan*.

The terms "masculine" and "neuter" mentioned above as well as "feminine" refer to grammatical genders such as occur in Modern German, Spanish, and French. Old English did not use natural gender based upon sex or sexlessness as Modern English generally does. As a result, pronouns referring back to a noun in Old English would be confusing to modern students. For example, the pronoun referring back to *wifmann* "woman" would be *hē* ("he") or one of the other masculine forms because *wifmann* is a masculine noun in Old English; the pronoun referring back to *bōc* ("book") would be *hēo* ("she") or one of the other feminine forms because *bōc* is a feminine noun in Old English; the pronoun referring back to *mægden* ("maiden, girl") would be *hit* ("it") or one of the other neuter forms because *mægden* is a neuter noun in Old English.

The modifiers of nouns in Old English had to agree in case, number, and grammatical gender with nouns that they modified, so there was a very complex inflectional system quite similar to that of Modern German. The demonstrative *sē, sēo,* ð*æt* (the masculine, feminine, and neuter nominative singular forms, respectively) from which modern *the* and *that* derive had different forms when they modified singular nouns in other than nominative cases, and there were different forms for the different cases when the nouns were plural as well. The same holds true for adjectives modifying nouns; different endings were added to the adjective depending on whether the noun was grammatically masculine, feminine, or neuter and on the case and number (singular or plural) of the noun. For example, in *swēte songas sungon þā scopas* ("sweet songs sang the poets") (notice the different word order from Modern English), the *-e* on *swēte* means that it is modifying a masculine plural accusative case noun, and the form *þā* means that it is modifying a masculine plural nominative plural noun (a masculine a-stem noun in both cases). To further complicate matters, the endings added to adjectives depended on whether there was a demonstrative in front of the adjective. In other words, there were two complete sets of adjective endings for the three grammatical genders in all cases in singular and plural: a strong set that was used when there was no demonstrative in front of the adjective and a weak set when there was. Notice the different forms of the adjectives in *þæm tilan mēare* ("to the good horse") and *tilum mēare* ("to [a] good horse").

Old English verbs were also much more highly inflected than Modern English verbs, inflecting not only for past tense and for third person singular present tense but also for person, number, and mood. As there are in Modern English, there were two major types of verbs (*be* and other exceptions already existed in Old English): weak verbs and strong verbs. Weak verbs are now considered "regular" verbs because they form their past tense with a dental suffix, usually *-ed*; this way of forming the past tense is a Germanic innovation that separates Germanic from the other branches of Indo-European. Strong verbs are now considered "irregular" verbs, but they form their past tense by an internal vowel change such as *sing-sang* in the same way that all Indo-European languages used to form their past tense. Many Old English strong verbs have been regularized into weak verbs in Modern English.

The verb *hȳran* ("hear") is illustrative of the Old English class 1 weak verbs, the most common of three Old English weak verb conjugations. The *-an* is an infinitive marker, and the person, number, mood, and tense markers are added to the base *hȳr-* after the infinitive inflection is removed. Notice that not all persons were marked by different forms, the plurals for all three persons always being reduced to one form, and that sometimes indicative, subjunctive, and imperative forms were not clearly differentiated from each other. However, the verb endings are clearly more complicated than those of Modern English verbs, which use only the base form of the verb for imperatives (commands) like *hear* and do not use a subjunctive form different from an indicative form except in constructions like *I asked that he hear this.* Students may be familiar with the use of subjunctives in modern foreign languages like Spanish, French, and German; if not, it is sufficient to tell them that subjunctives were used in Old English to indicate that something was not necessarily true or that it was contrary to fact as in *If I were king* (meaning that I am not king). The present participle of the verb *hȳran* illustrated here was *hȳrende* ("hearing"), and the part participle was *hȳred* ("heard"), sometimes with a *ge-* prefix, that is, *gehȳred*. The reason the ⟨e⟩ in the inflectional endings for second and third person present tense indicative is in parentheses is that the vowels in these inflectional endings were often omitted in late Old English.

Conjugation of *hȳran*

	Present Tense Indicative	Past Tense Indicative
First Person Singular	hȳre	hȳrede
Second Person Singular	hȳr(e)st	hȳredest
Third Person Singular	hȳr(e)ð	hȳrede
Plural for All Persons	hȳrað	hȳredon

	Present Tense Subjunctive	Past Tense Subjunctive
Singular for All Persons	hȳre	hȳrede
Plural for All Persons	hȳren	hȳreden

	Present Tense Imperative
Second Person Singular	hȳr
Second Person Plural	hȳrað

Strong verbs in Old English can be illustrated by the class 3 strong verb *bindan* ("bind"). There were seven classes of strong verbs in Old English, each with a different set of vowel alternations in their principal parts. The vowel alternation in the root syllable for this type of class 3 strong verb is *-i-* in the infinitive, *-a-* in the first and third person singular past indicative, *-u-* in the plural past indicative, and *-u-* in the past participle. In addition, as can be seen, endings for different persons, numbers, and moods are added to the stem besides the vowel changes. Notice that all of the present tense forms are based upon the vowel in the stem of the infinitive and that the vowel in the past subjunctive forms and in the second person singular form are based upon the vowel in the past plural indicative form. The present participle *bindende* is also based upon the infinitive. The past participle *(ge)bunden* only coincidentally has the same vowel as the past plural indicative form, however. The past tense of this verb in Modern English, *bound*, is based upon the past plural form here, but the past tense in Modern English is sometimes based on the first and third person singular past indicative as in *rose*, the past tense of *rise*, and *rode*, the past tense of *ride*.

Conjugation of *bindan*

	Present Tense Indicative	Past Tense Indicative
First Person Singular	binde	band
Second Person Singular	bindest	bunde
Third Person Singular	bindeð	band
Plural for All Persons	bindað	bundon

	Present Tense Subjunctive	Past Tense Subjunctive
Singular for All Persons	binde	bunde
Plural for All Persons	binden	bunden

	Present Tense Imperative
Second Person Singular	bind
Second Person Plural	bindað

Because of all of the inflectional endings indicating grammatical relationships, word order was somewhat flexible in Old English, as in Latin. However, the word order of Old English frequently did not differ much from that of Modern English. One exception is that in the common subject-verb-object type of sentence in Modern English, Old English preferred a subject-object-verb order, particularly if the object was a pronoun rather than a noun as in *Hē hine forbēah* ("He him passed").

LEARNING EXPERIENCES

Topic I: The External History of the Old English Period

- Using Reproduction Page 63, have the students locate the four main Old English dialect areas on the map.

- Using Reproduction Page 64, have the students locate the seven kingdoms of the Old English heptarchy on the map.

- Assign individual students to research the following and report back to the class:

   1.   Angles, Saxons, and Jutes

REPRODUCTION PAGE 63

OLD ENGLISH DIALECT AREAS

Directions: *Use different-colored pencils or crayons to shade in the areas on the map below where the four major Old English dialects were spoken (West Saxon, Kentish, Mercian, and Northumbrian). Use a fifth color to shade in the areas on the map where Celtic languages were still spoken during the Old English period.*

Source: Redrawn by permission of Harcourt Brace Jovanovich, Inc. from *Problems in the Origins and Development of the English Language*, 2d ed. (New York: Harcourt Brace Jovanovich, 1972), p. 107. © 1966, 1972 by Harcourt Brace Jovanovich, Inc.

REPRODUCTION PAGE 64

THE SEVEN KINGDOMS

Directions: *Identify the seven kingdoms of the Old English heptarchy on the map below by drawing whatever additional lines are necessary and labeling the appropriate areas: Kent, Wessex, Sussex, Essex, East Anglia, Mercia, and Northumbria.*

Source: John Nist, *A Structural History of English* (New York: St. Martin's Press, 1966), p. 76. Reprinted by permission.

2. Pope Gregory I

3. St. Augustine (not the African-born author of *The City of God*)

4. Cædmon

5. Alfred the Great

6. Bede

7. Bede's *The Ecclesiastical History of the English People*

8. Alfred's Preface to *Pastoral Care*

9. *The Anglo-Saxon Chronicle*

10. The conversion of Edwin, king of Northumbria

11. Pope Gregory I and the English slaves

12. The treaty between Alfred and Guthrum (Wedmore II)

13. St. Aidan

14. King Oswald of Northumbria

15. The Viking raids on England 787–878

16. The Viking conquest on England 991–1014

17. King Canute of England

18. Edward the Confessor

19. Cynewulf and Cyneheard

20. *Beowulf*

21. *The Wanderer*

22. *The Battle of Brunnanbush*

23. *The Battle of Maldon*

24. *The Dream of the Rood*

25. *Widsith*

26. *Deor*

27. *Judith*

28. *The Husband's Message*

29. *The Wife's Lament*

30. Ælfric

- Have each student write a short history of England from 400 to 1050 including the significant events and identifying significant historical figures of the period.

Topic II: Latin and Viking Influence on Old English

- After explaining the types of vocabulary influence which Latin and Old Norse had on Old English, use Reproduction Page 65 to have the class decide which source the following words were borrowed from during the Old English period. The answers are given below in parentheses but not on the Reproduction Page.

1. angel (Latin)	11. master (Latin)
2. bull (Old Norse)	12. priest (Latin)
3. candle (Latin)	13. root (Old Norse)
4. circle (Latin)	14. radish (Latin)
5. die (Old Norse)	15. school (Latin)
6. dirt (Old Norse)	16. scream (Old Norse)
7. egg (Old Norse)	17. sister (Old Norse)
8. give (Old Norse)	18. sky (Old Norse)
9. hymn (Latin)	19. ugly (Old Norse)
10. lily (Latin)	20. want (Old Norse)

- Use Reproduction Page 66 to have the class decide whether the following words were borrowed from Latin early in Old English or late in Old English. The early words are common words, and the later borrowings are more learned words. The answers are given below in parentheses but not on the Reproduction Page.

SOURCES OF OLD ENGLISH WORDS

Directions: *From what has been said in class about the types of words borrowed by Old English from Latin and Old Norse, try to figure out which language was the source of these words borrowed into Old English. Check a dictionary for the source of any words you are not sure of.*

1. angel
2. bull
3. candle
4. circle
5. die
6. dirt
7. egg
8. give
9. hymn
10. lily
11. master
12. priest
13. root
14. radish
15. school
16. scream
17. sister
18. sky
19. ugly
20. want

1. alms (early)	11. monk (early)
2. cancer (late)	12. noon (early)
3. cat (early)	13. paper (late)
4. centurion (late)	14. paralysis (late)
5. chest (early)	15. parsley (late)
6. heretic (late)	16. pear (early)
7. history (late)	17. peony (late)
8. lettuce (early)	18. pot (early)
9. martyr (late)	19. psalm (early)
10. mat (early)	20. talent (early)

TIME OF BORROWING

Directions: *From the following words borrowed from Latin into Old English, decide which are likely to have been borrowed during the period of Christianization (before 700) and which are likely to have been borrowed in late Old English (after 700). The first group will include common words, and the second group will include more learned words.*

1. alms
2. cancer
3. cat
4. centurion
5. chest
6. heretic
7. history
8. lettuce
9. martyr
10. mat
11. monk
12. noon
13. paper
14. paralysis
15. parsley
16. pear
17. peony
18. pot
19. psalm
20. talent

REPRODUCTION PAGE 67

OLD NORSE VS. ANGLO-SAXON

Directions: *Below are some common English words. Try to guess whether they are Old Norse borrowings or native Anglo-Saxon words. Then check with a dictionary to see which source each word came from.*

1. anger
2. child
3. dike
4. eat
5. fight
6. get
7. house
8. live
9. kid
10. knife
11. scrape
12. skill
13. skin
14. sleep
15. wife

- In order to show the easy integration of Old Norse words into Old English, use Reproduction Page 67 to have the students first guess which source, Old Norse or Anglo-Saxon, the common words listed are from and then check with a dictionary to see which the actual source is. It will be unusual if much more than half of their guesses are correct. The answers are given below in parentheses but not on the Reproduction Page.

1. anger (Old Norse)
2. child (Anglo-Saxon)
3. dike (Old Norse)
4. eat (Anglo-Saxon)
5. fight (Anglo-Saxon)
6. get (Old Norse)
7. house (Anglo-Saxon)
8. live (Anglo-Saxon)
9. kid (Old Norse)
10. knife (Old Norse)
11. scrape (Old Norse)
12. skill (Old Norse)
13. skin (Old Norse)
14. sleep (Anglo-Saxon)
15. wife (Anglo-Saxon)

- Have each student write a short essay discussing the different types of words borrowed from Latin and Old Norse during the Old English period.

Topic III: The Old English Language

- Using Reproduction Page 68, have the students translate the edited Old English passage below word for word. Old English writing symbols that do not look like modern writing symbols have been replaced by their modern equivalents. The translation is provided here but not on the Reproduction Page.

Sothlice sum mann haefde twegen suna. Tha cwaeth se gingra to his faeder, 'Faeder, sele
Truly [a] certain man had two sons. Then said the younger to his father, 'Father, give me
me minne dael minre aehte the me to gebyreth.' Tha daelde he him his aehta. Tha aefter
my share of my possessions which me to belongs.' Then gave he him his possessions. Then
feawum dagum eall his thing gegaderode se gingra sunu and ferde wraeclice on feorlen rice
after [a] few days all his things gathered the younger son and went abroad in [a] distant
and forspilde thaer his aehta, libbende on his gaelsan.
kingdom and wasted there his possessions, living in his pride.

REPRODUCTION PAGE 68

TRANSLATING OLD ENGLISH

Directions: *Using the glossary below, try to translate the edited Old English passage below word for word. The story may be familiar to you, but notice how the Old English word order differs from that of the familiar version.*

Sothlice sum mann haefde twegen suna. Tha cwaeth se gingra to his faeder, 'Faeder, sele me minne dael minre aehte the me to gebyreth.' Tha daelde he him his aehta. Tha aefter feawum dagum eall his thing gegaderode se gingra sunu and ferde wraeclice on feorlen rice and forspilde thaer his aehta, libbende on his gaelsan.

Glossary

sothlice	"truly"	gegaderode	"gathered"
tha	"then"	ferde	"went"
sele	"give"	wraeclice	"abroad"
dael	"share"	feorlen	"distant"
aehte	"possessions"	rice	"kingdom"
the	"which"	forspilde	"wasted"
gebyreth	"belong"	gaelsan	"pride"
daelde	"gave"		

Glossary

sothlice	"truly"	gegaderode	"gathered"
tha	"then"	ferde	"went"
sele	"give"	wraeclice	"abroad"
dael	"share"	feorlen	"distant"
aehte	"possessions"	rice	"kingdom"
the	"which"	forspilde	"wasted"
gebyreth	"belongs"	gaelsan	"pride"
daelde	"gave"		

- Using Reproduction Page 69, have the students write the Modern English equivalents of inflected case forms for the four Old English noun declensions indicated. The singular forms of *grund* will be *ground* except for genitive *ground's*. The plural forms of *grund* will be *grounds* except for genitive *grounds'*. The singular forms of *lufu* will be *love* except for genitive *love's*. The plural forms of *lufu* will be *loves* except for genitive *loves'*. The singular form of *man* will be *man* except for genitive *man's*. The plural forms of *man* will be *men* except for genitive *men's*. The singular form of *oxa* will be *ox* except for genitive *ox's*. The plural forms of *oxa* will be *oxen* except for genitive *oxen's*. The modern possessive forms come from the masculine a-stem genitive singular -*es*, which has been generalized to all declensions and the plural possessive. The plural forms come from the masculine a-stem nominative-accusative plural -*as* and the nominative-accusative plural forms of the last two declensions.

- Using Reproduction Page 70, have the students write the Modern English equivalents of the inflected verb forms for the Old English strong and weak verb forms conjugated there. The present indicative and imperative forms will be *sing* and *look* except for third person singular indicative forms *sings* and *looks*. These all come from dropping the person markers of Old English except for the -*s* forms, which are the result of borrowing an Old Norse inflection. The past indicative forms will be *sang*, whose source is obvious, and *looked*, which comes from dropping all of the Old English person markers. The present subjunctive forms will be *may sing* and *may look*, and the past subjunctive forms will be *might sing* and *might look*. These subjunctive equivalents come from dropping the number markers from the Old English verbs and adding auxiliary verbs.

DECLINING OLD ENGLISH

Directions: *Below you will find the forms for four Old English noun declensions. Indicate the form of the noun that would be used for each of the five cases in Modern English next to the Old English form. Then decide which of the Old English forms is the source of the Modern English forms and which Old English forms have been lost.*

grund ("ground"), Masculine a Declension

	Singular	Plural
Nominative	grund	grundas
Accusative	grund	grundas
Genitive	grundes	grunda
Dative	grunde	grundum
Instrumental	grunde	grundum

lufu ("love"), Feminine ô Declension

	Singular	Plural
Nominative	lufu	lufa
Accusative	lufe	lufa
Genitive	lufe	lufa
Dative	lufe	lufum
Instrumental	lufe	lufum

man ("man"), Masculine Radical Consonant Declension

	Singular	Plural
Nominative	man	men
Accusative	man	men
Genitive	mannes	manna
Dative	men	mannum
Instrumental	men	mannum

oxa ("ox"), Masculine n Declension

	Singular	Plural
Nominative	oxa	oxan
Accusative	oxan	oxan
Genitive	oxan	oxena
Dative	oxan	oxum
Instrumental	oxan	oxum

• Using Reproduction Page 71, have the students identify the Old English verbs below given in their infinitive and first person singular past indicative forms as either strong or weak verbs. Then have them give the modern past tense form and indicate whether the verbs are strong or weak in Modern English. The answers are given below but not on the Reproduction Page. This activity shows the historical trend to make strong verbs weak in Modern English.

Old English Verb	Strong or Weak	Modern Past Tense Form	Strong or Weak
1. bacan "bake," bōc	strong	baked	weak
2. blandan "blend," blēnd	strong	blended	weak
3. ceorfan "carve," cearf	strong	carved	weak
4. dēman "deem," dēmede	weak	deemed	weak
5. drincan "drink," dranc	strong	drank	strong
6. findan "find," fand	strong	found	strong
7. gifan "give," geaf	strong	gave	strong
8. hælan "heal," hælde	weak	healed	weak
9. hōn "hang," hēng	strong	hung	strong
		hanged	weak

REPRODUCTION PAGE 70

CONJUGATING OLD ENGLISH

Directions: *Below you will find the conjugations for two Old English verbs; singan is a strong verb, and lōcian is a weak verb. Indicate next to the Old English forms the form of the verb that would be used in Modern English instead of each of these Old English forms. Then decide which of the Old English forms are the sources of the Modern English forms and which Old English forms have been lost.*

singan ("sing") Strong Verb

Indicative

	Present Tense	Past Tense
First Person Singular	singe	sang
Second Person Singular	sing(e)st	sunge
Third Person Singular	sing(e)þ	sang
Plural for All Persons	singaþ	sungon

Subjunctive

	Present Tense	Past Tense
Singular for All Persons	singe	sunge
Plural for All Persons	singen	sungen

Imperative

	Present Tense
Second Person Singular	sing
Second Person Plural	singaþ

lōcian ("look") Weak Verb

Indicative

	Present Tense	Past Tense
First Person Singular	lōcie	lōcode
Second Person Singular	lōcast	lōcodest
Third Person Singular	lōcaþ	lōcode
Plural for All Persons	lōciaþ	lōcodon

Subjunctive

	Present Tense	Past Tense
Singular for All Persons	lōcie	lōcode
Plural for All Persons	lōcien	lōcoden

Imperative

	Present Tense
Second Person Singular	lōca
Second Person Plural	lōciaþ

10.	hȳran "hear," hȳrde	weak	heard	weak
11.	meltan "melt," mealt	strong	melted	weak
12.	scafan "shave," scōf	strong	shaved	weak
13.	scīnan "shine," scān	strong	shone	strong
			shined	weak
14.	sellan "sell," sealde	weak	sold	weak
15.	steppan "step," stōp	strong	stepped	weak
16.	styrian "stir," styrede	weak	stirred	weak
17.	teran "tear," tær	strong	tore	strong
18.	þancian "thank," þancode	weak	thanked	weak

- Using Reproduction Page 72, have the students identify the Old English personal pronouns that are the source of Modern English pronouns. There should be general agreement on *mīn* ("mine"), *mē* ("me"), *wē* ("we"), *ūs* ("us"), and the three masculine third person singular forms: *hē* ("he"), *his* ("his"), and *him* ("him"). In addition, *ic* is the source of *I*, *ūre* the source of *our*, *ēower* the source of *your*, *ēow* the source of *you*, *hire* the source of *her*, and *hit* the source of *it*.

REPRODUCTION PAGE 71

STRONG AND WEAK VERBS

Directions: *Below some Old English verbs in the infinitive and the first person singular past indicative are given. Tell whether each of the verbs was strong or weak in Old English. Then give the past tense form of the verb in Modern English. Is the verb strong or weak in Modern English? What does this tell you about the direction that Modern English is going in?*

Old English Verb	Strong or Weak?	Modern Past Tense Form	Strong or Weak?
1. bacan "bake," bōc			
2. blandan "blend," blēnd			
3. ceorfan "carve," cearf			
4. dēman "deem," dēmede			
5. drincan "drink," dranc			
6. findan "find," fand			
7. gifan "give," geaf			
8. hǣlan "heal," hǣlde			
9. hōn "hang," hēng			
10. hȳran "hear," hȳrde			
11. meltan "melt," mealt			
12. scafan "shave," scōf			
13. scīnan "shine," scān			
14. sellan "sell," sealde			
15. steppan "step," stōp			
16. styrian "stir," styrede			
17. teran "tear," tær			
18. þancian "thank," þancode			

- Have each student write a short essay on the types of grammatical categories that were used in Old English including inflectional categories that are no longer used in Modern English.

REPRODUCTION PAGE 72

OLD ENGLISH PRONOUNS

Directions: *Circle the Old English pronouns below that look like the Modern English pronouns with which you are familiar with only slight changes. All of the other forms have been dropped or replaced by other forms in Modern English.*

First Person	Singular	Dual	Plural
Nominative	ic "I"	wit "we two"	wē "we more than two"
Genitive	mīn	uncer	ūre
Dative	mē	unc	ūs
Accusative	mec, mē	unc	ūs

Second Person	Singular	Dual	Plural
Nominative	ðū "thou"	git "you two"	gē "you more than two"
Genitive	ðīn	incer	ēower
Dative	ðē	inc	ēow
Accusative	ðec, ðē	inc	ēow

Third Person	Masculine Singular	Feminine Singular	Neuter Singular	Plural
Nominative	hē "he"	hēo "she"	hit "it"	hīe "they"
Genitive	his	hire	his	hira
Dative	him	hire	him	him, heom
Accusative	hine	hīe	hit	hīe

ASSESSING ACHIEVEMENT OF OBJECTIVES

Ongoing Evaluation

The extent to which students have mastered the content of each topic can be measured by any of the activities assigned to the class as individuals, particularly the writing activities.

Final Evaluation

For an overall evaluation of the student's mastery of the content in this chapter, if the three topics in the chapter have been taught, a test constructed directly from the list of student objectives for the chapter as listed on page 190 can be used. As an alternative, one might consider a test composed from the following items:

1. Fill in the blanks below:

   A monk at the northern English monastery of Jarrow who wrote *The Ecclesiastical History of the English Nation* is the best source for the history of the early Old English period. His name is_____.

   At the beginning of the historical period, the earliest inhabitants of Britain were not speakers of Germanic languages but speakers of languages belonging to the_____ branch of Indo-European. In 43 A.D., they were partially conquered by speakers of an Italic language, the_____, who withdrew their legions from Britain in the year_____. Then the inhabitants of southern Britain were attacked by their northern neighbors, the_____ and the_____.

   The southern Britons then appealed to mercenary warriors in continental Europe to come to protect them for pay. These continental warriors spoke languages belonging to the_____ branch of Indo-European. Our historian says that these warriors came from three tribes: the_____, the_____, and the_____. They arrived in Britain in the year_____ and stayed on to occupy the lands of the southern Britons whom they had been hired to protect.

   In 597, Pope Gregory I sent Italian missionaries led by_____to convert these ancestors of the English to Christianity. As these missionaries worked upward from the south of Britain, another group of missionaries from _____were converting the ancestors of the English from the north of Britain downward. Nearly all of England was Christianized by 700.

   There were seven Old English kingdoms: 1_____, 2_____, 3_____, 4_____, 5_____, 6_____, and 7_____. There were, however, only four major Old English dialects: 1_____, 2_____, 3_____, and 4_____. Most of the Old English texts that survive today are in the_____dialect.

   The best source for the history of the late Old English period is_____. According to this document, attacks on the English by the_____began in 787. For almost a hundred years, these new invaders captured parts of England until they controlled nearly half of it. In 871, King_____came to the throne of the kingdom of_____. He led the English forces and won a major battle in 878 after which he made peace with the invaders, in essence giving them half of England and keeping the other half for himself. He and his heirs, however, gradually gained dominance over the part of England controlled by the invaders. His heirs ruled England until 1016.

However, new invaders also called _____began attacking England in the year_____. They gained the throne of England from 1014 to 1042. In 1042, the last English king who was descended from the famous king who established peace with the invaders in 878 became king of England. His name was _____, and he ruled until 1066.

2. Give two examples of Latin words borrowed into Old English during the period of Christianization and two examples of later Latin borrowing in Old English.

3. List five common words that were borrowed into Old English from Old Norse.

4. What kinds of things did Old English noun inflections show that Modern English nouns do not have?

5. What was the difference between the strong and weak adjective declensions in Old English?

6. What kinds of things did Old English verb inflections show that Modern English verbs do not have?

7. Explain the difference between strong verbs and weak verbs in Old English and give a modern example of each type of verb.

8. Where do the Modern English noun plural inflection and possessive inflection come from?

9. How does the Modern English article *the* differ from its ancestors in Old English?

10. Name two differences between Old English pronouns and Modern English pronouns.

RESOURCES FOR TEACHING ABOUT OLD ENGLISH

Below is a selected and annotated list of resources useful for teaching the topics in this chapter, divided into audiovisual and print materials and arranged in order of ascending difficulty. Special strengths and weaknesses are mentioned in the annotations. Addresses of publishers or distributors can be found in the alphabetical list on pages 263–265 in Appendix A. Films are black and white unless otherwise indicated.

I. THE EXTERNAL HISTORY OF THE OLD ENGLISH PERIOD

Audiovisual Materials

English History: Earliest Time to 1066. Film, 11 minutes, 1954, Coronet Instructional Media. Presents external history of the Old English period.

Anglo-Saxon England. Color film, 22 minutes, International Film Bureau, Inc. Presents a more sophisticated external history of the Old English period.

Print

"The Oldest Words in English," "The Tribes Called Angles," and "Terror from the Sea," pp. 10–21 in *The English Language: From Anglo-Saxon to American* by Charles Cutler. Provides a simple, abbreviated history of the Old English period and examples of vocabulary borrowings into Old English. Not recommended for older students. Paperbound, Xerox Educational Publications, 1968.

"The Celts and the Romans" and "The Angles, Saxons, and Jutes," pp. 33–44 in *The Story of British English* by J. N. Hook. Provides a short version of the external history of the Old English period, vocabulary borrowings into Old English, and suggested exercises. Paperbound, Scott, Foresman and Co., 1974.

"Old English (449–1100)," pp. 48–51, 55–56 in *A History of the English Language* by Garland Cannon. Gives a short overview of the external history of the period. Paperbound, Harcourt Brace Jovanovich, 1972.

"Angles, Saxons, and Jutes" and "To the Norman Conquest," pp. 83–93 in *The Scope of Language* by Howard K. Battles. Has a very readable history of the Old English period with suggested exercises. Paperbound, Silver Burdett, 1975.

"The Old English Period (449–1100)," pp. 113–121 in *The Origins and Development of the English Language*, 2d ed., by Thomas Pyles. Gives a concise overview of the external history of the Old English period. Hardbound, Harcourt Brace Jovanovich, 1971.

"The Early Growth of England," pp. 36–41 in *The Development of Modern English*, 2d ed., by Stuart Robertson and Frederic G. Cassidy. Provides a short history of the Old English period. Hardbound, Prentice-Hall, 1954.

"Anglo-Saxon Britain: The Beginnings," pp. 52–64 in *Origins of the English Language* by Joseph M. Williams. Provides a readable account of the Old English period and gives problems relating to lists of vocabulary items borrowed during various parts of the Old English period from the various contact languages. Hardbound, The Free Press, 1975.

"The Old English Period," pp. 94–103 in *The English Language* by James D. Gordon. Presents a readable but not very detailed external history of the Old English period. Hardbound, Thomas Y. Crowell Co., 1972.

"In the Beginning," pp. 25–37 in *Aspects of the History of English* by John C. McLaughlin. Provides a rather complete overview of the external history of the Old English period. Hardbound, Holt, Rinehart and Winston, 1970.

"Old English," pp. 47–61 in *A History of the English Language*, 2d ed., by Albert C. Baugh. Relates one of the more complete external histories of the Old English period. Hardbound, Appleton-Century-Crofts, 1957.

"The Scandinavian Influence: The Viking Age," etc., pp. 107–112 in *A History of the English Language*, 2d ed., by Albert C. Baugh. Gives a comprehensive history of the Viking activities during the Old English period. Hardbound, Appleton-Century-Crofts, 1957.

"The History of Old English 450–1150 A.D.," pp. 73–77, 90–91, 94–98, 103–107 in *A Structural History of English* by John Nist. Gives a detailed external history of the Old English period. Hardbound, St. Martin's Press, 1966.

"The Story of Cædmon" and "The Account by Bede of Cædmon's Inspiration," pp. 54–56 in *Old English* by Robert J. Kispert. Tells the story and illustrates the work of the first English poet. Hardbound, Holt, Rinehart and Winston, 1971.

"The Conversion of King Edwin" and "Two of King Edwin's Councillors Present Their Views of Christianity," pp. 62–66 in *Old English* by Robert J. Kispert. Recounts one of the famous tales from Bede's *Ecclesiastical History*. Hardbound, Holt, Rinehart and Winston, 1971.

"Scholarship and Learning in Anglo-Saxon England," pp. 83–86 in *Old English* by Robert J. Kispert. Shows something of Old English education and culture. Hardbound, Holt, Rinehart and Winston, 1971.

"The Anglo-Saxon Chronicle," pp. 108–110 in *Old English* by Robert J. Kispert. Explains the nature and the history of the document. Hardbound, Holt, Rinehart and Winston, 1971.

"King Knut and the Danish Domination of England," pp. 140–143 in *Old English* by Robert J. Kispert. Relates the history of the Viking rule of England in the eleventh century in detail. Hardbound, Holt, Rinehart and Winston, 1971.

II. LATIN AND VIKING INFLUENCES ON OLD ENGLISH

Audiovisual Materials

History of the English Language. Film, part of *Language and Linguistics* Series, 29 minutes, 1958, Indiana University Audio-Visual Center. Traces the external history of the English language and changes within the language due to this history.

Print

"Latin Loanwords" and "Scandinavian Loanwords," pp. 51-59 in *A History of the English Language* by Garland Cannon. Provides a short, simple overview of the types of Latin and Old Norse borrowings into English. Paperbound, Harcourt Brace Jovanovich, 1972.

"Christianization," pp. 33–34 in *Aspects of the History of English* by John C. McLaughlin. Illustrates the types of Latin borrowings into Old English as the result of the Christianization of the English. Hardbound, Holt, Rinehart and Winston, 1970.

"Linguistic Influence," pp. 37–41 in *Aspects of the History of English* by John C. McLaughlin. Shows in a very readable account the types of Scandinavian borrowings into Old English. Hardbound, Holt, Rinehart and Winston, 1970

"Latin Influence" and "Scandinavian Influence," pp. 98–103 in *A Structural History of English* by John Nist. Gives a good account of Latin borrowings into late Old English and one of the more complete discussions of Scandinavian borrowings into Old English. Hardbound, St. Martin's Press, 1966.

"Three Latin Influences on Old English," etc., pp. 86–106 in *A History of the English Language,* 2d ed., by Albert C. Baugh. Provides a scholarly and fairly comprehensive discussion of Latin borrowings into Old English. Hardbound, Appleton-Century-Crofts, 1957.

"The Relation of the Two Languages," etc., pp. 112–124 in *A History of the English Language,* 2d ed., by Albert C. Baugh. Provides a scholarly and fairly comprehensive discussion of Scandinavian borrowings into Old English. Hardbound, Appleton-Century-Crofts, 1957.

III. THE OLD ENGLISH LANGUAGE

Audiovisual Materials

Our Changing Language. LP record, 1975, NCTE. Provides a short discussion of and illustrative passage of Old English (as well as Middle English, Early Modern English, and thirteen modern American and Canadian dialects).

Seven Old English Poems. LP record and text, Educational Audio Visual, Inc. Has readings from seven famous Old English poems on the record and the texts and commentaries in the text.

Thousand Years of English Pronunciation, A. Two

LP records, Educational Audio Visual, Inc. Has readings from *Beowulf* and Old English prose (as well as Middle Early Modern English readings).

Beowulf-Chaucer. Tape, Educational Audio Visual, Inc. Gives readings of sections of *Beowulf* (and Chaucer).

Print

"The Language of King Alfred the Great," pp. 59–83 in *The Story of British English* by J. N. Hook.

Provides a simple but reasonably complete overview of Old English as a language. Paperbound, Scott, Foresman and Co., 1974.

"An Old English Text," pp. 63-65 in *A History of the English Language* by Garland Cannon. Provides a late West Saxon text, a literal translation, and a glossary of terms in the passage. Paperbound, Harcourt Brace Jovanovich, 1972.

"Gender and Number," "Case," and "Declensions," pp. 21-23 in *Old English* by Robert J. Kispert. Defines these concepts essential to understanding Old English nouns. Hardbound, Holt, Rinehart and Winston, 1971.

"Grammatical Gender," pp. 119-120 in *Problems in the Origins and Development of the English Language*, 2d ed., by John Algeo. Presents an exercise illustrating grammatical gender in Old English and the difference between grammatical and natural gender. Paperbound, Harcourt Brace Jovanovich, 1972.

"The Syntax of Nouns," pp. 123-124 in *Problems in the Origins and Development of the English Language*, 2d ed., by John Algeo. Provides a reasonably simple exercise illustrating the syntactic functions of the five cases of nouns in Old English. Paperbound, Harcourt Brace Jovanovich, 1972.

"Notes on Old English as a Language," pp. 32-41 in *A Survey of Modern Grammar*, 2d ed., by Jeanne H. Herndon. Presents a very detailed but incomplete short survey of the features of Old English grammar. Paperbound, Holt, Rinehart and Winston, 1976.

"Adjectives" and "Adverbs," pp. 134-136 in *The Origins and Development of the English Language*, 2d ed., by Thomas Pyles. Gives a complete but not easily read account of the strong and weak adjective declensions and the comparative and superlative adjective and adverb inflections. Hardbound, Harcourt Brace Jovanovich, 1971.

"Modern Survivals of Old English Inflections," pp. 122-123 in *Problems in the Origins and Development of the English Language*, 2d ed., by John Algeo. Presents exercises illustrating the inflections of Modern English nouns, adjectives, and adverbs and their Old English sources. Paperbound, Harcourt Brace Jovanovich, 1972.

"Indicative Forms of Verbs," and "Subjunctive and Imperative Forms," pp. 144-146 in *The Origins and Development of the English Language*, 2d ed., by Thomas Pyles. Illustrates the person, tense, number, and mood markers on Old English verbs. Hardbound, Harcourt Brace Jovanovich, 1971.

"Anglo-Saxon or Old English," pp. 18-29 in *The English Language: Yesterday and Today* by Charles B. Martin and Curt M. Rulon. Provides a short, readable description of the Old English language. Hardbound, Allyn and Bacon, 1973.

"Some Characteristics of Old English," pp. 60-71 in *A History of the English Language*, 2d ed. by Albert C. Baugh. Gives a concise description of the major features of the Old English language. Hardbound, Appleton-Century-Crofts, 1957.

"Personal Pronouns," pp. 23-24 in *Bright's Old English Grammar and Reader*, 3d ed., edited by Frederic G. Cassidy and Richard N. Ringler. Provides the best short discussion of Old English personal and interrogative pronouns. Has two exercises. Hardbound, Holt, Rinehart and Winston, 1972.

"Adjectives," pp. 35-38 in *Bright's Old English Grammar and Reader*, 3d ed., edited by Frederic G. Cassidy and Richard N. Ringler. Lists the strong and weak adjective inflections. Has a passage for translation. Hardbound, Holt, Rinehart and Winston, 1972.

"Nouns: the a-declension," etc., pp. 46-55 in *Bright's Old English Grammar and Reader*, 3d ed., edited by Frederic G. Cassidy and Richard N. Ringler. Provides the most complete short discussion of Old English noun inflections. Has exercises and passages for translation. Hardbound, Holt, Rinehart and Winston, 1972.

"Verb Classes," etc., pp. 59-77 in *Bright's Old English Grammar and Reader*, 3d ed., edited by Frederic G. Cassidy and Richard N. Ringler. Provides one of the most comprehensive short discussions of Old English verb classes and inflections. Has exercises and passages for translation. Hardbound, Holt, Rinehart and Winston, 1972.

"Old English (449-1100)," pp. 66-90 in *A History of the English Language* by Garland Cannon. Provides a complex transformational analysis of Old English syntax and morphology. Paperbound, Harcourt Brace Jovanovich, 1972.

11

Middle English

This chapter deals with the history of England during the Middle English period, the influence of French on the English language of the period, and the structure of the Middle English language. A practical application of this study should be an awareness of how the culture of speakers of English is the result of the fusion of two very different cultures, Germanic and Romance. Another practical application can be the development of an understanding of how language can change structurally yet still express the same concepts and relationships among words.

First, the student should be introduced to the history of England's ties with France from the Norman Conquest through the fifteenth century. This history includes both the occupation of England by the Norman-French and the later merger of the English and Norman-French into one people. It also includes the later relationship of the somewhat provincial English to the more cultural speakers of Parisian French.

If the teacher wishes, the topic of French vocabulary influence on Middle English can then be introduced. Both the borrowing from Norman French and the later borrowing from Parisian French reflect the influence of a superior culture in terms of government, cuisine, the arts, and many of the other criteria of civilization on an inferior culture.

Finally, the Middle English language itself may be examined. If the students have studied the chapter on Old English, they will be struck by how different (and to them much simpler) Middle English is from Old English because of the loss of most inflectional endings on nouns and adjectives and the simplification of verb inflections. These structural changes and the addition of French loanwords should make Middle English more recognizable to the students as English. Discussion of the pronunciation of Middle English has been omitted from the overview as inappropriate for study by secondary school students; however, the annotated bibliography does include readings of Middle English on records and tapes, so the students can be introduced to how Middle English sounds.

The first topic will probably be the most interesting to the students, and the last topic will be the most difficult. The teacher will need to decide whether the second topic should be introduced or not; one consideration should be whether the topic of English borrowing from other Indo-European languages in Chapter 9 has been taught and, if so, how thoroughly borrowings from French were discussed then.

OBJECTIVES

If the three topics in this chapter are taught by the teacher, the students should, at the end of the unit, be able to:

1. Explain the political events that led to the Norman Conquest of England
2. Explain the relationship between the Norman rulers of England and their English subjects and the changes in the relationship over the centuries
3. Identify the major Middle English dialects
4. Explain how one Middle English dialect gained prestige over the other dialects
5. Identify major historical figures of the Middle English period
6. Illustrate the types of loanwords borrowed from Norman-French and from Parisian French
7. Identify the major forces causing language change other than vocabulary change during the Middle English period
8. Discuss major differences in grammar between Middle English and Modern English (and between Middle English and Old English if Chapter 10 has been taught)

OVERVIEW

The External History of the Middle English Period

When the last Alfredian king of England, Edward the Confessor, died with no heir in 1066, his brother-in-law, Harold, was "elected" king of England by the other English lords. Harold, the son of the powerful Earl Godwin, was made king because of the compelling argument that he would seize the throne by force of his control of a large estate and many people on it and his military prowess if he were not elected.

The year 1066 is sometimes given as the end of the Old English period and the beginning of Middle English. One date is as good as another when no date is accurate, that is, the change was gradual. Syntactically and structurally, no date has any significance; however, in 1066 a new Latinate word stock was introduced into English vocabulary. Even then, the Norman-French vocabulary did not influence English vocabulary greatly for about two hundred years. The first recorded French words in an English document do not occur until the last entry of one manuscript of *The Anglo-Saxon Chronicle* in 1154. Generally, however, the English and Norman-French language were kept separate during early Middle English. Yet the admixture of Norman-French vocabulary to English is the most obvious major difference between Old English and Middle English.

The Anglo-Saxon Chronicle was updated yearly for less than a century after the Norman Conquest. Reflecting the English bias, the *Chronicle* is vague about the Normans but rich in detail of their battles, beginning with the Battle of Hastings in which Duke William of Normandy defeated the forces of King Harold. King Harold was killed in the battle, and Duke William proclaimed himself king of England. Until his death in 1086, William the Conqueror fought mopping-up operations against some of his unwilling English subjects and against Scandinavian kings and the king of France.

The *Chronicle* entry recording King William's death praises him for having brought law to England. Of course, the law was primarily for his benefit. He used it to kill or imprison many people who opposed him. Among his major achievements was the first survey of English land and cattle, *The Doomsday Book*. The purpose of this survey was to make his taxation of his subjects more efficient, however.

The Normans were descendants of Vikings or Danes like those who had conquered half of England by Alfred's time. The ancestors of the Normans (which means "Northmen") had attacked and settled the area in northern France that came to be called Normandy in the ninth and tenth centuries. As the Danes had done in England with Alfred, they, under William's great-great-grandfather, concluded a peace with the king of France that left them in control of the territory they had conquered. Since the kings of France had little power at the time, the Normans remained more or less autonomous in Normandy. As the Danes had done in England, the Normans forsook Old Norse and learned French. Because of an Old Norse substratum to their language, however, Norman French differed greatly from the other French dialects. Although the Normans were never integrated into the French mainstream (and still aren't), they learned military tactics for a regular army, the value of law and order, and the desirability of an efficient central government from the French before the Norman Conquest of England.

William, the bastard son of a bastardly father, Robert the Devil, and a tanner's daughter, became duke of Normandy at the age of eight. His position was maintained by advisors in Normandy until he was old enough to consolidate it for himself. By the time of Edward the Confessor's death in England, William had already asserted himself against the King of France and against his own Norman barons. He also had been preparing to lay claim to the throne of England upon Edward's death as his second cousin through Emma of Normandy, Edward's mother.

One can argue that the Norman Conquest really had begun with Edward's ascent to the throne of England. He was essentially a Norman monk who had fled to his mother's home in Normandy to escape the Scandinavian conquerors of England; he was only incidentally the son of the previous English king. When he was placed on the throne in 1042, he continued to be a Norman monk governed by a monastic rule. As a result, his marriage to Harold's sister had never been consummated—hence no heir. He installed Normans in high positions in England and showed little interest himself in governing.

In addition to William's tenuous blood ties with Edward as a claim to the throne, William particularly resented Harold's claiming the throne. At one time, Harold had been captured by William and given his freedom only with the understanding that he would support William's claim to the throne of England.

After William the Conqueror died, he was succeeded in England by William II and in Normandy by Duke Robert, his sons. His third son, Henry, inherited only money. William II's reign was a continuation of his father's. The *Chronicle* reports his wars with his brother, Duke Robert of Normandy, the Welsh, and the Scots. He kept his own nobles in line by blinding those who opposed him. In 1100, William II died after being shot with an arrow while hunting, possibly assassinated.

He was succeeded as king of England by his brother, Henry, who insured peace with Scotland by marrying the daughter of Malcolm, king of Scotland. This marriage left Henry free to fight on his southern front against his brother, Duke Robert of Normandy, and by 1120 he had control of all of Normandy and his brother in prison. The *Chronicle* reports his reign as one of high taxes and further strengthening of the Norman position in England. Like the rest of his family in England, Henry exercised cruelty to maintain his strength; for example, in 1125 he discouraged the counterfeiting of money by having the right hands and testicles of counterfeitors cut off. Nevertheless, the *Chronicle* entry for his death in 1135 describes him as a good man in whose reign men did not dare do evil.

The person making the entry in the *Chronicle* may have praised King Henry only in comparison with his successor and nephew, Stephen of Blois. King Steven was a mild and weak man whose reign was characterized by robbery and other social evils. His nobles rose against him, plundered the countryside, and held people for ransom. Steven was unable to stop these practices and died in 1154.

The last entry in *The Anglo-Saxon Chronicle* details the ascent of Count Henry of Anjou to the throne of England as Henry II, the first of the Plantagenets. Since the *Chronicle* ends with this entry, it was evidently recognized by this time that the Norman-French were going to continue to control England and that a history concerned originally with the Germanic-speaking English was no longer relevant.

French Influence on Middle English

The beginning of the Middle English period found England with two distinct linguistic groups living together on the island but ignoring each other's language and culture as much as possible. No doubt some of the English learned Norman-French and vice versa, because the two groups did have to deal with each other. However, for some time, speakers did not mix the two languages, so the languages remained unaffected by each other. England was a country in which the masses who had no power spoke English and the people in the government superstratum spoke Norman-French.

The early Norman kings and the later Plantagenets systematically placed Normans and then other Frenchmen in control of the lands, the church, and in the court. The kings during the early Middle English period clearly considered themselves French and an occupying power rather than English. William the Conqueror was buried in Normandy. The kings, with the exception of Henry I, married into French families rather than English ones. Henry II spent the majority of his time in France, of which he controlled two-thirds through hereditary rights and through marriage to Eleanor of Aquitaine in the south of France. Richard the Lionhearted who succeeded Henry II was always off crusading and left the government in the hands of his Archbishop of Canterbury, who governed in temporal as well as spiritual matters during Richard's reign (1189-1199).

Only the poor government of Richard's brother and successor, King John, brought about conditions that later encouraged the integration of the two linguistic groups and the two languages by which English triumphed and gained an enriched vocabulary through borrowing from French. To begin with, John lost Normandy and his other French lands to King Philip of France in 1204. Philip then told John's Norman barons either to come home and keep their Norman holdings or to stay in England and forfeit them. This meant that the close connection between England and Normandy was over. Then John's English barons of Norman descent forced him to sign the Magna Charta in 1215, ending the concept of absolute monarchy in England and establishing the rights to trial by one's peers and to taxation with representation. Although the rights applied only to "freemen," the precedent was established so that the principle would be extended to the masses later. The masses, of course, spoke English.

The Anglo-Norman nobility were given further impetus to consider themselves English rather than French during the reign of John's successor, Henry III, who still considered himself French. When Henry III became king, he gave high positions in his government to Frenchmen from Portou and Brittany, often displacing Anglo-Normans to do so. The barons, in order to maintain and extend their rights from the Magna Charta, forced the Provisions of Oxford on Henry III in 1258. The document was a clear clue of what was to come linguistically in that it was the first public document proclaimed in English by the crown in two hundred years (even though the English version was alongside the French and Latin versions). The leader of the barons who forced the Provisions on Henry III was the Anglo-Norman, Simon de Montfort, who further limited the power of the last truly French king of England by defeating Henry III's forces in 1264.

Edward I (1272-1307), who came to the throne upon Henry's death, had gotten the message. Although French was still the official legal language, Edward appointed many Englishmen to the government during his reign. This encouraged the use of English in government and among the upper classes where it was already becoming popular because of the conditions mentioned above as well as the intermarriage of the lower stratum of the French-speaking occupiers and the English.

Although French was still the language of polite society, members of the upper class were often forced to learn it as a second language. It is in the thirteenth century that books began to be written to teach upper-class children to speak French, indicating that it was no longer their first language. Similarly, English translations of French literature began to appear, perhaps indicating that the English wanted to read French literature but more likely indicating that the nobility no longer read or spoke French with ease. It was during this period that French vocabulary items began to appear increasingly in English (see the chapter overview and annotated bibliography of Chapter 9 for examples). It is important to note that the French that was borrowed into English at this time was Parisian French rather than the Norman-French of the earlier Middle English borrowings. This borrowing phenomenon suggests that even those who spoke French natively often felt the need to express themselves in English for those who did not speak French but, as anyone speaking a second language will do, introduced words from the first language, that is, French, into the second language when they could not think of the right words in the second language. One could make a strong argument that Middle English did not begin until this time, rather than at the end of the eleventh century; certainly it was not until the beginning of the fourteenth century that Middle English gained the strong French flavor that one associates with the most frequently read Middle English literature, that of Chaucer.

There is evidence to suggest that during the fourteenth century the upper classes came more and more to consider English their native language and French a necessary but burdensome second language. The borrowing of French words into English accelerated during the reigns of Edward II (1307-1327), Edward III (1327-1377), and Richard II (1377-1399). The fact that there were official attempts to promote French and to limit the use of English is testimony to the rise of English and the decline of French among the aristocracy. In the late thirteenth century, the Benedictine monasteries at Canterbury and Westminster prohibited the use of English by the novices and allowed only French in conversation. At Oxford in the early fourteenth century, regulations were drawn up requiring that students converse only in French and Latin. Even Parliament felt the need to get into the act, decreeing in 1332 that noblemen should see to it that their children learned French.

Besides the large number of Englishmen of all classes who spoke only English or English as their first language, there were two other causes that further militated against the use of French and encouraged the use of English. One was the Hundred Years' War (1337-1453), actually a series of wars lasting over a hundred years between England and France. One could hardly feel comfortable extolling the virtues of and using the language of one's enemy over one's own language. (Many high schools in the United States dropped German from the curriculum during World War I.) The other cause was the rise in prestige of Parisian French, the dialect of the Île de France. Since the French spoken by English nobility developed from Norman French primarily with an admixture of other French dialects in the thirteenth century, the French-speaking English nobles became rather uncomfortable speaking it knowing that it was not the "right" kind of French anyway.

The English who spoke French in the fourteenth century were obviously bilingual. Although French was the language of the law courts and Parliament, English was making inroads there. Near the end of the thirteenth century, English was sometimes used for explanations in courts. In 1337, a lawyer spoke English in Parliament, considering it more likely to be understood than French. Parliament was opened with a speech in English in 1362; this same Parliament passed the Statute of Pleading, which required that law cases be pled in English even though court records were kept in Latin. At the time of the Peasants' Revolt in 1381, Richard II spoke to the people in English, and the procedures and documents deposing him in 1399 were in both English and Latin. His successor, Henry IV, made his claim and acceptance of the throne in English.

Nevertheless, the records of Parliament were kept in French until 1423, and after that, often alternating with English. The laws of Parliament were also written in French from 1300 to 1485, at which time they were written in parallel texts of French and English until 1489. After that date, English was clearly the official language of England because Henry VII forbade the use of French in English laws in 1489. One might posit that year as the end of the Middle English period during which English was at first kept separate from French and then for nearly two hundred years rather freely mixed with French until many French words became English words.

There were five major dialects of Middle English. Important literary works were written in all of them, but the East Midland dialect is the one that teachers and students are most likely to be familiar with because it is the dialect Chaucer wrote in. In Middle English, the area of Mercian Old English divided into two dialect areas: East Midland, which was the dialect most influenced by French, and West Midland, which is sometimes further divided so that the northern part of the West Midland dialect is said to be the Middle English dialect least influenced by French. The other three Middle English dialects, Northern, Southern or Southwestern, and Kentish or Southeastern, correspond roughly to the geographic areas where Northumbrian Old English, West Saxon Old English, and Kentish Old English were spoken, respectively.

In late Middle English, the East Midland dialect of London became the prestige dialect because of the prestige of the people who lived there. London was not only the center of government but also the commercial center of England. As a result, the people with political power and the people with a great deal of money lived there. People who were ambitious, then, but were not speakers of the East Midland dialect often tried to imitate the dialects of fourteenth-century London in order to advance their own status and career, and many of them migrated to London from the other Middle English dialect areas.

The Middle English Language

Since Middle English is the name given to a period of the language covering about four centuries during which there was great change in and great dialect differences within the language, it is difficult to describe Middle English definitively. It is possible, however, to relate the direction of changes within the language, and it is customary to describe Middle English as the late-fourteenth-century East Midland dialect of London used by Chaucer, since that is the type of Middle English that students and teachers are most likely to encounter.

Structurally, the most important change from Old English to Middle English is the simplification of the Old English inflectional system. While this simplification was no doubt encouraged by the speech of Frenchmen speaking broken English without observing the niceties of declensional and case differences in nouns and adjectives or mood differences in verbs, the major cause of the decline and fall of the complex Old English inflectional system was a sound change. Although the sound change began in late Old English, during Middle English the short /a/, /e/, /o/ and /u/ vowels in unstressed syllables all fell together as the unstressed vowel /ə/ (the first vowel in *above*). This sound change, coupled with the minor sound change of the loss of final nasal sounds, meant that case, gender, and number distinctions that had been marked by different vowels in the inflectional endings of Old English could no longer be made in late Middle English.

For example, it was no longer possible to differentiate a nominative singular form of a feminine ō-declension noun ending in -*u* from its accusative, genitive, dative, and instrumental singular form ending in -*e* or from its nominative, accusative, or genitive plural form ending in -*a*; all of these vowels became /ə/ and were written with an ⟨e⟩ in late Middle English. Similarly, it was no longer possible to distinguish a masculine n-stem noun whose nominative singular form ended in -*a* from a feminine or neuter n-stem noun whose nominative singular form ended in -*e* because the nominative singular form of all three genders of n-stem nouns ended in /ə/, spelled with an ⟨e⟩. What evolved from the chaos caused by this sound change was a pattern of noun inflections for Middle English which discarded all markers of grammatical gender and all case distinctions except genitive (possessive) versus nongenitive. It maintained the number distinction between singular and plural and generalized the genitive singular -*es* (phonemically /əs/ in Middle English) inflection of masculine a-stem nouns and a few other declensions to all noun declensions. Unless the nominative-accusative plural forms were differentiated from the singular forms by an internal vowel change as in *mouse-mice,* Middle English generalized the Old English masculine a-stem -*as* nominative-accusative plural inflection to other nouns as well, also as -*es* (phonemically /əs/). The exceptions to this generalization about Middle English noun plurals include those Old English nouns that formed their nominative-accusative plurals in -*an,* so that the Middle English plural of *ox* was *oxen* and of *eye* was *eyen,* and those Old English nouns that had identical singular and plural nominative and accusative forms, so that the Middle English plural form of *sheep* was *sheep* and of *kind* was *kind.* Notice here that subsequently the "regular" *(e)s* plural has been added to the latter example in each set. Thus, the Middle English noun normally had two forms: a singular with no inflections and a singular possessive and a plural ending in -*es,* pronounced /əs/. The grammatical relationships that had been indicated by the lost case inflections came to be indicated by fixed word order and by prepositions in Middle English.

Because of the reduction of short vowels in unstressed syllables to /ə/ and the loss of all but genitive singular case distinctions in nouns, the adjective declensions also lost the ability to differentiate cases in both the strong and the weak adjective declensions. A distinction was maintained between singular and plural forms of strong adjectives but only if the adjective was monosyllabic and ended in a consonant. The singular strong form of a monosyllabic adjective like wīs "wise" was endless because of the generalization of the ∅ inflection of the Old English masculine nominative singular and the neuter nominative and accusative singular to all singular forms of strong adjectives. The plural strong form ended in -*e* (phonemically /ə/) as in wīse because of the generalization of the strong nominative-accusative forms ending in -*a,* -*e,* and -*u* (which became /ə/ spelled ⟨e⟩) to the other cases as well. As a result, strong adjectives had two forms, one endless and one ending in -*e* if the adjectives were monosyllabic and ended in a consonant; if the adjectives were polysyllabic or ended in a vowel, however, no -*e* was added to the plural, and only one form with no inflection remained. Weak adjectives in both the singular and plural kept an -*e* inflection from the reduction of unstressed vowels to /ə/ and the loss of final nasals but only if they were monosyllabic and ended in a consonant as in *smale* ("small"). The *-e* in *smale* came from the generalization of the nominative singular *-a* and *-e* endings and the nominative plural *-an* ending to all cases. Polysyllabic adjectives like *lītel* ("little") and adjectives ending in vowels like *frē* ("free") had no inflections added for singular or plural in either the strong or the weak positions.

The reduction of short unstressed vowels to /ə/ also caused a simplification of the verb inflections in Middle English. Specifically, the indicative present tense third person singular and plural forms and the imperative plural were no longer distinguishable because both *-eþ* and *-aþ* were reduced to /əΘ/, spelled *-eth* or *-eþ*, and the past tense indicative and subjunctive plural forms fell together as /ən/, spelled ⟨-en⟩, from both Old English *-on* and *-en*. The Midland dialects, including the East Midland of Chaucer, solved the problem of differentiating the third person singular present indicative from the plural present indicative at the expense of the distinction between indicative and subjunctive plurals by using *-eth* for third person singular and *-en* for plural present indicative forms, as shown in the conjugation of the weak verb *thanken* ("thank") below. Notice that the *-en* for present tense indicative plurals was sometimes reduced to *-e* because of the loss of final nasals and that final *-e*(/ə/) was sometimes lost in several verb forms. Chaucer sometimes used *-es*, which was the Northern Middle English form for both third person singular and plural present indicative forms of verbs, that is, *thankes,* but this practice was always to identify the speaker as a country bumpkin who did not speak the prestigious dialect. Other East Midland writers used the *-eth* form for plural present indicatives, which was the Southern and Kentish Middle English form, that is, *thanketh,* for the same purpose. Chaucer's use of *ar(e)n* as a plural form of *be* was also to identify the speaker as a Northern hick. Present participles ended in *-end(e)* or *-ing(e)* in East Midland English as in *thankend(e)* or *thanking(e)*; Southern and Kentish Middle English used *ind(e),* and Northern Middle English used *-and(e)* as dialect forms, however. Past participles of weak verbs still ended in *-ed,* sometimes with an *i-* or *y-* prefix as in *ithanked.*

Conjugation of *thanken*

	Present Tense Indicative	Past Tense Indicative
First Person Singular	thanke	thanked(e)
Second Person Singular	thankest	thankedest
Third Person Singular	thanketh (eþ)	thanked(e)
Plural for All Persons	thanke(n)	thanked(e)(n)

	Present Tense Subjunctive	Past Tense Subjunctive
Singular for All Persons	thanke	thanked(e)
Plural for All Persons	thanke(n)	thanked(e)(n)

	Present Tense Imperative
Second Person Singular	thank
Second Person Plural	thanketh(-eþ)

Strong verbs in Middle English underwent the same kind of simplification of their inflectional system as the weak verbs. In addition, they began to show a breakdown in the vowel alternation between the past indicative first and third person singular and the plural forms. The form *holp* below for first and third person singular past indicative is an analogical form based upon the base of the plural past indicative forms. The East Midland forms for the present participle of *helpen* were *helpend(e)* or *helping(e),* and the past participle forms were *(i)holpen* or *(y)holpen.*

Conjugation of *helpen*

	Present Tense Indicative	Past Tense Indicative
First Person Singular	helpe	halp, holp
Second Person Singular	helpest	holpe
Third Person Singular	helpeth (eþ)	halp, holp
Plural for All Persons	helpe(n)	holpe(n)

	Present Tense Subjunctive	Past Tense Subjunctive
Singular for All Persons	helpe	holpe
Plural for All Persons	helpe(n)	holpe(n)

	Present Tense Imperative
Second Person Singular	help
Second Person Plural	helpeth (-eþ)

The demonstratives were reduced in Middle English to forms not much different from Modern English demonstratives by the thirteenth century as grammatical gender and case distinctions were lost in nouns. The only late Middle English forms from the Old English *sē, sēo, þæt* demonstratives were *the, that,* and *tho* (sometimes spelled with ⟨þ⟩ instead of ⟨th⟩). *Tho* ("those") did not get an *-s* added to it (by analogy with the noun plural) in East Midland until the fifteenth century, although the Northern Middle English form contemporary with Chaucer, *thās,* had the *-s* by the fourteenth century. *This, thise,* and *these* developed in Middle English from the Old English *þēs, þēos, þis* demonstrative, the plural forms (as well as *those*) having a final *-e* by analogy with plural adjective forms.

Middle English pronouns were nearly as complex as Old English pronouns; although things like dual pronouns and separate accusative and dative forms were dropped in Middle English, new analogical second possessive or pronominal genitive forms were developed, and there was great dialectal difference in pronouns. For example, in Chaucer's Middle English, Old English third person singular masculine accusative *hine* and dative *him* had fallen together as a general objective form *him,* but *hine* was kept as a separate accusative form in Southern and Kentish Middle English. The analogical second possessive forms in East Midland like *ōures* ("ours") and *heres* ("hers") had developed by analogy with the possessive inflection *-es,* which had been generalized to all noun declensions. While Chaucer used nominative forms of the third person plural pronoun beginning with *th-* or *þ-* such as *they* and *thai,* he still used *h-* forms for the oblique cases: objective *hem* or *heom,* first possessive (before nouns) like *her* or *here,* and second possessives (not followed by nouns) like *heres.* It was not until the fifteenth century that East Midland adopted the Northern Middle English *th-* forms for the oblique cases: objective *thaim, thame,* or *them;* first possessive *their(e);* and second possessive *theires.*

LEARNING EXPERIENCES

Topic I: The External History of the Middle English Period

- Using Reproduction Page 73, have the students locate the five main Middle English dialect areas on the map.

- Using Reproduction Page 74, have the students locate London on the map and then explain why the dialect of London would be likely to borrow language forms from other dialects.

- Assign individual students to research the following and report back to the class:

  1. Edward the Confessor, king of England

  2. King Harold of England

  3. William the Conqueror

  4. The Normans

  5. *The Doomsday Book*

  6. King William II of England

MIDDLE ENGLISH DIALECTS

Directions: *Identify the major Middle English dialect spoken in each of the five numbered areas on the map below.*

Source: Redrawn by permission of Harcourt Brace Jovanovich, Inc. from *Problems in the Origins and Development of the English Language*, 2d ed. (New York: Harcourt Brace Jovanovich, 1972), p. 142. © 1966, 1972 by Harcourt Brace Jovanovich, Inc.

7. King Henry I of England

8. King Henry II of England

9. Eleanor of Aquitaine, queen of England

10. Richard the Lionhearted

11. King John of England

12. The Magna Charta

13. The Provisions of Oxford

14. King Henry III of England

15. The Hundred Years' War

16. The reintroduction of English into courts of law

17. The use of English in Parliament

18. *The Ormulum*

19. Barbour's *Bruce*

20. *The Owl and the Nightingale*

21. *The Ancrene Riwle*

MAJOR MIDDLE ENGLISH DIALECT AREAS

Directions: *Locate London on the map below. Then explain why the dialect of London would be likely to borrow language forms from other Middle English dialects.*

Source: John Nist, *A Structural History of English* (New York: St. Martin's Press, 1966), p. 154. Reprinted by permission.

22. Layamon's *Brut*

23. *Havelok the Dane*

24. *Cursor Mundi*

25. *Sir Gawain and the Green Knight*

26. *Piers Plowman*

27. The rise in prestige of the East Midland dialect of London

28. John Wycliffe

29. *The Canterbury Tales*

30. Geoffrey Chaucer

- Have each student write a short history of England from 1066 to 1476 including significant events and identifying historical figures of the period.

Topic II: French Influence on Middle English

- After explaining the types of vocabulary borrowed from French into Middle English, use Reproduction Page 75 to have the class decide which word in the pairs of words below is a French borrowing and which is the native English word. The answers are given below in parentheses but not on the Reproduction Page.

1. (French) action — deed (English)

2. (French) aid — help (English)

3. (French) amorous — loving (English)

4. (French) ancient — old (English)

5. (English) ask — demand (French)

6. (French) beef — cow (English)

7. (French) boil — seethe (English)

8. (English) calf — veal (French)

9. (French) cordial — hearty (English)

10. (French) cottage — hut (English)

11. (English) deep — profound (French)

12. (French) desire — wish (English)

13. (English) feather — plume (French)

14. (French) feeble — weak (English)

15. (English) feed — nourish (French)

16. (French) felicity — happiness (English)

17. (English) forgive — pardon (French)

REPRODUCTION PAGE 75

FRENCH BORROWING

Directions: *Decide which of the words in each pair below is a native English word and which is a French borrowing. Remember that the French borrowings in Middle English are often "fancier" words than their native English counterparts. Check the sources of words you are not sure of in a dictionary.*

	Source		Source
1.	_____	action-deed	_____
2.	_____	aid-help	_____
3.	_____	amorous-loving	_____
4.	_____	ancient-old	_____
5.	_____	ask-demand	_____
6.	_____	beef-cow	_____
7.	_____	boil-seethe	_____
8.	_____	calf-veal	_____
9.	_____	cordial-hearty	_____
10.	_____	cottage-hut	_____
11.	_____	deep-profound	_____
12.	_____	desire-wish	_____
13.	_____	feather-plume	_____
14.	_____	feeble-weak	_____
15.	_____	feed-nourish	_____
16.	_____	felicity-happiness	_____
17.	_____	forgive-pardon	_____
18.	_____	house-mansion	_____
19.	_____	mutton-sheep	_____
20.	_____	poignant-sharp	

NORMAN VERSUS PARISIAN FRENCH

Directions: Below are French words borrowed into Middle English from Norman-French and Parisian French. Since the Norman words were borrowed first, they are more likely to be words you say frequently than the Parisian words, which are more likely to occur only in your writing rather than your speech. Try to decide which of the two types of French is the source of the following words.

1. adolescence
2. affability
3. chapter
4. chattel
5. chiffon
6. crime
7. dress
8. fine
9. grape
10. immensity
11. judge
12. lesson
13. peace
14. real
15. royal
16. salad
17. sugar
18. sumptuous
19. supper
20. tax

18. (English) house — mansion (French)

19. (French) mutton — sheep (English)

20. (French) poignant — sharp (English)

- After explaining the types of vocabulary borrowed from Norman-French and Parisian French, use Reproduction Page 76 to have the class decide which of the two French sources the words below are most likely to have come from on the basis of whether the students would be likely to speak them or only to write them. The answers are given below in parentheses but not on the Reproduction Page.

1. adolescence (Parisian)	11. judge (Norman)
2. affability (Parisian)	12. lesson (Norman)
3. chapter (Norman)	13. peace (Norman)
4. chattel (Parisian)	14. real (Norman)
5. chiffon (Parisian)	15. royal (Parisian)
6. crime (Norman)	16. salad (Norman)
7. dress (Norman)	17. sugar (Norman)
8. fine (Norman)	18. sumptuous (Parisian)
9. grape (Norman)	19. supper (Norman)
10. immensity (Parisian)	20. tax (Norman)

- Have each student write a short essay discussing the different types of words borrowed into Middle English from French.

- Have each student write a short essay discussing the differences between tne types of words borrowed during Middle English from Norman-French and Parisian French.

TRANSLATING MIDDLE ENGLISH

Directions: *Translate the late Middle English passage below word for word. You should be able to recognize all of the words despite the different spelling. However, there are two verb phrases that may give you trouble:* ded do shewe *might best be translated as "caused to be shown," and* ben *is an East Midland form that has been replaced by "are" in your dialect.*

And fayn wolde I satysfye euery man, and so to doo toke an olde boke and redde therin; and certaynly the Englyssche was so rude and brood, that I coude not wele vnderstande it. And also my lorde abbot of Westmynster ded do shewe to me late certayn euydences wryton in olde Englysshe for to reduce it in-to our Englysshe now vsed; and certaynly it was wreton in suche wyse, that it was more lyke to Dutche than Englysshe; I coude not reduce ne brynge it to be vnderstonden. And certaynly our langage now vsed varyeth ferre from that whiche was vsed and spoken whan I was borne.

Topic III: The Middle English Language

- Using Reproduction Page 77, have the students translate the edited Middle English passage below word for word. The translation is provided here but not on the reproduction page. The forms *ded do shewe* and *ben* are explained on the Reproduction Page.

And fayn wolde I satysfye euery man, and so to doo toke an olde boke and redde therin;
And fain would I satisfy every man, and so to do took an old book and read therein; and
and certaynly the Englyssche was so rude and brood, that I coude not wele vnderstande
certainly the English was so rude and broad, that I could not well understand it. And also
it. And also my lorde abbot of Westmynster ded do showe to me late certayn euydences
my lord abbot of Westminster caused to be shown to me lately certain evidences
wryton in olde Englysshe for to reduce it in-to our Englysshe now vsed; and certaynly it
(writings) written in old English for to reduce (translate) it into our English now used;
was wreton in suche wyse, that it was more lyke to Dutche than Englysshe; I coude not
and certainly it was written in such [a] way, that it was more like to Dutch than English;
reduce ne brynge it to be vnderstonden. And certaynly our language now vsed varyeth
I could not reduce nor bring it to be understood. And certainly our language now used
ferre from that whiche was vsed and spoken whan I was borne.
varies far from that which was used and spoken when I was born.

- Using Reproduction Page 78, have the students write the Modern English forms of the following noun phrases. This exercise shows the differences between the strong singular and plural forms of monosyllabic adjectives ending in a consonant and

TRANSLATING NOUN PHRASES

Directions: *Translate the following Middle English noun phrases into their Modern English equivalents. Remember that possessive singulars like* boy's *and plurals like* boys *may both end in* -es *in Middle English; however, one can sometimes tell whether a noun is singular or plural by looking at the adjective in front of it.*

old man	_____	litel oxe	_____
old manes	_____	litel oxes	_____
olde men	_____	litel oxen	_____
old ground	_____	litel sone	_____
old groundes	_____	litel sones	_____
olde groundes	_____		_____
smal stone	_____	wis lord	_____
the smale stone	_____	the wise lord	_____
the smale stones	_____	the wise lordes	_____

between the strong and weak singular forms of the same adjective. It also shows that the singular possessive and the plural forms of some Middle English nouns were the same. The answers are given below in parentheses but not on the Reproduction Page.

old man (old man)	litel oxe (little ox)
old manes (old man's)	litel oxes (little ox's)
olde men (old men)	litel oxen (little oxen)
old ground (old ground)	litel sone (little son)
old groundes (old ground's)	litel sones (little son's / little sons)
olde groundes (old grounds)	
smal stone (small stone)	wis lord (wise lord)
the smale stone (the small stone)	the wise lord (the wise lord)
the smale stones (the small stone's / the small stones)	the wise lordes (the wise lord's / the wise lords)

- Using Reproduction Page 79, have the students write the Modern English equivalents of the inflected verb forms for the Middle English strong and weak verbs conjugated there. The present indicative and imperative forms will be *find* and *deem* except for

---

REPRODUCTION PAGE 79

MIDDLE ENGLISH VERBS

Directions: *Below you will find the conjugations for two Middle English verbs;* fīnden *is a strong verb and* dēmen *is a weak verb. Indicate next to the Middle English forms the form of the verb that would be used in Modern English instead of each of these Middle English forms. Then decide which of the Middle English forms are the sources of the Modern English forms and which Middle English forms have been lost.*

fīnden ("find"), Strong Verb

Indicative

	Present Tense	Past Tense
First Person Singular	finde	fōnd
Second Person Singular	findest	fōunde
Third Person Singular	findeth	fōnd
Plural for All Persons	finde(n)	fōunde(n)

Subjunctive

	Present Tense	Past Tense
Singular for All Persons	finde	fōunde
Plural for All Persons	finde(n)	fōunde(n)

Imperative

	Present Tense
Second Person Singular	find
Second Person Plural	findeth

dēmen ("deem" or "judge"), Weak Verb

Indicative

	Present Tense	Past Tense
First Person Singular	dēme	dēmde
Second Person Singular	dēmest	dēmdest
Third Person Singular	dēmeth	dēmde
Plural for All Persons	dēme(n)	dēmde(n)

Subjunctive

	Present Tense	Past Tense
Singular for All Persons	dēme	dēmde
Plural for All Persons	dēme(n)	dēmde(n)

Imperative

	Present Tense
Second Person Singular	dēm
Second Person Plural	dēmeth

MIDDLE ENGLISH PRONOUNS

Directions: *Circle the late East Midland Middle English pronouns below which, with only slight changes, look like the Modern English pronoun forms you are familiar with. All of the other forms have been dropped or replaced by other forms in Modern English. Many of the second possessive forms were new in Middle English, having been formed by analogy with noun possessives.*

First Person

	Singular	Plural
Nominative	ich, I	wē
Objective	mē	ūs
First Possessive	mīn, mī	ōures
Second Possessive	mīn	ōures

Second Person

	Singular	Plural
Nominative	thōu	yē
Objective	thee	yōu
First Possessive	thīn, thī	yōur(e)
Second Possessive	thīn	yōures

Third Person

	Masculine Singular	Feminine Singular
Nominative	hē	shē
Objective	him	her(e), hir(e)
First Possessive	his	her(e), hir(e)
Second Possessive	his	heres

	Neuter Singular	Plural for All Genders
Nominative	(h)it	they, thei, thay, thai
Objective	(h)it	hem, heom
First Possessive	his	her(e)
Second Possessive	his	heres

third person singular indicative forms *finds* and *deems.* These all come from dropping the person markers of Middle English except for the *-s* forms, which are the result of later borrowing of Northern Middle English forms. The past indicative forms will be *found,* whose source is obvious, and *deemed,* which comes from dropping all of the Middle English person markers. The present subjunctive forms will be *may find* and *might deem.* These subjunctive equivalents come from dropping the number markers from the Middle English verbs and adding auxiliary verbs.

- Using Reproduction Page 80, have the students identify the Middle English personal pronouns that are the source of Modern English pronouns. There should be no disagreement on *I, mē, ūs, yōu, hē, him, his, shē, (h)it,* and *they.* There also should be little disagreement about *mī* ("my"), *mīn* ("mine"), *ōur(e)* ("our"), *ōures* ("ours"), *yōur(e)* ("your"), *yōures* ("yours"), *her(e)* ("her"), and *heres* ("hers"). If your students read the King James or Douay versions of the Bible, they may circle *thōu, thee, thīn,* and *yē,* so it may be necessary to point out that they don't use those forms when speaking conversationally to each other. It may also be necessary to point out that the *his* forms for neuter third person singular have been replaced by *its,* although *his* still exists as a masculine form.

- Have each student write a short essay on the differences between Middle English grammatical forms and Modern English grammatical forms.

ASSESSING ACHIEVEMENT OF OBJECTIVES

Ongoing Evaluation

The extent to which students have mastered the content of each topic in the chapter can be measured by any of the activities assigned to the class as individuals, particularly the writing activities.

Final Evaluation

For an overall evaluation of the students' mastery of the content in this chapter, if the three topics in the chapter have been taught, a test constructed directly from the list of student objectives for the chapter as listed on page 212 can be used. As an alternative, one might consider a test composed from the following items:

1. Fill in the blanks below:
   The year 1066 is sometimes given as the year when Middle English began. While the change from Old English to Middle English was gradual, the events that occurred in 1066 did lead to major changes in English. During that year, England had three kings. The last descendant of Alfred the Great to rule England, _____, died with no heir. He was succeeded on the throne by King _____, who was his brother-in-law and had military and economic power. This second king of England in 1066 was killed during that year at the Battle of_____where his forces were defeated by the third person to claim the throne in 1066, _____.
   This third king of England was not an Englishman but a _____who ruled a section of the country of_____before he conquered England. His ancestors had been inhabitants of this country for only five or six generations, however; they were originally_____, who had conquered part of that country and settled there permanently. Since they did not speak the language of that country historically, when they learned it they spoke a dialect called _____, which differed from other dialects of that country. This language was then introduced into England and spoken by the upper-class people for several centuries.
   The third king to gain the throne of England was succeeded by two of his sons in succession. The first son,_____, was killed by an arrow while hunting in 1100. He may have been assassinated because he continued his father's cruelty while king. The second son,_____, who succeeded his brother as king, was also a stern ruler.
   The person who was king of England from 1189 to 1199 was called _____. He is better known for leading Crusades than for governing. His brother who succeeded him as king,_____, was forced to sign the Magna Charta in the year_____; this document established the idea of taxation with representation and the right to a trial by jury of one's peers in England.
   Later in the thirteenth century, the occupying forces began to think of themselves as English and no longer identified with their linguistic brothers across

the English Channel. As a result, they began to speak English more themselves, of course with frequent addition of words from their other language. This meant that many originally non-English words were added to English. By the fourteenth century, these recently naturalized Englishmen frequently could not speak the non-English language of their ancestors. As a result, they had to study that non-English language as a foreign language. However, they did not study the dialect spoken by their ancestors but the dialect of_____, which had greater prestige.

By the end of the fourteenth century, the English kings spoke English natively. In the year_____, Henry VII forbade the use of the non-English language of his ancestors in English laws and decreed that English was the appropriate language.

There were five major Middle English dialects: (1)_____, (2)_____, (3)_____, (4)_____, and (5)_____. In the fourteenth century, the_____dialect gained prestige over the other dialects because the city of_____was in this dialect area, and this city was the center of both government and commerce.

2. Give three examples of Norman-French borrowings in Middle English and comment on the types of words generally borrowed.

3. Give three examples of Parisian French borrowings in Middle English and explain how Parisian French borrowings differ from Norman-French borrowings.

4. Did Middle English noun inflections more resemble the noun inflections of Modern English or of Old English? Explain why.

5. Illustrate the difference between strong and weak adjectives in Middle English.

6. What kinds of things did Middle English verb inflections show that Modern English verb inflections do not?

7. Illustrate the difference between a strong verb and a weak verb in Middle English.

8. Name three differences between Middle English pronouns and Modern English pronouns.

9. Did Middle English use grammatical gender or natural gender? Explain the difference between the two concepts.

10. What major sound change caused a simplification of the inflectional system of Middle English from that of Old English?

RESOURCES FOR TEACHING ABOUT MIDDLE ENGLISH

Below is a selected and annotated list of resources useful for teaching the topics in this chapter, divided into audiovisual and print materials and arranged in order of ascending difficulty. Special strengths and weaknesses are mentioned in the annotations. Addresses of publishers or distributors can be found in the alphabetical list on pages 263–265 in Appendix A. Films are black and white unless otherwise indicated.

I. THE EXTERNAL HISTORY OF THE MIDDLE ENGLISH PERIOD

Audiovisual Materials

History of the English Language. Film, part of *Language and Linguistics* Series, 29 minutes, 1958, Indiana University Audio-Visual Center. Relates the external history of the English language and changes within the language due to this history.

Print

"Upper-Class Words" and "A New Look," pp. 23–29 in *The English Language: From Anglo-Saxon to American* by Charles Cutler. Provides a very simple history of the Norman Conquest and Chaucer's time with passing reference to French loanwords in Middle English. Not recommended for older students. Paperbound, Xerox Educational Publications, 1968.

"The Norman Conquest," pp. 44–49 in *The Story of British English* by J. N. Hook. Gives an abbreviated history of the Norman Conquest and discusses the French loanwords in Middle English. Has suggested exercises. Paperbound, Scott, Foresman and Co., 1974.

"Middle English (1100–1500)," pp. 93–96, 101–104 in *A History of the English Language* by Garland Cannon. Gives a short overview of the external history of the Middle English period. Paperbound, Harcourt Brace Jovanovich, 1972.

"The Background of the Norman Conquest," pp. 152–154 in *The Origins and Development of the English Language,* 2d ed., by Thomas Pyles.

Provides a short discussion of the Normans and the Norman Conquest. Hardbound, Harcourt Brace Jovanovich, 1971.

"The Middle English Period," pp. 103–111 in *The English Language* by James D. Gordon. Gives a short overview of the external history of the period. Hardbound, Thomas Y. Crowell Co., 1972.

"The Norman Invasion," pp. 41–47 in *Aspects of the History of English* by John C. McLaughlin. Provides a short, readable external history of the Middle English period. Hardbound, Holt, Rinehart and Winston, 1970.

"From Middle English to Modern English," pp. 65–86 in *Origins of the English Language* by Joseph M. Williams. Gives the history of the Middle English period in chronicle form with questions for discussion after each series of events chronicled. Hardbound, The Free Press, 1975.

"The Decline and Subjection of Old English, 1042–1154" and "The History of Middle English 1150–1500 A.D.," pp. 103–107, 141–148, 158–160, 171–173 in *A Structural History of English* by John Nist. Gives the most complete short external history of the Middle English period. Hardbound, St. Martin's Press, 1966.

"The Norman Conquest and the Subjection of English, 1066–1200" and "The Re-Establishment of English," pp. 127–187 in *A History of the English Language,* 2d ed., by Albert C. Baugh. Provides a very detailed scholarly history of the Middle English period. Hardbound, Appleton-Century-Crofts, 1957.

II. FRENCH INFLUENCE ON MIDDLE ENGLISH

Audiovisual Materials

English Language: Story of Its Development. Film, 11 minutes, Coronet Instructional Media. Traces the history of English with the various influences of other languages.

Print

"The Norman Conquest," pp. 44-49 in *The Story of British English* by J. N. Hook. Discusses French loanwords in Middle English. Has suggested exercises. Paperbound, Scott, Foresman and Co., 1974.

"The Early Growth of English," pp. 45-51 in *The Development of Modern English,* 2d ed., by Stuart Robertson and Frederic G. Cassidy. Gives a very simple general overview of the French influence on Middle English. Hardbound, Prentice-Hall, 1954.

"The French Element," pp. 155-161 in *The Development of Modern English,* 2d ed., by Stuart Robertson and Frederic G. Cassidy. Gives a short overview of French vocabulary borrowings during Middle English. Hardbound, Prentice-Hall, 1954.

"The French Influence," pp. 48-55 in *Aspects of the History of English* by John C. McLaughlin. Provides a good discussion of French borrowings into Middle English and illustrates them in Chaucer's "Prologue" to *The Canterbury Tales* and *Sir Gawain and the Green Knight.* Hardbound, Holt, Rinehart and Winston, 1970.

"Influx of Norman French" and "French Influence," pp. 151-154, 160-165 in *A Structural History of English* by John Nist. Provides an excellent discussion of Norman-French and Parisian French borrowings into Middle English. Hardbound, St. Martin's Press, 1966.

"French Influence on the Vocabulary," pp. 200-218 in *A History of the English Language,* 2d ed., by Albert C. Baugh. Gives a rather thorough account of French borrowings and displacement of native English words during the Middle English period. Hardbound, Appleton-Century-Crofts, 1957.

III. THE MIDDLE ENGLISH LANGUAGE

Audiovisual Materials

Our Changing Language. LP record, 1975, National Council of Teachers of English. Provides a short discussion of and illustrative passage of Middle English (as well as of Old English, Early Modern English, and thirteen modern American and Canadian dialects).

Thousand Years of English Pronunciation, A. Two LP records and text, Educational Audio Visual, Inc. Has readings from six Middle English authors (as well as Old and Early Modern English readings).

Beowulf-Chaucer. Tape, Educational Audio Visual, Inc. Has readings from Chaucer's *The Canterbury Tales* and *Troilus and Criseyde* (as well as *Beowulf*).

Songs and Ballads of the Scottish Wars 1290-1745. LP record, Folkways Records. Provides songs in Middle English (as well as in Early Modern English).

Early English Ballads from the Percy and Child Collections. LP record, Folkways Records. Has some Middle English songs, but mostly Early Modern English ones.

Print

"Notes on Middle English as a Language," pp. 43-48 in *A Survey of Modern Grammars,* 2d ed., by Jeanne H. Herndon. Presents a short overview of the differences in pronunciation, vocabulary, inflections, and syntax between Chaucer's Middle English and Modern English. Paperbound, Holt, Rinehart and Winston, 1976.

"Middle English Dialects," etc., pp. 30-34 in *The English Language: Yesterday and Today* by Charles B. Martin and Curt M. Rulon. Provides a short, reasonably simple description of late Middle English morphology. Hardbound, Allyn and Bacon, 1973.

"The Language," pp. 148-151 in *A Structural History of English* by John Nist. Gives a good summary of the types of grammatical change which occurred from Old English to Middle English. Hardbound, St. Martin's Press, 1966.

"The Reduction of Inflections" etc., pp. 166-180 in *The Origins and Development of the English Language,* 2d ed., by Thomas Pyles. Provides a good, readable discussion of Middle English grammar and the grammatical changes from Old English to Middle English. Hardbound, Harcourt Brace Jovanovich, 1971.

"Morphology" and "Syntax," pp. 184-200 in *A Structural History of English* by John Nist. Gives one of the most complete descriptions of Middle English as a language. Recommended for teachers. Hardbound, St. Martin's Press, 1966.

Exercises, pp. 153-159 in *Problems in the Origins and Development of the English Language,* 2d ed., by John Algeo. Provides exercises dealing with Middle English inflections of nouns, adjectives, and verbs as well as pronoun forms and word order. Paperbound, Harcourt Brace Jovanovich, 1972.

"Middle English," pp. 189-200 in *A History of the English Language,* 2d ed., by Albert C. Baugh. Gives a rather scholarly description of the changes in grammar from Old English to Middle English. Hardbound, Appleton-Century-Crofts, 1957.

"Middle English (1100-1500)," pp. 99-101, 104-124 in *A History of the English Language* by Garland Cannon. Illustrates and explains Middle English with passages from *The Ormulum,* Chaucer, and the *Wycliffe Bible,* but presents a complex analysis of the grammar of the passages. Paperbound, Harcourt Brace Jovanovich, 1972.

12

Early Modern English

This chapter deals with the Renaissance vocabulary and spelling influence on Early Modern English; the development of prescriptive grammar, usage, and spelling; and the structure of the Early Modern English language. A practical application of this study should be an awareness of the multiple levels of English vocabulary reflecting native elements and learned foreign elements. However, the most important practical result of studying this chapter should be the development of a healthy skepticism about self-proclaimed authorities in linguistic as well as other matters.

First the students should be introduced to the effect of the Renaissance on English vocabulary and spelling. While the students may be familiar with some of the English vocabulary borrowings of the period from Chapter 9, they will not be aware of the conscious and unconscious reasons for some of the adoptions or the opposition during Early Modern English to many borrowings as "inkhornisms."

Then the students should be made aware of how the traditional school grammars developed from Early Modern English grammars, which were based inappropriately on Latin and Greek grammars and which prescribed usage at the whim of the authors. They should also be made aware how spellings were standardized by various dictionaries whose authors took it upon themselves to prescribe spelling as they pleased. Students should also have explained to them why these prescriptions were generally accepted.

Finally, the Early Modern English language itself should be examined. The students will be struck by the fact the Early Modern English morphology simplified from that of Middle English to the extent that it greatly resembles that of Modern English. They should be interested in the few differences between Early Modern English and Modern English morphology, however. They are also likely to think Early Modern English syntax "funny" where it differs from that of Modern English.

The first topic might be omitted if the teacher has covered the topic extensively in Chapter 9. The students will most likely be quite interested in the second topic if they dislike traditional grammar or have trouble with spelling. The third topic will be most interesting to students who have read some Shakespeare or the King James or Douay versions of the Bible.

OBJECTIVES

If the three topics in this chapter are taught by the teacher, the students should, at the end of the unit, be able to:

1. Explain the effect of the Renaissance on Early Modern English
2. Define "inkhornism" and explain the inkhornism controversy
3. Explain the demand for prescriptive grammar, usage, and spelling books during the Early Modern English period
4. Identify theoretical assumptions underlying the Early Modern English grammars and explain the weaknesses of these assumptions
5. Name major Early Modern English grammars, their authors, and their attitudes toward acceptable usage
6. Trace the development of English dictionaries during the Early Modern English period and identify major dictionaries of the period
7. Point out differences between Early Modern English and Modern English nouns
8. Discuss the major changes in personal pronouns during Early Modern English
9. Identify characteristics of Early Modern English adjectives and adverbs which differ from their characteristics in Modern English
10. Explain the simplification of verb inflections in Early Modern English and identify the major inflectional and phrasal changes in verbs from Middle English to Early Modern English to Modern English

CONTENT OVERVIEW

Renaissance Influence on Vocabulary and Spelling

Both the times of the beginning of the Early Modern English period and its duration are debatable. Many authorities say that it began around 1500 and extended to 1700 or even 1800. The beginning of the Early Modern English period is usually assumed to have begun with the Renaissance in England, but, of course, there is no agreement as to when the Renaissance reached England either. Perhaps 1476 when William Caxton, the first English printer, introduced movable type into England and made books, including translations from other languages, available to non-upper-class Englishmen would be a reasonable date to assign for the beginning of both events.

Even an earlier date is possible, however. The Renaissance was characterized, in addition to its humanistic concerns, by an interest in the vernacular languages and a rediscovery of the literature, arts, and philosophy of classical antiquity. It began on the Continent earlier than it did in England. In 1303, Dante wrote in a Latin treatise, *De Vulgare Eloquentia,* that the vernacular languages were suitable vehicles for serious literature and that authors should not be required to write in Latin to be taken seriously, and both Dante and Boccaccio wrote in their native Florentine Italian in the fourteenth century. Provençal and Spanish writers had already begun to write in their vernaculars. When these authors, who had been educated to write medieval Latin, wrote in their vernaculars, however, they could not help but introduce Latin words into their vernaculars. Chaucer did the same thing in late Middle English when he wrote in English but added many French and Latin words from his sources into his English.

Translations of literature in the vernacular languages as well as some of the pre-Christian Latin and Greek literature were available to the upper class in England as early as the fourteenth century; they became available to much of the middle class at the end of the fifteenth century. These translations often included words from the original language in the English version, so new words were introduced into English because the words were already familiar to the translators. These new words are a clear sign that the Renaissance had begun in England and that the Early Modern English period had begun. The majority of these new English words were from Latin, but many came from Greek and French and a few from Italian and Spanish.

While this carry-over of words from non-English languages to English by authors and translators familiar with the non-English languages was inevitable, many Englishmen objected to these new words as "inkhornisms," meaning that they were born in the inkpots the authors dipped their pens in and therefore were not part of the English language. Many of the Early Modern English borrowings are very much a part of English now, however. These include, from Latin, *abject, conspicuous, delineation, dexterity, dimension, education, encyclopedia, expensive, extinguish, function, idiom, insane, meditate, penetrate,* and *scientific;* and, from Greek, *anonymous, catastrophe, criterion, ostracize, tantalize, thermometer,* and *tonic.* However, other inkhornisms were not accepted and have disappeared with little harm to anyone except students of Renaissance literature. These include, from Latin, *abusion, dispone, fecundius, palestral,* and *reclinatory* and, from Greek, *enchiridion* (replaced by the Latin *encyclopedia*). See also the overview and annotated bibliography for Chapter 9.

A great debate raged among educated Englishmen in the sixteenth century about the acceptability of using Latin and Greek Renaissance borrowings in English. One side argued that English was enriched by these borrowed words, many of which had no one-word equivalents in native English words (or earlier borrowings into English). The other side argued that the words were not only strange but that they were used only by pedantic writers who wanted both to be obscure and to show their own erudition. As usual when there are two diametrically opposed positions, there was justification on both sides, and what actually happened within the language was a compromise. Many of the borrowed words survive in the language as near synonyms for native words like *rise* and *ascend, ask* and *interrogate,* or *go* and *exit,* which, because they have different connotations, allow speakers of English to convey nuances of meaning not available to speakers who do not have a double vocabulary. However, the recognition that the excessive use of borrowed words rather than Anglo-Saxon words is characteristic of phony people who have pretensions or choose to be obscure did not disappear in the sixteenth century. Shakespeare satirized it in Holofernes' speech in *Love's Labor's Lost,* and teachers who are accused of sounding like teachers today are not always being complimented.

The introduction of Latin words into English during the Early Modern English period caused the respelling of many native words and earlier borrowings by analogy with the spelling of these newly borrowed Latin words or just with Latin spelling. The ⟨s⟩ in *island* was added during Early Modern English by analogy with Latin *insula,* although the word comes from Old English *igland.* Although the words were all borrowed from French, the following words all had consonants added during the Renaissance to reflect alleged Latin origins: ⟨b⟩ added to *debt* and *doubt;* ⟨c⟩ added to *perfect* and *verdict* (and now pronounced); ⟨d⟩ added to *advantage* (and pronounced); ⟨g⟩ added to *foreign* and *sovereign;* ⟨l⟩ added to *fault* and *vault* (and pronounced); ⟨p⟩ added to *receipt*

The Development of Prescriptive Grammar, Usage, and Spelling

By the end of the Middle English period, the division between the upper class and lower class was becoming less clear due to the appearance of a middle class between the two older classes. The middle class were aware that their language use was a criterion for upward mobility; they were also aware that their speech was not exactly like that of the upper class. Of course, they wanted to learn the "right" kind of English then. As usual, when someone is willing to pay someone else to tell the first person what is correct, authorities arose to meet the need. These authorities offered prescriptions in three broad areas: grammar, usage, and spelling.

Just as Latin and Greek had influenced the vocabulary of Early Modern English, they also provided the models for the first grammars of English during the Early Modern English period. Of course, Early Modern English had a completely different grammatical structure from that of classical Latin or Greek.

Nevertheless, some traditional grammars still follow the Latin tradition of the first Early Modern English grammar, William Bullokar's *Bref Grammar for English* (1586), and talk about nominative, accusative, genitive, dative, and ablative cases for Modern English, for which such terms are totally inappropriate. The first important grammar of Early Modern English was John Wallis's *Grammatica Linguae Anglicanae* (1653). It equated Latin verb inflections with Early Modern English auxiliaries to give English a full repertoire of tenses, but English, like all other Germanic languages, has only two tenses—past and nonpast or present—marked in the verb itself. Other time relations are shown, not by tense, but by auxiliaries. Many traditional grammars still conjugate verbs as if they were Latin verbs with six inflections, one for each person in the singular and plural. In reality, Modern English has only two forms in the present indicative (one with -*s* and one without) and only one form in the past.

In defense of the Early Modern English grammarians, however, it should be pointed out that Latin and Greek grammars were the only grammars that they knew. It was only natural that they would describe English as if it were Latin or Greek, particularly since they had figured out that any idea could be expressed in any language and concluded that there must be a "universal grammar" underlying all languages. This practice of using a Latin model was followed for other Early Modern English grammars until the last half of the eighteenth century.

Bishop Robert Lowth's *A Short Introduction to English Grammar* (1762), while still influenced by Latin models and the idea of universal grammar, did attempt to describe the grammar of English as English, but he tried to describe English as he thought it should be, not as it was. As a result, Lowth found errors in the writings of all of the great literature of the period. Unfortunately, his prescriptive grammar and habit of looking for deviations from his prescriptions have survived into the twentieth century as the traditional grammar taught in schools. Although George Campbell's *Philosophy of Rhetoric* (1776) suggested that usage determined the correct grammar of English, most other grammars, such as Anselm Bayly's *The English Accidence* (1771) and Lindley Murray's *English Grammar* (1795), perpetuated Lowth's ideas that no one spoke or wrote English correctly, since usage did not conform to their prescriptions.

With regard to questions of usage rather than of grammatical structure, the Early Modern English grammarians set up many rules by which unlearned speakers of English could be identified as such. It mattered little that the usage prescribed was not that of cultivated speakers of English. John Wallis produced the usage rule that *shall* should be used for first person and *will* for second and third person to indicate simple future; Robert Lowth perpetuated that myth but decided the reverse was true for questions. Lowth also introduced the usage rule that two negatives make a positive (as in mathematics and logic) in English. He also decided that "smarter than *me*" was unacceptable usage while "smarter than *I*" was acceptable. While such usage rules were Early Modern English fabrications, they may still be found in school grammars in the twentieth century. The rule against "split infinitives" was concocted during this same period by analogy with Latin and Greek infinitives, which are distinct grammatical forms with distinct inflectional endings. Since Latin and Greek inflections were never separated from the root of the infinitive, it was decided that nothing should intervene between *to* and the base form of a verb, *to understand*. The problem of course is that *to* was never part of an English infinitive (see content overview in Chapter 10); the decision to create an English infinitive consisting of *to* plus the base form of the verb was made during the Early Modern English period, since English infinitives had lost their inflectional endings and it was assumed that every language must have a separate infinitive form like Latin and Greek. The addition of "interjection" as an English part of speech was made at the same time because Greek had eight parts of speech and English must have eight too.

There were two major forces which supported the standardization of English spelling during the Renaissance in addition to the desire of the middle class to spell the "right" way for their own social advancement. The first was the introduction of movable print into England by William Caxton in 1476, so that books became available to people other than the very rich and literacy increased. The second was the Renaissance introduction into English of learned Latin and Greek words which only those with a classical education would know how to spell. Once a spelling was written in print, it exerted a great power as *the* way to spell a word. It is true that Shakespeare spelled his last name four different ways, so proper spelling was not yet the shibboleth in Early Modern English that it is in Modern English, but there was increasing pressure on spelling consistently and "correctly."

Beginning in the seventeenth century, dictionaries were introduced to tell the linguistically uncertain the "proper" spellings, pronunciations, and meanings of English words. Prior to that time, there were foreign-language–English dictionaries and attempts at spelling reform like Richard Mulcaster's *Elementarie* (1582). The first English dictionary, Robert Cawdrey's *A Table Alphabeticall* (1604), supposedly dealt only with borrowed terms in English, but actually contained some native words as well. The other early English dictionaries also included only "hard" words and did not pretend to be complete, such as John Bullokar's *English Expositour* (1616), Henry Cockeram's *The English Dictionarie* (1623), and Thomas Blount's *Glossographie* (1658).

Later dictionaries sometimes claimed to be complete dictionaries of the English language, but they usually were not. Nathaniel Bailey's *Universal Etymological English Dictionary* (1721) is the most famous example. Bailey was the first to put accent marks on words in his dictionary; Samuel Johnson's *A Dictionary of the English Language* (1755) followed this practice. William Kenrick's *New Dictionary* (1773) was the first to indicate vowel sounds. All of these dictionaries were the works of individual lexicographers who, although sometimes professing to be recording the usage of their time, arbitrarily spelled and defined words the way they wanted to and recorded only their own personal usage.

The Early Modern English Language

Since the process of generalizing the *-es* possessive and the *-es* plural to nearly all nouns had already begun in late Middle English, Early Modern English nouns do not differ greatly from their Modern English developments. The *-(e)n* plural was still used for some nouns that have since then adopted the regular *-(e)s* plural such as *eyen* ("eyes"), *fleen* ("fleas"), *fon* ("foes"), *kine* ("cows"), and *kneen* ("knees"). Some nouns like *hors* and *kind* still had unchanged plurals like Modern English *deer* but have subsequently been regularized. A peculiarity of Early Modern English nouns was the use of the *his*-possessive as in *the King his son,* but this spelling probably was pronounced in the same way as *the King's son* would be now. The group genitive as in *the King of England his son* developed in Early Modern English, but the older form *the King his son of England* still occurred.

The changes in Early Modern English pronouns are more significant. The most important changes involved second person pronouns. The second person singular forms *thou, thy, thine,* and *thee* developed an aura of intimacy or condescension like the Modern Spanish and French *tu* and German *du*. As a result, the second person singular forms could be used only to persons one was close to or persons of low status. In contrast, the *ye, your, yours, you* second person plural forms began to be used when addressing only one person when one wished to maintain a degree of formality or to show respect just like the modern use of French *vous*, Spanish *usted*, and German *Sie*. Shakespeare made frequent use of these conventions when he had characters in his plays address each other with either *thou* or *ye* forms and frequently shift from one to the other as their relationships changed in the course of a play. By the end of the Early Modern English period, the *thou* forms had been discarded as offensive, and the *you* forms generalized to both singular and plural second person. The early-seventeenth-century Bible translations maintained the *thou* and *ye* distinctions, but the translations were consciously archaic in this usage even for their time. Another Early Modern English second person pronoun change was the generalization of *you* to nominative function (replacing *ye*) as well as objective function. The usual explanation for this phenomenon is that both *ye* and *you* were usually unstressed and pronounced /jə/, so it was difficult to keep them separate when writing. Again, the seventeenth-century Bible translations do keep them separate, but that separation was already an archaism at the time of translation.

The other pronoun changes of the period include the completion of the adoption of the *th-* third person plural forms *them, their,* and *theirs,* and the development of the third person singular neuter possessive *its* (replacing *his*, which would be confused with the masculine form) by analogy with the noun possessive and the second possessive form of other pronouns. The complementary distribution of *my-mine* and *thy-thine* with the first form used before words beginning with a consonant sound and the second before a vowel sound (as in the Modern English distribution of *a-an*) was generally maintained in Early Modern English until the eighteenth century. The relative pronoun *who* was introduced in the sixteenth century, but the use of the relative *which* was still used to refer to people (unlike in Modern English) and things.

Adjectives and adverbs in Early Modern English did not differ much from those of Modern English. The distinction between the strong singular and all the other forms from Middle English was lost entirely (partly due to the loss of final *-e/ə/* in pronunciation). The comparative and superlative forms used *-er* and *-est* or *more* and *most* as in Modern English, but the distinction between base adjectives and adverbs (of one or two syllables) taking *-er* and *-est* and derived adjectives or adverbs (formed from another word with a derivational affix and thus polysyllabic) using *more* and *most* was not as rigorous as it is today. As a result, one finds Early Modern English forms like *impudentest* and *more fast* and double comparatives and superlatives like *more better* and *most worst.* Some Early Modern English adjectives and adverbs had comparative and superlative forms with a different vowel in the base of the inflected forms like archaic Modern English *old-elder-eldest;* these included *long-lenger-lengest* and *strong-strenger-strengest,* which have since been regularized. Not all adverbs that end in *-ly* today had the *-ly* added during Early Modern English, so one finds expressions like *wondrous strange* rather than *wondrously strange* from that period.

With the loss of final *-e/ə/* in Early Modern English, present tense forms of verbs were reduced to a second person singular form in *-(e)st,* a third person singular form in *-(e)th,* and an endingless form for first person singular and for the plural of all persons. Of course, the *-(e)st* form disappeared when the *thou* forms of the pronouns disappeared, and the Northern third person singular form in *-(e)s* gradually replaced the *-(e)th* form during Early Modern English. The past tense forms were reduced to one form that had no personal endings after the second person singular form in *-(e)st* disappeared with the disappearance of the *thou* pronouns. The frequency of the use of "progressive" verb phrases with *be* and the present participle as in *He is working* increased during Early Modern English. The major differences between Early Modern English and Modern English verb forms lie in the differences in contracted forms and the Early Modern English use of impersonal constructions. Early Modern English contracted forms *'tis, 'twas,* and *'twill* are no longer used; *it's* and *it'll* are modern forms, but there is no contracted form for *it was* in Modern English. Impersonal constructions from Early Modern English like *methinks* ("it seems to me") and *it yearns me* are now considered archaic. There was also much confusion of past tense and past participle forms in Early Modern English as many strong verbs changed to weak verbs like *melt* with Early Modern English past forms *malt* and *melted* and past participle *molten* and *melted* and as some strong verbs vacillated between past tense forms from the Middle English first and third person singular forms and the plural forms like *write* with Early Modern English past tense forms *wrote* and *writ.*

The major syntactic differences between Early Modern English and Modern English involve the formations of questions and negative sentences. Minor differences involve different prepositions in certain idioms and the addition or omission of articles in certain idioms. Questions in Early Modern English did not require the use of the dummy auxiliary *do* in inversions like *Did you eat yet?* or *When did he die?* In Early Modern English simple inversions like *Ate you yet?* or *When died he?* were quite acceptable. On the other hand, *do* might be added in Early Modern English where it would not be now except for emphasis as in *Who did take it?* Similarly, negatives did not require the use of the auxiliary *do* in an Early Modern English sentence like *I hear not your words.* On the other hand, double or triple negatives were acceptable in Early Modern English for emphasis as in *I will not bow to no man.* Prepositional differences include things like Early Modern English *I bought two after threepence* each (rather than *at*). Different article use in Early Modern English is obvious in phrases like *at the length* for Modern English *at length* and *singing like bird* for Modern English *singing like a bird.*

LEARNING EXPERIENCES

Topic I.   Renaissance Influence on Vocabulary and Spelling

- After explaining Renaissance borrowing to the class, have the students form two groups to debate opposite sides of the topics: Renaissance borrowing from other languages into Early Modern English improved the language, or Renaissance borrowing from other languages into Early Modern English complicated the language unnecessarily.

- Using Reproduction Page 81, have the students identify which word in the pairs of synonyms below is a Renaissance borrowing into Early Modern English. The Renaissance borrowings are marked with an *R* in parentheses below but not on the Reproduction Page. The borrowings are from Latin unless identified as Greek below.

1. (R) advent—coming
2. (R-Greek) antipathy—hatred
3. (R) ascend—rise
4. catlike—feline (R)
5. (R-Greek) climax—end
6. (R) communicate—speak
7. (R) conduct—lead
8. (R) conflagration—fire
9. dig—excavate (R)
10. earthly—terrestrial (R)
11. (R) educate—teach
12. (R) emancipate—free
13. evil—malignant (R)
14. fast—secure (R)

REPRODUCTION PAGE 81

RENAISSANCE BORROWING

Directions: *From the pairs of synonyms below, identify which word in each pair is a Renaissance Latin or Greek borrowing. Remember that the Renaissance borrowings are likely to be difficult or learned words. Check the source of any words you are not sure of in a dictionary.*

Source		Source
1. _____	advent-coming	_____
2. _____	antipathy-hatred	_____
3. _____	ascend-arise	_____
4. _____	catlike-feline	_____
5. _____	climax-end	_____
6. _____	communicate-speak	_____
7. _____	conduct-lead	_____
8. _____	conflagration-fire	_____
9. _____	dig-excavate	_____
10. _____	earthly-terrestrial	_____
11. _____	educate-teach	_____
12. _____	emancipate-free	_____
13. _____	evil-malignant	_____
14. _____	fast-secure	_____
15. _____	free-liberate	_____
16. _____	fortitude-strength	_____
17. _____	kingly-regal	_____
18. _____	manifest-show	_____
19. _____	meditate-think	_____
20. _____	tantalize-tease	_____

15. free—liberate (R)

16. (R) fortitude—strength

17. kingly—regal (R)

18. (R) manifest—show

19. (R) meditate—think

20. (R-Greek— tantalize—tease

- Using Reproduction Page 82, have the students use a dictionary to determine which letters in the following words were added during the Renaissance because the words were assumed to have come directly from Latin. The added letters are given in parentheses below but not on the Reproduction Page.

    1. advance (d)

    2. advantage (d)

    3. adventure (d)

    4. aisle (s)

    5. debt (b)

    6. doubt (b)

    7. fault (l)

    8. foreign (g)

    9. island (s)

    10. perfect (c)

    11. receipt (p)

    12. sovereign (g)

REPRODUCTION PAGE 82

SPELLING CHANGES

Directions: *Below are words that had letters added to their spelling during Early Modern English to reflect their real or imagined Latin origins. Use a dictionary to see the source of each word in English and then determine what letter was added to the spelling of each during the Early Modern English period. Are these letters pronounced now, or are they ignored in pronunciation?*

1. advance
2. advantage
3. adventure
4. aisle
5. debt
6. doubt
7. fault
8. foreign
9. island
10. perfect
11. receipt
12. sovereign
13. vault
14. verdict
15. victuals

13. vault (l)

14. verdict (c)

15. victuals (c)

- Have individual students research and report back to the class on the following:

  1. William Caxton

  2. Sir Thomas Elyot's *The Governour*

  3. Sir Thomas Wyatt and Henry Howard, earl of Surrey

  4. Thomas Wilson's *Art of Rhetorique*

  5. Richard Mulcaster's *Elementarie*

  6. John Skelton

  7. Edmund Spenser's use of archaic morphology

  8. Sir John Cheke

  9. inkhornisms

- Have each student write a short essay on Early Modern English vocabulary borrowings from Latin and Greek.

Topic II: The Development of Prescriptive Grammar, Usage, and Spelling

- After the spelling practices of the Early Modern English period have been discussed, have the students form two groups to debate opposite sides of the topic: consistency in spelling is unnecessary.

- Using Reproduction Page 83, have the students compare the Latin and Early Modern English verb paradigms to determine why the Latin pattern is inappropriate for describing Early Modern English. (Latin has six different forms for each tense, while Early Modern English has three forms in the present and two in the past.) The students are asked to change the Early Modern English forms to Modern English (*see, sees,* and *saw*) and to decide whether the Latin paradigm is more or less appropriate for Modern English than for Early Modern English (less because of further reduction in distinctive person forms).

- Using Reproduction Page 84, have the students compare the Latin and Early Modern English noun paradigms to determine why the Latin pattern is inappropriate for describing Early Modern English. (Latin has four forms for each number, dative and ablative being the same in the example, while Early Modern English has only two forms in the singular and one in the plural.) The students are asked to change the Early Modern English forms to Modern English (*son, son's, sons,* and *sons',* but it may be necessary to explain the modern convention of the apostrophe, which developed in very late Early Modern English) and to decide whether the Latin paradigm is appropriate for Modern English (obviously not).

- Have individual students research and report back to the class on the following:

  1. William Bullokar's *Bref Grammar for English* (1586)

LATIN VS. ENGLISH VERB PATTERNS

Directions: *Below you will find present and preterite indicative forms of the Latin verb* vidēre *("see") and the corresponding present and past indicative forms of the Early Modern English verb* see. *Why is the Latin pattern of verb forms inappropriate for giving the forms of the Early Modern English verb? (Hint: How many different forms do the two languages each have?) Change the Early Modern English forms to their Modern English equivalents. Is the Latin more or less appropriate for Modern English than for Early Modern English?*

	vidēre	see
	Present Indicative	
First Person Singular	video	see
Second Person Singular	vidēs	seest
Third Person Singular	videt	seeth/sees
First Person Plural	vidēmus	see
Second Person Plural	vidēmus	see
Third Person Plural	vident	see
	Preterite Indicative	
First Person Singular	vīdī	saw
Second Person Singular	vīdistī	sawest
Third Person Singular	vīdet	saw
First Person Plural	vīdimus	saw
Second Person Plural	vīdistis	saw
Third Person Plural	vīdērunt	saw

2. John Wallis's *Grammatica Linguae Anglicanae* (1653)

3. Robert Lowth's *A Short Introduction to English Grammar* (1762)

4. Anselm Bayly's *The English Accidence* (1771)

5. Lindley Murray's *English Grammar* (1795)

6. Robert Cawdrey's *The Table Alphabeticall* (1604)

7. John Bullokar's *English Expositour* (1616)

8. Henry Cockeram's *The English Dictionary* (1623)

LATIN VS. ENGLISH NOUN PATTERNS

Directions: *Below you will find the inflected forms of the Latin noun* filius *("son") and the Early Modern English noun* sone *("son"). Why is the Latin pattern of indicating five cases, both singular and plural, inappropriate for giving the forms of Early Modern English nouns? (Hint: How many different forms do the two languages have?) Change the Early Modern English forms to their Modern English equivalents. Is the Latin pattern appropriate for Modern English?*

	filius	sone
	Singular	
Nominative (subject)	filius	son(e)
Genitive (possessive)	filī	son(e)s
Dative (indirect object)	filiō	son(e)
Accusative (direct object)	filium	son(e)
Ablative (with certain prepositions)	filiō	son(e)
	Plural	
Nominative	filiī	son(e)s
Genitive	filiōrum	son(e)s
Dative	filiīs	son(e)s
Accusative	filiōs	son(e)s
Ablative	filiīs	son(e)s

    9. Thomas Blount's *Glossographie* (1658)

   10. Nathaniel Bailey's *Universal Etymological English Dictionary* (1721)

   11. Samuel Johnson's *A Dictionary of the English Language* (1755)

   12. Daniel Defoe's call for the establishment of an Academy in *Essay Upon Projects* (1697)

   13. Jonathan Swift's call for the establishment of an Academy (1712)

- Have each student write a short essay on one of the following topics:

   1. The development of prescriptive rules of usage in English

   2. The development of English grammars during Early Modern English

   3. The development of English dictionaries during Early Modern English

   4. The standardization of spelling during Early Modern English

Topic III: The Early Modern English Language

- If your students are reading any of Shakespeare's plays, have them analyze the use of second person pronouns (*thou* and *ye* forms) in a scene to see what that usage conveys about the relationships among characters in the play. Suggested scenes are: *Antony and Cleopatra,* V.ii; *As You Like It,* IV.i; *Hamlet,* III.iv; *Henry IV, Part 1,* III.ii–iii; *Love's Labor's Lost,* I.i; *The Merchant of Venice,* IV.i; *Much Ado About Nothing,* IV.i; *Richard III,* I.ii; *Two Gentlemen of Verona,* V.iii.

- If your students are reading anything by an Early Modern English author, have each student make a list of grammatical features of nouns, verbs, adjectives, and adverbs he or she finds in the reading that differ from their forms in Modern English.

- Using Reproduction Page 85, have the students translate the edited passage of a letter from Queen Elizabeth I to the future King James I and then list the grammatical changes from Early Modern English to Modern English as shown by their translations. A glossary is provided for words and phrases that are not easily understood.

- Using Reproduction Page 86, have the students translate the following Early Modern English phrases into Modern English. The Early Modern English usage illustrated is identified below but not on the Reproduction Page.

   1. most unkindest (double superlative)

   2. within this mile and half (different idiomatic use of article; add *a*)

   3. at the last (different idiomatic use of article; delete *the*)

   4. creeping like turtle (different idiomatic use of article; add *a*)

   5. more happier (double comparative)

   6. two eyen (n-stem plural of *eye*)

   7. the king's of England nose (non-group-genitive: . . . *England's*)

TRANSLATING EARLY MODERN ENGLISH

Directions: *Translate the passage from an Early Modern English letter written by Queen Elizabeth I to the later King James I into Modern English. Then make a list of the grammatical changes from Early Modern English to Modern English as shown by your translation. The glossary below explains points that you might not be able to figure out.*

my deare brother, Hit hathe sufficiently infourmed me of your singular care of my estat and brething that you haue sent one, in suche diligence, to understand the circumstances of the treasons wiche lately wer lewdly attempted and miraculously vttred. Of whiche I had made participant your embassador afore you lettars came. And now am I to shewe you, that, as I haue receaved many writings from you of great kindnis, yet this last was fraughted with so careful passion. . . . If I shuld not seak to decerue it . . . , I were ill-wordy suche a frind . . .

Glossary

one	"someone"
made participant	"informed"
fraughted	"filled"
careful	"concerned," literally "full of care"
passion	"emotion"
decerue	"deserve" (creative spelling)
were	"would be" (subjunctive form of verb)
ill-wordy	"ill-worthy" (misspelling)

8. as red as Mars his heart (his possessive: *Mars's* or *Mars'*)

9. most boldest (double superlative)

10. his shoon (n-stem plural of *shoe*)

11. more near (use of *more* as comparative of base adjective: *nearer*)

12. beautifullest (use of inflection as superlative of derived adjective: *most beautiful*)

TRANSLATING EARLY MODERN ENGLISH PHRASES

Directions: *Translate the following Early Modern English phrases into Modern English. What kinds of changes have you made?*

1. most unkindest
2. within this mile and half
3. at the last
4. creeping like turtle
5. more happier
6. two eyen
7. the king's of England nose
8. as red as Mars his heart
9. most boldest
10. his shoon
11. more near
12. beautifullest
13. grievous sick
14. stay lenger
15. mine aunt
16. the man which
17. thou art sick
18. ye discovered it
19. well completed of you
20. married of him

13. grievous sick (adverb without -ly: *grievously*)

14. stay lenger (umlaut comparative: *longer*)

15. mine aunt (use of possessive pronoun in -*n* before noun beginning with a vowel: *my*)

16. the man which (use of *which* as a relative referring to people: *who*)

17. thou art sick (use of second person singular pronoun and verb forms: *you are*)

18. ye discovered it (use of nominative form of second person plural pronoun before *you* assumed nominative function)

19. well completed of you (different idiomatic use of preposition: *by*)

20. married of him (different idiomatic use of preposition: *by* or *to*)

- Using Reproduction Page 87, have the students write the Early Modern English questions below in Modern English. The students are asked to identify any patterns of change (addition of auxiliary *do* to put before the subject so the verb, except for *be*, will still follow the subject; replacement of second person singular by second person plural forms). The Modern English equivalents are given below in parentheses but not on the Reproduction Page.

  1. Worked you long yesterday? (Did you work long yesterday?)

  2. Is that your dog? (no change)

  3. Will she be here? (no change)

  4. When came she? (When did she come?)

  5. What think you about it? (What do you think about it?)

  6. Do you understand, John? (no change)

REPRODUCTION PAGE 87

WORD ORDER CHANGES

Directions: *Write the Early Modern English questions below in Modern English word order. What kinds of changes have you made? Is there a pattern? Some sentences will require no change in word order.*

1. Worked you long yesterday?

2. Is that your dog?

3. Will she be here?

4. When came she?

5. What think you about it?

6. Do you understand, John?

7. How many hast thou eaten?

8. What sayst thou to that?

9. Who did tell that lie?

10. Went they?

7. How many hast thou eaten? (How many have you eaten?)

8. What sayest thou to that? (What do you say to that?)

9. Who did tell that lie? (Who told that lie? unless *did* is stressed)

10. Went they? (Did they go?)

- Using Reproduction Page 88, have the students rewrite the Early Modern English negatives below in Modern English. The students are asked to identify any patterns of change (addition of auxiliary *do* before negative and movement of negative to before the verb, except for *be*; deletion of double negatives). The Modern English equivalents are given below in parentheses but not on the Reproduction Page.

1. He understands not the meaning. (He does not understand the meaning.)

2. That is not the cause neither. (That is not the cause either.)

3. She saw him not. (She did not see him.)

4. Never shall none be fairer. (Never shall any be fairer or There shall be none fairer.)

5. I like not him. (I do not like him.)

6. I not doubt his word. (I do not doubt his word.)

7. I eat not meat, nor fowl neither. (I do not eat meat or fowl either.)

8. I will not move for no man. (I will not move for any man or I will move for no man.)

9. He never did no harm to no one. (He never did any harm to anyone.)

10. It not appears to me so. (It does not appear to me so.)

REPRODUCTION PAGE 88

CHANGES IN NEGATIVE SENTENCES

Directions: *Write the Early Modern English negative sentences below in Modern English. What kinds of changes have you made? Is there a pattern?*

1. He understands not the meaning.

2. That is not the cause neither.

3. She saw him not.

4. Never shall none be fairer.

5. I like not him.

6. I not doubt his word.

7. I eat not meat, nor fowl neither.

8. I will not move for no man.

9. He never did no harm to no one.

10. It not appears to me so.

- Have each student write a short essay on the morphological and syntactical differences between Early Modern English and Modern English.

ASSESSING ACHIEVEMENT OF OBJECTIVES

Ongoing Evaluation

The extent to which students have mastered the content of each topic in the chapter can be measured by any of the activities assigned to the class as individuals, particularly the writing activities.

Final Evaluation

For an overall evaluation of the students' mastery of the content in this chapter, if the three topics in the chapter have been taught, a test constructed directly from the list of student objectives for the chapter as listed on page 232 can be used. As an alternative, one might consider a test composed from the following items:

1. Give three examples of words borrowed from Latin or Greek during Early Modern English.

2. Give two examples of words that were respelled by analogy with Latin words during Early Modern English.

3. What were the major arguments for and against borrowing words from other languages during Early Modern English?

4. Why were grammars of English written during the Early Modern English period?

5. Name two weaknesses of Early Modern English grammars.

6. What criteria did the authors of Early Modern English grammars use to determine what was acceptable usage?

7. Identify two major Early Modern English grammarians.

8. Describe the first English dictionaries.

9. Identify two Early Modern English dictionaries (or authors of dictionaries).

10. Give an example of an Early Modern English noun plural that differs from its Modern English equivalent.

11. Name two Early Modern English pronouns that no longer exist in Modern English.

12. Give an example of an Early Modern English comparative or superlative form of an adjective that differs from its Modern English equivalent.

13. Identify an Early Modern English verb inflection that has been dropped by the time of Modern English.

RESOURCES FOR TEACHING ABOUT EARLY MODERN ENGLISH

Below is a selected and annotated list of resources useful for teaching the topics of this chapter, divided into audiovisual and print materials and arranged in order of ascending difficulty. Special strengths and weaknesses are mentioned in the annotations. Addresses of publishers or distributors can be found in the alphabetical list on pages 263-265 in Appendix A. Films are . black and white unless otherwise indicated.

I. RENAISSANCE INFLUENCE ON VOCABULARY AND SPELLING

Audiovisual Materials

Speaking of Spelling. Sound filmstrip (sound on LP record or cassette tape), 22 minutes, 1975, Guidance Associates. Presents a short discussion of the development of writing systems, influences on the English writing system, and regularities in Modern English spelling.

Print

"Some Greek and More Latin," pp. 34-37 in *The English Language: From Anglo-Saxon to American* by Charles Cutler. Discusses Renaissance and other Latin borrowings into English. Not recommended for older students. Paperbound, Xerox Educational Publications, 1968.

"Some Examples of Early Modern English" and "Vocabulary Growth," pp. 109-119, 128-132 in *The Story of British English* by J. N. Hook. Illustrates and discusses Early Modern English spelling and Renaissance vocabulary borrowings Has discussion questions. Paperbound, Scott, Foresman and Co., 1974.

"Early Modern (1500-1660): History," etc., pp. 125-129 in *A History of the English Language* by Garland Cannon. Discusses the Early Modern English period and Latin borrowing. Paperbound, Harcourt Brace Jovanovich, 1972.

"The History of Early Modern English 1500-1650," pp. 210-217, 223-233 in *A Structural History of English* by John Nist. Provides a clear discussion of the causes of vocabulary expansion in Early Modern English and documents it copiously. Hardbound, St. Martin's Press, 1966.

"Nature and Extent of the Movement" and "The Movement Illustrated in Shakespeare," pp. 280-282 in *A History of the English Language,* 2d ed., by Albert C. Baugh. Discusses and illustrates the extent of Latin borrowings into Early Modern English. Hardbound, Appleton-Century-Crofts, 1957.

"Excess and Reaction" and "The Establishment of Modern English," pp. 87-92 in *Origins of the English Language* by Joseph M. Williams. Discusses Latin influence on Early Modern English vocabulary. Provides exercises. Hardbound, The Free Press, 1975.

"The Renaissance," pp. 55-66 in *Aspects of the History of English* by John C. McLaughlin. Explains the Renaissance in England, Latin borrowings, and reactions against inkhornisms. Provides exercises. Hardbound, Holt, Rinehart and Winston, 1970.

"Derivation," pp. 124-133 in *Origins of the English Language* by Joseph M. Williams. Lists and discusses the principal prefixes and suffixes, many of them Renaissance borrowings, by which English derives new words. Provides exercises. Hardbound, The Free Press, 1975.

"The Problem of Enrichment," etc., pp. 257-272 in *A History of the English Language,* 2d ed., by Albert C. Baugh. Presents a rather scholarly discussion of Renaissance vocabulary borrowing, opposition to inkhornisms, and the fate of various Latinisms. Hardbound, Appleton-Century-Crofts, 1957.

II. THE DEVELOPMENT OF PRESCRIPTIVE GRAMMAR, USAGE, AND SPELLING

Audiovisual Materials

Dictionary in Action, The. Part 1. Filmstrip, 1961, Educational Filmstrips. Traces the history of English dictionaries from their beginning to the present.

Print

"Why the Rule Books Were Written," pp. 42–45 in *The English Language: From Anglo-Saxon to American* by Charles Cutler. Discusses how traditional English grammars were concocted by false analogy with Latin and Greek grammars. Paperbound, Xerox Educational Publications, 1968.

"Language-Teaching Manuals," "Spellers," and "Dictionaries," pp. 129–133 in *A History of the English Language* by Garland Cannon. Discusses the major prescriptive grammars, spelling books, and dictionaries of the Early Modern English period. Paperbound, Harcourt Brace Jovanovich, 1972.

"Authoritarian English, 1660-1800," pp. 154–161 in *A History of the English Language* by Garland Cannon. Provides a good discussion of late Early Modern English calls for an English academy to fix the language and grammarians of the period. Paperbound, Harcourt Brace Jovanovich, 1972.

"Changing Attitudes toward English," pp. 92–97 in *Origins of the English Language* by Joseph M. Williams. Discusses attempts to standardize the English language during the Early Modern English period. Hardbound, The Free Press, 1975.

"Grammatical Principles," etc., pp. 68–82 in *Aspects of the History of English* by John C. McLaughlin. Recounts Early Modern English efforts to standardize spelling, meanings of words, and English grammar (using a Latin model). Hardbound, Holt, Rinehart and Winston, 1970.

"Dictionaries of Hard Words," pp. 279–280 in *A History of the English Language*, 2d ed., by Albert C. Baugh. Discusses the first English dictionaries of English words. Hardbound, Appleton-Century-Crofts, 1957.

"Orthographic Practices," pp. 217–221, and "The Rise of Lexicography," pp. 233–234, in *A Structural History of English* by John Nist. Discusses Early Modern English spelling practices, spelling reform, and English dictionaries. Hardbound, St. Martin's Press, 1966.

"Spelling," "Dictionaries," and "Grammars," pp. 330–334 in *The Development of Modern English*, 2d ed., by Stuart Robertson and Frederic G. Cassidy. Gives an overview of Early Modern English spelling changes and prescriptive dictionaries and grammars. Hardbound, Prentice-Hall, 1954.

"The Problem of Orthography," pp. 250–257 in *A History of the English Language*, 2d ed., by Albert C. Baugh. Discusses the confusing spelling variation of the Early Modern English period, attempts to reform and standardize spelling, and the gradual tendency toward uniform spelling. Hardbound, Appleton-Century-Crofts, 1957.

"The Rise of the Prescriptive Tradition," pp. 252–261 in *The English Language* by James D. Gordon. Explains the causes of prescriptivism and discusses some of the Early Modern English prescriptive dictionaries and grammars. Hardbound, Thomas Y. Crowell Co., 1973.

"The Recovery of Meaning," pp. 164–167 in *Origins of the English Language* by Joseph M. Williams. Illustrates and discusses entries in Early Modern English dictionaries. Provides exercises. Hardbound, The Free Press, 1975.

"The Early Modern English Period to 1800," pp. 204–208, 221–228 in *The Origins and Development of the English Language*, 2d ed., by Thomas Pyles. Discusses the development of prescriptive rules of usage and of dictionaries during the Early Modern English period. Hardbound, Harcourt Brace Jovanovich, 1971.

"The Appeal to Authority, 1650-1800," pp. 306–348 in *A History of the English Language*, 2d ed., by Albert C. Baugh. Discusses various calls for, and attempts to, standardize the English language through prescriptive grammars and dictionaries and establishing an academy to decide what is acceptable English. Hardbound, Appleton-Century-Crofts, 1957.

"The Early Dictionaries" and "Eighteenth-Century Attitudes Toward Language," pp. 216–227 in

Problems in the Origins and Development of the English Language, 2d ed., by John Algeo. Provides passages from Early Modern English dic-

tionaries and a grammar and exercises dealing with them. Paperbound, $6.95, Harcourt Brace Jovanovich, 1972.

III. THE EARLY MODERN ENGLISH LANGUAGE

Audiovisual Materials

Our Changing Language. LP record, 1975, National Council of Teachers of English. Provides a short discussion of and an illustrative passage of Early Modern English (as well as of Old English, Middle English, and thirteen modern American and Canadian dialects).

A Thousand Years of English Pronunciation. Two LP records and text, Educational Audio Visual, Inc. Has readings from Shakespeare and eight other Early Modern English authors (as well as Old and Middle English readings).

Songs and Ballads of the Scottish Wars, 1290-1745. LP record, Folkways Records. Provides songs in Early Modern English (as well as Middle English).

Early English Ballads from the Percy and Child Collections. LP record, Folkways Records. Presents Early Modern English songs (and a few Middle English ones).

British Traditional Ballads in the Southern Mountains, Vols. 1 and 2. Two LP records, Folkways Records. Presents survivals of Early Modern English songs in the Appalachian Mountains.

Print

"The Age of Elizabeth," pp. 38-41 in *The English Language: from Anglo-Saxon to American* by Charles Cutler. Discusses the language of Shakespeare and the King James Bible. Not recommended for older students. Paperbound, Xerox Education Publications, 1968.

"Some Examples of Early Modern English," pp. 119-124, and "The Grammar of Early Modern English," pp. 133-139, in *The Story of British English* by J. N. Hook. Illustrates and provides a short overview of Early Modern English morphology and syntax. Has discussion questions. Paperbound, Scott, Foresman and Co., 1974.

"Early Modern English," pp. 34-37 in *The English Language: Yesterday and Today* by Charles B.

Martin and Curt M. Rulon. Gives a short overview of Early Modern English morphology and syntax and how they differ from those of Modern English. Hardbound, Allyn and Bacon, 1973.

"Grammatical Features," pp. 234-236 in *A Structural History of English* by John Nist. Provides an overview of distinctive morphological and syntactical features of Early Modern English. Hardbound, St. Martin's Press, 1966.

"Grammatical Features," pp. 290-300 in *A History of the English Language,* 2d ed., by Albert C. Baugh. Provides a good description of the morphology of Early Modern English nouns, adjectives, pronouns, and verbs with passing reference to syntactic differences between Early Modern and Modern English. Hardbound, Appleton-Century-Crofts, 1957.

"The Modern English Period to 1800," pp. 195-204, 208-223 in *The Origins and Development of the English Language,* 2d ed., by Thomas Pyles. Provides a fairly complete overview of morphological and syntactical changes in Early Modern English, including the his genitive, the group genitive, and relative and interrogative pronouns. Hardbound, Harcourt Brace Jovanovich, 1971.

"Modern English," pp. 187-239 in *The English Language* by James D. Gordon. Provides a thorough description of Early Modern English morphology and syntax, illustrated with literary examples of the period. Hardbound, Thomas Y. Crowell Co., 1973.

Exercises, pp. 203-216 in *Problems in the Origins and Development of the English Language,* 2d ed., by John Algeo. Provides some fairly difficult exercises dealing with Early Modern English pronouns, verbs, prepositions, and syntax. Paperbound, Harcourt Brace Jovanovich, 1972.

"Structure of Early Modern English," pp. 140-151 in *A History of the English Language* by Garland Cannon. Analyzes passages from Early Modern English using a transformational model. Not recommended for students. Paperbound, Harcourt Brace Jovanovich, 1972.

13

Modern Dictionaries

This chapter focuses on the procedures used in modern lexicography, the prescriptive and descriptive traditions' influence on modern dictionaries, and how one should use a modern dictionary. A practical application of this study should be a recognition that dictionaries are not arbiters of linguistic questions and that to appeal to a dictionary as an authority is a misuse of a dictionary. On the other hand, another practical application of this unit should be to make students aware of all of the proper uses of a dictionary.

First, the time-consuming work that goes into making a dictionary should be introduced to the students. It should also be explained that the dictionary makers do not decide what the meaning of a word should be but what the meaning is as the word is currently used. Students should also become aware that dictionaries include different kinds of information, depending on whom the dictionary is intended for, so that not all dictionaries will have the same definitions or include the same information.

Then the issue of descriptive versus prescriptive functions of dictionaries should be discussed. It will turn out that modern dictionaries often combine both functions but with different emphases on one or the other of the two functions. It should be pointed out that most dictionaries that profess to be descriptive of language use are incomplete and thus not totally descriptive. It should also be pointed out that prescriptive usages, spellings, and pronunciations should not necessarily be accepted if those prescriptions fly in the face of what the students know about the English language as it is used.

Finally, the students should be taught the proper and improper uses of a dictionary and shown how to use a dictionary to find the information they are interested in about a word. The latter activity will have to be individualized to the particular student dictionary the students all have, but it would be wise to explain how to use larger dictionaries that are available in the school too.

The first topic may be omitted without damage to the discussion of the other two topics in the chapter. The second topic is crucial to the students' understanding of what a dictionary is, but the teacher may not care to go into the issue as deeply as suggested in this chapter. The third topic is the one teachers are likely to consider the most important.

OBJECTIVES

If all of the topics in this chapter are chosen by the teacher, the students, at the end of the unit, should be able to:
1. Identify the processes involved in making a dictionary
2. Explain differences among dictionaries and the reasons for these differences
3. Explain the difference between descriptive and prescriptive
4. Determine to what degree their own dictionaries are descriptive or prescriptive
5. Explain what specific usage labels mean
6. Identify proper uses of dictionaries and improper ones
7. Show familiarity with the introductory material at the front of the dictionary they use in school
8. Identify the various kinds of information found in the entries of the dictionary they use
9. Demonstrate their ability to find specific information in a dictionary

---

CONTENT OVERVIEW

How Dictionaries Are Made

Unlike the Early Modern English dictionaries, modern dictionaries, with the possible exception of short technical dictionaries for particular fields, are the result of many people working together for a long period of time. Publishers of large general dictionaries have large staffs who are always working on the next edition of those publishers' dictionaries. These staffs include readers or excerpters and definers as well as editorial and clerical personnel.

Since most modern dictionaries profess to be describing the language as it is used, it is necessary to know the current uses of words. The usual procedure is to have a large number of readers who excerpt current published works for current uses of words. This procedure involves marking passages in which the words in question are used, so the meanings of the words in question are made clear in the context of the passage. Frequently the readers are experts in the particular field in which they are reading. The passages are then placed on file slips with the word the excerpter is interested in at the top as a headword, the citation including the word, and the source from which the excerpt comes. In order to be complete, there is usually some sort of random sampling of printed materials in addition to the excerpts made by readers such as making a slip for the first word of every fifth or tenth line in the printed sources used.

These slips are then grouped together by the same headword for the purposes of defining the headwords. Sometimes slips with related headwords like *deep, deepen, deeply, depth,* and *deepness* will be considered together in defining the headwords, since the meanings of related words will also be related. The job of the definers is to study all of the citation slips with the same headword to see what meaning or meanings that word has in the citations. Many words can be accurately defined with only one definition that will encompass the sense of the word used in all of the citations on the slips, but other words will have more than one sense and require more than one definition. If there are multiple senses or definitions to a word, the definers will number them 1, 2, and so on. Some dictionary makers editorially decide to list these multiple definitions in terms of frequency of occurrence in the citations; others order multiple definitions chronologically. Some lexicographers use the law of substitutability in defining: the definition of the word should be substitutable for the word in the citations on the slips. It is also the practice in some dictionaries to define one word in a group of related words like *deep* completely and then to define related words like *deepen* and *depth* less completely with the intention that the reader will refer back to *deep*.

Once the excerpting and defining have been done (in accordance with the editorial policy of the particular publisher), several other editorial decisions must be made concerning the form of dictionary entries, whether all words are to be included (many dictionaries are abridged), and what kinds of information in addition to definitions will be included. These decisions are made with the targeted reading population for the dictionary in mind. School dictionaries have to have definitions with only simple terms, but technical dictionaries may have definitions that contain other technical terms. A general rule of thumb for all dictionaries, however, is that no definition will contain any words that are more technical than the word being defined. An exception to this general rule used by some lexicographers is using a core vocabulary to define all words, with the result that words in the core vocabulary may be defined in more technical terms themselves.

Dictionaries nearly always begin an entry with the word to be defined in bold faced type and broken for syllabication. General dictionaries follow the word to be defined with pronunciations. Modern dictionaries usually indicate different pronunciations in order of frequency without indicating a preference; however, *The Harcourt Brace School Dictionary* (1972) gives only one pronunciation for *roof.* Dictionaries also usually indicate the part of speech of the word defined and sometimes contractions or inflected forms. Some dictionaries also include area usage labels. All dictionaries will include the definition or definitions of the word defined. General dictionaries, but not school or technical dictionaries, often include etymologies or synonyms. All kinds of dictionaries are likely to include illustrative quotations showing collocations in which the word defined commonly appears. They are also likely to include some encyclopedic information about the word. How much of this information will be included is determined by the publisher of the dictionary, keeping in mind the intended market and the publication costs of including various kinds of information in the entries.

Descriptive Versus Prescriptive Dictionaries

Probably the major editorial decision made by publishers of dictionaries is how closely their dictionaries will follow the descriptive tradition, which most of them give lip service to in the prefaces to their dictionaries, and how much they will yield to the prescriptive tradition that most of their potential reading public expects them to follow. The prescriptive tradition goes back to the first monolingual English dictionaries of the Early Modern English period (see overview of Chapter 12) and was accepted editorially by publishers of general dictionaries into the twentieth century. The descriptive tradition began with work on the *Oxford English Dictionary* in the last half of the nineteenth century and was accepted editorially but not usually practiced by publishers of general dictionaries in the first part of the twentieth century. Even *Webster's Third New International Dictionary* (1961), which raised the hackles of prescriptivists who, for the first time, read the statement of descriptive editorial principles in a major dictionary, still used usage labels like *substandard* and *nonstandard* that are prescriptive in nature, although *proscriptive* might be a better word in this case.

Usage labels or notes are the most obvious carry-over of the prescriptive tradition into modern dictionaries, but there are more subtle ways that the prescriptivist tradition is reflected in some dictionaries that profess to be descriptive. While many sophisticated modern dictionaries have gotten rid of pejorative usage labels like *illiterate* or even *substandard* and labels that have been misinterpreted like *colloquial* (which only means "spoken" as opposed to "written"), labels like *nonstandard, informal,* and *dialect* will still be considered prescriptive or proscriptive by most readers of American dictionaries. If the publishers decide not to list *all* alternative spellings of a word that are found on citation slips or *all* alternative pronunciations of a word in a dictionary entry, this editorial decision (whether intentionally prescriptive or made only in the interest of economy) produces a prescriptive dictionary. The best dictionaries include quotations using the word defined from identified sources. Obviously, a quotation by a person of prestige using a word in a particular sense implies that that usage is acceptable, but a quotation using the word in a particular sense and attributed to a well-known gangster, stripper, or person of little intelligence or taste implies that that usage may be questionable. It is also interesting to note that most popular dictionaries (with one major exception), while professing to be descriptive, do not include the traditional four-letter Anglo-Saxon obscene terms in their entries.

It may well be that it is impossible for a general dictionary to be completely descriptive because of the time lag between collecting citation slips, the expectations of the reading public, and the necessity of providing usage labels or notes. It may not even be desirable, since part of the description of the language involves levels of usage. However, the reading public should be made aware that "the dictionary" is, like the unicorn, a mythical beast. They should also be educated not to take any dictionary information as authoritative, since nearly all dictionaries exclude some information about a word in the interest of economy and usage labels are usually decided by usage boards that include prescriptivists as well as descriptivists. Anyone who has played Scrabble knows that different dictionaries exclude or include different English words and allow or disallow certain spellings of particular words. We should not get any more telephone calls from drunken Ph.D.'s in English at parties who want someone to settle an argument about the pronunciation or meaning of a particular word by looking it up in a dictionary.

How to Use a Modern Dictionary

As a general rule, dictionaries may be used to corroborate what one already knows about a word and to give some general idea about the meaning, pronunciation, and so on, of an unfamiliar word. Dictionaries should not be used to eliminate a particular pronunciation or usage from one's speech if most other people with whom one has contact use it. Students, until they have been brainwashed by teachers, generally will use the dictionaries correctly in these aspects.

Students use dictionaries mainly for the same two purposes as adults: to check spellings of words they are writing and to look up meanings of unfamiliar words. They may even be unaware of the other kinds of information that dictionaries provide. A good place to begin to teach students to use a dictionary for all of the information it provides is to have them read the introductory material at the front of their dictionary.

Any modern school dictionary will include an explanation about the form of each entry, identifying each type of information provided in order for an entry. Most such dictionaries will also include a statement of adherence to the descriptive principle, but the teacher will have to examine the dictionary to see how closely the principle is adhered to. They also provide information about how to find a particular word in the dictionary.

In teaching students to use a dictionary, it may be necessary to emphasize certain points that the teacher is likely to take for granted. First, it may be necessary to point out that words are listed alphabetically in English dictionaries and to explain what that means about looking at the second, third, fourth letters in a word. Dictionaries of other languages such as Chinese and Hebrew are not organized on the alphabetic principle. Second, the use of the guide words at the top of each page of dictionary entries should be explained to facilitate the students' task of finding words in a dictionary. Third, the pronunciation keys at the bottom of the entry pages and in the front material of the dictionary should be pointed out and explained. It may also be necessary to explain syllabication and stress marks used in the particular dictionary.

It would be wise to go through a couple of entries in the students' dictionaries with them to point out and explain the different types of information provided there. Different dictionaries may alter the order in which some of the information is presented, but they all begin with the main form of the word in boldface followed by the pronunciation in parentheses or brackets. Alternate spellings may be given next or later. The grammatical category is usually given next in italics and abbreviated; it may be necessary to point out the abbreviations for grammatical categories that are usually listed at the front of the dictionary. If the students' dictionaries use *vt* as symbol for transitive verbs, it would be helpful to point out that most transitive verbs in English have intransitive homophones, whether the dictionary lists them or not. Next, one usually finds inflected forms of the base word also in bold faced type, particularly if the inflected forms involve a spelling change or are irregular. The definition or numbered definitions follow, usually with illustrative collocations. Usage notes or labels and area and field labels may follow. General dictionaries often provide etymologies, but most student dictionaries do not. Student dictionaries as well as other types often end an entry with related words formed from the main form by derivational affixes; they may also provide synonyms. Larger dictionaries sometimes provide encyclopedic information about some words beyond definitions.

LEARNING EXPERIENCES

Topic I: How Dictionaries Are Made

- Have students break into small groups and ask each group to come up with three words they use or have read in current periodicals. Then assign each group to find as many sentences as possible using each word from current periodicals and write the sentences on individual note cards. When the slips have been written, ask each group to define each of their three words to encompass all of the meanings of each word as used in the sentences on the notecards. (There may only be one sense or definition to each word as used in the sentences on the note cards.)

- Have the students break into small groups and have each group think of as many meanings of the word *class* as they can and then write a definition of the word. Compare each group's definitions to see if it encompasses all of the meanings of the word and then compare the definitions with those of available dictionaries. You will probably discover that the students have all defined the noun *class* rather than the verb. They may also have provided more definitions (overdifferentiated) than the school dictionary, but have also left out some meanings.

- Assign small groups to define *some, but, the, above, many,* and *yet.* Since these are function words rather than lexical parts of speech, they have little lexical meaning and the students will have difficulty coming up with much beyond grammatical meaning. Compare the students' definitions with those of a school dictionary.

- Assign individual students to read the introductory material at the front of each of the general dictionaries in the library and report back to the class what they have learned about how each dictionary was constructed.

- Divide the class into small groups and ask each group to find as many different dictionaries as possible in the school library.

- Have each student write a short essay on dictionary making (lexicography).

Topic II: Descriptive Versus Prescriptive Dictionaries

- Ask the students to find the usage labels and notes used in their desk dictionaries. These may be listed in one place at the front of the dictionary. If not, ask each student to find the usage notes or labels used in a different ten-page section of the dictionary. Once all of the usage labels and notes have been found, ask the students whether they want to continue to use the words with each of the different usage labels or notes. The two points of this exercise are to make the students aware of the different usage labels and notes and to point out how such labels and notes are perceived as prescriptive.

- Have the students form two groups to debate the issue: dictionaries should tell a person how a word is used rather than how it should be used.

- Have the students form two groups to debate the proposition: the meanings of words should be fixed once and for all so as not to introduce confusion into the language.

- Have individual students look up the treatment of *ain't* in the different dictionaries in the library and report back to the class on whether they consider the particular dictionary they looked at to be primarily descriptive or primarily prescriptive on the basis of its treatment of this word.

- If conditions permit it, have individual students look for the long-established obscene four-letter English words like *shit, piss,* and so on, in the different dictionaries in the library and report back to the class on which dictionaries are descriptive with regard to these words and which are prescriptive (or proscriptive, in this case) by not even including these well-known words.

- Have each student write a short essay on the topic of descriptivism versus prescriptivism in dictionaries.

Topic III. How to Use a Modern Dictionary

- Using Reproduction Page 89, have the students arrange the following words in alphabetical order to make sure they understand the principle by which dictionary entries are listed.

1. person	6. red	11. hot	16. angry
2. anger	7. since	12. knife	17. zebra
3. boy	8. personal	13. read	18. giraffe
4. honor	9. angrily	14. sincere	19. noise
5. pneumonia	10. buy	15. personnel	20. psychology

REPRODUCTION PAGE 89

ALPHABETICAL ORDER

Directions: *Arrange the following words in alphabetical order. This will indicate the order they will be found in in a dictionary.*

1. person
2. anger
3. boy
4. honor
5. pneumonia
6. red
7. since
8. personal
9. angrily
10. buy
11. hot
12. knife
13. read
14. sincere
15. personnel
16. angry
17. zebra
18. giraffe
19. noise
20. psychology

USING HEADWORDS

Directions: *List the headwords at the top of the page in your dictionary where the following words would be found.*

Headwords

1. brain
2. cause
3. concern
4. destructive
5. example
6. fail
7. famous
8. grief
9. impossible
10. incapable
11. murder
12. pity
13. primarily
14. section
15. statement
16. sword
17. take
18. time
19. weep
20. word

- Using Reproduction Page 90, have the students list the headwords at the top of the page in their student dictionary on which the following words will be found. Since different schools require their students to use different dictionaries, no answers can be provided below.

1. brain	6. fail	11. murder	16. sword
2. cause	7. famous	12. pity	17. take
3. concern	8. grief	13. primarily	18. time
4. destructive	9. impossible	14. section	19. weep
5. example	10. incapable	15. statement	20. word

- Using Reproduction Page 91, have the students use their dictionaries to mark the syllable breaks in the following words. The syllable breaks are indicated below in parentheses with spaces between syllables but not on the Reproduction Page.

1. antonym (an to nym)	11. kitchenette (kitch en ette)
2. barrel (bar rel)	12. local (lo cal)
3. conspire (con spire)	13. marriage (mar riage)
4. difficulty (dif fi cul ty)	14. neither (nei ther)
5. event (e vent)	15. official (of fi cial)
6. fixture (fix ture)	16. pastoral (pas to ral)
7. government (gov ern ment)	17. readability (read a bil i ty)
8. harness (har ness)	18. sediment (sed i ment)
9. intelligent (in tel li gent)	19. testimony (tes ti mo ny)
10. Japan (Ja pan)	20. underbrush (un der brush)

- Using Reproduction Page 92, have the students use their dictionaries to find the pronunciations of the following words. Most dictionaries will give more than one pronunciation. The students are asked to circle their pronunciation from among

MARKING SYLLABLE BREAKS

Directions: *Use your dictionary to determine the breaks between syllables in the following words and write the words with the syllables divided as in your dictionary. You will have to know where syllables in words end when you are writing and cannot get an entire word on a line.*

1. antonym
2. barrel
3. conspire
4. difficulty
5. event
6. fixture
7. government
8. harness
9. intelligent
10. Japan
11. kitchenette
12. local
13. marriage
14. neither
15. official
16. pastoral
17. readability
18. sediment
19. testimony
20. underbrush

those given. They are also asked whether they should stop using their pronunciation if everyone they know uses it if their pronunciation is not given in the dictionary.

1. aunt	6. garage	11. roof	16. vehicle
2. brooch	7. greasy	12. root	17. wash
3. catch	8. homage	13. route	18. which
4. creek	9. luxury	14. strength	19. with
5. forehead	10. orange	15. tourney	20. wreaths

IS YOUR DICTIONARY CORRECT?

Directions: *List the pronunciations given in your dictionary for the following words. Then circle the pronunciation you use, if it is given. If your pronunciation is not given but everyone you know pronounces the word the way you do, should you stop using that pronunciation?*

1. aunt
2. brooch
3. catch
4. creek
5. forehead
6. garage
7. greasy
8. homage
9. luxury
10. orange
11. roof
12. root
13. route
14. strength
15. tourney
16. vehicle
17. wash
18. which
19. with
20. wreaths

PRONUNCIATION SYMBOLS

Directions: *What symbols does your dictionary use to represent the vowel sounds in the following words? Rather than look up each word individually, try to figure out what the symbols would be by referring to the pronunciation key in your dictionary.*

Symbol representing the vowel sound

1. sheet
2. pick
3. wait
4. dread
5. fat
6. shoot
7. wood
8. boat
9. bought
10. crop
11. loud
12. high
13. joy
14. shun
15. (first syllable of) around

- Using Reproduction Page 93, have the students use their dictionaries to find the symbols to represent the vowel sounds in the words below. No answers are provided, since different dictionaries use different symbols.

1. sheet	6. shoot	11. loud
2. pick	7. wood	12. high
3. wait	8. boat	13. joy
4. dread	9. bought	14. shun
5. fat	10. crop	15. (first syllable of) around

- Using Reproduction Page 94, have the students determine how many entries (usually numbered) their dictionaries have for the following words and what part of speech

MULTIPLE ENTRIES

Directions: *List the number of entries your dictionary has for the words with the spellings below. List what parts of speech these different entries are identified as.*

1. affect
2. batter
3. chow
4. down
5. ell
6. fell
7. grate
8. heel
9. in- (prefix)
10. jet
11. keel
12. lap
13. mark
14. nip
15. ooze
16. pawn
17. rack
18. see
19. stalk
20. well

each entry is identified as. Again, since the answers will vary depending upon the particular dictionary used, no answers are provided below.

1. affect	6. fell	11. keel	16. pawn
2. batter	7. grate	12. lap	17. rack
3. chow	8. heel	13. mark	18. see
4. down	9. in- (prefix)	14. nip	19. stalk
5. ell	10. jet	15. ooze	20. well

- Have each student write a short essay on the kinds of information available in a dictionary entry.

- Have each student write a short essay on how to find a particular word in a dictionary.

ASSESSING ACHIEVEMENT OF OBJECTIVES

Ongoing Evaluation

The extent to which students have mastered the concepts covered under each topic can be measured by any of the activities assigned to the class as individuals, particularly the writing activities.

Final Evaluation

For an overall evaluation of the students' mastery of the concepts in this chapter, if all topics in the chapter have been taught, a test constructed directly from the list of student objectives for the chapter as listed on page 250 can be used. As an alternative, one might consider a test composed from the following items:

1. Name three types of dictionaries.

2. Explain how dictionary definitions are arrived at.

3. Explain what *descriptive* and *prescriptive* mean when applied to dictionaries.

4. What does *abridged* mean when applied to dictionaries?

5. Identify two usage labels used by your dictionary and explain what they mean.

6. What are four things a dictionary may be used for?

7. Identify two sections of your dictionary that appear before the dictionary entries begin.

8. List as many parts of a dictionary entry as you can.

9. Where is the pronunciation key in your dictionary?

10. What are guide words?

11. How are the words listed in your dictionary?

12. What does the letter *n.* in italics mean in your dictionary?

13. What is an etymology?

14. Explain why no dictionary that has been published can be a complete record of the English language.

15. Why should a dictionary not be used to settle arguments about the meaning or pronunciation of a word?

RESOURCES FOR TEACHING ABOUT MODERN DICTIONARIES

Below is a selected and annotated list of resources useful for teaching the topics in this chapter, divided into audiovisual materials and print materials and arranged in order of ascending difficulty. Special strengths and weaknesses are mentioned in the annotations. Addresses of publishers or distributors can be found in the alphabetical list on pages 263–265 in Appendix A. Films are black and white unless otherwise indicated.

I. HOW DICTIONARIES ARE MADE

Audiovisual Materials

Dictionaries: Words and Languages. Film, 11 minutes, 1973, Coronet Instructional Media. Illustrates how dictionaries record changes in language and modern techniques of lexicography.

Hiding Behind the Dictionary. Film, part of *Language in Action* Series, 30 minutes, 1958, Indiana University Audio-Visual Center. Explains how dictionaries are constructed as records of usage rather than legislators of usage and how meanings of words are learned from contexts.

Print

"Dictionaries," pp. 62–63 in *Linguistics and Language* by Julia S. Falk. Explains how the processes of dictionary making place limitations on dictionaries as records of the language. Paperbound, Xerox College Publishing, 1973.

"Language and Lexicons," by Wallace L. Pretzer, pp. 199–201 in *Language: An Introductory Reader,* edited by J. Burl Hogins and Robert M. Yarber. Discusses the function of a lexicographer. Provides a comprehension quiz, discussion questions, and writing suggestions. Paperbound, Harper and Row, 1969.

"Words and Where to Find Them: Dictionaries," pp. 157–164 in *Words, Words, Words* by Charlton Laird. Explains how a lexicographer works and provides exercises comparing and contrasting entries from an old and a recent dictionary. Paperbound, Harcourt Brace Jovanovich, 1972.

"Word Census: English Dictionaries Through the Years," pp. L177–L208 in *Structure and Plan* by Albert R. Kitzhaber et al. Discusses compilation of Early Modern English dictionaries, reproduces representative pages from various dictionaries, and provides exercises dealing with the pages reproduced. Hardbound, Holt, Rinehart and Winston, 1974.

"Preface to Random House Dictionary," by Jess Stein, pp. 191–195 in *Language: An Introductory Reader,* edited by J. Burl Hogins and Robert M. Yarber. Relates procedures, problems, and goals in producing a dictionary. Provides a comprehension quiz, discussion questions, and writing suggestions. Paperbound, Harper and Row, 1969.

"Problems in Editing Commercial Monolingual Dictionaries," by C. L. Barnhart, pp. 457–475 in *Readings in Applied English Linguistics,* 2d ed., edited by Harold B. Allen. Explains and illustrates how decisions are made about what to include in a dictionary and in a dictionary entry.

Not recommended for younger students. Paperbound, Appleton-Century-Crofts, 1964.

"The Process of Dictionary-Making, or Every Man His Own Lexicographer," p. 26 in *Problems in the Origins and Development of the English Language,* 2d ed., by John Algeo. Provides a fairly sophisticated exercise in lexicography for students utilizing the procedures by which modern dictionaries are constructed. Paperbound, Harcourt Brace Jovanovich, 1972.

II. DESCRIPTIVE VERSUS PRESCRIPTIVE DICTIONARIES

Print

"The Dictionary," pp. 286–292 in *Aspects of Language* by Dwight Bolinger. Contrasts dictionaries as authorities and dictionaries as records, and discusses limitations of dictionaries. Paperbound, Harcourt, Brace and World, 1968.

"British and American Spelling," pp. 266–268 in *The Origins and Development of the English Language,* 2d ed., by Thomas Pyles. Illustrates specific spelling changes prescribed by Noah Webster and accepted in the United States. Hardbound, Harcourt Brace Jovanovich, 1971.

"Noah Webster and an American Language," etc., pp. 424–433 in *A History of the English Language,* 2d ed., by Albert C. Baugh. Relates Webster's prescriptive influence on American English spelling and pronunciation. Hardbound, Appleton-Century-Crofts, 1957.

"Present-Day Attitude," pp. 344–353 in *The Development of Modern English,* 2d ed., by Stuart Robertson and Frederic C. Cassidy. Discusses prescriptivism of popular American dictionaries before 1950 and acceptance by most Americans of dictionaries as linguistic arbiters rather than linguistic records. Hardbound, Prentice-Hall, 1954.

"The Oxford English Dictionary," pp. 395–400 in *A History of the English Language,* 2d ed., by Albert C. Baugh. Discusses the compilation of, principles behind, and the influence of the *Oxford English Dictionary.* Hardbound, Appleton-Century-Crofts, 1957.

"The Modern Dictionary: A Reflector of Language," pp. 416–426 in *Reading About Language,* edited by Charlton Laird and Robert M. Gorrell. Gives the entries for "horse" in the *Oxford English Dictionary* and three other modern dictionaries showing the descriptive rather than prescriptive nature of modern dictionaries. Provides suggested exercises. Paperbound, Harcourt Brace Jovanovich, 1971.

"But What's a Dictionary For?" by Bergen Evans, pp. 212–223 in *Language: An Introductory Reader,* edited by J. Burl Hogins and Robert E. Yarber. Discusses the functions of dictionaries. Provides a comprehension quiz, discussion questions, and writing suggestions. Paperbound, Harper and Row, 1969.

"The *Oxford English Dictionary,*" "*Dictionary of American English,*" and "Modern Language Study and the *Third International,*" pp. 263–265, 267–273 in *The English Language* by James D. Gordon. Discusses the major historical descriptive dictionaries and the controversy when *Webster's Third International* adopted a descriptive rather than a prescriptive editorial policy. Has suggested exercises. Hardbound, Thomas Y. Crowell Co., 1972.

"The New Webster Dictionary: A Critical Appraisal," by Albert C. Marckwardt, pp. 476–485 in *Readings in Applied Linguistics*, 2d ed., edited by Harold B. Allen. Explains editorial decisions made in publishing *Webster's Third New International Dictionary* (1961) and why those who expected a dictionary to be prescriptive criticized it. Paperbound, Appleton-Century-Crofts, 1967.

"Dictionaries and the English Language," by Albert C. Marckwardt, pp. 236–248 in *A Linguistics Reader,* edited by Graham Wilson. Discusses the differences between descriptive and prescriptive dictionaries in light of the controversy surrounding the publication of *Webster's Third New International Dictionary* (1961). Has discussion questions. Paperbound, Harper and Row, 1967.

III. HOW TO USE A MODERN DICTIONARY

Audiovisual Materials

Dictionary in Action, The. Parts 2 and 3, Slide strips, 1961, Educational Filmstrips. Provides simple explanation of how to use modern school dictionaries for various purposes. Not recommended for older students.

Print

"How to Use a Dictionary," pp. 78-93 in *Patterns of Communicating* (Grade 7) by Allan A. Glatthorn and Jane Christensen. Discusses use of guide words and pronunciation keys as well as the types of information found in dictionary entries. Hardbound, D. C. Heath and Co., 1975.

"Using Your Dictionary," pp. U109-U128 in *Purpose and Change* by Albert R. Kitzhaber et al. Explains information found in and problems with dictionary entries. Provides many simple exercises. Hardbound, Holt, Rinehart and Winston, 1974.

"Using Your Dictionary," pp. U91-U112 in *Invention and Style* by Albert R. Kitzhaber et al. Identifies types of information found in and problems with dictionary entries. Provides many simple exercises. Hardbound, Holt, Rinehart and Winston, 1974.

"Using Your Dictionary," pp. U103-U115 in *Substance and Process* by Albert R. Kitzhaber et al. Explains information found in dictionary entries: pronunciation, parts of speech, numbered definitions, etymologies, inflected forms, usage labels and notes, and synonyms. Provides exercises. Hardbound, Holt, Rinehart and Winston, 1974.

"Using Your Dictionary," pp. U99-U111 in *Structures and Plan* by Albert R. Kitzhaber et al. Identifies information found in dictionary entries: pronunciation, parts of speech, numbered definitions, etymologies, inflected forms, usage labels and notes, and synonyms. Has exercises. Hardbound, Holt, Rinehart and Winston, 1974.

"Usage and the Dictionary," pp. 16-17 in *Problems in the Origins and Development of the English Language,* 2d ed., by John Algeo. Provides an exercise dealing with usage labels in modern dictionaries. Paperbound, Harcourt Brace Jovanovich, 1972.

"Words and Dictionaries," pp. 123-132 in *English: An Introduction to Language* by Thomas Pyles and John Algeo. Discusses different kinds of dictionaries and information found in dictionary entries. Provides exercises. Paperbound, Harcourt, Brace and World, 1970.

"The Dictionary," pp. 519-535 in *Warriner's English Grammar and Composition* (complete course) by John E. Warriner and Francis Griffith. Discusses the content and uses of the dictionary and identifies different types of dictionaries. Has exercises. Hardbound, Harcourt Brace Jovanovich, 1973.

"How to Read a Dictionary," by Mortimer J. Adler, pp. 181-190 in *Language: An Introductory Reader,* edited by J. Burl Hogins and Robert E. Yarber. Presents a rambling explanation of how to use a dictionary. Provides a comprehension quiz, discussion questions, and writing suggestions. Paperbound, Harper and Row, 1969.

"How to Use Your Dictionary," by Dimmes McDowell, pp. 15-49 in *The Harcourt Brace School Dictionary,* edited by Harrison Gray Platt. Provides a lengthy but clear explanation of how to use this particular dictionary. Hardbound, Harcourt Brace Jovanovich, 1972.

"Some Practical Matters," pp. 215-225 in *Working with Aspects of Language* by Mansoor Alyeshmerni and Paul Taubr. Provides four lengthy exercises: three using *Webster's Third New International Dictionary* (1961) and one using the student's desk dictionary. Paperbound, Harcourt, Brace and World, 1970.

"The Oxford English Dictionary: The Treatment of Entries" and "Using the Oxford English Dictionary," pp. 17-26 in *Problems in the Origins and Development of the English Language,* 2d ed., by John Algeo. Presents two sophisticated exercises in obtaining various kinds of information from entries in the *Oxford English Dictionary.* Paperbound, Harcourt Brace Jovanovich, 1972.

APPENDIX
A

Addresses of Producers of Resources

Allyn and Bacon, Inc.
470 Atlantic Avenue
Boston, Massachusetts 02210

Appleton-Century-Crofts
521 Fifth Avenue
New York, New York 10036

Bantam Books
666 Fifth Avenue
New York, New York 10019

Center for Applied Linguistics
1611 North Kent Street
Arlington, Virginia 22209

Center for the Humanities, Inc.
2 Holland Avenue
White Plains, New York 10603

Coronet Instructional Media
65 East South Water Street
Chicago, Illinois 60601

Thomas Y. Crowell Co.
666 Fifth Avenue
New York, New York 10019

Educational Audio Visual, Inc.
Pleasantville
New York 10570

Educational Filmstrips
1401 Nineteenth Street
Huntsville, Texas 77340

Encyclopaedia Britannica Educational Corp.
425 North Michigan Avenue
Chicago, Illinois 60611

Filmfair Communication, Inc.
10820 Ventura Boulevard
Studio City, California 91604

Filmstrip House
6633 West Howard Street
Niles, Illinois 60648

Folkways Records
701 Seventh Avenue
New York, New York 10036

The Free Press
866 Third Avenue
New York, New York 10022

Globe Book Company
175 Fifth Avenue
New York, New York 10010

Guidance Associates
757 Third Avenue
New York, New York 10017

Harper and Row, Publishers, Inc.
10 East Fifty-Third Street
New York, New York 10022

Harcourt Brace Jovanovich
757 Third Avenue
New York, New York 10017

D. C. Heath and Company
125 Spring Street
Lexington, Massachusetts 02173

Holt, Rinehart & Winston
383 Madison Avenue
New York, New York 10017

Houghton Mifflin Co.
2 Park Street
Boston, Massachusetts 02107

Indiana University Audio-Visual Center
Film Library
Audio-Visual Center
Bloomington, Indiana 47401

International Film Bureau
332 South Michigan Avenue
Chicago, Illinois 60604

J. B. Lippincott Company
East Washington Square
Philadelphia, Pennsylvania 19105

Macmillan, Inc.
866 Third Avenue
New York, New York 10022

McGraw-Hill Book Co.
1221 Avenue of the Americas
New York, New York 10020

National Council of Teachers of English
1111 Kenyon Road
Urbana, Illinois 61801

W. W. Norton and Co.
55 Fifth Avenue
New York, New York 10003

Oxford University Press
200 Madison Avenue
New York, New York 10016

Prentice-Hall, Inc.
Educational Books Division
Englewood Cliffs, New Jersey 07632

Random House, Inc.
201 East Fiftieth Street
New York, New York 10022

Henry Regnery Co.
180 North Michigan Avenue
Chicago, Illinois 60601

The Ronald Press Co.
79 Madison Avenue
New York, New York 10016

St. Martin's Press
175 Fifth Avenue
New York, New York 10010

Scott, Foresman and Co.
1900 East Lake Avenue
Glenview, Illinois 60025

Charles Scribner's Sons
597 Fifth Avenue
New York, New York 10017

Silver Burdett Company
Morristown, New Jersey 07960

Stuart Finley, Inc.
3428 Mansfield Road
Falls Church, Virginia 22041

Syracuse University Film Rental Library
1455 East Colvin Street
Syracuse, New York 13210

Teachers College Press
1234 Amsterdam Avenue
New York, New York 10027

University of Massachusetts Press
P.O. Box 429
Amherst, Massachusetts 01002

The University of Michigan Press
615 East University
Ann Arbor, Michigan 48106

University of Pennsylvania Press
3933 Walnut Street
Philadelphia, Pennsylvania 19104

Vintage Books
201 East Fiftieth Street
New York, New York 10022

Winthrop Publishers, Inc.
17 Dunster St.
Cambridge, Massachusetts 02138

Xerox College Publishing
c/o Ginn and Company
191 Spring Street
Lexington, Massachusetts 02173

Xerox Education Publications
Education Center
1250 Fairwood Avenue
Columbus, Ohio 43216

APPENDIX
B

Reproduction Pages

The pages that follow have been provided to facilitate the reproduction of exercises and other materials needed for activities suggested in the preceding pages. Each page is perforated to make removal from this book easy. Once removed, the page can be used in any of three ways:

1. *For projection with an opaque projector.* No further preparation is necessary if the page is to be used with an opaque projector. The page may simply be inserted in the projector for viewing by the whole class.

2. *For projection with an overhead projector.* The Reproduction Page must be converted into a transparency for use with an overhead projector. To produce the transparency, overlay the Reproduction Page with a blank transparency and run both through a copying machine.

3. *For duplication with a spirit duplicator.* A master can be made from the Reproduction Page by overlaying it with a special heat-sensitive spirit master and running both through a copying machine. The spirit master can then be used to reproduce 50–100 copies on paper.

Please note that all material appearing on Reproduction Pages (as well as all other material in this book) is protected under the United States Copyright Law. Allyn and Bacon, Inc., grants to readers the right to make multiple copies of reproduction pages for nonprofit educational use only. All other rights are reserved.

SEMANTIC DISTINCTIONS

Directions: *Fill in the feature matrices below to describe these common English kinship terms with + if the word has the feature and — if the feature is absent. Notice that English does not specify one feature for cousin that it does for the other terms. The first term is marked for you.*

Feature \ Term	Mother	Father	Sister	Brother	Aunt	Uncle	Cousin	Grand-mother	Grand-father
Same generation as speaker	−	−	+	+	−	−	+	−	−
One generation older than speaker									
Two generations older than speaker									
Female									

Directions: *Fill in the feature matrices below to describe these common domesticated animals with + if the word is associated with the feature and — if the feature is absent. Notice that the features might be different for the same word in different cultures. What other features might have been used?*

Feature \ Term	Cow	Horse	Cat	Dog	Sheep	Goat	Pig
Pet							
Source of milk							
Source of meat							
Source of transportation							
Skin used by man							
Hair used by man							
Guard animal							

MORE SEMANTIC DISTINCTIONS

Directions: *Take common breeds of dogs and define them in terms of feature matrices. Some common breeds and some possible features are given, but you may add other breeds and other features to differentiate the breeds further.*

Term \ Feature	Irish setter	German shepherd	Chihuahua	Collie				
Large								
Hunting								
Watchdog								
Stock dog								
Long hair								
Solid color								

PHONEMIC SYMBOLS FOR ENGLISH CONSONANTS

/p/   The first sound in *pin*, second in *spin*, last in *nip*
/t/   The first sound in *tick*, second in *stick*, last in *kit*
/k/   The first sound in *cat*, second in *scat*, last (ck) in *tack*
/b/   The first sound in *ban*, last in *nab*
/d/   The first sound in *dog*, last in *mad*
/g/   The first sound in *go*, last in *lag*
/č/   The first sound (ch) in *chin*, last (tch) in *watch*
/ǰ/   The first sound in *Jim* or *gym*, last (dge) in *fudge*
/f/   The first sound in *fall*, last (gh) in *laugh*
/θ/   The first sound (th) in *thick*, last (th) in *breath*
/s/   The first sound in *sin*, last (ss) in *hiss*
/š/   The first sound (sh) in *shake*, last (sh) in *smash*
/v/   The first sound in *vine*, last (ve) in *love*
/ð/   The first sound (th) in *then*, last (the) in *breathe*
/z/   The first sound in *zeal*, last in *his*
/ž/   The medial consonant in *vision*, last sound (ge) in *rouge*
/m/   The first sound in *man*, second in *smear*, last (mb) in *crumb*
/n/   The first sound (kn) in *know*, second in *snip*, last in *mean*
/ŋ/   The last sound (ngue) in *tongue*
/l/   The first sound in *laugh*, second in *slice*, last (ll) in *fall*
/r/   The first sound (wr) in *write*, last in *door*
/j/   The first sound in *you* or *ewe*
/w/   The first sound in *woo* or *one*
/h/   The first sound in *his* or (wh) *whole*

PHONEMIC SYMBOLS FOR ENGLISH VOWELS AND DIPHTHONGS

/i/   The vowel sound in *he* and *sneak*
/ɪ/   The vowel sound in *pit* and *bin*
/e/   The vowel sound in *way* and *plain*
/ɛ/   The vowel sound in *pet* and *dead*
/æ/   The vowel sound in *nap* and *laugh*
/u/   The vowel sound in *who* and *boot*
/ʊ/   The vowel sound in *put* and *look*
/o/   The vowel sound in *go* and *moan*
/ɔ/   The vowel sound in *law* and *bought*

/ʌ/	The vowel sound in *but* and *tough*
/a/	The vowel sound in *rob* and *father* (first syllable)
/ə/	The unstressed vowel sound in the first syllable of *above* and the second syllable of *sofa*
/aɪ/	The diphthong in *my* and *kind*
/aʊ/	The diphthong in *out* and *cow*
/ɔɪ/	The diphthong in *boy* and *coin*

TRANSCRIBING FROM PHONEMIC SYMBOLS

Directions: *Use the list of Phonemic Symbols to help you write the words below in current English spelling.*

1. /dɪp/ _____	26. /kaʊ/ _____	51. /hæf/ _____
2. /dip/ _____	27. /šev/ _____	52. /tu/ _____
3. /šɛl/ _____	28. /gʊd/ _____	53. /ju/ _____
4. /šek/ _____	29. /tɔl/ _____	54. /skɔld/ _____
5. /ful/ _____	30. /praɪz/ _____	55. /saɪ/ _____
6. /wʊl/ _____	31. /fjud/ _____	56. /ek/ _____
7. /sop/ _____	32. /pɪg/ _____	57. /luz/ _____
8. /sɔ/ _____	33. /ɛb/ _____	58. /lus/ _____
9. /pæd/ _____	34. /mum/ _____	59. /aʊr/ _____
10. /hʌg/ _____	35. /tæks/ _____	60. /bam/ _____
11. /waɪf/ _____	36. /čæf/ _____	61. /wʊrk/ _____
12. /ǰab/ _____	37. /ðe/ _____	62. /əbaʊt/ _____
13. /slaʊč/ _____	38. /wo/ _____	63. /sofə/ _____
14. /mɔɪst/ _____	39. /hɔk/ _____	64. /šʊrt/ _____
15. /pju/ _____	40. /taʊn/ _____	65. /grop/ _____
16. /tič/ _____	41. /ǰʌǰ/ _____	66. /skrim/ _____
17. /pæɵ/ _____	42. /ɵru/ _____	67. /splæš/ _____
18. /ǰæm/ _____	43. /rɔŋ/ _____	68. /strɛč/ _____
19. /jæm/ _____	44. /sam/ _____	69. /əraʊnd/ _____
20. /pamp/ _____	45. /vju/ _____	70. /smak/ _____
21. /juɵ/ _____	46. /hɪm/ _____	71. /snɔr/ _____
22. /pʊl/ _____	47. /bɪld/ _____	72. /pliz/ _____
23. /ðoz/ _____	48. /bʌŋk/ _____	73. /slɪk/ _____
24. /ɵɪŋ/ _____	49. /flu/ _____	74. /trʌbəl/ _____
25. /gloz/ _____	50. /mjul/ _____	75. /rɪtən/ _____

TRANSCRIBING INTO PHONEMIC SYMBOLS

Directions: *Use the list of Phonemic Symbols to help you write the following words in phonemic transcription.*

1. sick	21. rest	41. caps
2. dig	22. tooth	42. cads
3. fad	23. cat	43. picks
4. hive	24. sail	44. pigs
5. rough	25. crutch	45. wreaths
6. shun	26. brick	46. times
7. thick	27. love	47. rakes
8. this	28. shout	48. pails
9. rang	29. child	49. toes
10. saw	30. tribe	50. walks
11. hot	31. these	51. things
12. stand	32. cheat	52. gives
13. would	33. wretch	53. robs
14. book	34. which	54. robbed
15. wait	35. wild	55. popped
16. grow	36. ouch	56. dreamed
17. toil	37. brain	57. banged
18. brief	38. match	58. raced
19. sheet	39. sign	59. rushed
20. drive	40. wood	60. missed

INDICATING PRIMARY STRESS

Directions: *Indicate which syllable is stressed in the words below by marking over the vowel that is the center of the stressed syllable. What generalizations can you draw about the stress patterns of nouns and verbs that are spelled alike (1–12)?*

1. conflict (verb)

2. conflict (noun)

3. pervert (verb)

4. pervert (noun)

5. suspect (noun)

6. suspect (verb)

7. contract (noun)

8. contract (verb)

9. permit (verb)

10. permit (noun)

11. relay (verb)

12. relay (noun)

13. belief

14. differ

15. phoneme

16. window

17. utilize

18. operate

19. operation

20. silly

PITCH AND MEANING

Directions: *Answer the questions below about the meanings of the sentences for which pitch patterns are indicated by putting the letter of the sentence in the space after each question.*

1. Which sentence is a question?_____ Which sentence might indicate fear?_____ Which sentence is just an average statement? _____

    a. ^{2}I failed the ^{3} test^1

    b. ^{2}I failed the ^{3} test^3

    c. ^{2}I failed the ^{4} test^1

2. Which of the following would you expect to be followed by "but he is leaving soon"? _____ Which of the following is a question?_____ Which of the following is a statement *and* the end of the sentence?_____

    d. ^{2}He is ^{3} here^1

    e. ^{2}He is ^{3} here^2

    f. ^{2}He is ^{3} here^3

3. Which of the following should you respond to with "Yes" or "No"?_____ Which of the following should you respond to with "Pie" or "Cake"?_____

    g. ^{2}Do you want ^{3} pie^3 ^{2}or ^{3} cake^1?

    h. ^{2}Do you want ^{3} pie^3 ^{2}or ^{3} cake^3?

4. Which of the following could be either a command to a dog or a response to the question "Where is your brother?" _____ Which of the following is a question?_____

    i. ^{3}Home^1

    j. ^{3}Home^3

JUNCTURE PHONEMIC SYMBOLS

Directions: *Supply the appropriate juncture phoneme symbols to differentiate among the following words and phrases:*

1. Indicate where open juncture /+/ occurs in the following phrases that have the same segmental phonemes:

   a. yellowed rug vs. yellow drug

   b. nitrate vs. night rate

   c. a board vs. aboard

   d. an ale vs. a nail

   e. I scream vs. ice cream

   f. That's tough vs. that stuff

2. Indicate where a sustained terminal juncture /|/, a rising terminal juncture /||/, and a falling terminal juncture /#/ would be used in the following sentences:

   g. He has gone, hasn't he?

   h. "He is gone," I thought.

   i. She brought two books, a pencil, and a notebook.

   j. Our dog, Abby, is sick.

   k. If you'll wait, I'll get some for you.

   l. These are the ones you wanted?

LONG OR SHORT ALLOPHONES

Directions: *Indicate whether the allophones of the consonant phonemes used at the beginning and end of the words below are long or short by writing the words* long *or* short *after* initially *and* finally *below. Can you draw any general conclusion about the distribution of long and short allophones of these consonant phonemes? The generalization will also hold true for the allophones of /v/, /θ/, /ð/, and /ž/.*

/r/
rear /rɪr/
roar /rɔr/
rare /rɛr/
initially:
finally:

/s/
cease /sis/
Sis /sɪs/
sass /sæs/
initially:
finally:

/n/
noon /nun/
nun /nʌn/
Nan /næn/
known /non/
noun /naʊn/
nine /naɪn/
initially:
finally:

/m/
mum /mʌm/
Mom /mam/
mime /maɪm/
maim /mem/
initially:
finally:

/l/
lull /lʌl/
Lil /lɪl/
initially:
finally:

/f/
fife /faɪf/
initially:
finally:

/z/
zoos /zuz/
initially:
finally:

/š/
shush /šʌš/
initially:
finally:

/č/
church /čʊrč/
initially:
finally:

/ǰ/
judge /ǰʌǰ/
initially:
finally:

ASPIRATED, UNASPIRATED, AND UNRELEASED ALLOPHONES

Directions: *Determine the complementary distribution and free variation pattern of the aspirated* [kʰ] *allophone, the unaspirated* [kʳ] *allophone, and the unreleased* [k˺] *allophone of the /k/ phoneme in the words below by identifying the environment in which each of the allophones occurs in complementary distribution and the environment where all three allophones occur in free variation. Indicate your conclusions by completing the sentences that follow:*

[kʰæp]	[skʳæmp]	[læk˺t]	[lʊkʰ]
[kʰip]	[skʳi]	[lik˺t]	[lʊkʳ]
[kʰʌp]	[skʳʌm]	[plʌk˺t]	[lʊk˺]
[kʰep]	[skʳet]	[ek˺t]	

Complementary Distribution:
The [kʰ] allophone occurs . . .

The [kʳ] allophone occurs . . .

The [k˺] allophone occurs . . .

Free Variation:
The [kʰ] allophone, the [kʳ] allophone, and the [k˺] allophone may all occur . . .

ALLOPHONE DISTRIBUTION

Directions: *Determine the complementary distribution pattern of the very long* [i:] *allophone, the long* [i.] *allophone, the nonlong* [i] *allophone, and the long, nasalized* [ĩ.] *allophone of the* /i/ *phoneme in the words below by identifying the environment in which each of the allophones occurs in complementary distribution. Indicate your conclusions by completing the sentences which follow.*

[ti:]	[ti.z]	[šit]	[sĩ.m]
[si:]	[si.d]	[sit]	[sĩ.n]
[ski:]	[li.g]	[bič]	[krĩ.m]
[tri:]	[li.v]	[lik]	[lĩ.n]

Complementary Distribution:
The [i:] allophone occurs . . .

The [i.] allophone occurs . . .

The [i] allophone occurs . . .

The [ĩ.] allophone occurs . . .

ALLOPHONE PATTERNS

Directions: *The allophones of the /h/ phoneme that occur before vowels are themselves corresponding voiceless vowels. You may test by saying the initial /h/ as if you were going to say each of the words below. You are given the phonetic transcription for each of the words below. Write the complementary distribution pattern for the allophones of the /h/ phoneme below the words. Note that a vowel symbol with a ̥ below it indicates a voiceless vowel.*

he [i̥i]   his [ɪ̥ɪz]
hit [ɪ̥ɪt]   hoot [u̥ut]
hate [e̥et]   hoe [o̥o]
head [ɛ̥ɛd]   hide [ḁaɪd]
hat [æ̥æt]   has [æ̥æz]
who [u̥u]   house [ḁaʊs]
hurt [ʊ̥ʊrt]   hill [ɪ̥ɪl]
hold [o̥old]   heard [ʊ̥ʊrd]
halt [ɔ̥ɔlt]   hop [ḁap]
hot [ḁat]   home [o̥om]
height [ḁaɪt]   hick [ɪ̥ɪk]
hound [ḁaʊnd]   hike [ḁaɪk]
hoist [ɔ̥ɔɪst]   haze [e̥ez]
hut [ʌ̥ʌt]   hum [ʌ̥ʌm]

Complementary Distribution:
The [u̥] allophone occurs . . .

The [ʊ̥] allophone occurs . . .

The [o̥] allophone occurs . . .

The [ɔ̥] allophone occurs . . .

The [ḁ] allophone occurs . . .

The [ʌ̥] allophone occurs . . .

The [i̥] allophone occurs . . .

The [ɪ̥] allophone occurs . . .

The [e̥] allophone occurs . . .

The [ɛ̥] allophone occurs . . .

The [æ̥] allophone occurs . . .

INITIAL CONSONANT CLUSTERS

Directions: *Write an English word that begins with each of the following initial consonant clusters. Three of the consonant clusters do not occur in English, so do not get frustrated when you cannot think of words that begin with some of these sequences of sound.*

1. /skr-/

2. /spl-/

3. /skw-/

4. /stn-/

5. /str-/

6. /sf-/

7. /pr-/

8. /sm-/

9. /ky-/

10. /tw-/

11. /fl-/

12. /šw-/

13. /sl-/

14. /fr-/

15. /šr-/

16. /st-/

17. /Ɵr-/

18. /sn-/

19. /sŋ-/

20. /pl-/

FINAL CONSONANT CLUSTERS

Directions: *Write an English word that ends with each of the following final consonant clusters. Three of the consonant clusters do not occur in English, so do not get frustrated when you cannot think of words that end with some of these sequences of sound.*

1. /-mps/

2. /-ksθ/

3. /-rst/

4. /-lfθ/

5. /-plt/

6. /-nč/

7. /-lǰ/

8. /-st/

9. /-ŋk/

10. /-ks/

11. /-ls/

12. /-sk/

13. /-hm/

14. /-lθ/

15. /-mp/

16. /-fθ/

17. /-st/

18. /-sp/

19. /sŋ/

20. /-nt/

CONSONANT–VOWEL PATTERNS

Directions: *In the formulas for English words below, C stands for any consonant phoneme and V stands for any vowel or diphthong phoneme. Write an English word that has the consonant-vowel pattern indicated in the formulas below. One of the formulas is not a possible formula for an English word, so you will not be able to find a word with that sound pattern in it.*

1. VC

2. CV

3. CVC

4. VCC

5. CCV

6. CCVC

7. CVCC

8. CCVCC

9. CVCCC

10. CCCVCC

11. CCVCCC

12. CCCVCCC

13. CCCCVCC

14. VCV

15. VCVC

16. VCCVC

17. CVCVC

18. CCVCVC

19. CVCCV

20. CCVCVC

DIVIDING WORDS INTO MORPHS

Directions: *Divide the words below into the morphs (meaningful units of sound) that make up the various parts of words.*

1. resharpen

2. quickly

3. watches

4. clarify

5. multicolored

6. unresponsive

7. inactive

8. waited

9. players

10. snowy

11. prettier

12. scholarship

13. clearance

14. policeman

15. duckling

16. idolize

17. biology

18. troublesome

19. orange

20. unfolding

ADDING -ED

Directions: *The past tense of verbs is often indicated by adding -ed to the simple form of a verb, but the -ed may be pronounced as a /t/, a /d/, or /əd/. After the past tense forms listed below, indicate whether the -ed is pronounced /t/, /d/, or /əd/. Then indicate what kinds of sounds the different pronunciations of -ed follow. As a clue, notice which sounds are voiced and which are voiceless.*

1. snowed

2. rained

3. patted

4. wished

5. hoped

6. hated

7. played

8. copied

9. screamed

10. clapped

11. folded

12. tricked

13. missed

14. raised

15. needed

16. breathed

17. groaned

18. laughed

19. cried

20. shoveled

PARTS OF SPEECH

Directions: *Indicate how many different parts of speech each of the words below can be and then use each word in a sentence illustrating its use as each of these parts of speech.*

1. treasure

2. kind

3. relay

4. group

5. orderly

6. bear

7. trains

8. bored

9. flies

10. cooler

AFFIXES

Directions: *Indicate whether the prefixes and suffixes underlined in the words below are inflectional or derivational affixes.*

1. fool<u>ish</u>

2. <u>anti</u>social

3. teach<u>er</u>

4. teacher<u>s</u>

5. watch<u>ed</u>

6. tall<u>er</u>

7. care<u>ful</u>

8. careful<u>ly</u>

9. <u>re</u>assess

10. deep<u>est</u>

11. activ<u>ate</u>

12. coach<u>es</u>

13. convention<u>al</u>

14. <u>un</u>conventional

15. music<u>ian</u>

16. musician<u>'s</u>

17. driv<u>en</u>

18. man<u>ly</u>

19. <u>im</u>practical

20. king<u>dom</u>

INFLECTIONS

Directions: *Add each of the inflections indicated to each word below and then use the word in its inflected form in a sentence.*

1. girl (a noun)
    A. With the {Plural} inflection:

    B. With the {Possessive} inflection:

2. talk (a verb)
    A. With the {Present} inflection:

    B. With the {Past} inflection:

    C. With the {Past Participle} inflection:

    D. With the {Present Participle} inflection:

3. sick (an adjective)
    A. With the {Comparative} inflection:

    B. With the {Superlative} inflection:

4. fast (an adverb)
    A. With the {Comparative} inflection:

    B. With the {Superlative} inflection:

PREFIXES AND SUFFIXES

Directions: *Write down as many words as possible ending in the following derivational suffixes or beginning with the following derivational prefixes:*

1. nouns ending in *-ness*

2. nouns ending in *-ism*

3. nouns ending in *-ity*

4. nouns ending in *-er*

5. nouns ending in *-ment*

6. nouns ending in *-ance*

7. verbs beginning with *re-*

8. verbs beginning with *dis-*

9. verbs ending in *-ate*

10. verbs ending in *-ify*

11. verbs ending in *-en*

12. verbs ending in *-ize*

13. adjectives beginning with *un-*

14. adjectives ending in *-ful*

15. adjectives ending in *-less*

16. adjectives ending in *-ive*

17. adjectives ending in *-able*

18. adjectives ending in *-al*

19. adverbs ending in *-ly*

20. adverbs ending in *-wise*

NOUN IDENTIFIERS

Directions: *Identify the determiners, inflections, derivational suffixes, word order positions, and stress patterns that identify the nouns as nouns in the following sentences. Not all devices will necessarily be used to identify any particular noun.*

1. Some musicians study music seriously.

2. Those children need nourishment.

3. The suspect is a sailor.

4. My nargships are valuable.

VERB IDENTIFIERS

Directions: *Identify the auxiliaries, inflections, derivational affixes, word order positions, and stress patterns that identify the verbs as verbs in the following sentences. Not all devices will necessarily be used to identify any particular verb.*

1. Both men had clarified their positions.

2. The new surroundings disoriented the prisoners.

3. Mr. Smith will conduct the investigation.

4. My dog has stricated before.

ADJECTIVES

Directions: *Form the comparative and superlative form of the adjectives below. Some of the adjectives will take the {Comparative} and {Superlative} inflections, but others will form their comparative and superlative forms with the qualifiers* more *and* most. *After you have done the first part of the exercise, see if you can draw any generalizations about the types of adjectives that take the inflections and those that do not.*

	Comparative Form	*Superlative Form*
1. quick		
2. lavish		
3. traditional		
4. remarkable		
5. strange		
6. useful		
7. marvelous		
8. small		
9. large		
10. significant		
11. devoted		
12. interesting		
13. sharp		
14. careless		
15. hot		

IDENTIFYING ADJECTIVES

Directions: *Since not all words that modify nouns are adjectives and since adjectives may be preceded by qualifiers like* quite, *determine which of the words below are adjectives by seeing if they will fit in both blanks in each of the sentences below.*

1. That _____ person is quite _____.

   A. mysterious

   B. fat

   C. interesting

   D. sleeping

   E. murdered

   F. tired

   G. terrible

   H. alone

   I. intelligent

   J. foolish

2. The _____ room was quite _____.

   A. crowded

   B. reading

   C. dirty

   D. cold

   E. sun

ADVERBS

Directions: *Write appropriate adverbs in the blanks in the following sentences. What derivational affixes mark some of these adverbs as adverbs? What derivational suffix is used most frequently?*

1. The man walked＿＿＿＿＿＿＿＿＿down the road.

2. Those girls＿＿＿＿＿＿＿＿＿eat dinner together.

3. After＿＿＿＿＿＿＿＿＿opening the letter, he began reading it.

4. He told her lies＿＿＿＿＿＿＿＿＿.

5. The＿＿＿＿＿＿＿＿＿famous writer died.

6. He drove the car＿＿＿＿＿＿＿＿＿.

7. Staring＿＿＿＿＿＿＿＿＿at the book, he continued to read.

8. Your hat is＿＿＿＿＿＿＿＿＿where you left it.

9. Mary laughed＿＿＿＿＿＿＿＿＿.

10. The student worked very＿＿＿＿＿＿＿＿＿.

NOUN MODIFIERS

Directions: *Write a sentence in which the noun* man *is modified by each of the words or constructions below. You may have other modifiers of* man *in each sentence as well. Then write a sentence in which another noun is modified by each of the same kinds of words or constructions.*

1. a   (a determiner)

2. music   (a noun)

3. old   (an adjective)

4. singing   (a verb)

5. upstairs   (an adverb)

6. in the car   (a prepositional phrase)

7. kind and friendly   (a structure of coordination)

8. eating candy   (a structure of complementation)

9. who spoke to me   (a structure of predication—relative clause)

10. wanted by the police   (a structure of modification)

VERB MODIFIERS

Directions: *Write a sentence in which the verb* run *is modified by each of the words or constructions below. You may have other modifiers of* run *in each sentence as well. Then write a sentence in which another verb is modified by each of the same kinds of words or constructions.*

1. should   (an auxiliary)

2. often   (an adverb)

3. limping   (a verb)

4. true   (an adjective)

5. miles   (a noun)

6. in races   (a prepositional phrase)

7. frequently but slowly   (a structure of coordination)

8. chasing a ball   (a structure of complementation)

9. very rapidly   (a structure of modification)

10. when they are frightened   (a structure of predication—included clause)

ADJECTIVE MODIFIERS

Directions: *Write a sentence in which the adjective* green *is modified by each of the words or constructions below. You may have other modifiers of* green *in each sentence as well, and you may need to use inflected forms of* green. *Then write a sentence in which another adjective is modified by each of the same kinds of words or constructions.*

1. very   (a qualifier)

2. unusually   (an adverb)

3. light   (an adjective)

4. pea   (a noun)

5. to eat   (a verb)

6. as grass   (a prepositional phrase)

7. pale and sickly   (a structure of coordination)

8. very dark   (a structure of modification)

9. than I had seen before   (a structure of predication--included clause)

FINDING ADVERB-HEADED MODIFIERS

Directions: *Underline the adverb-headed structures of modification in the paragraph below.*

Some people can write quite rapidly. Other people write unusually slowly. Although no one can write as fast as Superman, some students will have very nearly finished a paper while others are pages away from the end. No one should be expected to write faster than he or she can, but students who write habitually and unnecessarily slowly can be shown right away that their lack of speed handicaps them rather greatly academically.

DISTINGUISHING SUBJECTS FROM PREDICATES

Directions: *Draw a line between the subjects and the predicates in the sentences below.*

1. The high school basketball team has won its last three games.

2. That young man who is waiting for Mary is her fiancé.

3. Cheating at cards is dishonest.

4. From here to there is thirty yards.

5. That the treasure once existed has been established.

6. The old deserve some respect.

7. Children sometimes speak the truth at inappropriate times.

8. Ben, Barry, and Ron came for dinner.

9. Killing animals is sadistic.

10. Some people from Alabama speak with a drawl.

11. Frequently is too often.

12. Chasing rainbows seems futile.

13. A penny saved won't buy much.

14. Whoever did that should be punished.

15. The kind old man from New York gave Mary his handkerchief.

16. My father's house needs paint.

17. To forgive is divine.

18. Living comfortably requires some money.

19. Whatever happens will happen.

20. Electing him chairman was a terrible mistake.

WRITING SENTENCES WITH SUPPLIED SUBJECTS

Directions: *Write a sentence using each of the following words or structures as the subject or as the head in a structure of modification used as the subject. Then write other sentences in which the same parts of speech or structures are used as the subjects.*

1. girls   (a noun)

2. poor   (an adjective)

3. to tell   (a verb)

4. then   (an adverb)

5. in the water   (a prepositional phrase)

6. who did it   (a structure of predication)

7. reading books   (a structure of complementation)

8. Dick and Jane   (a structure of coordination)

WRITING SENTENCES WITH SUPPLIED PREDICATES

Directions: *Write a sentence using the following structures involving verbs within the predicate. Other elements may also be added to the predicate than just those indicated.*

1. a verb modified by an auxiliary

2. a verb modified by an adverb

3. a verb modified by a prepositional phrase

4. a verb modified by an included clause

5. a verb with a complement

6. a verb with a complement but modified by an adverb

7. a verb with a complement but modified by an auxiliary

8. a verb with a complement but modified by an included clause

9. two verbs in a structure of coordination

10. a verb modified by two auxiliaries

WRITING SENTENCES WITH SUPPLIED DIRECT OBJECTS

Directions: *Use each of the following words or structures as a direct object in a sentence. Then write other sentences in which the same parts of speech or structures are used as direct objects.*

1. men (a noun)

2. the sick (an adjective-headed structure of modification)

3. out (an adverb)

4. to fly (a verb)

5. taking tests (a structure of complementation)

6. that the pencil should be here (a structure of predication)

7. Debbie and Sue (a structure of coordination)

WRITING SENTENCES WITH SUPPLIED SUBJECT COMPLEMENTS

Directions: *Use each of the following words or structures as a subject complement in a sentence. Then write other sentences in which the same parts of speech or structures are used as subject complements.*

1. a nut   (a noun-headed structure of modification)

2. neat   (an adjective)

3. here   (an adverb)

4. to believe   (a verb)

5. from California   (a prepositional phrase)

6. winning money   (a structure of complementation)

7. wet and dirty   (a structure of coordination)

8. what he wanted   (a structure of predication)

IDENTIFYING SENTENCE PARTS

Directions: *Indicate above each complement underlined below whether it is a subject complement, direct object, indirect object, or object complement.*

1. They opposed his election.

2. Wendy and Kate are upstairs.

3. Ed supposed Mary the hostess.

4. Mr. Jones is a teacher.

5. He seems rather tired.

6. The chickens chose Chanticleer their spokesman.

7. Mark has become an alienated person.

8. Priscilla considered John's proposal a joke.

9. Scott was in the backyard.

10. The organization sent him a yellow rose.

11. The styles were quite strange.

12. I mailed Jane a love letter.

13. The big dog scratched its fleas.

14. They found Walter quite happy.

15. A wedding is a strange ritual.

16. A sow's ear remains a sow's ear.

17. The company gave its seven top employees large raises.

18. People eat breakfast in the morning.

19. The class voted Tim the person most likely to succeed.

20. Bernie seemed a nice person.

IDENTIFYING COORDINATING STRUCTURES

Directions: *Underline the structures of coordination in the following sentences:*

1. I am studying algebra, biology, English, French, and history this semester.

2. I have traveled far and seen much.

3. Romeo and Juliet were lovers.

4. I like chicken but hate turkey.

5. They watch television sporadically and infrequently.

6. Either Sally or Betty must have broken it.

7. David is a young and innocent child.

8. Tom, Dick, or Harry brought the pickles.

9. She is pretty but dumb.

10. Some people prefer coffee rather than tea.

11. Phil hates chemistry, but Carl likes it.

12. I lost or misplaced my pen.

13. Ben likes sweet-and-sour pork.

14. They are from Poland or Russia.

15. Harry brought Tom and Jim their coats.

16. John is tired, yet he refuses to rest.

17. The Porters raise tomatoes, lettuce, and carrots.

18. Snow and rain are types of precipitation.

19. Mr. Rice teaches mathematics and coaches basketball.

20. I just met Kim and Bruce.

WRITING SENTENCES USING COORDINATION

Directions: *Write sentences in which the following structures of coordination are used. Then write other sentences in which the same kinds of words or structures are used in structures of coordination.*

1. basketball and football   (nouns)

2. rich and handsome   (adjectives)

3. cry and eat   (verbs)

4. slowly but surely   (adverbs)

5. of the people, by the people, and for the people   (prepositional phrases)

6. who did it and when it happened   (structures of predication)

7. purple cows and pink elephants   (structures of modification)

8. acting the fool and playing the clown   (structures of complementation)

MAP 1   WORD GEOGRAPHY OF THE EASTERN STATES

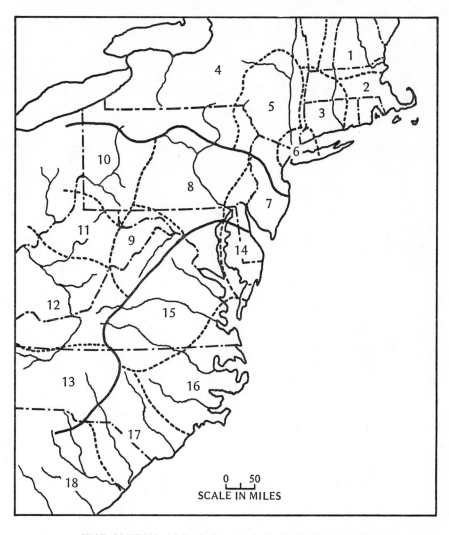

SCALE IN MILES

THE SPEECH AREAS OF THE EASTERN STATES

The North
1. N.E. New England
2. S.E. New England
3. S.W. New England
4. Upstate New York and W. Vermont
5. Hudson Valley
6. Metropolitan New York

The Midland
7. Delaware Valley
8. Susquehanna Valley
9. Upper Potomac and Shenandoah Valleys
10. Upper Ohio Valley
11. N. West Virginia
12. S. West Virginia
13. W. No. and W. So. Carolina

The South
14. Delmarva (E. Shore of Maryland and Virginia, and S. Delaware)
15. Virginia Piedmont
16. N.E. No. Carolina (Albemarle Sound and Neuse Valley)
17. Cape Fear and Peedee Valleys
18. So. Carolina

Source: Hans Kurath, *A Word Geography of the Eastern United States* (Ann Arbor, Michigan: University of Michigan Press, 1949).

MAP 2   DIALECT AREAS OF THE UNITED STATES

ATLANTIC SEABOARD AREAS (AFTER KURATH). TENTATIVE DIALECT BOUNDARIES.
Arrows indicate direction of migrations.

The North

1. Northeastern New England
2. Southeastern New England
3. Southwestern New England
4. Inland North (western Vermont, Upstate New York & derivatives)
5. The Hudson Valley
6. Metropolitan New York

The Midland

North Midland
  7. Delaware Valley (Philadelphia)
  8. Susquehanna Valley
  10. Upper Ohio Valley (Pittsburgh)
  11. Northern West Virginia

South Midland
  9. Upper Potomac & Shenandoah
  12. Southern West Virginia & Eastern Kentucky
  13. Western Carolina & Eastern Tennessee

The South

14. Delmarva (Eastern Shore)
15. The Virginia Piedmont
16. Northeastern North Carolina (Albemarle Sound & Neuse Valley)
17. Cape Fear & Peedee Valleys
18. The South Carolina Low Country (Charleston)

Source: W. Nelson Francis, *The Structure of American English* (New York: The Ronald Press Co., 1958), pp. 580–581. Reprinted by permission of John Wiley & Sons, Inc.

MAP 3

DIALECT AREAS
IN THE
GREAT LAKES REGION

NORTHERN

M I D L A N D

Small areas indicate
mixed usage

MAP 4

NORTH
DAKOTA

MINNESOTA

SOUTH
DAKOTA

IOWA

NEBRASKA

Source: Adapted from "Dialect Distribution and Settlement Patterns in the Great Lakes Region" by Alva L. Davis. *Ohio State Archeological and Historical Quarterly,* 60: 48–50 (1951). Reprinted with permission of the Ohio Historical Society.

CLASSIFYING YOUR DIALECT

Directions: *Classify your dialect as primarily Northern, Midland, or Southern on the basis of the following vocabulary items. Do not be surprised if you use some words in more than one column, since dialect mixing is not uncommon, or if you use other words than those in the lists.*

Northern	Midland	Southern
string bean	green beans	snap beans
pail	bucket	bucket
sweet corn/corn on the cob	roasting ears	roasting ears
swill "garbage fed to hogs"	slop	slop
corn husks	corn husk (North)/corn shucks (South)	corn shucks
brook "small stream"	run (North)/branch (South)	branch
clapboards "finished siding"	weatherboards	weatherboards
shades "window covering on roller"	blinds	shades
distance	piece "distance"	distance
escort "take someone someplace"	escort	carry
wishbone "breast bone of chicken"	wishbone (North)/pulley bone (South)	pulley bone
cherry pit	cherry pit (North)/cherry seed (South)	cherry seed

FURTHER CLASSIFYING YOUR DIALECT

Directions: *See if you can classify your dialect even further after you have decided whether it is Northern, Midland, or Southern on the basis of the following vocabulary items, which break the three broad dialect areas down into subdivisions. Do not be surprised if you use some words in more than one column, because dialect mixing is not uncommon, or if you use other words than those in the lists. Not all Southern dialects are represented here.*

Northern Dialects

Eastern New England	Inland North	New York City and Hudson Valley
pigsty "pigpen"	pigpen	pigpen
apple dowdy "deep-dish apple pie"	deep-dish apple pie	deep-dish apple pie
buttonwood	sycamore	sycamore
porch/piazza	porch/stoop	stoop (NYC)/porch (HV)
sour milk cheese/Dutch cheese "cottage cheese"	Dutch cheese	pot cheese
bonny-clabber "curdled milk"	lobbered milk	
haystack	haystack	barrack
ground beef/hamburg	ground beef/hamburg(er)	chopped meat (NYC)/ ground beef/hamburg(er)(HV)

Midland Dialects

North Midland	South Midland	Eastern Pennsylvania	Western Pennsylvania
run "creek"	creek	creek	creek
smearcase "cottage cheese"	cottage cheese	cottage cheese	cottage cheese
baby buggy	baby carriage	baby coach	baby cab
sidewalk	sidewalk	pavement	sidewalk
ghost	ghost	spook	ghost
curdled milk	clabber milk	thick milk	crudded milk
sugar maple	sugar tree	sugar maple	sugar tree

Southern Dialects

Eastern Virginia	South Carolina–Georgia Low Country
evening "afternoon"	evening "afternoon"
batter bread "spoonbread"	awendaw "spoonbread"
goobers "peanuts"	pinders "peanuts"
lumber room "storeroom"	
	savannah "grassland"

CLASSIFYING DIALECTS BY PRONUNCIATION

Directions: *See if you can classify your dialect as primarily Northern, Midland, or Southern on the basis of the following pronunciations. You may have pronunciations from more than one column because of dialect mixing, but your dialect will be classified as predominantly one of three broad categories.*

Northern

different vowels in *horse* and *hoarse* (except for New York City and Hudson Valley)
same vowels in *Mary* and *merry* (except for eastern New England and New York City)
/s/ in *grease* (verb) and *greasy*
/s/ in the middle of *Mrs.*
different vowels in *tin* and *ten*
/r/ not pronounced in *park* (except for Inland North and Hudson Valley)
wash not pronounced with /r/
vowel sound of *put* in *root*
last sound of *breathe* in *with*

Midland

same vowel in *horse* and *hoarse* (except in South Midland)
same vowels in *Mary* and *merry*
/z/ in *grease* and *greasy* (except for Eastern North Midland)
/s/ in the middle of *Mrs.*
same vowels in *tin* and *ten*
/r/ pronounced in *park*
wash pronounced with /r/
vowel sound of *boot* in *root*
last sound of *breath* in *with*

Southern

same vowels in *horse* and *hoarse*
different vowels in *Mary* and *merry*
/z/ in *grease* and *greasy*
/z/ in the middle of *Mrs.*
same vowels in *tin* and *ten*
/r/ not pronounced in *park*
wash not pronounced with /r/
vowel sound of *boot* in *root*
last sound of *breath* in *with*

FURTHER CLASSIFYING DIALECTS

Directions: *See if you can classify your dialect even further after you have decided whether it is Northern, Midland, or Southern on the basis of the following pronunciations, which break the three broad dialect areas into subdivisions. Do not be surprised if you use pronunciations in more than one column, because dialect mixing is not uncommon. Not all Southern dialects are represented here.*

Northern Dialects

Eastern New England	Inland North	New York City and Hudson Valley
/r/ not pronounced in *park*	/r/ pronounced in *park*	/r/ not pronounced in *park* (NYC)/ /r/ pronounced in *park* (HV)
/r/ added to *idea* of it	/r/ not added to *idea* of it	/r/ added to *idea* of it (NYC)/ /r/ not added to *idea* of it (HV)
different vowels in *Mary* and *merry*	same vowels in *Mary* and *merry*	
different vowels in *rode* and *road*	same vowels in *rode* and *road*	same vowels in *rode* and *road*
different vowels in *coil* and *curl*	different vowels in *coil* and *curl*	same vowels in *coil* and *curl*
vowel sound of *hot* in *aunt*	vowel sound of *hat* in *aunt*	vowel sound of *hat* in *aunt*
vowel sound of *fought* in *fog*	vowel sound of *hot* in *fog*	vowel sound of *hot* in *fog*
/g/ not pronounced in *song*	/g/ not pronounced in *song*	/g/ pronounced in *song*

Midland Dialects

North Midland	South Midland
vowel sound of *thick* in *creek*	vowel sound of *eat* in *creek*
vowel sound of *fought* in *fog*	vowel sound of *fought* in *fog*
vowel sound of *boot* in *food*	vowel sound of *boot* in *food*
vowel sound of *pie* in *nice*	vowel sound of *hot* (lengthened) in *nice*
same vowels in *horse* and *hoarse*	different vowels in *horse* and *hoarse*
vowel sound of *ooze* in *Tuesday*	sounds of *you* in *Tuesday*

Eastern Pennsylvania	Western Pennsylvania
vowel sound of *eat* in *creek*	vowel sound of *eat* in *creek*
vowel sound of *hot* in *fog*	vowel sound of *fought* in *fog*
vowel sound of *boot* in *food*	vowel sound of *foot* in *food*
vowel sound of *pie* in *nice*	vowel sound of *pie* in *nice*
same vowels in *horse* and *hoarse*	same vowels in *horse* and *hoarse*

Southern Dialects

Eastern Virginia	North Carolina	South Carolina–Georgia Low Country
different vowels in *out* and *loud*	same vowels in *out* and *loud*	different vowels in *out* and *loud*
different vowels in *right* and *ride*	same vowels in *right* and *ride*	same vowels in *right* and *ride*
/hw/ sounds in *why*	/hw/ sounds in *why*	no /h/ before /w/ in *why*
vowel sound of *hot* in *crop*	vowel sound of *hot* in *crop*	vowel sound of *fought* in *crop*
vowel sound of *hot* in *long*	vowel sound of *hot* in *long*	vowel sound of *fought* in *long*
vowel sound of *hit* in *fish*	vowel sound of *heat* in *fish*	vowel sound of *hit* in *fish*
afraid rhymes with *head*	*afraid* rhymes with *made*	*afraid* rhymes with *made*
vowel sound of *put* in *bulk*		vowel sound of *putt* in *bulk*

CLASSIFYING DIALECTS BY GRAMMAR

Directions: *See if you can classify your dialect as primarily Northern, Midland, or Southern on the basis of the following grammatical forms. You may not have some of the distinctive grammatical forms given here because some of them are considered nonstandard or old-fashioned.*

Northern	Midland	Southern
youse (plural of *you*)	you-uns/you-all (South)	you-all
who (plural of *who*)	who all	who
dove (past tense of *dive*)	dived	dived
clim (past tense of *climb*)	clum	clim/clome (eastern Virginia)
see (past tense of *see*)	seen/seed (South)	seed/see (eastern Virginia)
woke up	woke up/got awake (eastern Pennsylvania)	waked up
have gone	have gone/have went	have gone
have drank	have drunk	have drunk

FURTHER CLASSIFYING BY GRAMMAR

Directions: *If your dialect is Midland or Southern, see if you can classify your dialect further on the basis of the following grammatical forms. Some of these forms are old-fashioned or nonstandard, so do not be upset if you do not use all of the forms indicated for your dialect.*

Midland

North Midland	South Midland
you-uns (plural of *you*)	you-uns/you-all
seen (past tense of *see*)	seen/seed
woke up	woke up
did (past tense of *do*)	done did
didn't use to	use to didn't
might be able	might could
not sure	not for sure

Eastern Pennsylvania	Western Pennsylvania
you-uns	you-uns
seen	seen
got awake	woke up
did	did
didn't use to	didn't use to
might could	might be able
not sure	not sure

Southern

Eastern Virginia	South Carolina—Georgia Low Country
clome (past tense of *climb*)	clim
see (past tense of *see*)	seed

CLASSIFYING DIALECTS BY SYNTACTIC DIFFERENCES

Directions: *See if you can classify your dialect as primarily Northern, Midland, or Southern on the basis of the following ways of saying things. Although you may say some things in more than one column, the majority of your expressions will be in only one column.*

Northern	Midland	Southern
as well as	all the better	as well as
as far as	all the further	as far as
all to once/all at once	all at once	all at once
quarter to/quarter of (the hour)	quarter till	quarter to
want to get off	want off	want to get off
wait for (someone)	wait on (not *serve* someone)	wait for
hadn't out (to do something	oughtn't (except Eastern North Midland)	oughtn't
sick to one's stomach (except in southeastern New England, New York City, and Hudson Valley)	sick at one's stomach/ sick in one's stomach (eastern Pennsylvania)	sick at one's stomach/ sick in one's stomach (eastern Virginia)

FURTHER CLASSIFYING DIALECTS

Directions: *See if you can classify your dialect even further after you have decided whether it is primarily Northern, Midland, or Southern on the basis of the following expressions. Again you may not use all of the expressions in the particular column representing your dialect, because some of them are used only by older persons.*

Northern

Eastern New England	Inland North	New York City and Hudson Valley
in line	in line	on line
lives on Pleasant Street	lives on Pleasant Street	lives in Pleasant Street
are buttons on the coat	are buttons on the coat/are buttons onto the coat	are buttons on the coat
burn coal in the stove	burn coal into the stove/burn coal in the stove	burn coal in the stove
sick to one's stomach/sick at one's stomach (southeastern New England)	sick to one's stomach	sick at one's stomach

Midland

North Midland	South Midland
didn't use to	use to didn't
bitten by a dog	dog-bit
sick at one's stomach	sick at one's stomach
tire "become tired"	give out
met	met
all gone	all gone
woke up	woke up/waked up (eastern Kentucky)

Eastern Pennsylvania	Western Pennsylvania
didn't use to	didn't use to
bitten by a dog	bitten by a dog
sick on one's stomach	sick at one's stomach
tire	tire
met	ran onto
all "all gone"	all gone
got awake	woke up

Southern

Eastern Virginia	South Carolina–Georgia Low Country
ran up on "met"	met
bitten by a dog	dog-bit
for purpose	on purpose
sick in one's stomach/sick at one's stomach	sick at one's stomach

SOUNDS OF BLACK ENGLISH

Directions: *From what you have learned in class about the sound system of some black English dialects, indicate which sounds would be left out and which sounds would be changed to other sounds in contrasting the way most people would say these sentences in your area and the way they might be said in black English. Then decide whether the black English of your area would really make all of these changes and whether some nonblack speakers would make the same changes in their dialect.*

Sentences	Black English
1. The test was hard.	1.
2. Three tests in one day are too many.	2.
3. Four tests are even worse.	3.
4. Bathe the dog.	4.
5. Both pencils are sharpened.	5.
6. Whose fault is that?	6.
7. Help me with this problem.	7.
8. I laughed during the whole class.	8.
9. She glimpsed the truth.	9.
10. He called the police.	10.
11. I know that he's here.	11.
12. She told the teacher a lie.	12.
13. She is going to fail.	13.
14. Their cats scratched him.	14.
15. What's the length of this room?	15.

GRAMMAR OF BLACK ENGLISH

Directions: *From what you have learned in class about grammatical features of some black English dialects, indicate what changes would be made in the following sentences if you were translating them into black English. Then decide whether the black English of your area would really make all of these changes and whether some nonblack speakers would make the same changes in their dialect.*

Sentences	Black English
1. I didn't do anything.	1.
2. He doesn't have his books.	2.
3. There is a bug on the floor.	3.
4. He is her boyfriend.	4.
5. She is fat.	5.
6. He looked tired yesterday.	6.
7. She'll do it later.	7.
8. He'd rather not go.	8.
9. He always is on time.	9.
10. They were sleeping in class.	10.
11. They have been winning for years.	11.
12. She talks too much.	12.
13. I haven't seen her.	13.
14. I already did it.	14.
15. She's forgotten their lunch.	15.

SOUNDS OF SPANISH-FLAVORED ENGLISH

Directions: *From what you have learned in class about Spanish-flavored English, indicate what sounds would be omitted or added and which sounds would be changed if the following sentences were spoken in Spanish-flavored English. Then decide whether the people with Spanish surnames in your area would actually make all of these changes and whether the same changes would be made by anyone else in your community.*

Sentences	Spanish-flavored English
1. She beat him.	1.
2. They made an arrest.	2.
3. The strike is over.	3.
4. His suit is tan.	4.
5. John cut his finger.	5.
6. He saw the roses.	6.
7. The pool was empty.	7.
8. Both valves were stuck.	8.
9. Snow is cold.	9.
10. Can George sing?	10.
11. Have you seen Spain?	11.
12. The garage was full.	12.
13. The sheets were dirty.	13.
14. A funny thing happened.	14.
15. Their shares disappeared.	15.

GRAMMAR OF SPANISH-FLAVORED ENGLISH

Directions: *From what you have learned in class about Spanish-flavored English, indicate what grammatical and idiomatic changes would be made in changing the following sentences into Spanish-flavored English. Then decide whether the people with Spanish surnames in your area would actually make all of these changes.*

Sentences	Spanish-flavored English
1. The table cannot clean itself.	1.
2. Juan married Maria	2.
3. He understood nothing.	3.
4. The pretty house appeared clean.	4.
5. I want some cotton shirts for men.	5.
6. You are a student?	6.
7. He wanted two red apples.	7.
8. Bring it (the book) here.	8.
9. I sat on the chair yesterday.	9.
10. Is he here?	10.

THE INDO-EUROPEAN LANGUAGE FAMILY

Directions: Circle the language or languages your ancestors spoke other than English. From how many branches of Indo-European have you circled languages?

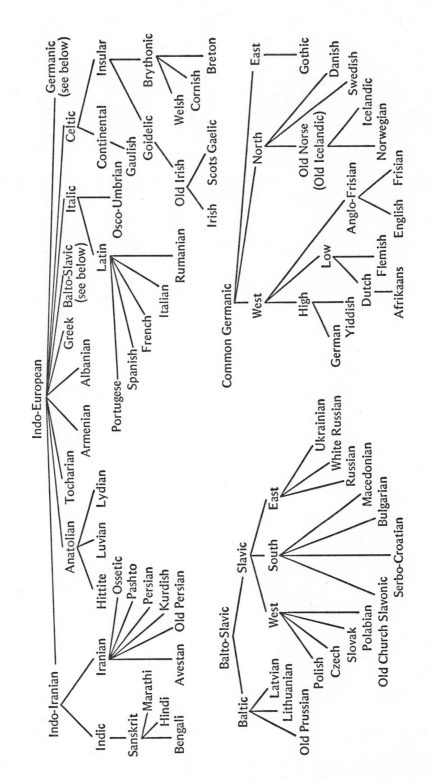

Source: Anthony Arlotto, *Introduction to Historical Linguistics* (Boston: Houghton Mifflin Co., 1977), p. 107.

THE INDO-EUROPEAN LANGUAGES IN PRESENT-DAY EUROPE

Directions: *Place an X on each place on the map below from which you have ancestors. Which branches of Indo-European do you have represented?*

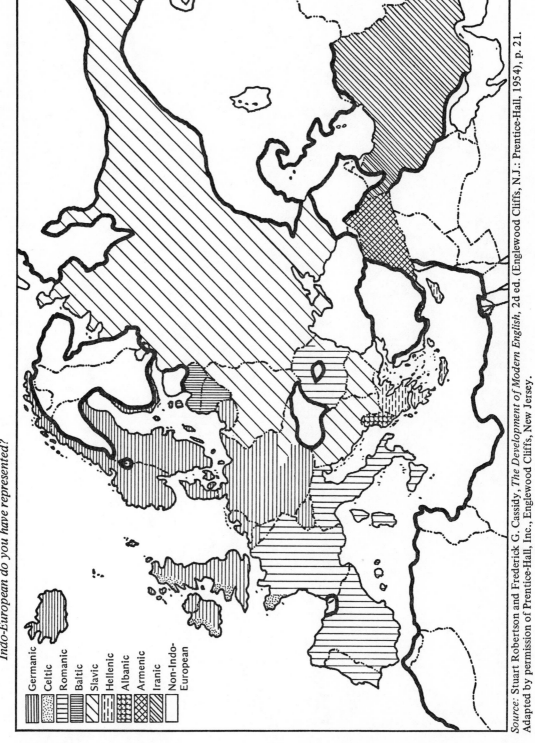

Germanic
Celtic
Romanic
Baltic
Slavic
Hellenic
Albanic
Armenic
Iranic
Non-Indo-European

Source: Stuart Robertson and Frederick G. Cassidy, *The Development of Modern English,* 2d ed. (Englewood Cliffs, N.J.: Prentice-Hall, 1954), p. 21. Adapted by permission of Prentice-Hall, Inc., Englewood Cliffs, New Jersey.

LOCATING INDO-EUROPEAN LANGUAGES

Directions: *Match the numbers in the areas of the map below with the branches of Indo-European spoken in those areas. The non-Indo-European languages spoken in the area have already been marked for you.*

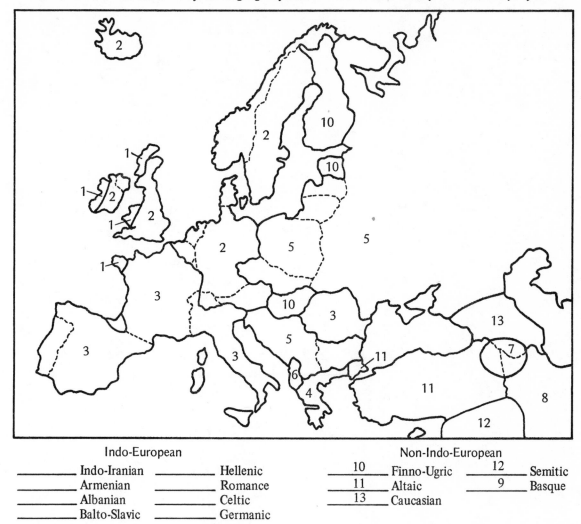

Indo-European		Non-Indo-European	
_____ Indo-Iranian	_____ Hellenic	__10___ Finno-Ugric	__12___ Semitic
_____ Armenian	_____ Romance	__11___ Altaic	__9___ Basque
_____ Albanian	_____ Celtic	__13___ Caucasian	
_____ Balto-Slavic	_____ Germanic		

Source: John Algeo, *Problems in the Origins and Development of the English Language,* 2d ed. (New York: Harcourt Brace Jovanovich, 1966 and 1972), p. 84. Redrawn by permission of Harcourt Brace Jovanovich, Inc.

ORIGINS OF WORDS

Directions: *Identify the source language from which English borrowed these words and then identify to which Indo-European branch that source language belongs. You will need to use your dictionary for this exercise.*

	Source Language	Indo-European Branch
1. clan		
2. street		
3. egg		
4. history		
5. adventure		
6. tundra		
7. bishop		
8. pajamas		
9. law		
10. schooner		
11. angel		
12. knife		
13. innumerable		
14. slogan		
15. poverty		
16. spinach		
17. cypress		
18. army		
19. plum		
20. bungalow		
21. sister		
22. idiosyncrasy		
23. curse		
24. obedient		
25. radish		
26. violin		
27. paraffin		
28. tiger		
29. mosquito		
30. splint		

MAJOR LANGUAGE GROUPS OF AFRICA

Directions: *Place an X in each place on the map below from which you have ancestors.*

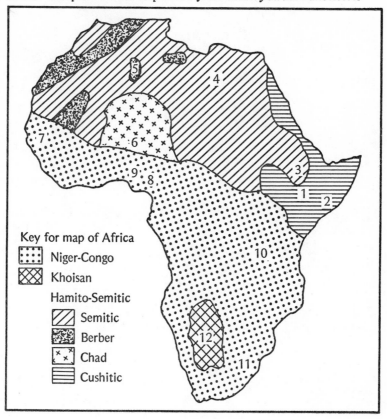

Key for map of Africa
- Niger-Congo
- Khoisan

Hamito-Semitic
- Semitic
- Berber
- Chad
- Cushitic

Familiar Languages

1. Gulla	5. Tuareg	9. Yoruba
2. Somali	6. Hausa	10. Swahili
3. Amharic	7. Wolof	11. Zulu
4. Arabic	8. Ibo	12. Bushman

Source: Anthony Arlotto, *Introduction to Historical Linguistics* (Boston: Houghton Mifflin Co., 1972), p. 56.

MAJOR LANGUAGE GROUPS OF ASIA

Directions: *Place an X in each place on the map below from which you have ancestors.*

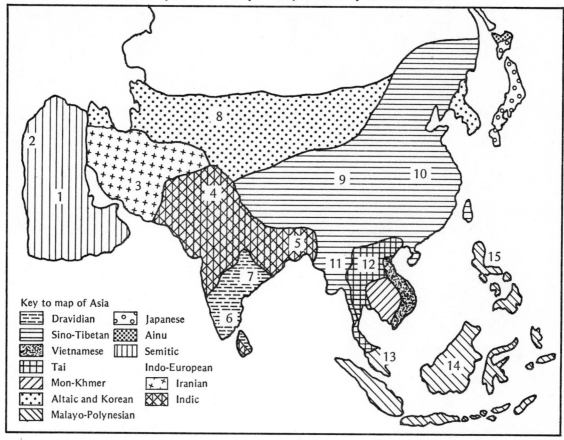

Key to map of Asia

Dravidian		Japanese	
Sino-Tibetan		Ainu	
Vietnamese		Semitic	
Tai		Indo-European	
Mon-Khmer		Iranian	
Altaic and Korean		Indic	
Malayo-Polynesian			

Familiar Languages

1. Arabic	6. Tamil	11. Burmese
2. Hebrew	7. Telegu	12. Thai
3. Persian	8. Uzbek	13. Malay
4. Hindi	9. Tibetan	14. Dayak
5. Bengali	10. Chinese	15. Tagalog

Source: Anthony Arlotto, *Introduction to Historical Linguistics* (Boston: Houghton Mifflin Co., 1972), p. 51.

LANGUAGE FAMILIES OF THE EASTERN HEMISPHERE

Directions: *Match the numbers in the areas of the map below with the families of languages spoken in those areas.*

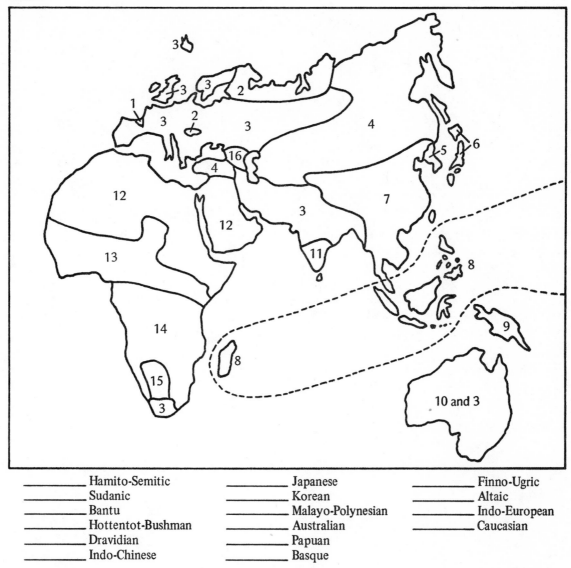

_____ Hamito-Semitic	_____ Japanese	_____ Finno-Ugric
_____ Sudanic	_____ Korean	_____ Altaic
_____ Bantu	_____ Malayo-Polynesian	_____ Indo-European
_____ Hottentot-Bushman	_____ Australian	_____ Caucasian
_____ Dravidian	_____ Papuan	
_____ Indo-Chinese	_____ Basque	

Source: John Algeo, *Problems in the Origins and Development of the English Language,* 2d ed. (New York: Harcourt Brace Jovanovich, 1966 and 1972), p. 83. Redrawn by permission of Harcourt Brace Jovanovich, Inc.

MAJOR LANGUAGE GROUPS OF AMERICA NORTH OF MEXICO

Directions: *From the map below, find the native American language grouping which was originally spoken in your area. What particular language or languages from that group were spoken in your area? Do you know of others that are not listed below?*

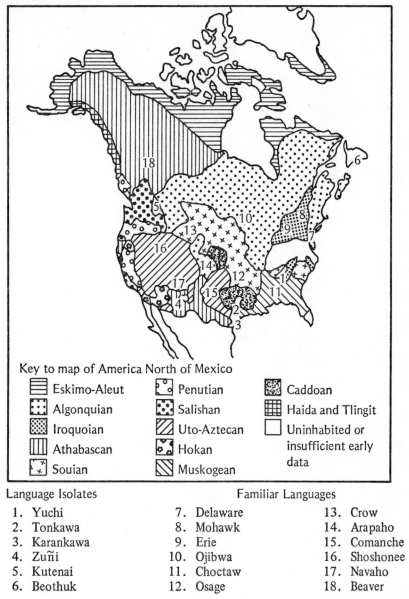

Key to map of America North of Mexico

▤ Eskimo-Aleut	⬚ Penutian	▨ Caddoan
⬚ Algonquian	⬚ Salishan	▦ Haida and Tlingit
▨ Iroquoian	▨ Uto-Aztecan	☐ Uninhabited or
▥ Athabascan	⬚ Hokan	insufficient early
⬚ Souian	◩ Muskogean	data

Language Isolates

Familiar Languages

1. Yuchi	7. Delaware	13. Crow
2. Tonkawa	8. Mohawk	14. Arapaho
3. Karankawa	9. Erie	15. Comanche
4. Zuñi	10. Ojibwa	16. Shoshonee
5. Kutenai	11. Choctaw	17. Navaho
6. Beothuk	12. Osage	18. Beaver

Source: Anthony Arlotto, *Introduction to Historical Linguistics* (Boston: Houghton Mifflin Co., 1972), p. 59.

SOURCES OF ENGLISH WORDS

Directions: *Use your dictionary to find the source language from which English borrowed the following words and then identify the non-Indo-European language family to which that source language belongs.*

		Source Language	Language Family
1.	safari		
2.	vampire		
3.	cinnamon		
4.	mugwump		
5.	mango		
6.	judo		
7.	tea		
8.	bamboo		
9.	kangaroo		
10.	khaki		
11.	harem		
12.	goulash		
13.	pariah		
14.	hogan		
15.	okra		
16.	coffee		
17.	chipmunk		
18.	giraffe		
19.	karate		
20.	kibbutz		
21.	squash		
22.	tycoon		
23.	ukulele		
24.	banjo		
25.	geisha		
26.	raccoon		
27.	horde		
28.	taboo		
29.	yam		
30.	almanac		

OLD ENGLISH DIALECT AREAS

Directions: *Use different-colored pencils or crayons to shade in the areas on the map below where the four major Old English dialects were spoken (West Saxon, Kentish, Mercian, and Northumbrian). Use a fifth color to shade in the areas on the map where Celtic languages were still spoken during the Old English period.*

Source: Redrawn by permission of Harcourt Brace Jovanovich, Inc. from *Problems in the Origins and Development of the English Language*, 2d ed. (New York: Harcourt Brace Jovanovich, 1972), p. 107. © 1966, 1972 by Harcourt Brace Jovanovich, Inc.

THE SEVEN KINGDOMS

Directions: *Identify the seven kingdoms of the Old English heptarchy on the map below by drawing whatever additional lines are necessary and labeling the appropriate areas: Kent, Wessex, Sussex, Essex, East Anglia, Mercia, and Northumbria.*

ANGLES

Humber River

CELTS

ANGLES

Thames River

JUTES

SAXONS

CELTS

English Channel

Source: John Nist, *A Structural History of English* (New York: St. Martin's Press, 1966), p. 76. Reprinted by permission.

SOURCES OF OLD ENGLISH WORDS

Directions: *From what has been said in class about the types of words borrowed by Old English from Latin and Old Norse, try to figure out which language was the source of these words borrowed into Old English. Check a dictionary for the source of any words you are not sure of.*

1. angel

2. bull

3. candle

4. circle

5. die

6. dirt

7. egg

8. give

9. hymn

10. lily

11. master

12. priest

13. root

14. radish

15. school

16. scream

17. sister

18. sky

19. ugly

20. want

TIME OF BORROWING

Directions: *From the following words borrowed from Latin into Old English, decide which are likely to have been borrowed during the period of Christianization (before 700) and which are likely to have been borrowed in late Old English (after 700). The first group will include common words, and the second group will include more learned words.*

1. alms

2. cancer

3. cat

4. centurion

5. chest

6. heretic

7. history

8. lettuce

9. martyr

10. mat

11. monk

12. noon

13. paper

14. paralysis

15. parsley

16. pear

17. peony

18. pot

19. psalm

20. talent

OLD NORSE VS. ANGLO-SAXON

Directions: *Below are some common English words. Try to guess whether they are Old Norse borrowings or native Anglo-Saxon words. Then check with a dictionary to see which source each word came from.*

1. anger

2. child

3. dike

4. eat

5. fight

6. get

7. house

8. live

9. kid

10. knife

11. scrape

12. skill

13. skin

14. sleep

15. wife

TRANSLATING OLD ENGLISH

Directions: *Using the glossary below, try to translate the edited Old English passage below word for word. The story may be familiar to you, but notice how the Old English word order differs from that of the familiar version.*

Sothlice sum mann haefde twegen suna. Tha cwaeth se gingra to his faeder. 'Faeder, sele me minne dael minre aehte the me to gebyreth.' Tha daelde he him his aehta. Tha aefter feawum dagum eall his thing gegaderode se gingra sunu and ferde wraeclice on feorlen rice and forspilde thaer his aehta, libbende on his gaelsan.

Glossary

sothlice	"truly"	gegaderode	"gathered"
tha	"then"	ferde	"went"
sele	"give"	wraeclice	"abroad"
dael	"share"	feorlen	"distant"
aehte	"possessions"	rice	"kingdom"
the	"which"	forspilde	"wasted"
gebyreth	"belong"	gaelsan	"pride"
daelde	"gave"		

403

DECLINING OLD ENGLISH

Directions: *Below you will find the forms for four Old English noun declensions. Indicate the form of the noun that would be used for each of the five cases in Modern English next to the Old English form. Then decide which of the Old English forms is the source of the Modern English forms and which Old English forms have been lost.*

grund ("ground"), Masculine a Declension

	Singular	Plural
Nominative	grund	grundas
Accusative	grund	grundas
Genitive	grundes	grunda
Dative	grunde	grundum
Instrumental	grunde	grundum

lufu ("love"), Feminine ō Declension

	Singular	Plural
Nominative	lufu	lufa
Accusative	lufe	lufa
Genitive	lufe	lufa
Dative	lufe	lufum
Instrumental	lufe	lufum

man ("man"), Masculine Radical Consonant Declension

	Singular	Plural
Nominative	man	men
Accusative	man	men
Genitive	mannes	manna
Dative	men	mannum
Instrumental	men	mannum

oxa ("ox"), Masculine n Declension

	Singular	Plural
Nominative	oxa	oxan
Accusative	oxan	oxan
Genitive	oxan	oxena
Dative	oxan	oxum
Instrumental	oxan	oxum

CONJUGATING OLD ENGLISH

Directions: *Below you will find the conjugations for two Old English verbs;* singan *is a strong verb, and* lōcian *is a weak verb. Indicate next to the Old English forms the form of the verb that would be used in Modern English instead of each of these Old English forms. Then decide which of the Old English forms are the sources of the Modern English forms and which Old English forms have been lost.*

singan ("sing") Strong Verb

Indicative

	Present Tense	Past Tense
First Person Singular	singe	sang
Second Person Singular	sing(e)st	sunge
Third Person Singular	sing(e)þ	sang
Plural for All Persons	singaþ	sungon

Subjunctive

	Present Tense	Past Tense
Singular for All Persons	singe	sunge
Plural for All Persons	singen	sungen

Imperative

	Present Tense
Second Person Singular	sing
Second Person Plural	singaþ

lōcian ("look") Weak Verb

Indicative

	Present Tense	Past Tense
First Person Singular	lōcie	lōcode
Second Person Singular	lōcast	lōcodest
Third Person Singular	lōcaþ	lōcode
Plural for All Persons	lōciaþ	lōcodon

Subjunctive

	Present Tense	Past Tense
Singular for All Persons	lōcie	lōcode
Plural for All Persons	lōcien	lōcoden

Imperative

	Present Tense
Second Person Singular	lōca
Second Person Plural	lōciaþ

STRONG AND WEAK VERBS

Directions: *Below some Old English verbs in the infinitive and the first person singular past indicative are given. Tell whether each of the verbs was strong or weak in Old English. Then give the past tense form of the verb in Modern English. Is the verb strong or weak in Modern English? What does this tell you about the direction that Modern English is going in?*

Old English Verb	Strong or Weak?	Modern Past Tense Form	Strong or Weak?
1. bacan "bake," bōc			
2. blandan "blend," blēnd			
3. ceorfan "carve," cearf			
4. dēman "deem," dēmede			
5. drincan "drink," dranc			
6. findan "find," fand			
7. gifan "give," geaf			
8. hǣlan "heal," hǣlde			
9. hōn "hang," hēng			
10. hȳran "hear," hȳrde			
11. meltan "melt," mealt			
12. scafan "shave," scōf			
13. scīnan "shine," scān			
14. sellan "sell," sealde			
15. steppan "step," stōp			
16. styrian "stir," styrede			
17. teran "tear," tær			
18. þancian "thank," þancode			

OLD ENGLISH PRONOUNS

Directions: *Circle the Old English pronouns below that look like the Modern English pronouns with which you are familiar with only slight changes. All of the other forms have been dropped or replaced by other forms in Modern English.*

First Person	Singular	Dual	Plural
Nominative	ic "I"	wit "we two"	wē "we more than two"
Genitive	mīn	uncer	ūre
Dative	mē	unc	ūs
Accusative	mec, mē	unc	ūs

Second Person	Singular	Dual	Plural
Nominative	ðū "thou"	git "you two"	gē "you more than two"
Genitive	ðīn	incer	ēower
Dative	ðē	inc	ēow
Accusative	ðec, ðē	inc	ēow

Third Person	Masculine Singular	Feminine Singular	Neuter Singular	Plural
Nominative	hē "he"	hēo "she"	hit "it"	hīe "they"
Genitive	his	hire	his	hira
Dative	him	hire	him	him, heom
Accusative	hine	hīe	hit	hīe

MIDDLE ENGLISH DIALECTS

Directions: *Identify the major Middle English dialect spoken in each of the five numbered areas on the map below.*

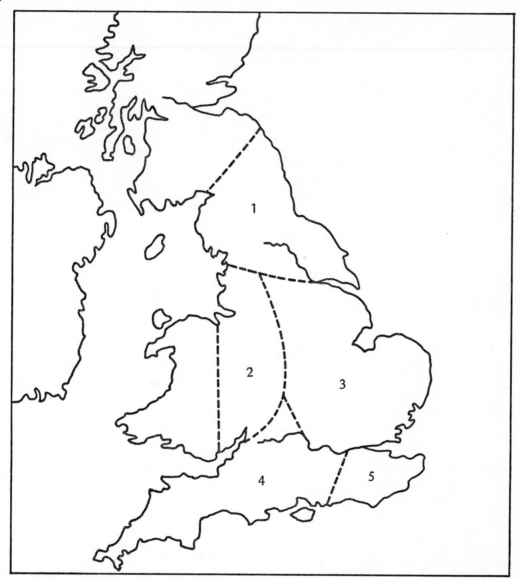

Source: Redrawn by permission of Harcourt Brace Jovanovich, Inc. from *Problems in the Origins and Development of the English Language,* 2d ed. (New York: Harcourt Brace Jovanovich, 1972), p. 142. © 1966, 1972 by Harcourt Brace Jovanovich, Inc.

MAJOR MIDDLE ENGLISH DIALECT AREAS

Directions: *Locate London on the map below. Then explain why the dialect of London would be likely to borrow language forms from other Middle English dialects.*

Source: John Nist, *A Structural History of English* (New York: St. Martin's Press, 1966), p. 154. Reprinted by permission.

FRENCH BORROWING

Directions: *Decide which of the words in each pair below is a native English word and which is a French borrowing. Remember that the French borrowings in Middle English are often "fancier" words than their native English counterparts. Check the sources of words you are not sure of in a dictionary.*

	Source		Source
1.	_____	action-deed	_____
2.	_____	aid-help	_____
3.	_____	amorous-loving	_____
4.	_____	ancient-old	_____
5.	_____	ask-demand	_____
6.	_____	beef-cow	_____
7.	_____	boil-seethe	_____
8.	_____	calf-veal	_____
9.	_____	cordial-hearty	_____
10.	_____	cottage-hut	_____
11.	_____	deep-profound	_____
12.	_____	desire-wish	_____
13.	_____	feather-plume	_____
14.	_____	feeble-weak	_____
15.	_____	feed-nourish	_____
16.	_____	felicity-happiness	_____
17.	_____	forgive-pardon	_____
18.	_____	house-mansion	_____
19.	_____	mutton-sheep	_____
20.	_____	poignant-sharp	_____

NORMAN VERSUS PARISIAN FRENCH

Directions: *Below are French words borrowed into Middle English from Norman-French and Parisian French. Since the Norman words were borrowed first, they are more likely to be words you say frequently than the Parisian words, which are more likely to occur only in your writing rather than your speech. Try to decide which of the two types of French is the source of the following words.*

1. adolescence
2. affability
3. chapter
4. chattel
5. chiffon
6. crime
7. dress
8. fine
9. grape
10. immensity
11. judge
12. lesson
13. peace
14. real
15. royal
16. salad
17. sugar
18. sumptuous
19. supper
20. tax

TRANSLATING MIDDLE ENGLISH

Directions: *Translate the late Middle English passage below word for word. You should be able to recognize all of the words despite the different spelling. However, there are two verb phrases that may give you trouble:* ded do shewe *might best be translated as "caused to be shown," and* ben *is an East Midland form that has been replaced by "are" in your dialect.*

And fayn wolde I satysfye euery man, and so to doo toke an olde boke and redde therin; and certaynly the Englyssche was so rude and brood, that I coude not wele vnderstande it. And also my lorde abbot of Westmynster ded do shewe to me late certayn euydences wryton in olde Englysshe for to reduce it in-to our Englysshe now vsed; and certaynly it was wreton in suche wyse, that it was more lyke to Dutche than Englysshe; I coude not reduce ne brynge it to be vnderstonden. And certaynly our langage now vsed varyeth ferre from that whiche was vsed and spoken whan I was borne.

TRANSLATING NOUN PHRASES

Directions: *Translate the following Middle English noun phrases into their Modern English equivalents. Remember that possessive singulars like* boy's *and plurals like* boys *may both end in* -es *in Middle English; however, one can sometimes tell whether a noun is singular or plural by looking at the adjective in front of it.*

old man _____   litel oxe _____

old manes _____   litel oxes _____

olde men _____   litel oxen _____

old ground _____   litel sone _____

old groundes _____   litel sones _____

olde groundes _____   _____

smal stone _____   wis lord _____

the smale stone _____   the wise lord _____

the smale stones _____   the wise lordes _____

MIDDLE ENGLISH VERBS

Directions: *Below you will find the conjugations for two Middle English verbs;* finden *is a strong verb and* dēmen *is a weak verb. Indicate next to the Middle English forms the form of the verb that would be used in Modern English instead of each of these Middle English forms. Then decide which of the Middle English forms are the sources of the Modern English forms and which Middle English forms have been lost.*

fīnden ("find"), Strong Verb
Indicative

	Present Tense	Past Tense
First Person Singular	fīnde	fōnd
Second Person Singular	fīndest	fōunde
Third Person Singular	fīndeth	fōnd
Plural for All Persons	fīnde(n)	fōunde(n)

Subjunctive

	Present Tense	Past Tense
Singular for All Persons	fīnde	fōunde
Plural for All Persons	fīnde(n)	fōunde(n)

Imperative

	Present Tense
Second Person Singular	fīnd
Second Person Plural	fīndeth

dēmen ("deem" or "judge"), Weak Verb
Indicative

	Present Tense	Past Tense
First Person Singular	dēme	dēmde
Second Person Singular	dēmest	dēmdest
Third Person Singular	dēmeth	dēmde
Plural for All Persons	dēme(n)	dēmde(n)

Subjunctive

	Present Tense	Past Tense
Singular for All Persons	dēme	dēmde
Plural for All Persons	dēme(n)	dēmde(n)

Imperative

	Present Tense
Second Person Singular	dēm
Second Person Plural	dēmeth

MIDDLE ENGLISH PRONOUNS

Directions: *Circle the late East Midland Middle English pronouns below which, with only slight changes, look like the Modern English pronoun forms you are familiar with. All of the other forms have been dropped or replaced by other forms in Modern English. Many of the second possessive forms were new in Middle English, having been formed by analogy with noun possessives.*

First Person

	Singular	Plural
Nominative	ich, I	wē
Objective	mē	ūs
First Possessive	mīn, mī	ōures
Second Possessive	mīn	ōures

Second Person

	Singular	Plural
Nominative	thōu	yē
Objective	thee	yōu
First Possessive	thīn, thī	yōur(e)
Second Possessive	thīn	yōures

Third Person

	Masculine Singular	Feminine Singular
Nominative	hē	shē
Objective	him	her(e), hir(e)
First Possessive	his	her(e), hir(e)
Second Possessive	his	heres

	Neuter Singular	Plural for All Genders
Nominative	(h)it	they, thei, thay, thai
Objective	(h)it	hem, heom
First Possessive	his	her(e)
Second Possessive	his	heres

Copyright © 1978 by Allyn and Bacon, Inc. Reproduction of this material is restricted to use with <u>A Guidebook for Teaching About the English Language</u>, by John Cormican and Gene Stanford.

RENAISSANCE BORROWING

Directions: *From the pairs of synonyms below, identify which word in each pair is a Renaissance Latin or Greek borrowing. Remember that the Renaissance borrowings are likely to be difficult or learnèd words. Check the source of any words you are not sure of in a dictionary.*

	Source		Source
1.	_____	advent-coming	_____
2.	_____	antipathy-hatred	_____
3.	_____	ascend-arise	_____
4.	_____	catlike-feline	_____
5.	_____	climax-end	_____
6.	_____	communicate-speak	_____
7.	_____	conduct-lead	_____
8.	_____	conflagration-fire	_____
9.	_____	dig-excavate	_____
10.	_____	earthly-terrestrial	_____
11.	_____	educate-teach	_____
12.	_____	emancipate-free	_____
13.	_____	evil-malignant	_____
14.	_____	fast-secure	_____
15.	_____	free-liberate	_____
16.	_____	fortitude-strength	_____
17.	_____	kingly-regal	_____
18.	_____	manifest-show	_____
19.	_____	meditate-think	_____
20.	_____	tantalize-tease	_____

SPELLING CHANGES

Directions: *Below are words that had letters added to their spelling during Early Modern English to reflect their real or imagined Latin origins. Use a dictionary to see the source of each word in English and then determine what letter was added to the spelling of each during the Early Modern English period. Are these letters pronounced now, or are they ignored in pronunciation?*

1. advance

2. advantage

3. adventure

4. aisle

5. debt

6. doubt

7. fault

8. foreign

9. island

10. perfect

11. receipt

12. sovereign

13. vault

14. verdict

15. victuals

LATIN VS. ENGLISH VERB PATTERNS

Directions: *Below you will find present and preterite indicative forms of the Latin verb* vidēre *("see")
and the corresponding present and past indicative forms of the Early Modern English verb* see. *Why is the
Latin pattern of verb forms inappropriate for giving the forms of the Early Modern English verb? (Hint:
How many different forms do the two languages each have?) Change the Early Modern English forms to
their Modern English equivalents. Is the Latin more or less appropriate for Modern English than for Early
Modern English?*

	vidēre	see
Present Indicative		
First Person Singular	videō	see
Second Person Singular	vidēs	seest
Third Person Singular	videt	seeth/sees
First Person Plural	vidēmus	see
Second Person Plural	vidēmus	see
Third Person Plural	vident	see
Preterite Indicative		
First Person Singular	vīdī	saw
Second Person Singular	vīdistī	sawest
Third Person Singular	vīdet	saw
First Person Plural	vīdimus	saw
Second Person Plural	vīdistis	saw
Third Person Plural	vīdērunt	saw

LATIN VS. ENGLISH NOUN PATTERNS

Directions: *Below you will find the inflected forms of the Latin noun* filius *("son") and the Early Modern English noun* sone *("son"). Why is the Latin pattern of indicating five cases, both singular and plural, inappropriate for giving the forms of Early Modern English nouns? (*Hint: *How many different forms do the two languages have?) Change the Early Modern English forms to their Modern English equivalents. Is the Latin pattern appropriate for Modern English?*

	filius	sone
Singular		
Nominative (subject)	filius	son(e)
Genitive (possessive)	filī	son(e)s
Dative (indirect object)	filiō	son(e)
Accusative (direct object)	filium	son(e)
Ablative (with certain prepositions)	filiō	son(e)
Plural		
Nominative	filiī	son(e)s
Genitive	filiōrum	son(e)s
Dative	filiīs	son(e)s
Accusative	filiōs	son(e)s
Ablative	filiīs	son(e)s

TRANSLATING EARLY MODERN ENGLISH

Directions: *Translate the passage from an Early Modern English letter written by Queen Elizabeth I to the later King James I into Modern English. Then make a list of the grammatical changes from Early Modern English to Modern English as shown by your translation. The glossary below explains points that you might not be able to figure out.*

my deare brother, Hit hathe sufficiently infourmed me of your singular care of my estat and brething that you haue sent one, in suche diligence, to understand the circumstances of the treasons wiche lately wer lewdly attempted and miraculously vttred. Of whiche I had made participant your embassador afore you lettars came. And now am I to shewe you, that, as I haue receaved many writings from you of great kindnis, yet this last was fraughted with so careful passion. . . . If I shuld not seak to decerue it . . . , I were ill-wordy suche a frind . . .

Glossary

one	"someone"
made participant	"informed"
fraughted	"filled"
careful	"concerned," literally "full of care"
passion	"emotion"
decerue	"deserve" (creative spelling)
were	"would be" (subjunctive form of verb)
ill-wordy	"ill-worthy" (misspelling)

TRANSLATING EARLY MODERN ENGLISH PHRASES

Directions: *Translate the following Early Modern English phrases into Modern English. What kinds of changes have you made?*

1. most unkindest

2. within this mile and half

3. at the last

4. creeping like turtle

5. more happier

6. two eyen

7. the king's of England nose

8. as red as Mars his heart

9. most boldest

10. his shoon

11. more near

12. beautifullest

13. grievous sick

14. stay lenger

15. mine aunt

16. the man which

17. thou art sick

18. ye discovered it

19. well completed of you

20. married of him

WORD ORDER CHANGES

Directions: *Write the Early Modern English questions below in Modern English word order. What kinds of changes have you made? Is there a pattern? Some sentences will require no change in word order.*

1. Worked you long yesterday?

2. Is that your dog?

3. Will she be here?

4. When came she?

5. What think you about it?

6. Do you understand, John?

7. How many hast thou eaten?

8. What sayst thou to that?

9. Who did tell that lie?

10. Went they?

CHANGES IN NEGATIVE SENTENCES

Directions: *Write the Early Modern English negative sentences below in Modern English. What kinds of changes have you made? Is there a pattern?*

1. He understands not the meaning.

2. That is not the cause neither.

3. She saw him not.

4. Never shall none be fairer.

5. I like not him.

6. I not doubt his word.

7. I eat not meat, nor fowl neither.

8. I will not move for no man.

9. He never did no harm to no one.

10. It not appears to me so.

ALPHABETICAL ORDER

Directions: *Arrange the following words in alphabetical order. This will indicate the order they will be found in in a dictionary.*

1. person

2. anger

3. boy

4. honor

5. pneumonia

6. red

7. since

8. personal

9. angrily

10. buy

11. hot

12. knife

13. read

14. sincere

15. personnel

16. angry

17. zebra

18. giraffe

19. noise

20. psychology

USING HEADWORDS

Directions: *List the headwords at the top of the page in your dictionary where the following words would be found.*

Headwords

1. brain   _____   _____

2. cause   _____   _____

3. concern   _____   _____

4. destructive   _____   _____

5. example   _____   _____

6. fail   _____   _____

7. famous   _____   _____

8. grief   _____   _____

9. impossible   _____   _____

10. incapable   _____   _____

11. murder   _____   _____

12. pity   _____   _____

13. primarily   _____   _____

14. section   _____   _____

15. statement   _____   _____

16. sword   _____   _____

17. take   _____   _____

18. time   _____   _____

19. weep   _____   _____

20. word   _____   _____

MARKING SYLLABLE BREAKS

Directions: *Use your dictionary to determine the breaks between syllables in the following words and write the words with the syllables divided as in your dictionary. You will have to know where syllables in words end when you are writing and cannot get an entire word on a line.*

1. antonym

2 barrel

3 conspire

4. difficulty

5. event

6. fixture

7. government

8. harness

9. intelligent

10. Japan

11. kitchenette

12. local

13. marriage

14. neither

15. official

16. pastoral

17. readability

18. sediment

19. testimony

20. underbrush

IS YOUR DICTIONARY CORRECT?

Directions: *List the pronunciations given in your dictionary for the following words. Then circle the pronunciation you use, if it is given. If your pronunciation is not given but everyone you know pronounces the word the way you do, should you stop using that pronunciation?*

1. aunt
2. brooch
3. catch
4. creek
5. forehead
6. garage
7. greasy
8. homage
9. luxury
10. orange
11. roof
12. root
13. route
14. strength
15. tourney
16. vehicle
17. wash
18. which
19. with
20. wreaths

PRONUNCIATION SYMBOLS

Directions: *What symbols does your dictionary use to represent the vowel sounds in the following words?*
Rather than look up each word individually, try to figure out what the symbols would be by referring to
the pronunciation key in your dictionary.

Symbol representing the vowel sound

1. sheet

2. pick

3. wait

4. dread

5. fat

6. shoot

7. wood

8. boat

9. bought

0. crop

11. loud

12. high

13. joy

14. shun

15. (first syllable of) around

MULTIPLE ENTRIES

Directions: *List the number of entries your dictionary has for the words with the spellings below. List what parts of speech these different entries are identified as.*

1. affect

2. batter

3. chow

4. down

5. ell

6. fell

7. grate

8. heel

9. in- (prefix)

10. jet

11. keel

12. lap

13. mark

14. nip

15. ooze

16. pawn

17. rack

18. see

19. stalk

20. well

APPENDIX
C

Feedback Form

Your comments about this book will be very helpful to us in planning other books in the *Guidebook for Teaching* Series and in making revisions in *A Guidebook for Teaching about the English Language.* Please tear out the form that appears on the following page and use it to let us know your reactions to *A Guidebook for Teaching about the English Language.* The authors promise a personal reply. Mail the form to:

Dr. John Cormican and
Dr. Gene Stanford
c/o Longwood Division
Allyn and Bacon, Inc.
470 Atlantic Avenue
Boston, Massachusetts 02210

Your school:_____

Address:_____

City and state:_____

Date:_____

Dr. John Cormican and
Dr. Gene Stanford
c/o Longwood Division
Allyn and Bacon, Inc.
470 Atlantic Avenue
Boston, Massachusetts 02210

Dear John and Gene:

My name is_____and I want to tell
you what I thought of your book *A Guidebook for Teaching about the English Language.* I
liked certain things about the book, including:

I do, however, feel that the book could be improved in the following ways:

There were some other things I wish the book had included, such as:

Here is something that happened in my class when I used an idea from your book:

Sincerely yours,

_____